African American Students' Career and College Readiness

Race and Education in the Twenty-First Century

Series Editor: Kenneth Fasching-Varner and Roland Mitchell

This series asks authors and editors to consider the role of race and education, addressing questions such as "how do communities and educators alike take on issues of race in meaningful and authentic ways?" and "how education work to disrupt, resolve, and otherwise transform current racial realities?" The series pays close attention to the intersections of difference, recognizing that isolated conversations about race eclipse the dynamic nature of identity development that play out for race as it intersects with gender, sexuality, socioeconomic class, and ability. It welcomes perspectives from across the entire spectrum of education from Pre-K through advanced graduate studies, and it invites work from a variety of disciplines, including counseling, psychology, higher education, curriculum theory, curriculum and instruction, and special education.

Titles in Series

Big Box Schools: Race, Education, and the Danger of the Wal-Martization of Public Schools in America by Lori Latrice Martin

African American Students' Career and College Readiness: The Journey Unraveled edited by Jennifer R. Curry and M. Ann Shillingford

African American Students' Career and College Readiness

The Journey Unraveled

Edited by
Jennifer R. Curry
and
M. Ann Shillingford

LEXINGTON BOOKS
Lanham • Boulder • New York • London

Published by Lexington Books
An imprint of The Rowman & Littlefield Publishing Group, Inc.
4501 Forbes Boulevard, Suite 200, Lanham, Maryland 20706
www.rowman.com

Unit A, Whitacre Mews, 26-34 Stannary Street, London SE11 4AB

Copyright © 2015 by Lexington Books

All rights reserved. No part of this book may be reproduced in any form or by any electronic or mechanical means, including information storage and retrieval systems, without written permission from the publisher, except by a reviewer who may quote passages in a review.

British Library Cataloguing in Publication Information Available

Library of Congress Control Number: 2015949369
ISBN: 978-1-4985-0686-1 (cloth : alk. paper)
ISBN: 978-1-4985-0688-5 (pbk. : alk. paper)
ISBN: 978-1-4985-0687-8 (electronic)

∞™ The paper used in this publication meets the minimum requirements of American National Standard for Information Sciences—Permanence of Paper for Printed Library Materials, ANSI/NISO Z39.48-1992.

Printed in the United States of America

For Daniel, I hope you will always seek truth, justice, and fairness for yourself and others. May peace, love, and compassion follow you all the days of your life.
—Jennifer R. Curry

To Justin and Summer Joy: My most precious gifts of hope, justice, and love...
—M. Ann Shillingford-Butler

Contents

Series Foreword ix

1. African Americans and Career and College Readiness 1
   Jennifer Curry

2. Education and Race Case Law and Legislation: The Impact on the Career and College Readiness of African American Students 17
   Jennifer R. Curry and Shandricka E. Jackson

3. Making a Way Out of No Way: A Contextualized History of African Americans in Higher Education 39
   Berlisha R. Morton and Dana C. Hart

4. Holland Codes and STEM Careers: Cultural Values and Individual Interests in Career Development for African American Students 55
   Tristen Bergholtz

5. Talent Development as Career Development and College Readiness in Gifted African American Youth 85
   Andrea Dawn Frazier, Jennifer Riedl Cross, and Tracy L. Cross

6. Rigor, Course Choice, and Educational Excellence: Positioning African American Students for Future Success 109
   D'Jalon J. Jackson

7. Supporting the Transition of African American Students with Specific Learning Disabilities into Post-secondary Education 131
   Sharon H. deFur and Elizabeth Auguste

8	African Americans Students and Financial Literacy *M. Ann Shillingford, Brian Kooyman, and S. Kent Butler*	153
9	Employability Skills and Career Development *Ashley Churbock and Lauren Treacy*	167
10	African American First-Generation College Students *Cyrus Williams, Michael T. Garrett, and Eric Brown*	187
11	Historically Black Colleges and Universities: Relevance in Modern Education *J. Richelle Joe and Pamela N. Harris*	207
12	African American Students at PWIs *Natoya Haskins and Brandee Appling*	227
13	Engaging a Discourse of Policy Analysis and Curriculum that Addresses Poverty and Race: Democracy through Collective Impact Models *Jessica Exkano*	259
14	African American Males: A Career and College Readiness Crisis *Christopher T. Belser*	279
15	African American Athletes and Higher Education *Linwood Vereen, Nicole R. Hill, and Michelle Lopez*	309
16	African American Students Navigating Higher Education Through a Wellness Approach *M. Ann Shillingford and Amy Williams*	341
Index		355
About the Contributors		361

Series Foreword

DuBois some 100 plus years ago suggested that "the world problem of the twentieth century is the problem of the color line." Despite claims of a twenty-first century evolution into a postracial society, the reality of our times suggests that systemic oppression, marginalization, and alienation continue to play out along color lines. The Race and Education series asks authors and editors to consider "what is the role of race and education?," "how do communities and educators alike take on issues of race in meaningful and authentic ways?," and "how might education (from womb to tomb) work to disrupt, resolve, and otherwise transform current racial realities?"

While much scholarly attention has been paid to race over the last 100 years very little substantive and systemic change seems to occur. Simultaneously in nonacademic settings, the election of the nation's first president of color has prompted many to suggest that we have achieved racial nirvana—that the Obama-era has ushered in a postracial reality. The vast majority of children of color continue to live in poverty, attend largely re-segregated public schools, are taught by predominantly white teachers, and have little supported access to institutions of higher education. If we live in a postracial moment, the highlights of those times include intensified segregation with little opportunity to openly dialogue about the realities, opportunities, and challenges of race. This series is a necessary addition to the literature because it works to understand race (1) through interdisciplinary lenses, (2) draws on educational perspectives across the entire spectrum of education from Pre-K through advanced graduate studies, and (3) confronts the contributions between the articulation of being postracial and the very racial realities of the times.

The Race and Education series covers a broad range of educational perspectives and contexts, drawing upon both qualitative/quantitative and empirical/

theoretical approaches to understanding race and education. Further the series will contextualize the relationship between race and education not just in the United States, but also in a variety of transnational settings. Disciplines such as counseling, psychology, higher education, curriculum theory, curriculum and instruction, and special education all contribute to the larger dialogue in the series. The series pays close attention to the intersections of difference, recognizing that isolated conversations about race eclipse the dynamic nature of identity development that play out for race as it intersects with gender, sexuality, socioeconomic class, and ability (among others). Consequently, the series provides readers with multiple opportunities to examine the importance of race and education in both breadth and depth as it plays out in the human experience.

African American Students' Career and College Readiness: The Journey Unraveled is the second book in the series and the first edited collection. Curry and Shillingford have brought together a broad range of scholarly perspectives on what it means for African Americans to be college ready, particularly in a complex context where day-to-day survival is becoming more and more difficult. Drawing upon both success and roadblocks to success, this collection pushes readers to think deeply about the pragmatic, policy, and social implications of college access and readiness. The editors have done a superb job bringing light to these perspectives, some of which go unheard or others of which remain ignored. As the series develops we look forward to bringing you a wide range of perspectives and ideas about race and education.

—*Kenneth Fasching-Varner and Roland Mitchell,*
Series Editors

Chapter 1

African Americans and Career and College Readiness

Jennifer Curry

INTRODUCTION

On July 1, 2014 the First Lady of the United States, Michelle Obama, unveiled her *Reach Higher* initiative to the American School Counselor Association (ASCA) (www.whitehouse.gov). Reach Higher is a national campaign to increase college preparation access for all students, particularly the most underserved students such as minorities and students from low income schools. Yet, as Mrs. Obama noted, the challenges are critical and in many ways, seemingly greater in scope than ever before and the disadvantages faced by marginalized groups a generation ago are as pervasive today as they were for past generations.

Indeed, historic landmark legislation, the 1954 passage of *Brown v. The Board of Education, Topeka, Kansas*, marked in the American conscience a moment that many believed would change the educational landscape permanently by providing equal opportunity for all. Yet time and again, we are reminded that we are falling short of this goal. In a seminal, and explosive, 1991 release of the book *Savage Inequalities: Children in America's Schools*, Jonathan Kozol documented the reality of public schools in modern America that are largely African American and urban with conditions that are incomprehensible. Conditions documented by Kozol ranged from a total lack of learning materials (i.e., books, paper, pencils), buildings and facilities in complete disrepair, understaffed and overcrowded classrooms, and busing that took kids hours to get to and from school. And while the physical conditions of schools remain a constant disparity between White and Black, poor and wealthy, the data and the challenges of our time are crystalizing and becoming substantially even more high stakes. Specifically, college and postsecondary training pay off and those who do not receive this kind of education are systematically denied access to high paying, high prestige careers creating pervasive, lifelong disadvantages. As stated by Boo (2004, p. 165) and cited in Farmer–Hinton (2008), "College preparation inequities are the 'civil rights issue of our time" (p. 73).

According to an August 2011 Executive Summary report released by the Georgetown University Center on Education and the Workforce, over their lifetime, individuals with a high school degree earn on average 1.3 million whereas those with a Bachelor's degree earn an approximate 2.27 million (Carnevale, Rose, & Cheah, 2011). In general, the greater the degree acquired, the greater the lifetime earnings for individuals (see Figure 1.1). However, for every education level attained, the amount earned differs significantly by gender and by race, fundamentally disadvantaging African Americans and Latinos (Carnevale et al., 2011).

Although progress across race is being made, the achievement gap is still persistent. According to the U.S. Department of Education's National Center for Education Statistics (NCES) report, *The Condition in Education* (2014), from 1990 to 2013 the high school graduation rates for Whites and Blacks rose. For Whites the rate went from 90 to 94%, for Blacks 82–90%. So although Black students had higher gains in high school graduation rates, they are still behind their White counterparts by 4%. And the picture is far more concerning at the collegiate level. In regard to attaining a Bachelor's degree or higher, from 1990 to 2013 Whites aged 25–29 increased from 26 to 40% while Blacks aged 25–29 increased from 13 to 20%, a more modest gain but

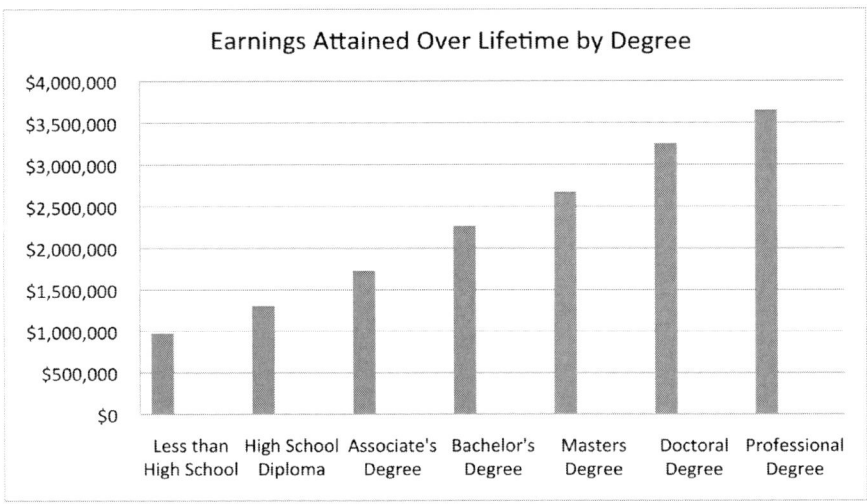

Figure 1.1 **Earnings Attained Over Lifetime by Degree.** *Source*: Adapted from Carnevale et al. 2011

the achievement gap between groups is still firmly intact at the Bachelor's degree attainment level or higher (NCES, 2014). So, while 90% of Black students in the United States graduate from high school, only 20% receive Bachelor's degrees or higher. What accounts for those who do not? The conundrum is notably more dismal according to Holland (2010), who noted that African American high school students are just as likely to aspire to college degrees and to realistically understand the long-term benefits of attending college as do White high school students. So, why does a four-year college degree continue to elude so many African American students? To better understand the data one must first address what career and college readiness actually is and what it means for twenty-first-century African American students.

DEFINING CAREER AND COLLEGE READINESS

There are many definitions of career and college readiness but in order to fully understand these terms, we can define them first as academic concepts and secondly as social and political constructs. For example, an academic definition of *career readiness* according to the Association for Career and Technical Education (ACTE; 2010),

> Career readiness involves three major skill areas: *core academic skills* and the ability to apply those skills to concrete situations in order to function in the workplace and in routine daily activities; *employability skills* (such as critical thinking and responsibility) that are essential in any career area; and *technical, job-specific skills* related to a specific career pathway. (p. 1)

Similarly, Conley (2007) described the college ready student as one who is

> able to understand what is expected in a college course, can cope with the content knowledge that is presented, and can take away from the course the key intellectual lessons and dispositions the course was designed to convey and develop. In addition, the student is prepared to get the most out of the college experience due to a thorough understanding of the culture and structure of postsecondary education and the ways of knowing and intellectual norms that prevail in this academic and social environment. The student has both the mindset and disposition necessary to enable this to happen. (pp. 5–6)

Yet, we may also consider the social and political meanings of college and career readiness. Farmer-Hinton and McCullough (2008) propose that, based on social capital theory, career and college preparation is actually school-based social capital due to the implications for increased positive social, political, economic, and life transformations when students are given access to postsecondary opportunity. Conversely, when denied such opportunity due to inequity, students are faced with a downward spiral of decreased capital.

Because many African American students are first-generation college students from low socioeconomic backgrounds, they often have less economic and planning resources available at home to prepare them for college (Farmer-Hinton & McCullough, 2008). Holland (2010) points out that social capital can be either *formal* or *informal*. A family system comprised of family members, family friends and acquaintances, and members of the family's immediate surroundings (i.e., community members, neighbors) are part of the informal social capital structure. Institutions and their members that individuals come in contact with, such as school personnel, are formal social capital. We can apply this to college preparation. For example, if no one in a student's family has ever filled out a college application, visited a college campus, accessed resources for financial aid and scholarships, or learned about degree program admission requirements, then all of this information has to be provided for students to even recognize that it is critical information they need to know. So, first-generation and low-income African American students come into P-12 schools with low *informal* career and college readiness social capital. Beyond the family members themselves, neighbors and close friends of the family may also have limited knowledge of career and college readiness. In other words, because the college transition is new to their family system, their support network may not be able to provide the tools or skills to know how to navigate exploring careers and preparing for college. Therefore, individuals with low informal social capital for career and college readiness must then turn to more formal social capital means (such as the school system via teachers, counselors, mentors) to provide support. Thus, many African American students may need more college advisement and academic support than their White counterparts in order to learn about college opportunities and how to access postsecondary training and education (Farmer-Hinton & McCullough, 2008; Farmer-Hinton, 2008). But how much equality is there in college counseling, advisement, and academic preparation in twenty-first century schools? In other words, how much access do African American students have to career and college preparation formal capital structures?

Academic and College Advisement: Pervasive Inequity

In order to more fully examine how social capital is gained or lost in career and college readiness it is first important to understand a few key terms, how they relate, and how they differ: career exploration, career maturity, academic advisement, and college counseling. Career exploration is a necessary part of career development for all youth. *Career exploration* can be described as the process by which students learn about occupations, the relationships between occupations, projected outlook for the growth of careers, median salary and income ranges, training and educational requirements, and the skills necessary to be successful in a given career (Curry & Milsom, 2013). *Career maturity* is the process by which individuals begin to be able to make career decisions they truly understand, have comprehensively explored, and planned for effectively (Curry & Milsom, 2013). Students with high career maturity make choices that reflect deep consideration of their personal values, interests, and aptitudes related to career (Sharf, 2006). What is most notable is that career maturity does not just develop on its own, like most developmental tasks, the environment and opportunities to explore careers, with adults who are knowledgeable about careers and can serve as resources, foster this type of growth.

Academic advisement is the process whereby a counselor with career and academic counseling certification, generally a certified school counselor, assists a student in aligning academic curriculum choices with future career plans. During academic advisement, a school counselor helps students make choices about taking rigorous courses that will promote critical thinking and problem solving and will assist the students in developing study habits that are necessary for college success. *College counseling* is a process of helping students explore postsecondary training and education options that match their career goals; providing education on the application and admissions process; helping students access financial options for paying for college including loans, work study, grants and scholarships, learning about resources and activities available to them on college campuses; and establishing a college-going culture through expectations that students will go to college (Curry & Milsom 2013, Farmer-Hinton & McCullough, 2008). So what is the difference between career exploration opportunities, academic advisement, and college counseling services provided to African American students and their White counterparts?

Career and College Counseling

The American School Counselor Association (2012) recommends a school counselor to student ratio of 1:250. School counselors are conduits of career and college readiness curriculum; they provide one-to-one college counseling, transition services, classroom career exploration activities beginning in elementary school, and help students connect academics to the world of work. However, the recommended 1:250 ratio is not only uncommon in public schools across the country, it is outright rare. To be pointed, based on U.S. Department of Education data from 2010 to 2011, reported by the American School Counselor Association (2011) only 4 states or U.S. territories had school counselor to student ratios equal to or less than

1:250 (New Hampshire, Vermont, Wyoming, and the U.S. Virgin Islands). Moreover, twelve states had greater than 1:500 ratios with California at the top with a 1:1016 counselor-to-student ratio. First Lady Michelle Obama summed up the numbers,

> While school counselors at private schools have an average caseload of 106 students, and ASCA recommends no more than 250 students per counselor, the national average is one school counselor for every 471 students. And that is outrageous. Outrageous. And one in five American high schools doesn't have any school counselors at all – none. And that's appalling. (www.whitehouse.gov)

These numbers are so critical because a school counselor is necessary to promote student career development, foster career maturity, and to support college and postsecondary decision making. In short, school counselors are formal, social capital for students' career and college access. While students in private schools have the intense, high touch personal attention of school counselors with small case loads, they are often the same students who have the social capital and resources of parents with better socioeconomic circumstances and have a higher likelihood of having parents with some college education (Stephan, 2013). According to a large-scale study utilizing NCES data conducted by Bryan, Holcomb-McCoy, Moore-Thomas, and Day-Vines (2009), results indicated that in schools with smaller student-counselor rations, students were more likely to seek out the school counselor for assistance in the college decision-making process. Conversely, African American public school students might not have a school counselor at all. For those public schools that do have school counselors, the counselors are likely to have a high student case load leaving the students in public schools with fewer resources to navigate the college exploration, application, and transition experience (Stephan, 2013). The impact of these high caseloads can be devastating. For example, Holland (2010) found that some students actually did not receive any college counseling or advisement until their senior year, when it was too late to meet college GPA and ACT requirements, leaving the students without options for going to college.

Moreover, public schools tend to have higher numbers of school counselors who are new and have never worked as a school counselor (Farmer Hinton & McCullough, 2008), so the ability to effectively provide college counseling is reduced as it can take time to gain experience and learn about requirements for different colleges and universities. Additionally, Farmer-Hinton and Adams (2006) asserted that many public school counselors in high need schools not only have high case loads, they are often relegated to duties that pull them from providing counseling resources: scheduling, testing, substitute teaching. In charter schools, to save money, instead of hiring a school counselor the school board may choose to hire a social worker or other helping professional with no training in career counseling or credentials in career training and development (Belser & Curry, submitted for review). Again, this lack of college counseling resources translates to lower students having lower career and college readiness social capital (Farmer-Hinton & Adams, 2006; Farmer-Hinton & McCullough, 2008; Farmer-Hinton, 2008).

Academic Advisement

Academic advisement is the process where a certified school counselor, ideally, works with students to align students' future career goals with curriculum choices throughout their secondary experience. As reported by Griffin and Allen (2006), there is a strong connection in data demonstrating that academic resources, rigorous curricula offerings, students' education outcomes and access to higher education all have strong correlations. For example, consider a student, Lamar, who is interested in becoming a veterinarian. Lamar will need high rigor math, and science courses. Further, he will need information on scores necessary for college entrance on the ACT/SAT, and how to be competitive for scholarships. A resource that might be particularly helpful is a weekend ACT preparatory course. Additional information Lamar needs will include options for Advanced Placement or honors courses, dual enrollment, and how to receive college credit for dual enrollment course work. Finally, Lamar's academic advisement should also include a discussion on how to think long term and choose wisely when considering extracurricular and service activities that will enhance learning opportunities (i.e., weekend volunteer work with an animal shelter, debate club, Olympics of the mind [math competition]) (Curry & Milsom, 2013). In order to adequately advise students, school counselors need access to one-on-one time with individual students where they can discuss the student's future plans and current academic path to achieving their career goals. As noted by Mrs. Obama, a counselor with a caseload of 106 students can give far more attention to students and delivering this important one-on-one service than a school counselor with 471 students.

Farmer-Hinton (2008) indicated that there is a dearth of rigorous courses offered in schools with high minority, low SES schools; particularly AP courses (Griffin & Allen, 2006). Students have little access to courses that will position them to be competitive for scholarships or will adequately prepare them to meet the demands of college coursework. Indeed, as purported by Curry and Milsom (2013), high rigor courses such as honors, AP, and dual enrollment prepare students not only for the academics of college, but also assist students in building the self-regulatory mechanisms necessary for college success (i.e., time management, stress management, ability to break projects down into manageable pieces, collaboration in groups, etc.). More shockingly, even when African American students attend schools where AP courses are offered, studies have shown that African American students are encouraged not to take these high rigor courses and are often tracked into regular or less rigorous courses (Griffin & Allen, 2006; West-Olatunji, Shure, Pringle, Adams, Lewis, & Cholewa, 2010). Holland (2010) further cited that when African American students perceive that their schools are not preparing them academically for college, they begin to disengage from the possibility of going to college and their aspirations to attend actually decreases. In concordance with Holland's findings, Bryan et al. (2009) found that students who perceived that their school counselor did not hold postsecondary aspirations for them subsequently did not seek contact with their counselor for college counseling and information.

STRENGTH ATTRIBUTES: CULTURE, RESILIENCE, OVERCOMING AND MAPPING THE PERSONAL JOURNEY

Griffin and Allen (2006) contended that while understanding the barriers and obstacles to African American students' career and college readiness success are imperative, equally critical is understanding how some African Americans overcome these difficulties and experience immense success. In other words, what cultural, personal, social, and environmental factors help African American students from low SES succeed in spite of a lack of monetary resources? In a study conducted by Farmer-Hinton and Adams (2006), participants pointed out that beyond academics and postsecondary preparation, African American students living in high poverty situations face a host of challenges including homelessness, community violence, mental and physical health issues, and parent incarceration that might impede their future career and college goals. Yet, a number of these disenfranchised students are able to rise above their societal challenges and secure a better future for themselves. Farmer-Hinton and Adams found that school counselors often tried to help students conceptualize life beyond the moment, a future where they could envision being economically stable, and assist each student in seeing his or her own unique potential.

Griffin and Allen (2006) pointed out that resilient students are able to translate difficult situations into a source of motivation; as a result, resilient students maintain their focus on goals and strategies to reach those goals. For instance, an African American student attending a predominantly White high school might face racism in the form of microaggressions, stereotypes, and open hostility. Rather than leaving the school, the student may choose to stay and persevere through the challenges.

According to qualitative data from a study conducted by Griffin and Allen (2006), African American students who faced racism in the college counseling process (i.e., being encouraged to attend a community college rather than a four-year university) were able to focus on and maintain their goals when they had positive support systems. One key support came from peers who were also college bound. It appears the students became a source of peer mentorship for each other, leading, encouraging and supporting one another (Griffin & Allen, 2006).

Once in college, it appears that these same students continue to be resilient for the same reasons: peer support, academic preparation, family support, teacher encouragement, personal motivation, and determination (Russell & Atwater, 2005). Additionally, students in Russell and Atwater's study noted that having experiences in their field of study (science) was also additive to their persistence in remaining in their major field of study. Of environmental factors studied by Small and Winship (2007), African American students' graduation from elite colleges was most dependent on their precollege academic preparation; this finding underscores the need to continue to improve rigor and persistence for all African American students.

WHAT DOES MAKE A DIFFERENCE?

Traditional Preparation

There is much promise for African American students and college access. Holland (2010) found that informal social capital in the form of support and encouragement from parents, elders in the community, and teachers was highly beneficial in pushing African American students to aspire to college. Subsequently, formal social capital structures that were tangible in nature (e.g., assistance from teachers in filling out applications and writing personal statements, teachers writing letters of recommendation) were also a significant source of help and support for college bound African American students. Other instances of formal social capital substantiated by Holland's (2010) study participants included course content and rigor as capital for college preparation. In short, when students felt challenged, they felt more prepared for college.

Making these kinds of supports available to African American students is key. Examples might include offering ACT/SAT preparation courses, having college and career curriculum for every student comprehensively throughout their high school career (ASCA, 2012), giving students access to career assessment and explaining results, and providing one-on-one academic and college advisement. Supplementary personnel may also be helpful such as career coaches, career mentors, and graduation coaches. Chicago Public Schools implemented a college coaching program that consisted of having coaches who developed school-based college fairs, organized college tours, and provided financial workshops (Stephan, 2013). So, while school counselors were providing individual academic advisement, the coaches were providing large-scale college exposure programming. More creative initiatives and clear intentionality behind programming may be necessary to promote postsecondary access for African American students.

Some concrete and outstanding examples of what does work are evidenced throughout the literature. So, although there is a plethora of research outlining the problems of promoting a career and college bound culture in schools, there are great strategies for improving school-based college preparation capital for students more than the expected and traditional practices already highlighted in this chapter. More appealing, some of these come with very little to no financial cost to schools, they simply must occur with planning, purpose and direction.

Innovative Approaches

Creating a college bound culture begins with getting the buy-in of the adults that work with students. The first requirement for changing the culture of a school is creating a belief that every student is capable and valuable, and unwavering attitude that postsecondary education and training access is critical for all. Providing staff and faculty professional development is essential to meeting this goal. Moreover, there should be an expectation that college talk will be infused formally and informally throughout the school day every day (Farmer-Hinton & McCullough, 2008; Farmer-Hinton, 2008). Recently, a high school chemistry teacher gave me (the author of this chapter) an example that she goes around the room in her class each week and asks students what future career they want. She then relates chemistry to their future career. She told me how shocked a young woman was to learn how much chemistry has to do with cosmetology (i.e., hair color). The teacher told me this practice has been very effective in engaging students in the chemistry curriculum. Another practice shared with this author came from a middle school principal. She said that each week her school counselor has a Friday Fun Fact that she gives during the morning announcement. The fun fact is information about a university or college. She talks about the college's mascot, their colors, what programs they are known for, where they are located, and something special (such as sports teams, debate team and arts). They don't have Friday Fun Facts about a highly popular university in their area. Instead, the announcement is always informational about a school they may not have heard of but is within their region. Then, at the end of each six weeks, students and teachers can wear the colors of a university or college they learned about that they thought was interesting and in homeroom everyone gets to talk about the colors they chose and why.

Another inexpensive way to convey the constant message that college and postsecondary life is important is to create tools and visual reminders throughout the environment such as pictures of graduating classes, career posters, timelines with benchmarks of important milestones for college access and more (Farmer-Hinton & Adams, 2006). One school counselor, who had a particular talent for sewing, designed beautiful college pennants for every university and college where her students chose to attend and hung them in the main office and counseling offices. Another very inexpensive and creative idea is to start a College Ambassadors Club (Stephan, 2013). Students in the Ambassadors Club can gather information on various colleges or universities, host admissions officers, give classroom presentations to underclassmen, and set up panel discussions with current college students about transitions to college. This type of peer leadership conveys that college is important to students, not just to adults in the school, and lends to social capital for both the Ambassadors and the students with whom they come into contact.

Rite of Passage Programs and Recognizing Achievements

Although the aforementioned practices are a great, and inexpensive way to get started with creating a college bound culture, there are far more extensive practices that can be implemented. In a study conducted by Farmer-Hinton and Adams (2006) one participant, a school counselor, told about having special blazers the Honors Club wears and how much pride the students take in earning those blazers. The blazers likely symbolized for the students more than just their accomplishments; these blazers marked them as students of great potential in a college bound culture that valued student achievement. Although recognizing achievements is certainly important, Rite of Passage (ROP) programs are far more in-depth and are one practice that can engage community partners, parents, and civic leaders in a school with a college bound culture (Brooks, West-Olatunji, & Baker, 2005; West-Olatunji & Conwill, 2011). ROPs are strength based, promoting a positive cultural identity for African American youth and engaging them civically through service learning opportunities and community building exercises. Students also have the opportunity to develop leadership, creative expression, communication and self-control skills, positive relationships with adults and mentors, problem solving and a sense of self as a learner. This is in direct juxtaposition with the negative experiences many African American students have felt in schools and classrooms, and it is what makes ROP programs so special and positive. By providing the ROP program opportunity to students, schools and communities can support a continued college bound culture (West-Olatunji & Conwill, 2011; West-Olatunji, Shure, Garrett, Conwill, & Torres, 2008).

Other types of leadership development can promote the college bound experience. Examples include challenge courses, wilderness camps, and outdoor adventure training, all of which take students out of their element and ask them to take risks. Most important, is to help students apply what they learn in these camp situations to how they problem-solve academics or how they will face the challenge of going to college. While some of these types of adventures are more costly, some can be funded by community partners. As a school counselor, this author found that the National Guard was willing to come to her school for free and offer a low ropes course for our 9th grade students (low-V, spider web, trust fall). Parents had to sign consent forms for participation, but the National Guard set up and facilitated the entire program which was meant to promote collaboration, critical thinking, and problem solving. Students loved it and the administration was highly supportive. Since it took an entire day we used it as a field day and had a local pizza parlor provide lunch. Students had a great time and they wrote reflection papers on what they learned from the low ropes course adventure and how it related to their future careers.

College Exposure and Leadership Development

College immersion exploration such as college tours provide students with exposure to a college campus. This type of exposure promotes college bound motivation and helps students envision college life and understand university organization and structure (Farmer-Hinton & Adams, 2006; Farmer-Hinton, 2008). Visiting a variety of campuses is ideal; seeing a Historically Black College or University (HBCU) as well as Predominantly White Institutions (PWI) can help students understand the structural differences and what resources might matter most to them.

Another type of immersion is to have students attend enrichment programs during the summer at universities (summer engineering camp, writing camp). Many students may be hesitant at first to give up time in the summer but these types of camps generally have field trips and lots of social and fun activities built in as well as academics. For example, at a summer camp in Louisiana designed to enhance literacy and creative writing, students take a field trip to the local zoo, visit the planetarium and science museum, go to a dairy store and make ice cream, and many other outings. These adventures are tied to reading modules and are used for writing prompts as well. As noted by Farmer-Hinton and Adams (2006), these camp experiences help the student and family acclimate to student going away and being away from home for bouts of time as will be necessary for college. So, camps become part of the real-world preparation for students.

IMPLICATIONS

Throughout this chapter it has been stated that teachers, counselors, administrators and all school staff need to continually give direct, clear and intentional messages about their expectations for students to go to college or postsecondary technical or career training (Bryan et al., 2009). These messages are only the beginning of creating the social exchanges necessary to generate enough social capital to assist African American students in gaining access to equitable college and careers but there is much more that must be done.

As mentioned by many researchers and scholars, for African American students to be adequately prepared for college, they must have access to high rigor courses throughout college (Curry & Milsom, 2013; Farmer-Hinton, 2008; Holland, 2010). This notion is somewhat problematic in that many African American students and their families don't know to advocate for themselves to receive more rigorous offerings. They may assume that what they are receiving is a standard high school education and is therefore sufficient college preparation as they may not understand the diversity in high school academic programming opportunities. This concern was confirmed in a study by Pitre (2006), who found that African American, high school freshmen college aspirations had no relationship with their actual academic achievement. This finding may indicate that the students in Pitre's study did not understand at the time that they were freshmen that their high school preparation and achievement would impact their ability to get into college. Subsequently, one might deduce that if students don't make the connection between academic achievement and college aspiration, they may not recognize the need to take high rigor courses or extracurricular academic opportunities. Furthermore, they may not understand the need to push themselves to excel academically until much later in high school when it is too late to make choices that will impact their ability to get into college bound curriculum. School personnel and community leaders should work with the school board to continually highlight this problem.

Even when African American students are college bound, they may not be aware of college activities and opportunities that might make them more marketable or enhance their college experience, such as international education and study abroad (Penn & Tanner, 2008), or how to pay for and access these opportunities. Providing workshops and activities that include parents and that give students information about transitioning to college and making the most of the college experience is an ideal practice (Bryan et al., 2009).

SUMMARY

Though African American students appear to aspire to college at the same rates as their White peers, college entrance and matriculation for African American students remain critically low. Pervasive disadvantages include schools with poor supports for college counseling and low rigor courses that inadequately prepare students for college. However, there are clear implications for how to change the current status quo including providing college expectations, creating peer advisement networks, increasing curricular rigor, and expanding college exposure programming.

REFERENCES

American School Counselor Association. (2012). *The ASCA national model: A framework for school counseling programs.* (3rd ed.). Alexandria, VA: Author.

American School Counselor Association. (2011). Student-to-school-counselor-ration 2010–2011. Retrieved online from http://www.schoolcounselor.org/asca/media/asca/home/ratios10–11.pdf

Association for Career and Technical Education (2010). *What is career ready?* Alexandria, VA: Author.

Belser, C. T., & Curry, J. (submitted for review). Changing the Tide: An Example of School Counselor Advocacy That Worked.

Brooks, M., West-Olatunji, C. A., & Baker, J. (2005). Rites of passage, youth empowerment and fostering resilience in African-American students. *Counseling Interviewer, 37,* 54–59.

Bryan, J., Holcomb-McCoy, C., Moore-Thomas, C., & Day-Vines, N. L. (2009). Who sees the school counselor for college information? A national study. *Professional School Counseling, 12*(4), 280–291.

Carnevale, A. P., Rose, S. J., & Cheah, B. (2011). *The college payoff: Education, occupations, lifetime earnings.* Retrieved from the Georgetown University Public Policy Institute, Center on Education and the Workforce website: http://cew.georgetown.edu/collegepayoff/

Conley, D. (2007). *Toward a more comprehensive conception of college readiness.* Educational Policy Improvement Center. Retrieved from: http://www.s4s.org/upload/Gates-College%20Readiness.pdf

Curry, J., & Milsom, A. (2013). *Career counseling in P-12 schools.* New York: Springer.

Farmer-Hinton, R. L., & Adams, T. L. (2006). Social capital and college preparation: Exploring the role of counselors in a college prep school for Black students. *The Negro Educational Review, 57*(1–2), 101–116.

Farmer-Hinton, R. L. (2008). Creating opportunities for college access: Examining a school model designed to prepare students of color for college. *Multicultural Perspectives, 10*(2), 73–81. doi: 10.1080/15210960802039148

Farmer-Hinton, R. L., & McCullough, R. G. (2008). College counseling in charter high schools: Examining the opportunities and challenges. *The High School Journal*, 77–90. doi: 10.1353/hsj.0.0006

Griffin, K. & Allen, W. (2006). Mo' money, mo' problems? High-achieving Black high school students' experiences with resources, racial climate, and resilience. *The Journal of Negro Education, 75*(3), 478–494. doi: 10.2307/40026816

Holland, N. E. (2010). Postsecondary education preparation of traditionally underrepresented college students: A social capital perspective. *Journal of Diversity in Higher Education, 3*(2), 111–125. doi: 10.1037/a0019249

Kozol, J. (1991). *Savage inequalities: Children in America's schools*. New York, Randon House.

National Center for Education Statistics. (2014). *The condition of education 2014*. NCES 2014–083. Washington, DC: U.S. Department of Education.

Obama, M. (July, 2014). Remarks by the First Lady to the American School Counselor Association Annual Conference. Speech presented at the ASCA Conference in Orlando, Florida. Retrieved online at http://www.whitehouse.gov/the-press-office/2014/07/01/remarks-first-lady-american-school-counselor-association-annual-conferen

Penn, E. B., & Tanner, J. (2009). Black students and international education: An assessment. *Journal of Black Studies, 40*(2), 266–282. doi:10.1177/0021934707311128

Pitre, P. E. (2006). College choice: A study of African American and white student aspirations and perceptions related to college attendance. *College Student Journal, 40*(3) 562–574.

Russell, M. L., & Atwater, M. M. (2005). Traveling the road to success: A discourse on persistence throughout the science pipeline with African American students at a predominantly White institution. *Journal of Research in Science Teaching, 42*(6), 691–715. doi: 10.1002/tea.20068

Sharf, R. S. (2006). *Applying career development theory to counseling* (4th ed.). Belmont, CA: Thomson.

Stephan, J. L. (2013). Social capital and the college enrollment process: How can a school program make a difference? *Teachers College Record, 115*(4), 1–39.

Small, M. L., & Winship, C. (2007). Black students' graduation from elite colleges: Institutional characteristics and between-institution differences. *Social Science Research, 36*, 1257–1275. doi:10.1016/j.ssresearch.2006.06.006

West-Olatunji, C. A. & Conwill, W. (2011). *Counseling & diversity: Counseling African Americans*. Belmont, CA: Brooks/Cole.

West-Olatunji, C., Shure, L., Garrett, M., Conwill, W., & Torres, E. (2008). Rite of passage programs as effective tools for fostering resilience among low-income African American male adolescents. *Journal of Humanistic Counseling Education and Development, 47*, 131–143. doi: 10.1002/j.2161-1939.2008.tb00053.x

West-Olatunji, C., Shure, L., Pringle, R., Adams, T., Lewis, D., & Cholewa, B. (2010). Exploring how school counselors position low-income African American girls as mathematics and science learners. *Professional School Counseling, 13*(3), 184–195.

Chapter 2

Education and Race Case Law and Legislation

The Impact on the Career and College Readiness of African American Students

Jennifer R. Curry and Shandricka E. Jackson

To conceptualize the challenges of today's African American youth in the areas of career and college preparation, it is necessary to understand the historical context of higher education in the United States. Moreover, issues of access and equity for African Americans and the legislative efforts to increase opportunity must be considered. In this chapter, we review key legislation and case law, the impact and intention of laws enacted, and the successes and failures of each. A note of caution to the reader, this subject could necessarily warrant a book in and of itself, therefore, this review is limited in scope and is meant to only highlight major efforts; therefore, this chapter does not exhaustively cover all race and education legislation impacting African American students' access to career and college preparation. In this chapter, we summarize, (1) the Morrill Land Grant Acts and legislation leading to the development of modern Land Grant institutions and Historically Black Colleges and Universities; (2) race and education case law impacting K-12 and higher education access for African Americans; and (3) legislative efforts aimed at ensuring quality, fairness, non-discrimination, and justice in education settings.

THE UNITED STATES LAND GRANT INSTITUTIONS AND RELATED ACTS

1862 Morrill Land Grant Act (PL 37–108)

Justin Smith Morrill was born in Vermont in 1810, the son of a blacksmith and his wife. Justin was the eldest of the Morrill's sons and, due to their humble earnings they only had enough money to send one son, Justin, to college. Justin Morrill chose not to attend university, foregoing the opportunity because his brothers could not also attend. Yet, in spite of his lack of a formal college education, Morrill became a successful merchant amassing a fortune through real estate, railroads and finance markets before retiring in 1848 at the age of 38. Morrill went on to pursue a second career, in politics, when he was elected to the House of Representatives in 1854 at the age of 44 (Biemiller, 2011; Rowland, 2014). A Republican who largely focused his legislative efforts on public finance, Morrill served six terms in the House and then sought, successfully, a seat in the U.S. Senate (Biemiller).

In 1857, three years into his career as a congressman, Representative Morrill began to seek support for a bill wherein he proposed using the proceeds of sales from government lands to fund the development of universities for "sons of toil" (Rowland, 2014, p. 54). Morrill envisioned an education for all and contended that these new colleges would serve the needs of the nonelite, individuals entering agricultural and mechanical fields, through accessible and affordable education for the working classes (Allen-Diaz, 2012; Gunn & Lucaites, 2010), rather than the prestigious Ivy League universities already serving the wealthiest (e.g., Harvard, Yale, William and Mary) (Loss, 2012). Although the bill struggled due to lack of popularity with southern Congressional leaders who viewed it as federal imposition in state and local education, it did pass through both houses of Congress. However, it was subsequently vetoed by President Buchanan (Biemiller, 2011; Loss, 2012; Rowland, 2014).

In 1860, after the election of Abraham Lincoln as the 16th president of the United States, and the consequential secession of southern Confederate states, Representative Morrill again proposed his Land Grant Colleges Act. This time it passed through the House and Senate and onto the desk of President Lincoln. Timing could not have been more predominant. The Homesteaders Act was signed into law on May 20, 1862 giving any U.S. citizen, including freed slaves and women, the right to 160 acres of land for up to five years. At the end of five years, the homesteader would file for a deed of title by demonstrating that he or she had improved the land by growing crops, building a 12 × 14 dwelling, and living on the land (Potter & Schamel, 1997). The need for agricultural education en masse was apparent and pressing. On the morning of July 2, 1862, Lincoln signed three bills into law. The first, to make the practice of polygamy illegal in the United States, the second, to create a loyalty oath for government officials, and the third bill signed into law that morning was the Morrill Land-Grant Colleges Act (Loss, 2012).

Representative Morrill's education for all concept was meant to help farmers and industrial workers learn cutting-edge techniques and to generate research that would help the country produce more effectively in the areas of agriculture and mechanical development and infrastructure. Thus, this act was foundational in creating a rich history that has been enjoyed by many of the original Land Grant institutions resulting in their becoming beacons of scholarship and innovation in both applied and basic research (Courant, Duderstadt, & Goldernberg, 2010). Hamilton (2013) contends that the 1860s Land-Grant and Homesteaders Acts set in motion a period of genuine concern for education, social welfare, and economic development for farmers. This is an important aspect to consider as much of the U.S. populace was rural and the family farm was the center of domestic life in the United States at that time. As noted by Allen-Diaz (2012), the Morrill Land-Grant Act undoubtedly contributed to the unique U.S. economy by creating a system of education for low-income workers that was the first of its kind in the world, thus, enabling advancements that set the stage for the United States to be an economic, political, and social world leader.

Successes and Failures of Morrill Land Grant Act

As with all legislation, the intended outcome and the actual realities are not always perfectly aligned. The Land Grant Act changed the landscape of U.S. higher education dramatically and literally opened doors of access to college for many; indeed, the impact of the Land Grant Act is nearly incomprehensible. Consider that nearly two-thirds of all research generated in the United States is conducted in Land Grant institutions and that there are more than 100 today (Rowland, 2014). Yet, the Land Grant Act did not create education for all as ideally or completely as Morrill might have imagined or hoped (Rowland, 2014). Specifically, race and gender were not addressed in the initial act, and as no mention was made of either, states were left to interpret the inclusion of minority populations in the higher education institutions created (Beck & Swanson, 2003). Beck and Swanson (2003) purport that many western and midwestern states chose to use the Land Grant legislation pragmatically and, given that free African Americans and women could own land and that pioneering communities needed the resources and faculties of all individuals engaged, many of those Land Grant institutions of 1862 chose to have fully integrated education from the beginning. This was not the same for many Southern and border states, necessitating the second Morrill Land Grant Act.

1890 Morrill-McComas Act

The Compromise of 1877 ushered a new era for the southern states. Post-Civil war regulation of the south by northern troops ended with the Compromise and the ensuing election of Rutherford B. Hayes as the 19th President of the United States (Harris & Worthen, 2004). The removal of troops left the southern states in a fragile imbalance with freed slaves highly vulnerable to angry ex-confederates; in particular, freed slaves were in dangerous physical circumstances, without protection, support, or legal recourse for their rights in many cases (Harris & Worthen, 2004). Moreover, African Americans, as previously noted, had been systematically excluded from most institutions of higher education, primarily in the southern states, after the passage of the original Morrill Land Grant Act, thus having no access to affordable agricultural or mechanical education. This was particularly problematic given that many of the freed slaves were now beginning to own land and needed practical knowledge of farming. Although many had worked as slaves on plantations, many had worked in highly skilled areas (blacksmithing, woodwork, equestrian training; specific crops) and had not received any basic education (reading, writing) or developed a well-rounded knowledge of running all aspects of a farm as an actual business.

The 1890 Morrill-McComas Land Grant assisted in the creation of Land Grant institutions that would be specifically for the education of African Americans and teacher educators for African American K-12 compulsory schools. According to Johnson (2014), "Under this second act, states had to demonstrate that existing colleges did not use race or color in determining admission. If they could not they had to designate a separate land grant college for African Americans" (p. 553). These Land Grant institutions are known today as the Historically Black Colleges and Universities (HBCUs). As reported by Brown (2002) the separate creation of the HBCUs and the 1862 Land Grants led to a dual system of higher education (racially segregated) in 19 border and southern states: Alabama, Arkansas, Delaware, Florida, Georgia, Kentucky, Louisiana, Maryland, Mississippi, Missouri, North Carolina, Ohio, Oklahoma, Pennsylvania, South Carolina, Tennessee, Texas, Virginia, and West Virginia. This dual system still exists today in many of these states, in spite of legislative efforts to desegregate college campuses (Brown).

Almost immediately after the creation of the 1890 institutions, there were notable differences in infrastructure and practice from the original 1862 Land Grant colleges. For example, Harris and Worthen (2004) point to the 1862 Land Grants' access to Hatch funds, a result of the Hatch Act of 1887 which created experimental research funding opportunities. According to Harris and Worthen, the 1890 Land Grants were denied access to these funds until the 1970s. Other differences were even greater in scope. Of particular importance, the 1890 Land Grant institutions served in areas where there was a paucity of education for Black students at the primary level. Therefore, much of the education at the Black Land Grants was primary and secondary education with basic instruction in reading, math, and writing skills as the focus (Harris & Worthen, 2004). The shift to collegiate training did not occur until around the 1920s. When a university training agenda did emerge it was highly infused with hard manual labor, particularly at the Tuskegee institute which followed the Hampton model under the direction of Samuel Chapman Armstrong and Booker T. Washington (Anderson, 1988). The concept was that Black students could be trained to be teachers but only after a heavy induction into manual labor that would include moral education (Harris & Worthen). Inequalities, injustices, and social oppression were not challenged under this model, and as contended by Anderson, were actually consented to through replication of existing social inequity. In other words, in the HBCUs like Tuskegee that followed the Hampton model, African Americans were trained as the continued labor force of the southern economic system. It was after much public debate and other models of education were proposed by African American leaders such as W. E. B. Dubois that changes to education at the HBCUs reflected greater resemblance to the research structure of the 1862 Land Grant institutions (Anderson, 1988).

Hatch Act of 1887 (PL 84–352)

According to the U.S. Department of Agriculture's Catalog of Federal Domestic Assistance, the Hatch Act of 1887, as previously mentioned, allowed federal money to be used to fund cooperative multistate and multidisciplinary research to solve agricultural problems at the identified State Agriculture Experiment Stations (www.cfda.gov, 2014). William Henry Hatch (1833–1896) is the individual for whom the Hatch Act of 1887 was named. Hatch was born in Kentucky, studied and practiced law, was a commissioned captain in the Confederate army during the Civil War, and was heavily involved in the agriculture industry. A representative from Missouri, Hatch was the chair of the Congressional Agriculture committee for numerous sessions of congress (bioguide.congress.gov, 2015). His congressional legacy is most certainly tied to his role in facilitating the Agriculture committee's development of a model for federal appropriations for research at the state Land Grant institutions.

However, a major problem with Hatch Act funds is that they were connected to the Land Grant institutions that existed at the time (i.e., the historically White Land Grant institutions). This funding model later caused a problem for the Land Grant institutions established in the Morrill-McComas Act of 1890 (i.e., Historically Black Colleges and Universities [HBCUs]). Although later legislation was written to correct this problem and allow HBCUs to receive Hatch funds, there appears to be an ongoing major discrepancy between what 1862 Land Grants and 1890 Land Grants receive. Specifically, based on report of findings from a policy brief published by the Association of Public and Land Grant Universities (2013), the resolution that provided for giving fiscal research support to the 1890 Land Grants did not come until the Evans-Allen Act of 1977 (90 years after the Hatch Act). However, the Hatch Act funds require a state match for 1862 Land Grants whereas no state match is required for the 1890 Land Grants and, in fact, a waiver of state funds may be requested on a year-to-year basis for 1890 institutions (Lee & Keys, 2013). Therefore, although the federal government and the U.S. Department of Agriculture might equitably dispense funds based on an agreed upon formula, not having the state one-to-one match for the HBCUs has left them pervasively disadvantaged. Thus, it is estimated that the 1890 Land Grant institutions (HBCUs) lost 57 million from 2010 to 2012 due to waivers for matching funds (Lee & Keys, 2013). This kind of inequity causes residual and pervasive underfunding of research, extension and cooperative programs, and compromises the ability of faculty at HBCUs to mentor students' research, provide students with lab opportunities, and assist students in the development of comprehensive research skill sets. Thus, students at HBCUs, as well as faculty, continue to be disadvantaged by this funding model.

Smith-Lever Act (PL 107–293)

The Hon. Bill Flores, of Texas, delivered a speech in the House of Representatives on Tuesday, January 7, 2014, imploring the U.S. Congress to consider May 8, 2014, a date to nationally commemorate the 100th anniversary of landmark legislation: the historic Smith-Lever Act of 1914. Hoke Smith, an attorney by training and the owner and editor of the *Atlanta Evening Journal*, was a former two-time governor of Georgia and state senator who introduced the bill in the senate (bioguide.congress.gov). Meanwhile, Asbury Francis Lever, a representative from South Carolina, introduced the bill in the House. The Smith-Lever Act of 1914 was proposed to develop a system whereby the Land Grant institutions would use research findings and distribute information, through cooperative extension programs, to local communities, schools, farms, and individuals needing information to improve farming practices and outputs. This system distributed information on agricultural techniques, livestock and crop disease control, nutrition and wellness information, and is even credited with the development of educational programs such as the national 4-H clubs.

The cooperative extension programs worked from a complicated matrix that used federal money set aside from the Smith-Lever Act that was then transferred to the U.S. Department of Agriculture. From there, money was dispersed to U.S. Land Grants established primarily by the Morrill Land Grant of 1862. The Land Grant institutions were instructed to use the money for research, development, and training in their surrounding communities and states. This fact is one of the most inherently problematic pieces of the Smith-Lever Act. Because the funding was primarily set aside for the 1862 Land Grant institutions, the majority of 1890 Land Grant institutions (those schools that became the HBCUs), with a few exceptions (i.e., Tuskegee under the direction of Booker T. Washington) were underfunded by this allocation for research and cooperative extension in a comprehensive way. This deficit was compounded over time and kept many of the HBCUs from having the seed funding to develop research infrastructure and to sustain stability of research faculty with the necessary skills to procure external grant funding. An effort to provide equity and fairness in the allocation of funding finally came in 1971. Colorado Representation, Frank E. Evans, amended the original funding formula to specifically allocate twelve and a half million dollars to the 1890 Land Grant institutions. Similarly, the funding formula was revised again in 1994 to include the Tribal Colleges, allowing the Native American populations to finally receive the community services offered through cooperative extension partnerships with universities.

CASE LAW

Plessy v. Ferguson

The Louisiana Separate Car Act was signed into law in 1890, mandating that individuals must occupy seats on passenger cars as assigned to their particular race. Specifically, White passengers were in White passenger cars and African Americans were in Black passenger cars. The constitutionality of the Louisiana Separate Car Act was challenged two years after it was signed into law. The question at the heart of the case was this: Did the fourteenth amendment to the U.S. Constitution mean to include racial integration, social equality, and enfranchisement of the African American populations? (Scott, 2008) The group that developed a plan to challenge the law was the *Comite des Citoyen,* a Creole organization from New Orleans (Hoffer, 2014). The plan included having a member of their organization intentionally arrested for riding in a "Whites-only" car and then presenting a test case in court to challenge the Separate Car Act (Golub, 2005).

The *Comite des Citoyens* of New Orleans was primarily comprised of members from the Creole professional class. Homer Adolph Plessy, a New Orleans Afro-Creole shoemaker, the plaintiff in the case *Plessy v. Ferguson*, was one of the members of the group (Scott, 2008). This group provided the organizational structure and the resources to bring a test case against the constitutionality of the Separate Car Act through a planned and coordinated effort. Beyond race, to fully understand the nature and context of the legal dispute, the location and culture of New Orleans and the Creole population must be considered (Golub, 2005).

Creoles were distinguished by language, culture, and ethnicity rather than color, including their largely French and Spanish influence, and many had already been given legal, social, and economic rights denied most African Americans (Golub, 2005). Many Creoles had always been free and did not view themselves as aligned with African Americans or the concerns of freedmen. Indeed, they often thought of themselves as a unique and far more liberated culture. This was primarily due to the fact that New Orleans' society was more open than the rest of the South to socially recognizing interracial relationships with greater freedoms and economic opportunities that could be enjoyed by mixed-race people (Golub, 2005). In addition, the city fostered a thriving community of free people of color (*gens de couleur libre*). This strong Creole culture is critical to the case as Plessy and the members of *Comite des Citoyens* were fighting against separation based on color because, for affluent Creoles in positions of prominence, separation threatened to destroy their culture and community and positioned them as second-class citizens along with African Americans (Golub, 2005). The Louisiana Separate Car Act actually cost affluent Creoles power and privilege by castigating them for their race. For the less affluent African Americans, the Louisiana Separate Car Act was a continuation of the status quo of racial inequality.

On the afternoon of June 7, 1892 Plessy purchased a first-class, one-way ticket aboard the Louisiana Railway, departing New Orleans and bound for Covington, Louisiana (Golub, 2005). Critical to this case were the physical characteristics of Homer Plessy. Plessy, by all accounts appeared to be as White as anyone else in the White passenger car (Golub, 2005; Hoffer, 2014). This is important because he easily boarded the White car undetected; however, it is assumed that once he boarded, as was planned, the conductor was tipped off by a member of the *Comite des Citoyens* or an affiliate of the group, as to the fact that he was indeed part African. A person with any African heritage at all was considered Black ("the one drop rule") and therefore, Plessy's choosing to sit in the White section was by definition an unlawful act. Although he appeared White, the conductor was expected to ask passengers, especially those who warranted suspicion of being of multi-race, "Are you Black?" Plessy, who had purposely boarded a White passenger car with the intent of being caught and arrested, answered, "Yes." After Plessy refused to move to the Colored Car, a detective had him removed from the train and taken immediately to jail.

Plessy's lawyer argued that the Louisiana Separate Car Act was in violation of the thirteenth amendment and fourteenth amendment (privileges and immunities clause) (Hoffer, 2014). On May 18, 1896 the U.S. Supreme Court's finding was delivered by Justice Henry Billings Brown. The findings were not unanimous (8–1) with one Justice, John Marshall Harlan, dissenting from the group. However, the majority was not in support of Plessy's appeal, and found that indeed separate facilities for Blacks and Whites were constitutional as long as they were equal, a ruling that became known as "Separate but Equal." This ruling set up an entire system of practices including separate facilities for shopping, entertainment, education and business. The laws supporting these practices became known as the Jim Crow laws and the time period around "separate but equal" is often referred to as the Jim Crow era. It is noted by Bernstein (1990) that this particular ruling likely enforced segregation in areas, such as New Orleans, that had previously experienced open racial integration and this case actually catapulted the South into the Jim Crow era. Most critically, the Supreme Court ruling in this case set the foundation for later legislation, specifically *Brown v. Board of Education of Topeka Kansas* in 1954, where the "separate but equal" precedence would be overturned. Still, the case remains relevant today, not only in the context of the Jim Crow Era and past racial oppression, but also for what it reveals about contemporary understandings of racial identity and legal rights. Indeed, as noted throughout this book, many schools today are still separate and unequal as African American students are largely still divided from their White peers by poverty, opportunity, and postsecondary access.

Gaines v. Canada

In 1935, Lloyd Lionel Gaines applied for admission to the University of Missouri Law School, having just obtained a Bachelor of Arts degree from Lincoln University. With no law school in the state of Missouri for African Americans, Gaines contacted the university's registrar, Sy Woodson Canada, who noticed the Lincoln transcript and referred Gaines to the University of Missouri's president. Gaines was told he could not be accepted into the university based on race, and as there was no law school in the state, he was referred to the Superintendent of Missouri Schools for an out-of-state scholarship application to find an institution to attend in another state. *Gaines v. Canada* is the first case taken all the way to the Supreme Court with the backing of the National Association for the Advancement of Colored People (NAACP) (Lavergne, 2012). Four years later, in 1938, it was heard. In 1939, findings were issued by the court including, (1) Missouri had to provide an equal educational experience for Gaines; (2) using out of state scholarships to avoid providing equal educational opportunity and experiences would no longer be acceptable practices by states; and (3) a promise of future educational opportunity (i.e., plans to build a law school for African Americans in the state soon) does not preclude the obligation to provide an equal educational experience. Therefore, the Supreme Court's ruling was that the University of

Missouri had to either create a law school for Gaines or admit him to the law school for which he applied (Lavergne, 2012).

Sweatt V. Painter

The groundwork for the most sweeping legal and civil rights reform in all of U.S. education history was planned and executed under the direction of the lead counsel of the National Association for the Advancement of Colored People (NAACP), Thurgood Marshall, in 1945. The plan, to bring a test case against a university to challenge Jim Crow segregation systems, and later to challenge elementary and secondary education segregation, was based on the premise that a segregated system by nature constitutes dual citizenry and that the possibility of true equality was simply unattainable (Goldstone, 2004). The chosen plaintiff, Heman Marion Sweatt, was an unlikely candidate in many ways. He was 33 years old, a veteran, a mail carrier, and an applicant to University of Texas Law School (Houston, 2009). He has been described as physically small in stature (five-foot six and only 135 pounds), with a meager physical presence (Goldstone). Yet, he had family members and friends that were heavily involved in social activism and he had been instilled with a sense of integrity in regard to human rights and dignity. So, when approached to join the NAACP's purpose, by using his circumstances as a test case, he obliged (Goldstone; Houston, 2009; Lavergne 2012).

The main crux of separate, but equal laws only work if in fact, resources are available to all parties. This became the point of contention in Sweatt's case. Sweatt, desiring a law degree, had no school in which to apply in the state of Texas. The closest school, University of Texas (UT), would not admit African Americans at the time. However, on February 26, 1946 Sweatt came to UT to register alongside all of the other students registering for spring trimester and was accompanied by a party of supporters from the Texas NAACP. It is noteworthy to mention that according to Lavergne (2012), Sweatt did meet all of the residency and academic requirements for admission to the UT Law School. The only factor keeping Sweatt from enrolling was race. When he was denied access to enrollment and registration, the group visited UT president, Theophilis Painter who admittedly had no in-state opportunity to equate to UT Law School for Sweatt to apply for, yet refused to admit Sweatt (Houston, 2009). Indeed, Sweatt could only apply for out-of-state scholarships (Goldstone, 2004). Sweatt did not accept out-of state scholarships and instead did apply for admission to UT. Subsequently, the Texas Attorney General directed Painter to not admit Sweatt (Lavergne, 2012).

Sweatt was denied admission and he filed a suit against UT in the 126th District Court of Travis County in April 1946, arguing that his exclusion on the basis of race denied him equal protection rights under the Fourteenth

Amendment (Heilig, Reddick, Hamilton, & Dietz, 2010–2011). Judge Archer denied Sweatt's petition to order the university to admit him (Goldstone, 2004). After many lengthy appeals, Sweatt v. Painter was finally heard by the U.S. Supreme Court four years later on April 4, 1950 and a ruling was made on June 5, 1950 (Heilig, et al.).

At the time of the hearing the term equality itself was challenged in a way never defined before. Prior to Sweatt v. Painter, only objective measures were applied to equality, including, as stated by Lavergne (2012), "wages, budgets, buildings, books, and student-teacher ratios" (p. 1). However, in Sweatt's case, the application of intangibles changed how equality was viewed as it was no longer a measurable objective. Specific application of intangibles in Sweatt's case, according to Lavergne, included the experience of the faculty at UT, the alumni base, and the prestige of the institution along with variety of courses offered and opportunities to specialize in different types of law (Merjian, 2010). These could not be replicated for African Americans by the development of buildings and through tangibles such as a law library. Therefore, equality was simply not possible through separation.

The Supreme Court ruled unanimously in favor of Sweatt, and the precedent for successfully challenging educational inequality, had been set. The Supreme Court ordered that Sweatt be admitted as the first African American to an all-White education institution in the United States. The groundwork was laid for *Brown v. Board of Education* (1954).

Brown v. The Board of Education, Topeka, Kansas

Brown v. Board of Education of Topeka, Kansas is recognized as one of the greatest Supreme Court decisions of the twentieth century. The case focused on the segregation of White and Black children in public education. Oliver Brown, the father of Linda Brown, a student who was denied access to one of Topeka's white schools because of her race, was the plaintiff in the original Brown v. Board of Education suit. Shortly after she was not accepted into the school in 1951 Brown filed a class action suit against the Board of Education of Topeka, Kansas (Zirkel & Cantor, 2004). Although Brown was the lead plaintiff and the court case bears his name, there were actually five separate cases involved that were merged into one case for the Supreme Court to hear: *Brown v. Board of Education of Topeka*, *Briggs v. Elliot*, *Davis v. Board of Education of Prince Edward County* (VA.), *Boiling v. Sharpe*, and *Gebhart v. Ethel* (www.uscourts.gov). All of the complainants had the same concern regarding the constitutionality of state sponsored, educational segregation based on race.

The case was funded by the NAACP and Thurgood Marshall was the lead counsel. The primary argument in *Brown* was that the racial segregation in Topeka violated the Constitution's Equal Protection Clause of the 14th Amendment. The basis for this contention was that schools serving African American children could never be equal to those serving White children. The case gained leverage in court through psychological studies demonstrating that African American girls in segregated schools suffered lower self-esteem than their White counterparts. Based on these studies, the Supreme Court determined that segregation actually produced psychological harm for African American children (McBride, 2006.).

The findings of the court were unanimous and clear. On May 14, 1954 Chief Justice Warren delivered the Supreme Court's ruling which included the following excerpt,

> Segregation of white and colored children in public schools has detrimental effect upon the colored children. The impact is greater when it has the sanction of the law; for the policy of separating the races is usually interpreted as denoting the inferiority of the Negro group. A sense of inferiority affects the motivation of a child to learn .... We conclude that in the field of public education the doctrine of "separate but equal" has no place. Separate educational facilities are inherently unequal. Therefore, we hold that the plaintiffs and others similarly situated for whom the actions have been brought are, by reason of the segregation complained of, deprived of the equal protection of the laws guaranteed by the Fourteenth Amendment (Brown v. Board of Educ., 347 U.S. 483, 1954)

As with all major change, the Supreme Court knew that this ruling would not be popular with all who were affected by it. Initially, states were free to consider how to implement desegregation. However a year later, on May 31, 1955, a second ruling, known as *Brown II* was handed down by the Supreme Court. In this ruling, it was stated that schools were to end segregation with "all deliberate speed." (www.uscourts.gov). Although many school districts tried to integrate through busing and the development of magnet programs, there is a long-lasting legacy of segregation by race that is still occurring in the United States today in spite of 60 years of *Brown v. Board of Education*.

Hopwood v. Texas

Undoubtedly, race has existed as an issue in higher education in spite of *Sweatt v. Painter* and *Brown v. the Board of Education*. Significant gains remain underscored by an abundance of questions. For example, although integration is mandated, to what degree is it actually occurring? How much do measures such as Affirmative Action help? As is noted throughout this book, measures such as Affirmative Action may be too little too late for African American students who come from P-12 schools that are severely under-resourced.

To be pointed, entrance into college or graduate school may be a moot point if one's preparation for such endeavor is lacking due to starkly insufficient infrastructure for educational and career preparedness necessary for success. Moreover, there have been challenges as to the constitutionality of efforts to support African Americans' academic integration initiatives. A particularly famous case in point is that of *Hopwood v. Texas*. Cheryle Hopwood was a White female applicant to UT-Austin School of Law and was denied. She filed a lawsuit claiming that less qualified minorities had been admitted. She was joined by three white males: Douglas Carvell, Kenneth Elliott, and David Rogers (Heilig et al., 2010–2011). The U.S. Court of Appeals for the 5th Circuit found in favor of the plaintiffs noting that the use of race for admissions decisions was not applicable under the 14th amendment to the constitution. This finding significantly changed the Affirmative Action practice in Texas universities which now operate under the Top Ten Percent Plan (Heilig, et al.). In sum, any student in Texas graduating in the top ten percent of his or her senior class in high school will be automatically admitted to their choice of state universities or colleges.

EDUCATION LEGISLATION

Although there are many pertinent cases that have influenced college access and career readiness for African Americans, it is beyond the scope of this chapter to cover all of them. Similarly, there has been a plethora of legislative acts issued over decades to improve educational quality for students. In this section we cover, briefly, a few major legislative acts that have had profound impact on academic equity, educational opportunity, and career and college readiness for African American students. Again, not every important Act is covered in this chapter.

National Defense Education Act (PL 85–864)

In 1958, the Soviet Union beat the United States in the Race to Space with the launch of Sputnik, sparking concern about the U.S. education system's ability to produce future scientists with the capability to keep the country as a global leader in technology and innovation. The National Defense Education Act (NDEA) of 1958 was in response to this concern. The NDEA allowed for curriculum improvement in science, math, and foreign language instruction beginning with elementary schools, allocated funds for graduate fellowships, and set up some of the first low interest student loans (U.S. Department of Education, 2012a). Additionally, school guidance counselors were placed in many secondary schools to promote vocational training and college transitions. However, little disaggregate data was collected on the impact of these initiatives in regard to promoting career and college transitions for African Americans as promoting diversity was not a main focus of the NDEA.

The Civil Rights Act (PL 88–352)

The Civil Rights Act, Public Law 88–352 (78 Stat. 241), was passed and signed into law in 1964 by Lyndon B. Johnson, 36th president of the United States. The Civil Rights Act barred employment discrimination (including promotions or termination) based on sex and race. The key title that addresses discrimination in education settings is Title VI of the Civil Rights Act and this legislation is reinforced through the U.S. Department of Education's Office of Civil Rights. The main regulatory functions of this office are to investigate reports of Civil Rights violations in education settings that receive federal appropriations (U.S. Department of Education, 2005). For example, the type of report that the OCR might receive and investigate is a report that minority students are being discriminatorily assigned to classes designed for students with learning disabilities.

Higher Education Act (PL 89–329)

The Higher Education Act (HEA), enacted in 1965, signed into law by President Lyndon B. Johnson, created one of the clearest visions in American life for a way to break the cycle of poverty and to give hope to families and children who were stuck in a cycle of government assistance and oppression, through opportunity and education. As stated by Johnson (2014), although postsecondary education is not a constitutional right, the Higher Education Act created greater accessibility to the American dream by making college affordable through the implementation of grants and loans. The Higher Education Act has been through eight reauthorizations since 1968, the year of the first reauthorization, evidence of the continued debate and conversation over what college access means, what constitutes affordability, and how institutions of higher education should be held accountable for funds. There are many successes of the HEA but there are also still problems. The initial impact of the HEA was undeniable. Prior to enactment of the HEA there were approximately 2.6 million students enrolled in higher education in the United States, by the first reauthorization, in 1968, that number was 7 million. Yet, while students were being given funding to attend universities, administrators were arguing that they needed greater resources to meet the demands of the growing populations at their institutions (Johnson, 2014). Further, issues addressed in later reauthorizations included increasing access through strengthening rigor in high school programs so that underprivileged and minority students would be truly prepared for college academics not just fiscal responsibilities of attending postsecondary programs (Burke, 2014).

Since its inception the Higher Education Act has funded multiple programs to increase equity, access, and fairness in college admissions and matriculation particularly for minority, low-income, and first-generation college students. These programs include, but are not limited to, the following:

1. Financial assistance to students including federal student aid, low interest student loans, federal work-study programs, Pell Grants, income-based repayment, and the College Navigator service (a listing of postsecondary institutions that receive federal funding and their annual tuition, fees, percent of tuition increase, a list of the lowest and highest price universities and more)
2. Institutional Aid: Monies are provided through the HEA to HBCUs and to colleges and universities providing Science, Technology, Engineering and Math experiential programs for K-12 minority and low-income students
3. Project GRAD: A program to increase the number of low-income students who graduate high school and attend college
4. Gaining Early Awareness and Readiness for Undergraduate Programs (GEAR UP) and TRIO: provides mentorship, tutoring, college counseling
5. Comprehensive college transition programs for students with disabilities (Burke, 2014)

All of these programs are substantial resources for students and have likely had significant impact on African American student success. However, the HEA continually undergoes reauthorization and is vulnerable to political environments and the ongoing financial backing of legislators.

Elementary and Secondary Education Act of 1965 (PL 89–10)

In 1965, as a continued effort in the war on poverty, and in response to the Civil Rights movement and the Civil Rights Act of 1964, Congress passed a sweeping education bill known as the Elementary and Secondary Education Act of 1965 (ESEA) that changed the financial structures of K-12 schools throughout the United States. President Johnson was a renowned supporter of the bill as part of his administration's efforts to eradicate poverty through social and education systems. The major crux of the ESEA was to ensure that all public schools had qualified teachers, sufficient facilities for educating students with adequate materials, and that all students had a right to a fair and equitable education. Because of this principle, the majority of funds were distributed to schools that had the highest concentration of low-income students (The Social Welfare History Project, 2014).

In the 133rd Congress, there were multiple proposals put forth for reauthorization of the ESEA. Based on a report submitted by the Congressional Research Service (Skinner, Kuenzi, Dortch, & McCallion, 2013), major features of the new proposed reauthorization pertinent to this chapter retained in the ESEA included: Magnet Schools assistance, rural and low-income school achievement program formula grants, and impact aid payments for eligible federally connected children (i.e., children with disabilities). New programs included improving literacy, STEM instruction and student achievement, increasing well-rounded education, financial literacy education, centers of excellence in early childhood, family engagement in education programs, and a college information demonstration program (Skinner et al., 2013).

Section 504 of the Rehabilitation Act of 1973 and Individuals with Disabilities Education Act (PL 94–142)

Section 504 of the Rehabilitation Act of 1973 was written and enacted to protect individuals from discrimination based on disabilities. In regard to education, Section 504 covers schools (including post-secondary) that receive federal financial assistance. In order to comply with Section 504, schools receiving federal financial assistance must provide every eligible student with a free appropriate public education (FAPE) regardless of the type or severity of the individual's disability (U.S. Department of Education, 2013). At the K-12 level, any student in the public school district must receive these services if they are identified with a disability requiring services and they are of an age that makes education mandatory in the state in which they reside. However, of specific interest, at the postsecondary level, students must meet the academic and technical requirements of the institution for admission. Section 504 outlines legal guidelines for what constitutes evaluation of an identified disability, how to deal with episodic versus temporary impairment, who makes final conclusions about student eligibility for services, parent consent and mediation procedures (U.S. Department of Education, 2013). Section 504 covers disabilities more broadly and is concerned with protecting the civil rights of an individual with a disability rather than producing measurable educational outcomes. In addition, the Americans with Disabilities Act (ADA) (PL 101–336) addresses access for students with disabilities at the postsecondary level from a civil rights perspective. Colleges and universities must ensure equal access to all students who are otherwise qualified. Accessibility may mean different things. For example, making buildings accessible through the use of wheelchair ramps, or having handicap parking available for students within a reasonable distance. Another example might include having wheelchair lifts available for on-campus transportation such as student shuttles. Of particular interest, since the ADA passed and accommodations for students have been mandatory, enrollments of students with disabilities at colleges and universities has continued to increase and this is likely due to the support services available to these students (Flexer, Simmons, Luft, & Baer, 2005; Henderson, 1999).

The Individuals with Disabilities Education Act (IDEA) was originally signed into law as the Education for All Handicapped Children Act, by the 38th president, Gerald Ford on November 29, 1975. The IDEA made educational provisions for young children (as young as birth to 2 years old) identified with disabilities to have access to a free appropriate public education (FAPE) in the least restrictive environment. This meant that students with disabilities would not automatically be separated from the general population in contained classrooms, but rather, where appropriate and possible, they would be educated alongside their peers (U.S. Department of Education, 2012b). The provisions of IDEA for individuals are highly specified and require that students make educational advances. The Individual Education Plan (IEP) may even be written to address additional services that will be offered (i.e., tutoring) and parent consent for the child's education plan is required. The IDEA has stringent re-evaluation guidelines that must be followed.

Although Section 504 and the IDEA has likely allowed many deserving students to receive services they definitively needed to be successful in education environments, it is imperative to consider the disproportionate identification of African American students (particularly males) as identified with learning disabilities. Greater contemplation of the evaluation process, support structures, and learning environments may yield more meaningful understandings of children's true abilities and potential rather than reflections on their race and socioeconomic circumstances. Further mindful thought of the labels applied to students and how to create a culture of acceptance, sensitivity, and respect for students' strengths and rights might assist in promoting change.

No Child Left Behind (PL 107–110)

In 2002, the 43rd president of the United States, George W. Bush, signed No Child Left Behind (NCLB) into law. NCLB, a reauthorization of the ESEA, was a bi-partisan effort aimed at ensuring every child has access to a quality education, and that there is a focus on academic gains and closing the achievement gap for minority populations (Chen, 2014; Curry & Milsom, 2013). NCLB outlined specific criteria for minimum teacher credentialing, school choice, school report cards, and required student proficiency on state assessments in order to gain federal funding. However, states were allowed to design their own student learning assessments. Because NCLB focused so heavily on Math and English/Language Arts many schools began to give more time and attention to these subjects to the loss of time in other curricula areas (Chen, 2014).

NCLB guidelines established a 12 implementation time frame for schools to close the achievement gap (Martin & Robinson, 2011). As noted in Chapter 1, this has not happened and was likely an unrealistic goal. Moreover, a major criticism of NCLB is that focus on standardized testing has led to teaching to the test and a less rounded education. As further iterations of NCLB are developed and refined, and data on the successes and failures of this legislation are reviewed, it will be critical to ascertain how effective this has been for all student populations including low SES and African American students. To date, the progress does not underscore that African Americans are still earning fewer college degrees and matriculating through college at a substantially lower rate than their White counterparts (please see Chapter 1 for statistics).

SUMMARY

In this chapter we reviewed pertinent legislation and case law affecting the career and college readiness of African American K-12 and postsecondary students. The information covered here was only a minimal review and readers are encouraged to more thoroughly review cases and legislation of interest. Although legislation and case law have resulted in significant gains and progress for African American students there is still much to be hoped for. At the conclusion of this chapter we salute the courage of individuals who filed lawsuits demanding their civil rights and the congressional leaders who represented access, equity and fairness in the bills that became laws that transformed schools and universities. We remain hopeful that change and equality are possible.

REFERENCES

Allen-Diaz, B. (2012). 150 years after Morrill Act, land-grant universities are key to healthy California. *California Agriculture, 66*(1), 1–2.

Anderson, J. D. (1988). *The education of Blacks in the south*. Chapel Hill, NC: University of North Carolina Press.

Beck, M. M., & Swanson, J. C. (2003). Value-added animal agriculture: Inclusion of race and gender in the professional formula. *Journal of Animal Science, 81*, 2895–2903.

Bernstein, D. (1990). The Supreme Court and "Civil Rights," 1886–1908. *The Yale Law Journal, 100*(3), 725–744.

Biemiller, L. (2011). A land-grant visionary's notion of home. *Chronicle of Higher Education, 58*(9), 37–38.

Biographical Directory of the United States Congress. (2015). Hatch, William Henry. Retrieved from http://bioguide.congress.gov/scripts/biodisplay.pl?index=H000339

Brown v. Board of Educ., 347 U.S. 483 (1954).

Brown, M. C. (2002). Good intentions: Collegiate desegregation and transdemographic enrollments. *The Review of Higher Education, 25*(3), 263–280. doi:10.1353/rhe.2002.0009

Burke, L. (2014). Reauthorizing the Higher Education Act: Toward policies that increase access and lower costs. Retrieved from http://www.heritage.org/research/reports/2014/08/reauthorizing-the-higher-education-acttoward-policies-that-increase-access-and-lower-costs

Catalog of Federal Domestic Assistance. (2014). Payments to agriculture experiment stations under the Hatch Act. Washington D.C.: U.S. Department of Agriculture. Retrieved from https://www.cfda.gov/index?s=program&mode=form&tab=core&id=5c58a96f8078d4a8c8d3e27dcbd4c51c

Chen, G. (Jan 30, 2014). Understanding No Child left Behind. Retrieved from http://www.publicschoolreview.com/blog/understanding-no-child-left-behind

Courant, P. N., Duderstadt, J. J., & Goldernberg, E. N. (2010). Needed: A National strategy to preserve public research universities. *Chronicle of Higher Education, 56*(17), 36.

Curry, J., & Milsom, A. (2013). *Career Counseling in P-12 Schools*. New York: Springer.

Flexer, R. W., Simmons, T. J., Luft, P., & Baer, R. M. (2005). *Transition planning for secondary students with disabilities* (2nd ed.). Upper Saddle River, NJ: Pearson.

Goldstone, D. N. (2004). "I don't believe in segregation": *Sweatt v. Painter* and the groundwork for *Brown v. Board of Education*. Judges' Journal,

Golub, M. (2005). Plessy as "passing": Judicial responses to ambiguously raced bodies in *Plessy v. Ferguson. Law & Society Review, 39*(3), 563–600.

Gunn, J. & Lucaites, J. L. (2010). The contest of faculties: On discerning the politics of social engagement in the academy. *Quarterly Journal of Speech, 96*(4), 404–412. doi:10.1080/00335630.2010.521176

Hamilton, N. D. (2013). Harvesting the law: Personal reflections on thirty years of change in agricultural legislation. *Creighton Law Review, 46*(4), 563–590.

Harris, R. P., & Worthen, H. D. (2004). Working through the challenges: Struggle and resilience within the Historically Black Land Grant institutions. *Education, 124*(3), 447–455.

Heilig, J. V., Reddick, R. J., Hamilton, C., & Dietz, L. (2010–2011). Actuating equity: historical and contemporary analyses of African American access to selective higher education from *Sweatt* to the Top 10 Percent law. *Harvard Journal of African American Public Policy, 17,* 11–27.

Henderson, C. (1999). *1999 college freshmen with disabilities statistical year 1998: A biennial statistical profile*. Washington, DC: American Council on Education, HEATH Resource.

Hoffer, W. J. H. (2014). Plessy v. Ferguson: The Effects of Lawyering on a Challenge to Jim Crow. *Journal of Supreme Court History*, 39(1), 1–21. doi:10.1111/j.1540–5818.2014.12037.x

Houston, R. (2009). The NAACP state conference in Texas: Intermediary and catalyst for change, 1937–1957. *The Journal of African American History.* 94(4), 509–528.

Johnson, T. L. (2014). Going back to the drawing board: Re-entrenching the Higher Education Act to restore its historical policy of access. *University of Toledo Law Review, 45*, 545–578.

Lavergne, G. M. (2012). *Sweatt v. Painter* (1950) and why Sweatt won his case: A chronicle of judicial appointments. *Southern Studies: An Interdisciplinary Journal of the South, 19*(1), 1–23.

Lee, J. M. & Keys, S. W. (2013). Land Grant but unequal: State one-to-one match funding for 1890 Land Grant institutions. Report No. 3000-PB1, Policy Brief, Association of Public and Land Grant Universities. Retrieved online www.aplu.org/OASreseaarch

Loss, C. P. (2012). Why the Morrill Land Grant Act still matters. *Chronicle of Higher Education, 58*(41), 17.

Martin, P. J., & Robinson, S. G. (2011). Transforming the school counseling profession. In B. T. Erford (Ed.), *Transforming the school counseling profession* (pp. 1–18). Upper Saddle River, NJ: Pearson.

McBride, A. (2006). Supreme Court history: Expanding civil rights. Retrieved online from http://www.pbs.org/wnet/supremecourt/rights/landmark_brown.html

Merjian, A. H. (2010). Relitigating Plessy in the 21st century: Separate and unequal education in California. *Texas Hispanic Journal of Law and Policy, 16*(1), 1–35.

Potter, L. A. & Schamel, W. (1997) The Homestead Act of 1862. *Social Education, 61*(6), 359–364.

Rowland, T. (2014). The 'do-something' congress. *America's Civil War 27*(5), 50–55.

Scott, R. J. (2008). Public rights, social equality, and the conceptual roots of the Plessy challenge. *Michigan Law Review*, 106(5), 777–804.

Skinner, R. R., Kuenzi, J. J., Dortch, C., & McCallion, G. (July 12th, 2013). ESEA Reauthorization propo9sals in the 113th congress: Comparison of major features. Congressional Research Service. 7–5700. www.crs.gov R43146

The Social Welfare History Project. (2014). The Elementary and Secondary Education Act of 1965. Retrieved online from http://www.socialwelfarehistory.com/events/elementary-and-secondary-education-act-of-1965/

United States Courts. (2015). Brown v. Board of Education. Retrieved from http://www.uscourts.gov/educational-resources/get-involved/federal-court-activities/brown-board-education-re-enactment/history.aspx

U.S. Department of Education. (2005). Education and Title IV. Retrieved online from http://www2.ed.gov/about/offices/list/ocr/docs/hq43e4.html

U.S. Department of Education. (2012a). The Federal role in education. Retrieved from http://www2.ed.gov/about/overview/fed/role.html

U.S. Department of Education. (2012b). The Office of Special Education and Rehabilitative Services celebrates 35 years of the Individuals with Disabilities

Education Act (IDEA). Retrieved from http://www2.ed.gov/about/offices/list/osers/idea35/index.html

U.S. Department of Education. (2013). Protecting students with disabilities. Retrieved from http://www2.ed.gov/about/offices/list/ocr/504faq.html

Zirkel, S., & Cantor, N. (2004). 50 years after Brown v. Board of education: The promise and challenge of multicultural education. *Journal of Social Issues, 60*(1), 1–15.

Chapter 3

Making a Way Out of No Way

A Contextualized History of African Americans in Higher Education

Berlisha R. Morton and Dana C. Hart

The history of African Americans in higher education is not a simple matter in the history of the United States higher educational enterprise; rather, it is a complicated part and parcel to the development of an educational system that predates the founding of the country (Mitchell, Dancy, Hart, & Morton, 2013). Accordingly, this historical narrative, as well as that of Historically Black Colleges and Universities (HBCUs), is an important part to the development of a democratic higher educational enterprise. The presence of African ascendant people (Dillard, 2012) in institutions of higher education before 1865 and the development of HBCUs after the Civil War document the struggles of a young nation's failures and triumphs in the democratic process. In *Democracy in America*, de Tocqueville (1835/1969) wrote, "The formidable evil threatening the future of the United States is the presence of the blacks on their soil" (p. 340). Often cited as a prediction for the Civil War and the ensuing racial contention in America, the next part of that passage is also very telling. He writes, "From whatever angle one sets out to inquire into the present embarrassments or future dangers facing the United States, one is almost always brought up against this basic fact" (p. 340). The outsider looking in perspective allowed for de Tocqueville's observations to take on a prophetic nature and created the angles in which the citizenry would have to evaluate the abolition of slavery and find solutions to the Negro problem.

Watkins (2001) explains this shift further when he writes, "Without question, the Civil War was the defining event in the shaping of industrial America. It represented at once an end to outdated agriculturalism, semi-feudal social relationships in the south, divisive regional governments, and international isolation" (p. 13). This environment nurtured the widespread development of

HBCUs, institutions that brought a previously enslaved population into the polity, and a true test of American democracy.

Higher education is the oldest formal system of education in the United States (Manning, 2013; Birnbaum, 1988). What is often thought to be the "American" system of higher education is derived from an Old World model of individuals self-organizing into guilds to study knowledge in a designated space (Manning, 2013; Thelin, 2004). However, while it has been acknowledged that the development of higher education began with Harvard in 1636 and predates the colonial project for independence by over a hundred years, the causal effects of studying a romanticized history of African Americans in postsecondary education have not been thoroughly interrogated. We confront this contextualized history of African Americans in education in this chapter, and present the history of HBCUs while unpacking complex questions concerning race and democracy.

The sociopolitical construct in which HBCUs were created is a critical element to their foundation and development. These institutions remain a vital component to the education of African Americans in the United States and they maintain a historic identity of promoting education, community, and racial uplift (Gasman, 2008). Developed within/against broader American society that was (and still is) dealing with its problems of race, HBCUs were tasked with educating and democratizing blacks into the citizenry. Therefore, in reality HBCUs did more with less, and in practice they did *more than* in promoting democracy and educational opportunity. In a separate-but-equal ethos, HBCUs did not discriminate or exclude, and they never systematically barred the admission of one race, gender, class, or faith.

It has been well documented by scholars (Anderson, 1988, 2012; Mills, 1997; Watkins, 2001; Brown & Davis, 2001) that the barriers to formal education of enslaved persons in Southern states were necessary for the socioeconomic structure to survive and thrive. Therefore, the monumental gains made by Southern Blacks after the Civil War provide a significant marking point to study the history of Blacks in higher education.

HISTORICAL CONTEXT

During the nation's infancy, the development of mercantilist economic systems in southern and northern colonies directly influenced the educational policies and laws for enslaved people and free people of color (Giddings, 1984; Williams & Ashley, 2004). In the northern colonies, although the rights and responsibilities of citizenship were inhibited through tangible inequality, the education of enslaved people and free people of color, however *"difficult and dangerous,*" was not illegal (Williams and Ashley, 2004). In the southern colonies, conversely, wherein the plantation economic system developed into what many scholars called a *slaveocracy*, educating enslaved people was deemed detrimental to the colonies' survival. For example, in 1740 and 1755 respectively, South Carolina and Georgia passed laws to limit and prohibit the education of enslaved people (Williams & Ashley, 2004). By the eighteenth century the social landscape in the United States slowly changed. Moreover, with the decline of slavery in the North after the Revolutionary War, states north of Maryland gradually abolished slavery by 1840. Yet, it remained illegal to educate slaves in the South, a punishable crime throughout the Civil War (Williams & Ashley, 2004). These events created a collective memory of abolitionist against slaveholders, in which the North represented a so-called bastion of educational opportunity and the South typified an educational wasteland.

From a national standpoint, higher education virtually excluded students of color until after the Civil War (Anderson, 1988). Although a few institutions emerged during the antebellum period, such as Lincoln and Cheney universities in Pennsylvania and Wilberforce in Ohio, from the Reconstruction era through the early twentieth century, black higher education in the United States largely developed within a system of private liberal arts colleges (Anderson, 1988). It should also be noted that Oberlin College in Ohio began accepting students of color in 1835, and by the 1840s and 1850s, African American students comprised from 4 to 5 percent of Oberlin's total enrollment. Yet, these first students of color did not escape the controversy and hostility perpetuated by many of their White classmates. At an address delivered at Oberlin College in 1891, for example, then secretary of the American Missionary Association, Reverend M. E. Strieby, recalled some of the initial resentment:

> When Father Shipherd ... wrote to the Trustees of Oberlin urging them to pass a vote to admit students *irrespective of color*, what a commotion it created! Some of the young ladies, who were students from New England, said that if colored people were admitted they would go home at once, if they had to wade Lake Erie to get there. But the vote was passed ... for after all discussions, moral and political, and all the bloodshed of the war, this word *irrespective of color* is still the pivotal point in one of the live questions of the day. Oberlin soon swung fully in line (Strieby, 1891).

As such, the development of HBCUs during the post-Civil War and Reconstruction eras, and the mass entrance of the freed people into the higher educational enterprise, has been studied and presented as the beginning of African Americans in higher education.

Post-Civil War Higher Education

Menand (2001) argues that the post-Civil War period marked the beginning of an intellectual tradition where the country's most prominent intellectuals wrote, lectured, and crafted court opinions about what democracy, liberty, and freedom meant in a modern America. While the primary concern of these thinkers was the preservation of the ideals of the Democratic experiment, Democracy would become more than an experiment as the newly emancipated entered the American populace. Anderson (1988) writes, "For a brief period during the late 1860s and 1870s, as free laborers, citizens, and voters, the ex-slaves entered into a new social system of capitalism, Republican government, and wage labor" (p. 19). However, full participation in these systems would not be possible without education for the newly emancipated. Anderson presents the postwar battles between the newly emancipated and the White planter class over the ramifications of universal education. These two groups understood that education was the path to realization of full social and economic citizenship and both worked tirelessly to reach two conflicting ends to this path. Anderson explains,

> They [ex-slaves] played a central role in etching the idea of universal public education into southern state constitutional law ... Black politicians and leaders joined with Republicans in southern constitutional conventions to legalize public education in the constitutions of the former Confederate states. (p. 19)

When the White planter class regained control of state legislatures from 1869 to 1877, the planters "kept universal schooling underdeveloped ...and generally discouraged the expansion of public school opportunities." (Anderson, 1988, p. 23).

When African Americans entered the postsecondary educational enterprise, there were intense debates, theories, and philosophies to unpack the curricular, socioeconomic, and moral needs of a people who were systematically denied access to education. However, the binding principle of these debates and essentially the history of African Americans in higher education is an understanding that higher education served a larger purpose than basic learning—it was an essential hope; a blind faith in the possibility of true "liberty and justice for all" in the United States. Therefore, in a volume where the focus is college readiness, it is necessary to present a chronological history that contextualizes this history, particularly in regard to the development of HBCUs, and understands the dual purpose of education—the pragmatic function to provide economic security and the pragmatic hope of uplifting an entire race. Thus, the history of African Americans in Higher Education, and subsequently HBCUs, cannot be told through institutional histories based on an Anglofied colonial ideal (Thelin, 2004), but should be told through the lens of political economy (Watkins, 2001).

DEMOCRATIZING HIGHER EDUCATION

With the understanding that Black colleges and universities were developed and nurtured within the same time period in which America redefined its intellectual, political, and economic identities, HBCUs were tasked with educating and democratizing Blacks into the American citizenry as both second and middle class citizens (Anderson, 1988; Watkins, 2001). However, what remains is the larger question of what *it meant for Blacks to be citizens*. To answer this question, many scholars turn to the intellectual debates of Booker T. Washington and W.E.B. DuBois, and for good reasons.

The theories behind the Washington/DuBois debates involve conceptualizations of the goals of educating Blacks. One goal, as espoused by Washington was a vocational model of a more applied nature, such as woodworking, sewing, fieldwork, and housekeeping. The opposing goal, most often affiliated with DuBois, was an education grounded in the values of a liberal arts tradition. These philosophical differences over the type of education Blacks should receive ultimately had an effect on the type and amount of support that HBCUs received from donors (Richardson, 1980). Accordingly, scholars such as Anderson (1988) and Watkins (2001) have produced formative texts that highlight the influence of ideology and political economy on the development of institutions for the higher education of Blacks. They pay particular attention to how White, mostly male, Northern philanthropists, in their motivations to gain new levels of wealth and influence, manipulated the development of Black education in general and higher education in particular. Specifically, significant investments were made in education models that supported the latter goal: vocational training. In so doing, northern philanthropists who were wishing to capitalize on the new postwar Southern economy would need a labor force that was skilled, inexpensive, and lacking in traditional education so that they could not escape the labor industry as a sole vocational path (Anderson, 1988).

Because of the historical exclusion of Black Americans from the larger sociopolitical polity, higher education highlights the contrasts between the ideology of the American Dream and the realities of racism. Scholars of African American higher education argue that African American education is often conceptualized in relation to the prevailing U.S. political economy. In her recounting of Carter G. Woodson's *The Education of the Negro Prior to 1861*, Evans (2007) suggested that the educational attainment of African ascendant people matched the ebb and flow of the socioeconomic and sociopolitical needs of the country as it moved from to colony to nation. She writes,

> From 1619 to 1750, the solidification of race-based enslavement narrowed opportunity, while from 1750 to 1800, the air of freedom exuded by American revolutionaries brought a relative loosening of educational restrictions.

From 1800 to the mid-1830s, African Americans aspiring to be educated experienced a backlash due to the Haitian Revolution and the subsequent revolts by Gabriel Prosser, Denmark Vesey, and Nat Turner (and reaction to David Walker's *Appeal*); and the period from the 1830s to 1860 was an era of intensified struggle for freedom.

Samuels (2004) made a relevant observation that while the tenets of the American Creed served as the basis for the arguments for the civil rights of Black Americans, "the American Creed tends to obscure the particulars of the African American Experience ... Despite the laudable goal of promoting racial harmony and understanding, applying the American Creed to racial issues often produces greater polarization between whites and African Americans" (original emphasis, p. 5). The centuries of systematic exclusion of Blacks from the higher educational enterprise and the subsequent decision to include Blacks through the creation of separate institutions marked the beginning of another era of debate. The most notable debates would occur over the Hampton-Tuskegee Model.

Which Way to Freedom?

The Hampton-Tuskegee Model began as the Hampton Idea. Watkins (2001) explains that the,

> Hampton Idea was about much more than education. It was about Nation building. It was about carefully situating the newly freed Black in a new sociopolitical and economic order ... it was about forging a social order rooted in apartheid, economic exploitation, oppression, and inequality. (p. 43)

General Samuel Chapman Armstrong founded Hampton Institute in the spring of 1868 with assistance from the American Missionary Association and Josiah King, a philanthropist from Pittsburgh, Pennsylvania. Of interest, W.E.B. Du Bois commented, "Easily the most striking thing in the history of the American Negro since 1876 is the ascendency of Mr. Booker T. Washington." (Du Bois, 1903/1997, p. 62) Du Bois was only born the year that Hampton opened. As such, the debates surrounding industrial versus classical education for the freed people existed long before the Washington/DuBois Debates. Although Du Bois was not the only critic of the Hampton-Tuskegee Model, his critiques were given the most visibility and credibility because of his stature as the "Renaissance man of African American letters during the first fifty years of the twentieth century" (Gates & McKay, 2004, p. 686). In other words, W. E. B. Dubois was seen as the leader of transformative political, social, and educative thought among many African Americans of his day and his harsh criticism of the Hampton-Tuskegee model was adopted by many other notable, and powerful, African American leaders. Specifically, Dubois wanted an academe of classics, a liberal education for African Americans; an education equivalent to the education of White students. Comparatively, the education given to African Americans in the Hampton-Tuskegee model was often vocational training in hard labor and rudimentary tasks.

To be sure, the nuances and peculiarities of the Washington/Du Bois curricular debate on the nature of Black education in the early twentieth century can fill an entire volume. However for this text, it is important to unravel the journeys that led to these debates. Washington and Du Bois represent more than two polarizing sides of the industrial versus classical education debate. These two men and their educational journeys led to educational philosophies that encapsulate the struggle of a people who believed that education could lead to freedom.

In his autobiography, *Up From Slavery*, Booker Taliferro Washington (1901/1963) describes the first time he heard of Hampton Normal and Agricultural Institute. According to Washington, he was working in a coal mine when he overheard "two miners talking about a great school for coloured people in Virginia" (p. 42). As he listened to them speaking of this school where "poor but worthy students could work out all or part of the cost of the board", he says,

> As they went on describing the school, it seemed to me that it must be the greatest place on earth, and not even heaven presented more attractions for me at that time than did the Hampton Normal and Agricultural Institute in Virginia … I resolved at once to go to that school, although I had no idea where it was, or how many miles away, or how I was going to reach it: I remembered that I was on fire constantly with one ambition, and that was to go to Hampton. This thought was with me day and night. (pp. 42–43)

Although penniless, Washington indeed made it to Hampton and became the premier African American leader of his generation and one of the most influential, yet controversial, thinkers in African American Higher Education. General Samuel Chapman Armstrong, founder of Hampton Institute, has been acknowledged by Washington and historians as having the strongest influence on Washington's educational philosophy. However, in any discussion of Washington's educational philosophy, his physical and metaphysical journey from enslavement to the steps of Hampton Institute must be included because Washington's journey is only exceptional due to the level of notoriety he obtained; however, it was not unique to the African American experience of that moment in history. To explain this idea, Watkins (2001) explains that Chapman and Washington were *"tailor-made for each other"* and further offers, "Armstrong was looking for students who would quickly and enthusiastically embrace his views on Negro socialization and education. Washington was looking for decent Whites not committed to the slaver's whip" (p. 59). As such, it becomes possible to understand Washington's dogmatic commitment to Armstrong and to what would become known as the Hampton-Tuskegee Model. Washington had an honest belief in the virtue of hard work because it was through hard work—manual and menial labor—that Washington was able to make the acquaintance of Armstrong.

Washington was born on April 5, 1856 on Bourrough's Plantation in Franklin County Virginia, and in 1865, his family moved to Malden, West Virginia (Hill, 1998). In Malden, Washington worked in a coal mine and eventually left the coal mine to work for the wife of General Lewis Ruffner, the owner of the salt furnace and coal mine. Of working for Mrs. Ruffner as a servant, Washington said that, "the lessons that I learned in the home of Mrs. Ruffner were as valuable to me as any education I have gotten anywhere since" (p. 44). In 1872, with funds acquired from his work with Mrs. Ruffner, his brother John, and "older coloured people who gave him 'a nickel, others a quarter, or a handkerchief" (p. 47). Washington traveled 500 miles from Malden, West Virginia to Hampton, Virginia. However, this was not an easy journey because according to Washington, "I had not been away from home many hours before it began to grow painfully evident that I did not have enough money to pay my fare to Hampton" (p. 47). Washington walked and begged for rides until he reached Richmond, Virginia. In Richmond, Washington worked for a chip captain unloading cargo until he earned enough money to travel the rest of the way to Hampton. Once he arrived at Hampton Institute, Washington described the experience as follows

> To me it had been a long, eventful journey; but the first sight of the large, three story, brick school building seemed to have rewarded me for all that I had undergone in order to reach the place. If the people who gave the money to provide that building could appreciate the influence the sight of it had upon me, as well as upon thousands of other youths, they would feel all the more encouraged to make such gifts. It seemed to me to be the largest and most beautiful building I had ever seen. The sight of it seemed to give me new life ... I felt that I had reached the promised land, and I resolved to let no obstacle prevent me from putting forth the highest effort to fit myself to accomplish the most good in the world. (pp. 50–51)

Washington worked as a janitor to pay for the cost of his room and board. In later years when he moved into his role as the embodiment of the Hampton-Tuskegee Model, Washington was able to relay the message so well because for him it genuinely resonated and was rooted in his lived experiences. Because Washington experienced enslavement, and education in the era of Reconstruction, his advocacy of industrial education seemed to be a plausible solution in its pragmatism and hopefulness (Anderson, 1988). Washington speaks of this in his autobiography when he wrote,

> I have spoken of my own experience of entering the Hampton Institute. Perhaps few if any, had anything like the same experience that I had, but about that same period there were hundreds who found their way to Hampton and other institutions after experiencing some of the same difficulties that I went through. The young men and women were determined to secure and education at any cost. (p. 53)

Washington graduated from Hampton institute in 1875. In 1881, he was selected by General Armstrong to lead Tuskegee Institute. Armstrong was a missionary, soldier, educator, and college president, and according to Watkins (2001), he was "an effective and farsighted social, political, and economic theorist working for the cause of a segregated and orderly South" (p. 43). When Armstrong's ideology of racial containment meshed with Washington's affinity for hard work, the Hampton-Tuskegee Model flourished.

If Washington's life story can be presented as insight into his educational philosophy and unwavering support for the Hampton-Tuskegee Model, W.E.B. Du Bois's life story can serve the same purpose. Whereas, Washington was a child of the South, Du Bois had a bittersweet love affair with the South. For Northern born Du Bois, the South was the place where he received an undergraduate education at Fisk University and an education in American racism. The South served as the inspiration for several of Du Bois's seminal texts, and institutions of higher education in the South served as ground zero for the Washington/Du Bois debates.

While the primary criticism of Du Bois's educational philosophy is the tone of elitism, concepts such as *the talented tenth*, his upbringing, although in a predominately White environment, was far from elite. In the introduction to their edited edition of the *Souls of Black Folk*, Blight and Williams (1997) provide biographical information of Du Bois's early life. William Edward Burghardt (W. E. B.) Du Bois was born in 1868 in Great Barrington, Massachusetts. Du Bois's mother was a domestic servant until she suffered a debilitating stroke in 1879. Du Bois worked several odd jobs which included selling and eventually becoming a correspondent for the *New York Globe*, a Black weekly newspaper. In 1884, Du Bois was the only African American in his graduating class of thirteen students, and when his mother died in 1885, local ministers and teachers organized a scholarship for him to attend Fisk University in Nashville, Tennessee. Fisk University was chartered in 1866 with support from the American Missionary Association. The University was named in honor of General Clinton B. Fisk of the Tennessee Freedman's

Bureau (Williams & Ashley, 2004). The first class consisting of freed people ranging in age from 7 to 70 convened in former Union barracks provided by General Fisk and reflected the Fisk commitment to educate newly emancipated. Fisk was the first HBCU to be awarded university status and in 1930 was the first HBCU to receive accreditation by the Southern Association of Colleges and School (Williams & Ashley, 2004).

When Du Bois left Massachusetts to attend Fisk University in Nashville, Tennessee, Gates and McKay (2004) explains that this was his "first foray into the South and southern racism, and more important, his first deep immersion in the lives of African Americans" (Gates & McKay, 2004, p. 687). Du Bois entered Fisk as a sophomore, and studied German, Greek, Latin, classical literature, philosophy, ethics, chemistry, and physics (Blight & Williams, 1997). Du Bois earned a Bachelor's degree from Fisk University in 1888. Du Bois had always aspired to attend Harvard, but was not afforded the opportunity (Blight & Williams, 1997). Upon his graduation from Fisk, Du Bois applied for and received a scholarship to Harvard, and he earned another bachelor's degree in philosophy from Harvard 1890. After receiving a master's degree in history from Harvard, Du Bois studied history, economics, and politics abroad at the Friedrich Wilhelm University in Berlin, German, and became the first African American to receive a PhD from Harvard in history in 1895.

Although Du Bois never formally received a degree in sociology, he is often referred to as a sociologist rather than a philosopher and historian. While this designation is due in part to the racist privileging of Eurocentric philosophies and philosophers, it is also not a completely unfair designation as Du Bois's seminal text, *The Souls of Black Folk*, is a sociological foray into the lives of Southern Blacks. A collection of thirteen essays and one short story, the book is "a moving evocation of black American folk culture and a critical response to the racism and economic subjugation afflicting black Americans at the end of the nineteenth century" (Blight & Williams, 1997, p. vii). In the third essay, *Of M. Booker T. Washington and Others*, Du Bois offers a respectful, yet harsh critique of Booker T. Washington and the Hampton-Tuskegee Model. Du Bois (1903/1997) wrote,

> One hesitates, therefore, to criticize a life which, beginning with so little, has done so much. And yet the time has come when one may speak in all sincerity and utter courtesy of the mistakes and shortcomings of Mr. Washington's career, as well of his triumphs, without being thought captious or envious, and without forgetting that it is easier to do ill than well in the world. (p. 63)

Du Bois carefully outlined what he believed to be flaws in Washington's accommodationist policies which, resulted in "1. The disenfranchisement of the Negro 2. The legal creation of a distinct status of civil inferiority for the Negro. 3. The steady withdrawal of aid from institutions for the higher training of the Negro." (p. 68). While Du Bois does not lay the blame of these phenomena solely at the feet of Washington, he does proclaim that "his propaganda has, without a shadow of a doubt, helped their speedier accomplishment" (p. 68). Du Bois further explains the "triple paradox of Washington's career," with the third paradox directly relating to higher education,

> He advocates common-school and industrial training, and depreciates institutions of higher learning: but neither the Negro common schools, nor Tuskegee itself, could remain open a day were it not for teachers trained in Negro Colleges, or trained by their graduates. (p. 68)

Although it is not historically inaccurate to position Washington and Du Bois as the figureheads of the polarizing debate between industrial versus liberal arts curricula, it is also important to note that these men, curricula, and institution were intertwined within an enterprise based on meritocracy and exclusion. Furthermore, they were two of the key players who have come to represent these philosophies. Many others were part of the larger debates.

Du Bois taught summer school at Tuskegee in 1903 and Washington served on Fisk's Board of Trustees; his children also attended Fisk (Fisk University History; Gasman & Geiger, 2012). Washington died on November 14, 1915, and was buried on the campus of Tuskegee University. Du Bois went on to pen surveys of Negro Colleges—the *College-Bred Negro* published in 1900 and *The College-Bred Negro American* published in 1910. Although the intent of these surveys were to strengthen Negro higher education by identifying their strengths and weaknesses (Gasman & Geiger, 2012), the long-term results proved detrimental for discourses surrounding what were to become HBCUs. The central thesis of these surveys was that the number of Negro colleges should be reduced to the strongest colleges, and both Du Bois's 1900 and 1910 surveys relied on ranking systems and methodologies advocated by prominent White male leaders within higher education such as Harvard president Charles Eliot and University of Chicago president William Rainey Harper (Gasman & Geiger, 2012). Du Bois argued that students and funding resources should be directed toward the strongest schools which included a small cadre of private liberal arts schools such as Howard, Lincoln, and Wilberforce (Gasman & Geiger, 2012). When Du Bois measured the quality of these schools against a Eurocentric model, however well intended, Du Bois reified a classification system of HBCUs that essentially privileged the small liberal arts colleges over the public colleges and this classification had detrimental effects for funding of these schools for years to come. For example, states are currently attempting to reconcile budget shortfalls with commitments to funding public institutions of higher education. Traditional accountability standards used to measure success at HBCUs are often in direct contrast to so-called equitable measures to fairly distribute funding to public universities (Minor, 2008). Budgetary and accountability conversations involving HBCUs are often misdirected to question the legacy and contributions of these colleges and universities. This leaves HBCUs fighting a war on two fronts and calls for them to justify their budgets and their very existence. As such, Roebuck and Murty's (1993) stinging critique of both Washington and Du Bois is not unfounded when they write, "They both failed, unfortunately, to join hands in seeking solutions to the pedagogical and political dilemma of blacks at a critical juncture in African-American history" (p. 31). Thus, Du Bois's critique that educational philosophies that undergird the creation and funding of HBCUs have equal potential for triumph and tragedy is prophetic.

MAKING A WAY OUT OF NO WAY

In the introduction to her 2008 text, *Making a Way of Out of No Way,* Coleman defines the concept of "making a way out of no way" as a "central theme in black women's struggles and God's assistance in helping them to overcome oppression" (p. 9). As a womanist theologian, Coleman defined and applied this concept in relation to the socioreligious experiences of Black women. However, this terminology and subsequent discussion of "making a way out of no way" is a pathway to learning from the past to be useful in explaining the concept of pragmatic hope within the development of HBCUs. Coleman incorporated postmodernist womanist theology to define the past. She informed readers that in order to learn from the past, we must acknowledge that *"those who have died have never left"* and that

> We *learn* from the past and then use what we have learned, what we have experienced, toward God's ideals of truth, beauty, adventure, art, peace, justice, and quality of life. Creative transformation remains the process, goal, and measure for "making a way out of no way." (p. 122)

Therefore, when applied to historical analysis, "making a way out of no way" can be considered as an onto-epistemology embedded in the collective consciousness of the history of HBCUs. This chapter has shown that within educational history, and particularly within the study of Black education, there is a modernist preoccupation with defining physical places through their curricula. While the foundational years of these schools are historicized as difficult and subpar, the administrators, faculty, staff, and students of the schools ensured their survival *in spite of* by essentially "making a way out of no way." For the HBCU community, making a way out of no way became a way of *being in knowing*—a tactic for surviving in a socioeconomic and political system designed for their failure.

The creation of the Negro College instantly created a racialized binary within historical studies of U.S. higher education. Surface level analyses that highlight the stark differences between Negro Colleges and White counterparts and insist that the early Negro Colleges were bastardizations of more established institutions are counterproductive because they ignore the pragmatic function of taking in persons with limited formal education, and preparing them to function within a collegiate setting. Administrators and teachers took in students of all ages who were underprepared for collegiate level work and developed a specialized curriculum of patience, community service, and faith. At their establishment, HBCUs and their foundational curriculums were criticized for their industrial and agricultural focus which in effect created "universities in name only." However, in spite of their narrow scope, the foundational curricula of HBCUs were indeed solid curricula that allowed for these schools to evolve into universities not "in name only."

If Negro Colleges are taken out of this racialized binary, it is then possible to illustrate that the foundational curriculums of Negro Colleges were intertwined with African ascendant (Dillard, 2012) educational philosophies. The early Negro Colleges have been analyzed for their role of creating a pathway for the freed people to enter sociopolitical and socioeconomic structure of the United States. They have not been examined in terms of the pragmatic function of performing this task. Herein rests the problem with conflating the history of HBCUs with the history of Blacks in higher education. When there is a myopic focus on defending the presence of these institutions within the larger higher educational enterprise, the totality of African American experience in higher education is glazed over. When the lens is broadened, it becomes possible to see that the pragmatic function of the curricula was sustained by educational philosophies that syncretized the African ascendant experience in America with a specialized understanding of the connections between, education, democracy and freedom.

IMPLICATIONS FOR COLLEGE READINESS

In one of the Amistad Murals, African American artist Hale Woodruff depicts the opening of Talladega College in Talladega, Alabama. Talladega College, founded in 1887, the edifice was originally constructed by slaves for the education of White students (Williams &Ashley, 2004). In vibrant colors, Woodruff depicts the freedmen dressed in the tattered clothes of sharecroppers bringing various goods—cattle, pigs, etc.—to barter as payment for their entrance into the college. The scene, while chaotic, expresses joy and anticipation. Even the animals appear to smile with an understanding of the gravity of the moment. These freedmen, men, who built a school building but were denied access to education, would now be participating in the crown jewel of the U.S. educational enterprise: higher education. Throughout their history, HBCUs have retained these complex identities as both safe havens of fairness and opportunity and shameful stains on the fabric of the higher education enterprise—reminders of a bygone era of enslavement, inequality, uncivility. To some, this piece of art would confirm the complexity of the mass entrance of the freed people into higher education through the institutions now referred to as Historically Black Colleges and Universities (HBCUs). HBCUs were founded within a context of educational containment, cultural elitism, and white supremacy (Anderson, 1988; Watkins, 2001); yet, they were undergirded by educational philosophies rooted in a belief in the mystical, transformative nature of education. When HBCUs are examined through the lens of African American educational philosophy, then it is possible to see these schools not as the embarrassments of U.S. higher educational enterprise, but as institutions that can help practitioners understand the pragmatic nature of college readiness.

The entrance of blacks into higher education in northern and border states prior to 1865, and development of Negro Colleges in the South after the Civil War represent a pragmatic triumph. The history of African Americans in higher education simultaneously represents the possibilities of the U.S. higher educational enterprise and the tenacity of a people who recognized education as freedom. This freedom can be described as pragmatic hope—a hope for entry into the citizenry and a hope to disprove the hegemonic power intellectual system of thought that presented African ascendant people as morally and intellectually inferior. As such, the history of Blacks in higher education must be told with the understanding that the presence of Blacks in colleges and universities served a higher function—and histories must take this into account.

As previously stated, the ongoing historical debate about the relevance of HBCUs is often tied to the socioeconomical tenure of the country. When the then named Negro Colleges are historicized as colleges in name only, and when this history is conflated into a larger history of African Americans in higher education, the contributions of African ascendant people and their allies are overlooked. Due to the physical and psychological trauma of enslavement, Jim Crow, etc., Black educators and allies more often than not had to do more with less—they had to make a way out of no way. Therefore instead of being ashamed of the curricula of the early Black colleges, they should be looked to as exemplars in the field of career readiness and an ongoing, relevant necessity in the postsecondary training of African American students.

REFERENCES

Anderson, J. (1988). *The education of Blacks in the South 1860–1935*. Chapel Hill, NC: University of North Carolina Press.

Anderson, J. (2012). Race in American higher education: Historical perspectives on current conditions. In *The racial crisis in American higher education*. Albany, NY: State University of New York Press.

Blight, D., & Gooding-Williams, R. (1997). Introduction: The strange meaning of being Black, Du Bois's American Tragedy. In D. Blight & R. Gooding-Williams (Eds.), *The Souls of Black Folk* (pp. 1–30). Boston, MA: Bedford Books.

Brown, M. C. & Davis, E. (2001). The historically Black college as social contract, Social capital, and social equalizer," in *Peabody Journal of Education 76*, (1), 31–49.

Coleman, M. (2008). *Making a way out of no way: A womanist theology*. Minneapolis, MN: Fortress Press.

Du Bois, W. (1997). *The Souls of Black Folk* (D. Blight & R. Gooding-Williams, Eds.). Boston, MA: Bedford Books.

Dillard, C. B. (2012). *Learning to (re)member the things we've learned to forget: Endarkened feminisms, spirituality, and the sacred nature of research and teaching*. New York, NY: Peter Lang.

Evans, S. (2007). *Black women in the ivory tower, 1850–1954: An intellectual history*. Gainesville, FL: University Press of Florida.

Fisk University History. (2014). Retrieved February 21, 2015, from http://www.fisk.edu/about/history

Gasman, M. (2008). *Understanding minority-serving institutions*. Albany, NY: State University of New York Press.

Gasman, M., & Geiger, R. (2012). Introduction: Higher Education for African-Americans before the Civil Rights Era, 1900–1964. In M. Gasman & R. Geiger (Eds.), *Higher education for African Americans before the civil rights era, 1900–1964*. New Brunswick, N.J.: Transaction.

Giddings, P. (1984). *When and where I enter: The impact of Black women on race and sex in America*. New York: W. Morrow.

Hill, P. (1998). *Call and response: The Riverside anthology of the African American literary tradition*. Boston, MA: Houghton Mifflin.

Menand, L. (2001). *The metaphysical club*. New York, NY: Farrar, Straus & Giroux.

Mills, C. W. (1997). *The racial contract*. New York, NY: Cornell University Press.

Minor, J. T. (2008). Contemporary HBCUs: considering institutional capacity and state priorities. A research report. Michigan State University, College of Education, Department of Educational Administration. East Lansing, MI.

Mitchell, R., Dancy, T., Hart, D., & Morton, B. (2013). Teaching to teach: African American faculty, HBCUs, and Critical Pedagogy. In R. Palmer, D. Maramba, & M. Gasman (Eds.), *Fostering Success of Ethnic and Racial Minorities in STEM: The Role of minority serving institutions* (pp. 72–85). New York: Routledge.

Roebuck, J., & Murty, K. (1993). *Historically black colleges and universities: Their place in American higher education*. Westport, Conn.: Praeger.

Richardson, J. (1980). *A history of Fisk university, 1865–1946*. Tuscaloosa, AL: University of Alabama Press.

Samuels, A.L. (2004). *Is separate unequal: Black colleges and the challenge to desegregation*. Lawrence, KS: University Press of Kansas.

Strieby, M. E. (1891). *Address, Oberlin and the American Missionary Association*. Washington D.C: Library of Congress.

Thelin, J. R. (2004). *A History of American Higher Education*. Baltimore, MD: Johns Hopkins University Press.

Tocqueville, A. (1969). *Democracy in America*. (George Lawrence, Trans.). New York, NY: Random House. (Original work published in 1835).

Washington, B. (1963). *Up from slavery, an autobiography*. Garden City, N.Y.: Doubleday. (Original work published in 1901).

Watkins, W. (2001). *The white architects of black education: Ideology and power in America, 1865–1954*. New York: Teachers College Press.

Williams, J., & Ashley, D. (2004). *I'll find a way or make one: A tribute to historically Black colleges and universities*. New York: Amistad.

Gates, H. L. & McKay, N. (2004). W.E.B. Du Bois. In H. L. Gates & N. McKay (Eds.), *The Norton anthology of African American literature* (2.nd ed., pp. 686–689). New York: W.W. Norton.

Chapter 4

Holland Codes and STEM Careers

Cultural Values and Individual Interests in Career Development for African American Students

Tristen Bergholtz

The career landscape of the twenty-first century is dramatically different than any other and there is an increasing demand for employees in science, technology, engineering, and mathematics (STEM) careers. According to the U.S. Department of Labor's Bureau of Labor Statistics (BLS) (2014c), STEM careers are projected to grow at a faster rate (13%) than all other occupations (11%) between 2012 and 2022. Carnevale, Smith, and Melton (2011) report 90% of STEM careers will require postsecondary education and training by 2018. On average, the majority of individuals who complete a postsecondary STEM degree compared to those with a non-STEM degree earn more money, even if they choose to pursue a non-STEM career. This significant difference in pay, no matter the career pursued, can be attributed to the skills STEM degree holders offer—critical thinking, deductive reasoning, and written, oral, and interpersonal communication skills, among others (BLS, 2014c). In addition to technological innovation, the creation and increase of STEM-related career opportunities, and the permeation of technology throughout almost all career fields, the high demand for STEM employees also comes as a result of the "baby boomer generation" entering or nearing retirement. The American Community Survey (ACS) reports that "Ten percent of all baby boomers with at least a Bachelor's degree—nearly 5 million workers—are in STEM occupations" (as cited in Carnevale et al., p. 68). With STEM jobs becoming available as baby boomers retire, the demand for STEM careers is at an all-time high.

    Despite these technological advances, changes to the career landscape, and increased number of STEM employment opportunities, the public education system remains as it was at the beginning of the twentieth century. As a result, the opportunity gap continues to grow, particularly for African

Americans. While the workforce seems to be moving in a direction where STEM is embraced, the U.S. Office for Civil Rights (OCR) (2012) found the education for African American students is not doing the same. Understanding the rigorous coursework "needed for selective colleges and future careers in science, technology, engineering and mathematics (STEM) careers," OCR found dire inequities when comparing schools serving predominantly White students versus those serving predominantly African American student populations. Examining a sample of 85% of the nation's public schools, OCR found 55% of all high schools offer calculus though only 29% of predominantly African American high schools offer this course. The percentages are similar for physics (66% vs. 40%) and Algebra II (82% vs. 65%) course offerings. This is especially troubling as Maltese and Tai (2011) found that exposure to advanced math and science course work in high school is positively correlated with postsecondary STEM major degree completion.

The lack of college preparatory courses offered to African American students is only one of many barriers preventing them from pursuing postsecondary degrees, let alone STEM majors and careers. These barriers further contribute to African Americans being underrepresented in prestigious, higher-paying careers such as STEM careers (Curry & Milsom, 2013). Furthermore, according to the National Science Foundation (NSF) (2013), only 4.98% of the science workforce and 3.57% of engineering jobs are currently occupied by African Americans. The focus of this chapter is career decision-making processes for African Americans with a specific focus on STEM; through an examination of cultural patterns, the influence cultural values and other ecosystemic forces has on vocational choices, as well as common misperceptions of scientists and the work they do. Additionally, John Holland's *Theory of Vocational Choice* will be discussed as it relates to current African American occupational patterns and the future implications for increasing the representation of African Americans in STEM careers.

PATTERNS IN COLLECTIVE AND COLLABORATIVE CULTURES VERSUS INDIVIDUALISTIC AND COMPETITIVE CULTURES

Individuals' worldviews, self-concepts, and particularly their values, are influenced tremendously by the cultures to which they belong. Culture is shaped by many variable traits such as socioeconomic status, education attainment level, spirituality/religion, race, ethnicity, gender, sexual orientation, disability/ability, and geographic location. These traits synergistically lead to the creation of shared group values and define individual member's worldviews; that is, the way one interprets and interacts with the world, events, and others. Due to their complex nature, culture and cultural values are typically conceptualized along a spectrum or continuum; the poles of this spectra being collectivistic, collaborative cultures or individualistic, competitive cultures. Table 4.1 provides a comparison of these poles and their respective cultural values.

When discussing cultural groups, it is important to remember that cultural groups are not homogenous or monolithic, as within each group differences exist. For example, individuals from the United States are seemingly more individualistic and competitive when compared to their international counterparts (Hofstede, 2001; Triandis & Gelfand, 1998), with value being placed on "both uniqueness and social status acquired through competition" (Gushue & Constantine, 2003, p. 5). However, racial minorities within the United States are much more collectivistic and collaborative than their White counterparts. It is also important to note that individuals may belong to more than one cultural group (e.g., African American, lesbian, disability) and may find their cultural values oriented more in one direction than the other and not necessarily prescriptively fitting into either end of the spectrum.

Oyserman, Coon, and Kemmelmeir (2002) developed a framework to describe cultural dimensions and how cultural values influence individuals, their worldviews, and ultimately their career decisions. The framework

Table 4.1 Comparison of Collectivistic, Collaborative and Individualistic, Competitive Cultural Values

Collectivistic, collaborative	*Individualistic, competitive*
Group-oriented, "we" mentality	Self-oriented, "I" mentality
Group success is valued	Individual success is valued
Extended family is valued and ties to the family and community are complex (e.g., unrelated individuals are considered family members)	Nuclear family is valued and ties to the family and community are simple (e.g., family vs. nonfamily members)
Shame or lose face within the group	Guilt or loss of self-respect
Pursue purpose in life	Pursue happiness
Standards and expectations vary depending upon the group's level of marginalization	Same set of standards and expectations apply to all people
High-context communication (e.g., togetherness does not require speaking)	Low-context communication (e.g., visits are filled with talking)
Emphasis on belonging	Emphasis on achievement and initiative
Associate with others based upon preexisting group ties	Associate with others based upon task and current needs
Purpose of education is to learn how to do and enter higher-status groups	Purpose of education is to learn how to learn and increase economic worth and/or self-respect

Source: Adapted from Hofstede (2001), Oyseryman, Coon, & Kemmelmeir (2002), Sue & Sue (2013).

developed by Oyserman and colleagues includes four domains: (1) self-concept, (2) well-being, (3) attribution style, and (4) relationality. All four domains of the framework are useful for examining individualistic and collectivistic cultural patterns. In general, the core element of each of these domains for individuals from collectivistic, collaborative cultures (i.e., African Americans, Asian Americans, Latino/a Americans, and Native Americans) is that there are mutual obligations and a sense of connectedness among group members. By contrast, the point of reference for each of these domains for individuals from individualistic, competitive cultures (i.e., European Americans) is typically the individual or self with a focus on "personal goals, personal uniqueness, and personal control" (p. 5). Following, each domain is described in detail according to Oyserman, Coon, and Kemmelmeir's framework.

Self-concept

Self-concept is the way in which a person perceives himself or herself, their goals, actions, values, and the world. Tending to orient their cultural values more toward the collectivistic, collaborative dimension, African Americans' self-concepts are filtered through a lens which emphasizes group membership as being a key component of their identity and values. Furthermore, African Americans tend to uphold beliefs of self-sacrificing for the good of all, as well as maintaining harmonious relationships with close others (Oyserman et al., 2002). These beliefs may often obligate individuals to stay close to home and pursue a career perceived as benefitting others (e.g., teacher, pastor). Conversely, individualistic, competitive self-concepts are centralized around the assumptions that everybody has the right to pursue self-fulfillment and happiness, experience success, positive feelings about oneself, and that "having many unique or distinctive personal attitudes are valued" (Oyserman et al., 2002, p. 5). The self-concept reflects the differences in cultural values listed in Table 4.1, such as pursuing one's purpose in life and the "we" mentality versus pursuing happiness and the "I" mentality.

Well-being

Well-being includes not only one's physical health, but one's overall health and wellness. Myers, Sweeney, and Witmer (2001) proposed five components of wellness: spirituality, self-direction, work and leisure, friends, and love. Well-being tends to be maintained in collectivistic, collaborative cultures through successfully carrying out roles, responsibilities and obligations to close others, avoiding failure in the process, and restraining emotion. Individualistic, competitive cultures foster well-being through the open expression of emotions and achievement of personal goals, as these are both thought to lead to life satisfaction (Oyserman et al., 2002). For example, White individuals tend to place an emphasis on low-context communication, achievement, and initiative, as opposed to African American individuals tending to emphasize high-context communication and belongingness.

Attribution Style

When events occur, individuals attribute the cause of the event to something—either internal or external locus of control. The locus of control can be determined based upon behaviors, events, or people. Individuals with more internal attribution styles direct the cause of events toward themselves and believe they have control, to some extent, over the circumstance in their life. Others possessing a more external attribution style infer the cause of situations to be factors outside of their control; individuals with an external attribution style generally do not believe they can influence others, their behaviors, or events. Typically, African Americans subscribe to an external attribution style with reasoning and causality being rooted in the physical, social, or situational context (Oyserman et al., 2002; Sue & Sue, 2013). One such reason may be as a result of the historical discrimination against African Americans in the United States. However, European Americans tend to contribute the causality of events to themselves, thus displaying more internalized attribution styles.

Relationality

Relationality is essentially the intentions behind our actions and the purpose of the relationships we share with others. Collectivistic, collaborative cultures regard relationships with close others as "facts of life," or ascribed and fixed, and to which one is expected to accommodate. Among African Americans, these permanent fixtures rarely change as relational boundaries between in-groups and out-groups are "stable, relatively impermeable, and important" (Oyserman et al., 2002, p. 5). Exchanges between in-groups members are not defined by selfishness, but instead generosity. Contrasting with this inclusive view, individualistic, competitive cultures approach relationships with a cost-benefit view; relationships with others help us attain our personal goals; this is one of the key purposes of "networking." Individuals who have internalized the individualistic, competitive cultural values perceive relationships as temporary and purposive. Individuals subscribing to individualistic, competitive cultural values leave relationships when the costs outweigh the benefits and develop new relationships as personal goals shift.

Understanding that culture itself is shaped by other cultures, society, and history, Oyserman et al. (2002) provide an approach that allows us to more specifically analyze how cultural values shape an individual's values and worldviews. In latter sections we will explore how African American collaborative and collective cultural values influence the career decision-making process and their occupational interests. For now, we turn to perceptions of science and scientists to examine how culture influences attitudes and beliefs toward both, which will help us better understand the dearth of African Americans in STEM careers.

PERCEPTION AS REALITY: DRAW A SCIENTIST TEST

In a graduate-level career and college readiness counseling course at a research university, a professor gave her students two minutes to read and follow the directions found on a worksheet similar to the one shown in Figure 4.1. This activity is known throughout the literature as the *"Draw a Scientist doing Science Test"* or *"Draw-A-Scientist-Test"* [DAST {1983}]. The professor then used a rubric developed by Pacific Northwest Aquatic and Marine Educators to compare and illustrate the stereotypes and perceptions commonly held about science and scientists. Applying the rubric to their own drawings, the students identified and analyzed the presence of the following representations of science and scientists: (a) physical characteristics of scientists (e.g., eyeglasses, lab coat); (b) symbols of research (e.g., microscope, test tubes); (c) symbols of knowledge (e.g., books); (d) signs of technology (e.g., machines); (e) gender; (f) race and ethnicity; and (g) personality (e.g., sinister, positive).

Upon conclusion of the activity, the majority of the students had drawn some variation of a White male wearing a white lab coat working alone in a sterile laboratory setting with Bunsen burners and beakers (representing mainly chemistry). Following up with this activity, the professor guided a class discussion on the various types of scientists there are (e.g., marine biologist), scientific equipment used (e.g., dive gear), diverse settings they work in (e.g., the ocean), and purpose of work done (e.g., preserving ocean life). After reflecting on the DAST, the class came to the consensus that, despite their diverse backgrounds, they had somehow collectively developed a limited, stereotypical perception of scientists and science over time. While these graduate students did not have any prior knowledge of the DAST or previous research studies, their drawings reflect the results of many other researchers who have administered the DAST have collected over the years (Chambers 1983; Finson, Beaver, & Cramond, 1995; Mason, Kahle, & Gardner, 1991; Symington & Spurling, 1990). These replications highlight the commonly-held, monolithic perceptions of scientists and the work they conduct, while also representing somewhat accurate portrayals of the current STEM labor market.

Holland Codes and STEM Careers   61

> Directions: Draw a scientist doing what a scientist does, working where a scientist works, and wearing what a scientist wears.

> Write a brief description of your drawing.

Figure 4.1 Draw a Scientist Test [DAST]. *Source*: Adapted from Finson, Beaver, and Cramond (1995)

Even though it is known that scientists are not inherently evil, have wild hair, work alone, and only conduct science experiments in sterile lab settings, the DAST results do illuminate the ever-present gender and racial disparities in science and related fields. The first DAST study was conducted by Chambers in 1983 and was the first of many studies to follow highlighting the pervasive cultural misperception of scientists and what science looks like. In this initial study, only 28 female scientists were drawn ($n = 4807$), or .58% of the study's participants depicted a female in their drawing of a scientist.

The results found from the graduate school DAST, as well as the studies conducted by Chambers (1983) and other researchers, illustrate that people are unlikely to think of females and racial minorities as scientists, they are also unlikely to think of science that looks different from chemistry (i.e., field observation, qualitative studies). Although they are not depicted in DAST results, it is understood that women and racial minorities can pursue STEM careers, yet both groups are still grossly underrepresented in these fields. According to the National Science Foundation (NSF; 2013), females comprise only 33.6% of those employed in science occupations and racial minorities account for only 30.81% of the science workforce. However, racial minorities include many other ethnicities beside African Americans. Specifically, African Americans only comprise 4.98% of the science workforce and 3.57% of engineering jobs. Science occupations were defined in the NSF study as biological/life, computer and information, mathematical, physical, psychological, and social scientists. Additionally, the common representation of science being drawn as chemistry indicates a general view of science as formulaic, predictable, as well as detached from the real world and others. This common misperception of science and other related fields fails to account for the many benefits to the common good STEM careers provide (e.g., safe roads, cures for diseases, prosthetic limbs, national security). Individual preferences, cultural values, and systemic issues will be evaluated in latter sections to further explore the realities and narrow views of STEM occupations.

Based upon the data collected by the NSF, it is clear that African Americans are markedly underrepresented in STEM careers. Underrepresentation leaves few STEM role models for African American students to learn from, an issue even more concerning given that role modeling is most effective when mentors and mentees share similar characteristics (e.g., race, culture, gender, shared experiences). This deficiency further highlights the need for more African American STEM role models. Finson, Beaver, and Cramond (1995) wrote the following on science education:

> If one of the goals of science education is to prepare students who are scientifically literate and to encourage students to pursue postsecondary study and careers in science and related fields, then students need to possess more positive images of scientists—the roles in which they themselves may function in the future. (p. 201)

When students can see themselves in a career, they are more likely to pursue an educational program that prepares them for that career (Finson et al.,

1995; MacCorquodale, 1984). This lack of role models also contributes to the already-present opportunity gap, which negatively impacts African Americans' career aspirations (Malone & Barabino, 2009) and self-concepts.

Although the relationship between being a scientist and self-concept is viewed as unimportant with regard to the advancement of science (Malone & Barabino, 2009), it is a salient point if the demographics of the science community and other related fields are to evolve. It is important to remember that one's self-concept has great influence on the way an individual perceives others, but especially himself or herself. Many important educational programming decisions are made at the high school and college levels in order to prepare students for postsecondary education and careers. These decisions are influenced not only by current experiences, but also by those learned at younger ages. Studying African American first through third grade students' self-concepts and perceptions of science and school, Varelas, Kane, and Wylie (2011) found the following:

> the children's ways of seeing science and their place in it were influenced by who they saw themselves and others being, how they saw themselves in interactions with their peers and teacher, and what they thought science as an intellectual domain was about. These different types of conceptions were intertwined, to different degrees, in the children's developing science ideologies .... They [African American students] act and react to various forces and interact with each other based on their past experiences and their conceptions and expectations for success. Furthermore, these conceptions and expectations are shaped by others' (people inside and outside their schools) conceptions about them and about their education. (pp. 22–25)

This study concludes that students with low self-concepts with respect to science are less likely to enter science programs in college, making science and related careers much more inaccessible. Furthermore, Odell, Hewett, Bowman, and Boone (1993) found students' images of self tend to match their perceptions about careers (as cited in Finson et al., 1995, p. 195). More specifically, when examining individuals' self-concepts and perceptions of science, Finson et al. found that females have lower levels than males and racial minorities have lower levels than Whites.

Another factor contributing to the paucity of African Americans pursuing STEM careers is the historical discriminatory methods used by scientists. After evaluating prior research studies, Malone and Barabino (2009) affirmed that the stereotypical DAST results (i.e., White, male) and low self-concepts associated with science are perpetuated by the way in which scientific studies have historically been conducted and presented: "Persons of color have been historically cast as less rational and as objects of scientific study rather than as scientists" (p. 490). And even when African

Americans pursue and achieve at high levels in STEM majors and careers, or as scientists, their work is less likely than their White counterparts to be recognized because of the "historical and prototypical notions of scientist" (Carlone & Johnson, 2007, p. 1207) as not being represented by non-White, non-male individuals. Essentially, people are unfamiliar and possibly uncomfortable with seeing African Americans as scientists, and have been for quite some time.

Underrepresentation in STEM careers; low cultural educational expectations; low self-concepts of self and science; social devaluation of STEM; lack of STEM role models; and discriminatory history of science experiments—all of these factors contribute to the current perception of scientists. The perception is paralleled in reality with the deficient representation of African Americans in such careers. The current STEM career culture offers little encouragement to African American students wishing to pursue STEM careers, thus preventing an increased presence of African Americans in STEM careers.

HOLLAND'S THEORY OF VOCATIONAL CHOICE

John Holland's Theory of Vocational Choice (1973, 1997) is conceptualized as a person-environment fit model. In this model, the highest levels of vocational satisfaction result from a best fit between an individual's personality and the work environment. Holland's theory proposes that individuals and work environments can both be classified using the Holland Occupational Themes, or Holland Codes. The Holland Codes are most often referred to as RIASEC, representing the six personality types and work environments he believes to exist: *R*ealistic, *I*nvestigative, *A*rtistic, *S*ocial, *E*nterprising, and *C*onventional (RIASEC). Table 4.2 provides a more detailed description of the Holland Codes. The Holland Codes define the interests, abilities, and values of a person, as well as those most likely to be represented in or relevant to a given work environment.

To better understand Holland's theory (1973, 1997), it is important to understand the four assumptions his theory is centered around:

1. People choose occupations that are an expression of their personality.
2. People with similar personality types will have careers in similar fields.
3. Because of their similar personality types, people in these similar career groups will react to challenges or events in similar ways.
4. The degree of personality type congruence between individuals and their work environment is positively correlated with levels of job satisfaction and achievement, as well as amount of time spent in the career.

Table 4.2 Holland Types

Type	Description	Possible Careers
Realistic	Prefers activities that are practical in nature including manipulation of tools, machinery, objects, and animals. Does not enjoy social, therapeutic, or educational activities. Views self as practical, mechanical, shy, hardheaded, and realistic.	Auto mechanic, carpenter, farmer, firefighter, florist, electrician, locksmith, locomotive engineer, painter, pilot, police officer, roofer, truck driver, ultrasound technologist
Investigative	Prefers to investigate physical, biological, and cultural phenomenon through observation, symbolism, and systematic processes with strong scientific and mathematical competence. Does not enjoy repetitive activities, selling things or ideas, leading or persuading people. Views self as precise, scientific, intellectual, critical, and methodical.	Anthropologist, architect, biologist, chemical engineer, chemist, computer systems analyst, dentist, economist, electrical technician, geologist, mathematician, medical technician, meteorologist, pharmacist, physician, physicist, statistician, surveyor, technical writer, veterinarian
Artistic	Prefers creative activities that involve the manipulation of physical, verbal, or human materials such as fine arts, performing arts, dance, and creative writing. Does not enjoy repetitive activities or highly structured, task-oriented activities. Views self as expressive, original, independent, complicated, and impulsive.	Actor/actress, art teacher, book editor, choreographer, clothes designer, comedian, copy writer, disc jockey, graphic designer, interior decorator, journalist, medical illustrator, museum curator, musician, photographer, sculptor, stage director
Social	Prefers activities that entail the manipulation of others to inform, train, educate, develop, enlighten, or cure in order to help others reach a goal. Does not enjoy mechanical or scientific activities. Views self as helpful, friendly, trustworthy, tactful, and responsible.	Athletic trainer, clinical psychologist, counselor, dental hygienist, dietician, historian, insurance claims examiner, librarian, nurse, parole officer, physical therapist, religious worker, social worker, speech therapist, teacher
Enterprising	Prefers activities that include selling things or ideas, leading or persuading people to attain economic gain, leadership, political or organizational change. Does not enjoy scientific, observational, or symbolic activities. Views self as energetic, ambitious, sociable, impulsive, and pleasure-seeking.	Business leader, buyer, city manager, emergency medical technician, hotel manager, interpreter, judge, lawyer, manager, producer, real estate agent, salesperson, school principal, sports promoter, television producer, travel agent
Conventional	Prefers activities that include interpretation of data, record keeping, filing materials, and organizing written and numerical data. Does not enjoy ambiguous, unstructured, or exploratory activities. Views self as orderly, systematic, conforming, careful, and efficient.	Accountant, administrative assistant, banker, bookkeeper, computer operator, cost estimator, court clerk, court reporter, editorial assistant, financial analyst, mail carrier, stenographer, title examiner

Source: Adapted from Curry & Milsom (2013, p. 172), Holland (1973, 1997), Jones (2011), Niles & Harris-Bowlsbey (2009).

People are typically given a three-letter Holland Code (e.g., IAS—*I*nvestigative, *A*rtistic, *S*ocial) after completing assessments such as Holland's Self-Directed Search. The three personality types indicated in the results are listed in descending order of prominence; the Holland Code describes a person's predominant preferences and the preferences most represented in work environments.

Applying Holland's four assumptions and the Holland Code example of IAS suggests the following: (1) IAS individuals are inclined to choose IAS occupations (e.g., sociologist, anthropologist); (2) other individuals with IAS personality types are likely to have careers in sociology, anthropology, or similar professions (e.g., political scientist); (3) people with IAS personalities are more likely to respond to events and challenges in similar ways (e.g., flexible, think about the situation analytically before responding, persistent); and (4) IAS work environments are most satisfying to people with IAS preferences, making it much more likely for them to feel job satisfaction, desire to maintain employment with their occupational choice, and achievement.

HOLLAND CODES: STEM AND AFRICAN AMERICANS

Carnevale, Smith, and Melton (2011) found the most prevalent code letters assessed for STEM careers and workers are Realistic and Investigative. The prevalence of these Holland Codes can be attributed to the working conditions in STEM occupations being nontraditional in the sense that they are less often in offices. STEM workers are more often working outside, with computers or in laboratory settings. The Realistic work environment demands STEM professionals to frequently engage in hands-on, highlyordered, mechanical, and sometimes outdoor tasks. Also, STEM careers typically require employees to be curious and use analytical, scientific, deductive-reasoning in order to find solutions or answers to broad questions or issues; these are the more Investigative characteristics of STEM occupations.

Considering race, culture and Holland Codes, Walker and Tracey (2012) found a difference in the preferences and perceptions of careers between African American and Whites. They found African Americans more frequently have a significantly stronger preference and higher level of prestige for Social and Enterprising occupations. Walker and Tracey suggested a link to African Americans' more collaborative, collectivistic culture and the high frequency of predominant preferences and high levels of prestige for Social and Enterprising careers. Given their history of discrimination, strong sense of community and lifelong bonds to community members, members of African American culture and communities may prefer and hold in higher prestige Social and Enterprising careers as they can be avenues to provide beneficial services to the community and its members (e.g., teacher, entrepreneur). Over time, this perception and frequent presence of such careers in African American communities may have led to an increase in preference toward and prestige levels for many African American individuals.

Reflecting these trends in Holland Codes among African Americans, Metz, Fouad, and Ihle-Helledy (2009) classified the career aspirations, expectations, and current labor market trends of college students. Comparing the career aspirations of racial minority students to nonminority students, Metz and colleagues found differences in their career aspirations but not in their career expectations. Minority students were more likely to indicate aspirations toward pursuing Social and Enterprising careers at significantly higher rates than their nonminority peers. The findings of the studies conducted on Holland Codes and the differences along racial lines support the notion that individuals are influenced by their cultural values, as a result, individual's career decisions are influenced by their cultural values. This is important to consider when examining the occupational interests of African American students. There is a disconnect between African American cultural values, career decision making, and the pursuit of STEM careers. If the goal is to increase the representation of African Americans in STEM careers, we must bridge this divide.

AFRICAN AMERICAN STUDENTS AND OCCUPATIONAL INTEREST

According to Brown and Pinterits (2001), poor education and training, a lack of socialization to nontraditional academic majors and career fields (e.g., STEM careers), and a number of other systemic factors have resulted in the underrepresentation of African Americans in high-earning, prestigious careers. Additionally, Hargrow and Hendricks (2001) defined *nontraditional* career fields as those in which African Americans are underrepresented and *traditional* career fields as those in which African Americans are represented in, at, or above the percentage level for which they make up the general population. While African Americans may not generally pursue nontraditional (i.e., STEM) careers or other occupations considered to be high-paying and prestigious, in a 2001 study based on 1997 U.S. Department of Labor's Bureau of Labor Statistics data, Hargrow and Hendricks found the following to be true of their occupational pursuits:

> The largest job sources for African American men and women have been in blue-collar, service-sector occupations .... African American women typically occupy positions as secretaries, nursing aids, cooks, cashiers, retail-sales

workers, elementary school teachers, cleaners, and janitors .... the largest sources of jobs for African American men were in fields such as correctional officers, security guards, cooks, motor vehicle operators (e.g., bus drivers, truck drivers, etc.), janitors, laborers, grounds keepers, and mechanics. (pp. 139–140)

Although unfortunately somewhat nebulous in presentation, the most recently released U.S. Department of Labor's Bureau of Labor Statistics (2014a) report demonstrates that these patterns are still present. With the exception of elementary school teachers, these occupations all share common characteristics. These jobs require little to no education, training, or prior experience. They offer little pay and few opportunities for career advancement. Moreover, these occupations are considered to be low prestige. This is the traditional career landscape for African Americans.

Conceptualizing the typical career path of African Americans using Holland Codes, the traditional occupations pursued can be classified as careers more likely to attract individuals with Social, Enterprising, or Realistic work preferences. STEM careers, which are nontraditional for African Americans, are more likely to attract employees with Realistic and Investigative work preferences. Even though African Americans are employed in jobs attracting Realistic personality types and work preferences at higher rates than any other work environment type, and STEM careers can be classified as Realistic, African Americans are much more likely to be employed in low-prestige Realistic positions. At the individual level, Miller, Springer, and Wells (1988) found the Social personality type to be the highest, most often recorded Holland Code for African Americans. Moreover, Social jobs are the most frequent source of high-level jobs for African Americans (Gottfredson, 1978).

If self-concept and culture are two of the most salient factors in career decision making for all persons, it is important to further examine the confluence of these two factors in order to better understand the underrepresentation of African Americans in nontraditional jobs and overrepresentation in others. Applying Lent, Brown, and Hackett's Social Cognitive Career Theory (1994), as well as Bronfenbrenner's Bioecological Theory (1977), we will consider how the patterns and pursuit of low-paying, low-prestige occupations persist among African Americans.

Social Cognitive Career Theory and Shaping the Self-concept

Social cognitive career theory (SCCT) (Lent, Brown, & Hackett, 1994) draws from Albert Bandura's concept of reciprocal determinism. Essentially, Bandura (1977) argues that decisions are made as a result of three interacting, interlocking mechanisms—personal attributes, the environment, and overt behaviors. Bandura (1997) asserted "that self-efficacy can be strengthened or weakened through the influence of a number of factors, with mastery experiences being one of the most influential factors" (as cited in Curry & Milsom, 2013, p. 228). The experiences individuals encounter shape their self-concept and can be thought to confirm or deny the perceptions they hold of themselves, the world, and others. The conclusion is that decisions aren't just made, but instead influenced by this triadic paradigm, making for a nuanced and complex decision-making process.

Considering these complexities, similar to those of cultural values and their influence on the individual, SCCT proposes that decision making does not boil down to the moment an opportunity is made available and the decision is made, but instead offers that it is an ongoing, malleable, and one could argue, optimistic, process. There are seven components to SCCT: (1) sources of self-efficacy and outcome expectations; (2) self-efficacy; (3) outcome expectations; (4) interests; (5) intentions/goals for activity involvement; (6) activity selection and practice; and (7) performance attainments. Figure 4.2 displays the interactions and relationships between each of these components. Each of these variables is individually unique and yet acts as a critical factor in the mutual interacting exchange between the other components of SCCT.

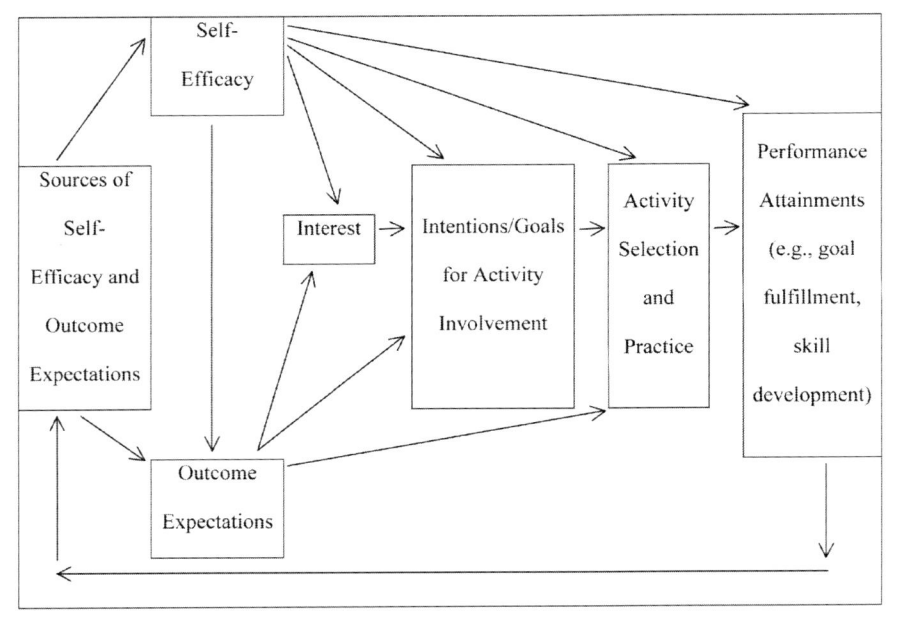

Figure 4.2 The Development of Basic Career Interests Over Time. *Source*: Adapted from Lent, et al. (1994)

Sources of *self-efficacy* and *outcome expectations* are derived from the *performance attainments*, or goal fulfillment and skill development, an individual achieves as the result of a learning experience. Self-efficacy is one's belief in their abilities to complete a task; an individual's self-efficacy is domain specific (e.g., one may have high self-efficacy toward calculus, but low self-efficacy toward drawing). Outcome expectations are the beliefs one holds about what will happen if they are to do something. For example, an individual may believe that taking a calculus exam is difficult and will require a lot of studying, but in the end the feelings of accomplishment and their efforts to prepare will be reflected in a high test grade and better understanding of math. However, this same individual may believe that no matter how much they practice or how long they study a figure, they will never be able to "make it look right" when drawing and see no purpose in even trying.

In SCCT, the definition of interests and goals for *activity involvement* is straightforward, but one's work interests and values should be considered when evaluating these components—how satisfied will an individual be doing a specific job or working in a certain work environment and what does the individual wish to get as a result of their work? Work interests and environments are typically classified using Holland Codes with a match between the individual's personality and the work environment most likely leading to the highest levels of fulfillment and satisfaction. Carnevale et al. (2011) provide examples of some of these work values: recognition, achievement, autonomy, advancement, independence, and social service. Work values central to African American culture (e.g., social service) tend to be less dominant and less essential in STEM careers. STEM occupations are typically defined by work values of achievement, independence, and recognition. As a result, these contrasting work values and interests tend to divert individuals from more collaborative cultures from pursuing a STEM-related major and career. For example, a student with high self-efficacy toward calculus is more likely to have interests related to math and may develop a personal goal of earning a perfect score on the math component of the ACT/SAT. He or she may choose to join the math club to prepare and improve his or her math skills.

Activity selection and practice are just that—how the individual goes about developing the required skills to accomplish a task. Performance attainments are the final results or product of the culmination of all of the SCCT components which interact and perpetuate this process while influencing each aspect of the model. For example, a student's ACT/SAT score report showed the student earned a score in the 99th percentile for the math portion of the test. The student now wants to apply to the nation's top engineering colleges.

"ALAIJAH" AND SCCT

Applying SCCT to a fictitious student, Alaijah, we see how all of these forces can confound the career decision-making process: Alaijah describes herself as always being someone who is helpful and loves talking with strangers (person inputs). Alaijah has lived in a large, urban city her entire life with her mom, who is a 911 operator, and three younger siblings (contextual factors). As the oldest sibling, Alaijah's mother has always encouraged her to take on a mentee/tutor role to her younger siblings (persuasion). Her dedication and concern for her siblings' academic success have led them to be honor roll students (positive reinforcement), which has led her to believe that she is good at helping others academically (self-efficacy beliefs). She believes that if she continues to support her siblings, they will continue to excel in school (outcome expectations). Her interest in providing this support to her siblings has influenced her goals to attend college and become an elementary teacher (personal goal). To fulfill her goal, Alaijah will continue to assist her siblings after school and continue working to meet the entry requirements to enroll in college (actions). Alaijah's family cannot afford for her to work after school at a tutoring center to better develop her teaching skills due to the amount of money needed to cover the costs of childcare for her siblings; she will also need to earn scholarships and rely on other sources of financial aid to cover the costs of college attendance (proximal contextual factors). Eventually, Alaijah was awarded an academic scholarship to a local college (performance attainment).

Considering all of the factors that had to coalesce in order for Alaijah to pursue her goals of attending college and becoming an elementary teacher, a change in any one of those variables could have easily changed the formula. Perhaps if Alaijah had been born a male, gender roles may have dictated her as not being responsible for her siblings and their academics (person inputs). Had Alaijah been born in a rural community in Asia or not had any siblings she may not have been so inclined to pursue a college degree, career in education, or to help others so willingly (contextual factors). Moreover, if she had provided academic support to her siblings and they did not earn honor roll status, she may believe that she is not capable of providing academic support to others and is, in fact, not helpful (self-efficacy as a result of learning experiences). Each of these happenstance variations could have resulted in dramatically different self-efficacy beliefs, outcome expectations, interests, goals, actions, and performance attainments for Alaijah.

Source: Adapted from Niles & Harris-Bowlsbey (2009, pp. 91–92).

Exhibit 4.1 Alaijah and SCCT

Bronfenbrenner's Bioecological Theory and Systemic Issues to Consider

Not only are cultural and personality traits influencing African Americans' career decisions, but systemic issues may also impede students from accessing opportunities to pursue STEM majors and careers. Bronfenbrenner (1977) proposes the bioecological theory, suggesting that an individual's self-concept is the most important determining factor in their development. However, there are additional layers of environments interacting over time which also influence the individual's development. The factors influencing personal development also guide career decision making. Bronfenbrenner's model has five levels: individual, microsystemic, mesosystemic, exosystemic, and macrosystemic, but we will focus mostly on the last four ecosystems as the individual's inputs were addressed in earlier sections. Outside of the individual, these broader levels influence the career decision-making process. Defining and examining each of these levels unveils a plethora of systemic barriers which contribute to the underrepresentation of African Americans in STEM majors and occupations.

First, the microsystemic level consists of an individual's relationship to their immediate environment (e.g., home, school, work) and the specific roles inhabited during specified times. This level includes one's relationship with their parents/guardians, siblings, teachers, peers, and supervisors. Next, the mesosystemic level can be defined as the interaction of microsystems, for example, the interaction that occurs during parent-teacher conferences (i.e., the home microsystem is intersecting with the school microsystem). On a broader level, the exosystemic level includes environments and others, the individual is not necessarily directly involved in or with. Instead, these environments and people are peripherally associated with the various microsystems to which the individual belongs (e.g., extended family, school board, mass media, parents' work environments) (Curry & Milsom, 2013). Finally, the macrosystemic level is comprised of abstract forces influencing an individual's life. Some of these macrosystemic forces include history, laws, the economy, and culture.

Considering these various levels of systemic influences as we conceptualize the career decision-making process for African American students, we find ecosystemic barriers across all levels. For instance, an overall lower persistence rate for African Americans in college; a lack of STEM professional mentors; lack of peer support; societal expectations; unwelcoming classroom climates; mainstream media biases; the flexibility of parents' work schedules; school board re-districting decisions; poverty; segregated schools; led-based paint; a culture of capitalism; food deserts; levels of discriminatory laws; and the history of slavery (Bronfenbrenner, 1977; Carnevale et al., 2011; Curry

& Milsom, 2013; Sasso, 2008; Strauss, 2011). Each of these barriers on its own creates a more difficult career decision-making process. However, with a multitude of ecosystemic barriers converging at once for many African Americans, the chances of pursuing a major and career in STEM or other higher level career fields can seemingly become impossible and the career decision-making process overwhelming.

According to Bingham and Ward (1994), it is expected that one-third of the twentieth-century workforce will comprise racial and ethnic minorities, yet there are currently overrepresentations and under representations in specific career groups due to ecosystemic barriers working to the disadvantage of African American students. In the next section, possible interventions that Pre-K through 12th grade preservice teachers and teachers, school counselors, and administrators, as well as higher education administrators can implement to help African American students pursue STEM majors and careers are suggested. These interventions might increase the number of African Americans in nontraditional, specifically STEM, occupations. However, as the preceding sections of this chapter have suggested, before changes can be made to the career landscape, the sources responsible for preventing this change from having occurred already must be understood. A clear understanding of the increased demand for STEM employees, occupational outlook of STEM careers, societal needs to continue employing STEM workers, as well as the cultural values, person-work environment preferences, and occupational interests of African American students is necessary in order to effectively take action. By doing so we are able to understand the ways in which African American students view themselves, opportunities, challenges, and STEM.

OVERCOMING THE SCIENTIST PERCEPTION: STEM AS A COMMUNAL CAREER CHOICE

As educators we have a shared understanding and universal intention for everything we do with or say to our students—to positively impact their futures. The junction of ecosystemic factors and education seems to be an apropos intersection to begin the work of shaping the career decision-making processes for African American students and their interests in STEM careers. With such a significant charge, it may seem impossible for Pre-K through 12th grade preservice teachers and teachers, counselors, and administrators, and higher education administrators to be responsible for justifying the need for African American students to pursue STEM majors and careers while also combatting the consistent misrepresentations of STEM workers and their work. Understanding both the importance and somewhat daunting nature of this work, this section provides comprehensive intervention suggestions for educators which embrace the cultural values, personality and work-environment preferences, and common occupational interests of African Americans, as well as systemic barriers they face. These interventions can be implemented at the Pre-K through 12th grade and postsecondary levels and aim to increase the representation of African Americans in STEM careers, as well as change the perception of STEM workers from being one that is typically defined by solitary, White male chemists to one of community helpers and inclusive of racial minorities.

Pre-K through 12th Grade

This section includes suggestions for preservice teachers, teachers, administrators, and school counselors working toward providing Pre-K through 12th grade African American students with a more equitable education. The proposed interventions offer educational opportunities which can better prepare and increase the number of African American students completing postsecondary degrees and pursuing high-paying, high-prestige occupations (e.g., STEM careers).

Preservice Teachers and Teachers

Applying Lent, Brown, and Hackett's Social Cognitive Career Theory (1994), it is important for teachers, regardless of their number of years of experience, to consider how students approach subjects, tasks, and ideas. Students approaching STEM-related subjects, activities, and discussions with a positive self-concept and understanding of what is expected of them are much more likely to experience success. Successful experiences are likely to breed future successful experiences. Specifically, when we consider how Pre-K through 12th grade African American students are approaching STEM-related subjects, assignments, and discussions we find several opportunities to close the STEM achievement gap for African American students and foster successful experiences for students.

Varelas, Kane, and Wylie (2011) studied how African American students perceive themselves, science and themselves as science learners. The results of their study concluded that when assigned a science exploration task by the teacher, African American students were more likely to be given positive praise for their on-task behaviors (e.g., listening to the teacher and working quietly) and for having large amounts of knowledge than they were for engaging in the true scientific nature of the task (e.g., active questioning and flexibility in their thoughts). Thus, teachers were misdirecting their praise by praising them for "doing science" (i.e., being docile) rather than praising African American students for experiencing science.

> Emphasis on and attention to regulatory behavioral norms communicate to children that what matters is being 'good' as judged by others, being good in terms of how they behave, not being good in terms of how they think, solve problems, ask questions, make sense of ideas, and come up with new ones. (Varelas, Kane, & Wylie, p. 834)

While persistence is arguably one of the most important keys to success in STEM degree completion and careers, our overemphasis on behavioral norms can disengage students and distort their views of STEM. Diverting our attentions as teachers away from the problem-solving process and toward student behavior during the activity leads many students to the belief that they are "bad at science." This can create a self-fulfilling prophecy for African American students as they are then more likely to be discouraged from attempting future STEM activities, taking STEM coursework in middle and high school, and pursuing STEM majors and careers in the future.

Additionally, teachers should encourage students to consider how the concepts they are learning and skills they are using during activities are used in various STEM careers to benefit people and their communities. For example, a cause and effect lesson in an English language arts class can easily be related to cancer researchers and the work they conduct to find and eliminate or prevent the use of cancer-causing agents. When a specific population experiences higher rates of cancer than others (effect), researchers can begin testing various common elements in the population members' environment to learn the cancer-causing source (cause). This example provides teachers with a cross-curricular opportunity to connect African American cultural values (e.g., "we" mentality) and common occupational interests (e.g., Social) to STEM careers, while also reinforcing students' abilities to identify and analyze causes and effects. Highlighting the importance and prestige of STEM careers not only piques student interest in STEM, but it promotes an increased, more positive self-concept.

School Counselors

Career guidance and counseling is critically important to the improvement of the "social, economic, political, and psychological" states for African Americans. Pre-K through 12th grade academic and career counseling can prevent the further "persistent bleeding of many African Americans from the educational pipeline" and STEM careers (Brown & Pinterits, 2001, p. 1). Further solidifying the argument and desire for such interventions in schools, studies conducted by Carter and Wilson (1992), Leong and Brown (1995), Stabb and Cogdal (1992), and Webster and Fretz (1978) all concluded that African American students want academic and career assistance and are willing to take advantage of academic and career counseling services. The implementation of a comprehensive Pre-K through 12th grade school counseling program focusing on the academic, emotional/social, and career needs of all students (American School Counselor Association [ASCA], 2012) ensures the delivery of these desired services. However, we must be aware of and address the systemic barriers preventing African American students from completing postsecondary degrees and entering or pursuing high-paying, high-prestigious careers.

In order to be effective in this comprehensive counseling model, school counselors must deliver their services in a culturally competent manner (Lapan, 2004). If we intentionally expose African American students to a variety of secondary and postsecondary education options, careers, and career role models who have shared characteristics or experiences, we begin to influence the student's self-concept. School counselors can also include the use of role models in their comprehensive school counseling lessons to provide students with observational learning experiences. When students see themselves in another person pursuing a particular career (e.g., engineering), their belief system and self-efficacy is enhanced.

Additionally, school counselors should consider their own relationship with STEM subjects, majors, and careers. West-Olatunji et al. (2010) suggested that a reflexive relationship exists between how the school counselor perceives himself or herself as a STEM learner and their perception of students as STEM learners. This reflexive relationship can determine whether or not school counseling is conducted using a deficit-oriented or "strength-based, culturally responsive approach" (p. 191). Just as the school counselor can be more effective in their delivery of services by becoming more aware of their own preferences, students should be encouraged to engage in interest inventories early on such as the *Self-Directed Search* (*SDS*) or *Strong Interest Inventory* (*SII*); both of these assessments provide students with results in the form of Holland Codes. By engaging in these self-exploration exercises, students learn about various careers they are most likely to enjoy and in which careers they are most likely to experience work satisfaction. Based upon their results, school counselors can expose students to STEM careers by highlighting some of the student's most-preferred Holland Codes and various STEM work environments and occupations that value the expression of those preferences. Starting this process before they enter their final years of high school allows students to explore a range of careers they may have never considered and prevents them from coming to the close of their secondary education experience without ever fully considering their postsecondary options.

Lastly, school counselors should encourage parental involvement in an effort to incorporate ecosystemic interventions and "to utilize more culturally responsive counseling techniques" (West-Olatunji et al., 2010, p.

185). Hargrow and Hendricks (2001) noted many studies in which African Americans in nontraditional career fields reported a high level of support from their families and communities. Students are more likely to invest in the messages they are hearing at school if they are echoed and reinforced at home.

Administrators

While school administrators have less direct interaction with students on a daily basis than teachers and school counselors, the decisions administrators may greatly impact the students attending their schools and each of these students' future education and occupational options. By hiring and retaining quality STEM teachers, ensuring rigorous, STEM-related courses are readily available to students, and fostering relationships with community stakeholders, Pre-K through 12th grade school administrators can markedly influence the career decisions of African American students and their interests in STEM majors and careers.

Teacher quality is one of the most significant determining factors as it relates to the quality of a child's education. Yet when we take into account the most underserved and resource-deserving students—African American and Hispanic students—in our nation's public schools, we find that schools with the highest rates of African American and Hispanic student enrollment are the ones most likely to employ the most inexperienced and least paid teachers (Office of Civil Rights [OCR], 2012). Research shows that having a major in the subject one teaches positively affects student achievement (Allen, 2003); however, when we specifically examine STEM subjects, math teachers are less likely to have majored and be certified in the subject they teach compared to teachers of other subject areas (U.S. Department of Education, 2011). The combination of inexperienced, underpaid, and unqualified teachers in our highest-needs schools underprepares African American students for career and college readiness at a disproportionate rate compared to their White counterparts.

In addition to the hiring of highly qualified STEM teachers, administrators should make a diverse and rigorous STEM course curriculum available to its students in order to prepare them to succeed in the twenty-first century college and career environments. The Office of Civil Rights [OCR] (2012) found that schools serving predominantly African American student populations lacked the rigorous coursework necessary to pursue STEM careers. Examining a sampling of 85% of the nation's public schools, OCR found the following course offering disparities: 55% of high schools offer calculus versus 29% of predominantly African American high schools; 66% of the nation's high schools offer physics versus 40% of predominantly African American high schools; and 82% of high schools offer Algebra II versus 65%

of predominantly African American high schools. This significant opportunity gap in course offerings for African American students systematically negatively impacts their readiness to complete postsecondary degrees and pursue high-paying, high-prestige careers.

Without question, there are many schools serving predominantly racial minority student bodies which are underfunded and underresourced; as a result of the financial and resource deficits, budgeting decisions for administrators become extremely difficult and complex. However, school stakeholders (i.e., school faculty, parents and guardians, and community partners) are invaluable resources that can provide financial relief to the school while also ensuring students are given access to an equitable education. Through networking with stakeholders, administrators gain awareness of community resources and build relationships with community partners who are integral to the development of African American students' interests and readiness to pursue STEM majors and careers. Curry and Milsom (2013) explain that by collaborating with stakeholders, schools gain career mentors, "career guest speakers, resources for career and technical fairs," and job-shadowing opportunities (p. 27). Additionally, partnering with local community colleges and neighboring schools provides students with opportunities to take rigorous STEM coursework, which their designated school may be unable to offer. The potential relationships administrators can build with stakeholders not only raises awareness and increases preparedness and interest in STEM, but also corrects the misconception that STEM is not a communal occupational choice.

Higher Education Administrators

The roles of higher education administrators are many and varied. Depending upon the size of the college or university and department one works in, a higher education administrator may be responsible for admissions, student records, student affairs, or coordinating the policies and activities of individual colleges or schools (U.S. Department of Labor's Bureau of Labor Statistics, 2014b). Despite these disparate roles, each plays a critical role in the efforts to increase the enrollment and degree-completion of African American students in STEM majors. Whether their focus is on enrollment or degree-completion, higher education administrators working in all departments should regularly disaggregate and analyze data points to identify areas of inequity disadvantaging certain student populations.

Enrollment

As admissions directors, recruitment efforts should be intentional and focused. Understanding the drastic underrepresentation of African Americans in STEM careers, promotional materials for the college or university and

STEM majors should be used as an opportunity to display the multifaceted nature of STEM and answer any misconceptions prospective students have regarding STEM majors and related coursework. Similar to the role Pre-K through 12th grade school administrators play in building relationships with stakeholders, higher education administrators working in student affairs should collaborate with the local community. For example, by coordinating service projects with the school's African American cultural center and STEM majors, student affairs administrators help promote degree-seeking behaviors and majoring in STEM careers among African American students in the local community. This also exposes community members to African American college students and STEM major students, who function as role models for younger students in the community. Additionally, such service projects emphasize the collaborative, collectivistic cultural values centered on giving back to one's local community by demonstrating community engagement at the college or university level.

Degree-completion

Administrators working in the registrar's office are responsible for scheduling students and ensuring they have met graduation requirements. During scheduled annual reviews of enrollment and graduation data, registrar administrators should take note of how African American students are performing across disciplines within the university and in STEM-related courses. Any patterns or areas of concern should be passed on to the administrators working directly within STEM colleges or schools.

Higher education administrators working for these individual colleges or schools are responsible for developing policies, appointing faculty members, and making budgeting decisions. With increasing the number of African American students majoring in STEM-related majors and completing degrees as a top priority, administrators at this level can work toward creating and implementing more equitable policies, faculty appointments, and budget decisions. Such an approach promotes diversity within the school at all levels, does not work to the detriment of any student population, and provides support systems which aid students in their degree-completion. For example, in response to a lack of rigorous coursework being offered at so many Pre-K through 12th grade schools in the nation serving predominantly African American student populations, administrators may notice a large number of African American students opting out of higher-level math and science courses. These findings can be sent to the higher education administrators, who can then make policy and financial decisions which will provide these students with remedial or supplemental courses in an effort to increase college and STEM major retention and degree-completion rates among African American students.

Regardless of whether we begin offering a wider variety of STEM courses, more rigorous courses, a comprehensive school counseling program, "STEM Career Day," partner with community businesses and leaders, or provide additional educational services to African American students, we must address the underlying force which shapes all career decision-making processes—culture. As mentioned at the onset and throughout this chapter, culture is influenced by many factors; these factors include, but are not limited to, perceptions of self, others, and the world, personality and work environment preferences, traditional occupational interests, and ecosystemic issues. Underscoring the disconnection between African American cultural values and STEM careers, Tracey and Walker (2012) found a correlation between perceived occupational prestige and levels of cultural identity for African Americans. African American students who had greater endorsement of African American identity and collaborative, collectivistic values reported higher prestige for Social and Enterprising occupations, but lower prestige for STEM careers. This study suggests that if the perception of scientists, science, and STEM careers is modified, we can create an opportunity to increase the number of African American students entering STEM majors and careers.

SUMMARY

Assisting students with their career and college decisions is no small task. And when we consider encouraging African American students to pursue STEM careers, this process can become extremely complex. While increasing exposure to STEM careers, eliminating discrimination, eradicating poverty, and improving the conditions of the other various ecosystemic forces will increase representation of African Americans in STEM careers, these are pervasive systemic issues that will take decades to overcome. Given the dire underrepresentation of African Americans in STEM careers, by embracing African American culture as opposed to continuing the historical rejection of it, we as educators can encourage these students to pursue STEM majors and careers. As we work to eliminate the opportunity and achievement gaps and increase access to an equitable education which prepares African American students to succeed in the twenty-first century, it is important we consider influences which will greatly determine the outcome of our efforts. These influences include: (1) collective and collaborative cultural values; (2) the underrepresentation of African Americans in STEM careers; (3) African American personality types and work environment preferences; (4) common occupational interests of African American students; and (5) how STEM is presented to students. By keeping these influences in mind, we as teachers, school counselors, and administrators can help African American students define their career and college paths for themselves instead of allowing systemic influences to override the career and college decision-making process.

REFERENCES

Allen, M. (2003). *Eight questions on teacher preparation: What does the research say?* Denver, CO: Education Commission of the States.

American School Counselor Association. (2012). *The ASCA national model: A framework for school counseling programs.* (3rd ed.). Alexandria, VA: Author.

Bandura, A. (1977). *Social learning theory.* Englewood Cliffs, NJ: Prentice Hall.

Bandura, A. (1997). *Self-efficacy: The exercise of control.* New York, NY: Freeman.

Bingham, R. P., & Ward, C. M. (1994). Career counseling with ethnic minority women. In W. Walsh & S. Osipow (Eds.), *Career counseling with women* (pp. 165–95). Hillsdale, NJ: Erlbaum.

Bronfenbrenner, U. (1977). Toward an experimental ecology of human development. *American Psychologist, 32*(7), 513–31. doi:10.1037/0003–066X.32.7.513

Brown, M. T., & Pinterits, E. J. (2001). Basic issues in career counseling of African Americans. In W. B. Walsh, R. P. Bingham, M. T. Brown, & C. M. Ward (Eds.), *Career counseling for African Americans* (1–26). Manwah, NJ: Lawrence Erlbaum Associates, Inc.

Carlone, H., & Johnson, A. (2007). Understanding the science experiences of success women of color: Science identity as an analytic lens. *Journal of Research in Science Teaching, 44*(8), 1187–218. doi:10.1002/tea.20237

Carnevale, A. P., Smith, N., & Melton, M. (2011). *STEM: Science, technology, engineering, mathematics.* Retrieved from the Georgetown University Public Policy Institute, Center on Education and the Workforce website: https://georgetown.app.box.com/s/cyrrqbjyirjy64uw91f6

Carter, D. J., & Wilson, R. (1992). *Minorities in higher education, 1991: Tenth annual status report.* Washington, DC: American Council on Education.

Chambers, D. W. (1983). Stereotypic images of the scientist: The draw-a-scientist-test. *Science Education, 67*(2), 255–65. doi:10.1002/sce.3730670213

Curry, J., & Milsom, A. (2013). *A practical approach to P-12 career guidance and counseling in schools: Developmental and contextual considerations.* New York, NY: Springer Publishing Company.

Finson, K. D., Beaver, J. B., & Cramond, B. L. (1995). Development and field test of a checklist for the draw-a-scientist test. *School Science and Mathematics, 95*(4), 195–205. doi:10.1111/j.1949–8594.1995.tb15762.x

Gottfredson, L. S. (1978). An analytical description of employment according to race, sex, prestige, and Holland type of work. *Journal of Vocational Behavior, 13*(2), 210–21. doi:10.1016/0001–8791(78)90046–5

Gushue, G., & Constantine, M. G. (2003). Examining individualism, collectivism, and self-differentiation in African American college women. *Journal of Mental Health Counseling, 25*(1), 1–15.

Hargrow, A. M., & Hendricks, F. (2001). Career counseling with African Americans in nontraditional career fields. In W. B. Walsh, R. P. Bingham, M. T. Brown, & C. M. Ward (Eds.), *Career counseling for African Americans* (139–60). Manwah, NJ: Lawrence Erlbaum Associates, Inc.

Hofstede, G. H. (2001). *Culture's consequences: Comparing values, behaviors, institutions, and organizations across nations* (2nd ed.). Thousand Oaks, CA: Sage Publications.

Holland, J. L. (1973). *Making vocational choices: A theory of careers.* Englewood Cliffs, NJ: Prentice Hall, Inc.

Holland, J. L. (1997). *Making vocational choices: A theory of vocational personalities and work environments* (3rd ed.). Odessa, FL: Psychological Assessment Resources.

Jones, L. K. (2011). *Holland's six personality types.* Retrieved from The Career Key website: http://www.careerkey.org/asp/your_personality/hollands_6_personalitys.asp

Lapan, R. T. (2004). *Career development across the K-16 years: Bridging the present to satisfying and successful futures.* Alexandria, VA: American Counseling Association.

Lent, R. W., Brown, S. D., & Hackett, G. (1994). Toward a unifying social cognitive theory of career and academic interest, choice, and performance. *Journal of Vocational Behavior, 45*(1), 79–122. doi:10.1006/jvbe.1994.1027

Leong, F. T. L., & Brown, M. T. (1995). Theoretical issues in cross-cultural career development: Cultural validity and cultural specificity. In W. B. Walsh & S. H. Osipow (Eds.), *Handbook of vocational psychology: Theory, research, and practice* (2nd ed., pp. 143–80). Mahwah, NJ: Lawrence Erlbaum Associates.

MacCorquodale, P. (1984, August). *Self-image, science and math: Does the image of the "scientist" keep girls and minorities from pursuing science and math?* Paper presented at the 79th annual meeting of the American Sociological Association, San Antonio, TX. Retrieved from http://files.eric.ed.gov/fulltext/ED253493.pdf

Malone, K. R., & Barabino, G. (2009). Narrations of race in STEM research settings: Identity formation and its discontents. *Science Education. 93*(3), 485–519. doi:10.1002/sce.20307

Maltese, A. V., & Tai, R. H. (2011). Pipeline persistence: Examining the association of educational experiences with earned degrees in STEM among U.S. students. *Science Education, 95*(5), 877–907. doi:10.1002/sce.20441

Mason, C. L., Kahle, J. B., & Gardner, A. L. (1991). Draw-a-scientist-test: Future implications. *School Science and Mathematics, 91*(5), 193–98. doi:10.1111/j.1949–8594.1991.tb12078.x

Metz, A. J., Fouad, N., & Ihle-Helledy, K. (2009). Career aspirations and expectations of college students: Demographic and labor market comparisons. *Journal of Career Assessment, 17*(2), 155–71. doi:10.1177/1069072708328862

Miller, M. J., Springer, T., & Wells, D. (1988). Which occupational environments do Black youths prefer? Extending Holland's typology. *School Counselor, 36*(2), 103–6. Retrieved July 9, 2014 from PsychINFO database.

Myers, J. E., Sweeney, T. J., & Witmer, J. M. (2001). Optimization of behavior: Promotion of wellness. In D. Locke, J. Myers, & E. Herr (Eds.), *The handbook of counseling* (pp. 641–52). Thousand Oaks, CA: Sage Publications.

National Science Foundation, National Center for Science and Engineering Statistics. (2013). *Women, minorities, and persons with disabilities in science and engineering: 2013*. Retrieved June 25, 2014, from http://www.nsf.gov/statistics/wmpd/

Niles, S. G., & Harris-Bowlsbey, J. (2009). *Career development interventions in the 21st century* (3rd ed.). Upper Saddle River, NJ: Merrill/Pearson.

Odell, M. R. I., Hewitt, P., Bowman, J., & Boone, W. J. (1993, April). *Stereotypical images of scientists: A cross-age study*. Paper presented at the 41st annual meeting of the National Science Teachers Association, Kansas City, MO.

Oyserman, D., Coon, H. M., & Kemmelmeir, M. (2002). Rethinking individualism and collectivism: Evaluation of theoretical assumptions and meta-analyses. *Psychological Bulletin, 128*(1), 3–72. doi:10.1037//0033–2909.128.1.3

Sasso, A. (2008). African-Americans studying STEM: Parsing the numbers. *Science Career Magazine*, May 16, 2008. Retrieved on July 9, 2014 from http://sciencecareers.sciencemag.org/career_magazine/previous_issues/articles/2008_05_16/caredit.a0800070. doi:10.1126/science.caredit.a0800070

Stabb, S. D., & Cogdal, P. A. (1992). Black college men in personal counseling: A five-year archival investigation. *Journal of College Student Psychotherapy, 7*, 73–86.

Strauss, V. (2011, August 17). 2011 ACT scores show problems with college readiness. *The Washington Post*. Retrieved online from http://www.washingtonpost.com/blogs/answer-sheet/post/2011-act-scores-show-problems-with-college-readiness/2011/08/16/gIQABKu4JJ_blog.html

Sue, D. W., & Sue, D. (2013). *Counseling the culturally diverse: Theory and practice* (6th ed.). Hoboken, NJ: John Wiley & Sons.

Symington, D., & Spurling, H. (1990). The 'draw a scientist test': Interpreting the data. *Research in Science & Technological Education, 8*(1), 75–77. doi:10.1080/02635100080107

Triandis, H. C., & Gelfand, M. J. (1998). Converging measurement of horizontal and vertical individualism and collectivism. *Journal of Personality and Social Psychology, 74*(1), 118–28. doi:10.1037/0022–3514.74.1.118

U.S. Department of Education, Institute of Education Sciences, National Center for Education Statistics. (2011, May). *Education and certification qualifications of departmentalized public high school-level teachers of core subjects: Evidence from the 2007–08 schools and staffing survey*, (NCES 2011–317). Retrieved from http://nces.ed.gov/pubs2011/2011317.pdf

U.S. Department of Labor, Bureau of Labor Statistics (2014a). *A-20: Employed persons by occupation, race, Hispanic or Latino ethnicity, and sex*. Retrieved July 1, 2014, from http://www.bls.gov/web/empsit/cpseea20.pdf

U.S. Department of Labor, Bureau of Labor Statistics (2014b). *Occupational outlook handbook, 2014–15 edition*. Retrieved July 31, 2014, from http://www.bls.gov/ooh/management/postsecondary-education-administrators.htm

U.S. Department of Labor, Bureau of Labor Statistics (2014c). *STEM 101: Intro to tomorrow's jobs*. By Dennis Vilorio. Retrieved June 11, 2014, from http://www.bls.gov/opub/ooq/2014/spring/art01.pdf

U.S. Office for Civil Rights. (2012, March 12). The transformed civil rights data collection. Retrieved from http://www2.ed.gov/about/offices/list/ocr/docs/crdc-2012-data-summary.pdf

Varelas, M., Kane, J. M., & Wylie, C. D. (2011). Young African American children's representations of self, science, and school: Making sense of difference. *Science Education*, 95(5), 824–51. doi:10.1002/sce.20447

Walker, T. L., & Tracey, T. J. G. (2012). Perceptions of occupational prestige: Differences between African American and White college students. *Journal of Vocational Behavior*, 80(1), 76–81. doi:10.1016/j.jvb.2011.06.003

Webster, D. W., & Fretz, B. R. (1978). Asian American, Black, and White college students' preferences for help-giving sources. *Journal of Counseling Psychology*, 25(2), 124–30. doi:10.1037/0022–0167.25.2.124

West-Olatunji, C., Shure, L., Pringle, R., Adams, T., Lewis, D., & Cholewa, B. (2010). Exploring how school counselors position low-income African American girls as mathematics and science learners. *Professional School Counseling*, 13(3), 184–95. doi:10.5330/PSC.n.2010–13.184

Chapter 5

Talent Development as Career Development and College Readiness in Gifted African American Youth

Andrea Dawn Frazier, Jennifer Riedl Cross, and Tracy L. Cross

Michael Jordan is considered a preeminent basketball player. His impact is so seminal that many *potentially* great players are cast in his shadow, with Jordan's prowess and accomplishments serving as the benchmark against which true prowess is determined. Considering his strength as an athlete, many expected his foray into baseball to be a runaway success. However, it turned out that Michael Jordan had long since aged past his ability to develop the visual motor skills necessary to hit a baseball expertly, thereby curtailing any ambition of becoming a talented baseball player (Klawans, 1996). Had Michael Jordan taken up baseball in childhood with the passion he brought to mastering basketball, the story about him as an athlete might well have been different.

Samuel Johansen[1] is a talented African American male from a low-income background. With the support of his family, he decided to attend a residential high school for students talented in math and science, a school noteworthy for being one of the finest high schools in the nation. During his first year in attendance, he enrolled in an introductory Japanese course. Prior to taking the course, Samuel had never spoken Japanese before. It became apparent that Samuel had a very good ear for Japanese, and for languages generally, and the Japanese instructor felt that Samuel was one of the best students he had ever had. Samuel is currently an assistant professor at an Ivy League university, with his research and teaching devoted to Japanese literature, performance studies, and art history.

Several years after Samuel graduated, Jeremiah Forester, another precocious African American male, attended the same high school. Jeremiah also had a passion drama. In a study exploring possible selves in high-ability African American males, Samuel was interviewed about his potential future selves. He described the school as being pivotal in helping him understand that drama was important for him, and he had already participated in several school plays by the time of the interview. However, in the course of describing his journey as a thespian, he recounted this story:

> I was in "Little Shop of Horrors" ... and I wanted to be like the main role for the guy, Seymour ... as soon as I walked in the door, the director said, I want you to sing "Feed Me." That's the song that the plant sings, and the plant's supposed to be like this big horrible creature, and it's supposed to have an Ebonic voice ... So, as soon as I walk in the door, they were like, "Sing that song." [I said] I've been practicing the song that Seymour sings for like a month now. And then they said you can sing "Feed Me" first and sing the other song later if you want to ... And then I turned out being the plant ... I did a really good job, but still, they didn't give me a chance (Frazier, 2012, p. 381).

At the time of the interview, Jeremiah was unsure of his future path. He wanted to pursue drama full time, but he was not confident in his ability to make drama his life's work, with some of this lack of confidence appearing to be due to the racism he was brushing up against (Frazier, 2012). It may be that the residential school that had been so positive for Samuel might not have been as positive a place for Jeremiah in helping him develop his potential.

In this chapter, we will discuss African American students who have exceptional academic potential and the supports necessary to ensure that they are prepared for success in college. Embedded within these vignettes are several themes that will be addressed in more detail when considering the role that talent plays in preparing highly able African American students for careers:

1. Though youth may be successful in a variety of ways, it is helpful to conceive of talent as domain specific (Subotnik, Olszewski-Kubilius, & Worrell, 2011) rather than generalized;
2. Talent development occurs along a trajectory, with the trajectory dependent on the domain (Subotnik et al., 2011);
3. It is important for children to have the opportunity to practice the skills of the domain in ways that are authentic. Mastery, as well as expectations that ratchet up based on level of expertise, indicate to an individual what they are capable of within the domain.
4. Proficiency in a talent domain needs to be recognized.
5. Schools are important to talent development to the degree they privilege academic press or challenge for all students, irrespective of ability;
6. Schools are not solely responsible for developing talent in children. Instead, talent development is embedded within and is influenced by a system of support that includes the home, the school, the child, and societal

influences (Subotnik et al., 2011; Ziegler & Phillipson, 2012). All are powerful entities.

Supporting the needs of African American students with exceptional potential begins with attention to the trajectory of their talent domain.

BECOMING HIGH ACHIEVERS

Who are gifted African American students? The only definition of giftedness accepted to a large degree in the United States appeared in a 1972 federal report to Congress. Marland (1972) proposed that gifted and talented children are

> those identified by professionally qualified persons who by virtue of outstanding abilities are capable of high performance. These are children who require differentiated educational programs and/or services beyond those normally provided by the regular school program in order to realize their contribution to self and society .... Children capable of high performance include those with demonstrated achievement and/or potential ability in any of the following areas, singly or in combination:
>
> 1. General intellectual ability
> 2. Specific academic aptitude
> 3. Creative or productive thinking
> 4. Leadership ability
> 5. Visual or performing arts
> 6. Psychomotor ability. (p. ix)

A follow-up report in 1993 clarifies this definition, adding, "Outstanding talents are present in children and youth from all cultural groups, across all economic strata, and in all areas of human endeavor" (U.S. Department of Education, 1993, p. 3). Historically, gifted education was built around providing services to a child who had been identified with gifts and talents. This tradition continues to be the prevalent model in schools. Designed to follow the example of special education, services for gifted and talented students begin when they are identified as meeting a definition, according to the criteria specified by the school district.

Increasingly, attention is being paid to the importance of identifying potentially gifted students as early in their development as feasible (National Association for Gifted Children [NAGC], 2006; Subotnik et al., 2011). One of the considerations supporting early identification is the relationship between identification and specific talent trajectories (Cross & Coleman, 2005; Feldman, 1986/1991). For example, female gymnasts now peak in their careers by age 17, while in the mid-1900s they tended to peak much later, often in their early 20s. Their physical development has also changed significantly, typically producing athletes who are much shorter and more muscular than in the 1950s. Likewise, their routines have become increasingly complex and challenging (Bloom, 1985).

The growing body of knowledge about developmental trajectories across talent domains allows for improved planning and increases world-class accomplishment. For example, world-class violinists began practicing violin at about 4 years of age and tend to come from homes where two parents are fine musicians and at least one parent is a very accomplished violinist (Bloom, 1985). Simply stated, families are very important to the process of developing world-class talent. Not enough is known about the trajectories dependent on academic learning (Subotnik, et al., 2011), but what patterns are known in various fields provide an advantage for parents in terms of preparing their child to develop in a particular talent domain. As knowledge is gained about these trajectories, the significance of appropriate early experiences becomes clear. When high-ability African American children do not have access to these early experiences, the effect on their later success in a field may be momentous.

In addition to information about specific developmental trajectories, other factors such as family financial resources, community resources, and cultural/societal prejudices can impact a child's development. Growth in some talent domains (e.g., gymnastics) begins early in the life of a student and requires obtaining specialized instruction and competition for the child to grow. This typically leads to considerable adult commitment (e.g., driving to competitions) and can even require moving to a location near a centralized training opportunity (Bloom, 1985). It is expensive to develop this form of talent. Families must commit to the process, and it is very helpful if communities have experts and facilities in place.

In areas like gymnastics, virtually all of the development occurs outside of school. In other types of talent domains such as mathematics, the school is typically the primary training ground where the student is provided the required resources. Early development is necessary, as evidenced by the positive relationship between, for example, early math performance and later college graduation (see Figure 5.1; Murnane, Willett, Duhaldeborde, & Tyler, 2000). Plus, the developmental trajectory is much longer, with world-class mathematicians revealing themselves after receiving a PhD in mathematics. In other words, instead of peaking by 17 years of age, receiving training outside of school, and moving to be near the best training, those who aspire to become mathematicians can develop their potential in their local schools, continue through college and graduate school and peak by age 45 or so.

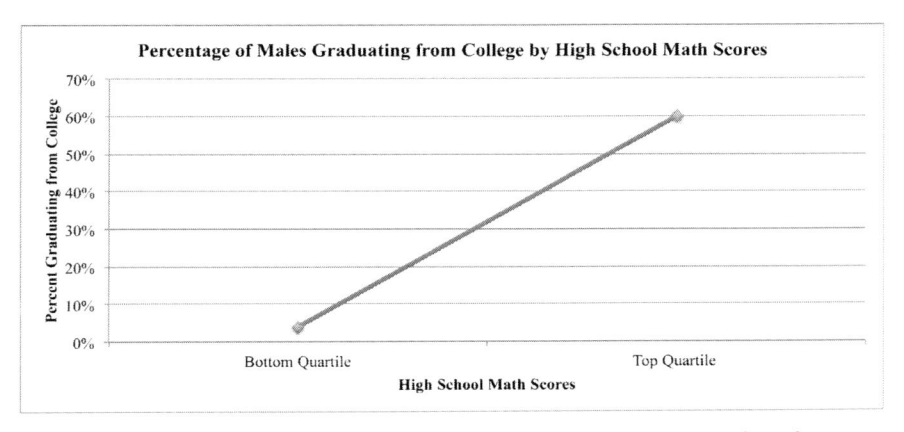

Figure 5.1 Percentage of Males Graduating from College by High School Math Scores. *Source*: High School & Beyond Dataset 1986–1992 (Murnane, Willett, Duhaldeborde, & Tyler, 2000)

An emphasis on developmental trajectories represents a shift in gifted education (Dai & Chen, 2013) away from the traditional focus on the individual gifted child, albeit this shift is in its early stages. Developing into a skilled gymnast or as a skilled mathematician reveals the range in developmental trajectories about which parents, educators, and counselors need to be informed. With limited information, families will struggle to help their children grow in their passion areas to their fullest extent. Sharing information about talent domains, the talent development process, identifying potential early, and effective counseling and guidance are all critical in the talent development of our able African American children.

Underrepresentation of High-Ability African American Students in Gifted Education

Most African American high-ability students will be educated in settings built around the identification of a gifted child. Despite the popular myth that gifted students will "do fine on their own" (NAGC, 2009), an education targeting average students will be inadequate for the full development of high potential in students. To ensure early success of African American students with exceptional academic ability, educators must be able to recognize them. Thus, the underrepresentation of African American students has been lamented for decades within the gifted education field (e.g., Ford, 2003; Ford, Grantham, & Whiting, 2008; Olszewski-Kubilius, Lee, Ngoi, & Ngoi, 2004; VanTassel-Baska & Stambaugh, 2007) and efforts have been made to increase the number of African American students in gifted and talented programs. Whereas an exceptional performance on a standardized test of intelligence or intellectual abilities was once the sole criterion for entrance to gifted and talented programs, multiple criteria are recommended as best practice (NAGC, 2014) and are now the norm rather than the exception. These multiple criteria allow consideration of such alternative indications of exceptional ability as nonverbal ability test scores; teacher, parent, peer or even self-nominations; or outstanding performances or products. Yet, even with the addition of multiple criteria to the identification process in the past few decades, African American students continue to be underrepresented in programs for gifted and talented students. Several broad explanations for this continued underrepresentation have been explored in the literature: teacher biases, test bias, and retention of identified students in gifted programming.

Teacher Biases

Teachers, who tend to be White and female in the United States (National Center for Education Statistics [NCES], 2008), are key to the identification process. Studies by Elhoweris, Mutua, Alsheikh and Holloway (2005) and McBee (2006, 2010) found that teachers most easily recognize the stereotypical White, middle-class gifted student and are more likely to identify White than African American students as gifted, even when presented with identical academic profiles. In his study of statewide nomination effectiveness, McBee (2006; 2010) found that teachers significantly under-nominated minority and economically disadvantaged students.

Ford and her colleagues (Ford, Harris, Tyson, & Trotman, 2002) proposed that many educators suffer from *deficit thinking*, an orientation that inhibits the development of their African American gifted students. Educators who engage in such deficit thinking view culturally different students as deprived or deficient and are unable to recognize their exceptional abilities or potential. Teacher training can increase numbers of accurate identifications (Hunsaker, Findley, & Frank, 1997) and deficit thinking can be ameliorated with targeted professional development that increases their cultural competence (Ford et al., 2002). Unfortunately, few states require teachers to have specialized training for working with or identifying gifted students (NAGC, 2013).

Test Biases

Standardized tests are often the single most important criteria used in the identification process, even when multiple criteria are considered. Since 1978, African American students have consistently scored lower than White students in both math and reading (Vanneman, Hamilton, Anderson, & Rahman, 2009). This achievement gap has barely changed, despite considerable attention to reducing the gap. Similar differentials are common in intelligence testing, as well. In a variety of ability tests, including nonverbal tests such as the *Raven's Progressive Matrices*, African American adults perform on average about one standard deviation below White adults (Valencia & Suzuki, 2001).

Both Valencia and Suzuki (2001) and Phillips, Crouse, and Ralph (1998) have challenged the popular acceptance of the ability and achievement test performance differences. Valencia and Suzuki cite a number of studies in which the inclusion of socioeconomic status in analyses of differences between African American and White intelligence test scores nearly eliminates differences. Phillips and colleagues controlled for earlier knowledge (e.g., first grade scores) in assessing achievement differences in reading and math. When earlier knowledge differences were controlled for, the achievement gaps at 9th and 12th grade were substantially smaller. These findings should be considered in light of the research of Turkheimer and colleagues (Harden, Turkheimer, & Loehlin, 2007; Turkheimer, Haley, Waldron, D'Onofrio, & Gottesman, 2003) who have found that environment explains more variance in intelligence scores than genetics for poor children, whereas genetics explains more variance than environment among their more advantaged peers.

The implication of these varied studies is that test scores must be interpreted with caution and with recognition of the importance of previous learning opportunities and the effects of an impoverished environment, where present. When students are sifted out of an identification process by their test scores, advocates should be able to challenge such a decision with alternative evidence of high ability. As the most common gatekeeper to special services for gifted students, test scores can be a particular hindrance to African American students, particularly those from low-income backgrounds.

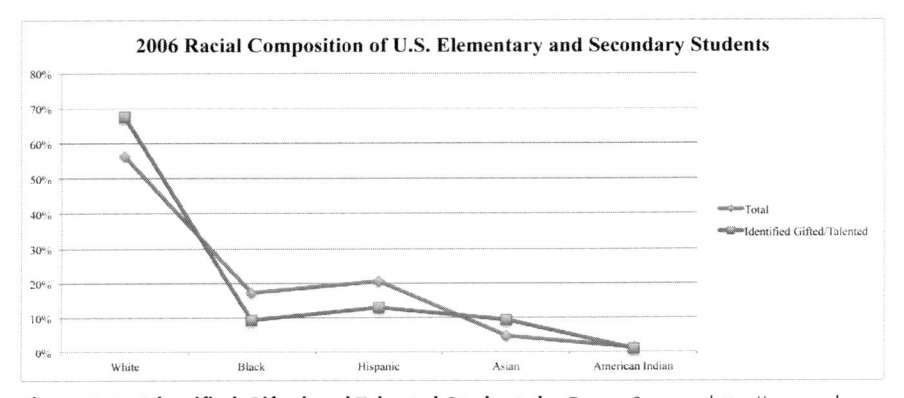

Figure 5.2 Identified Gifted and Talented Students by Race. *Source*: http://nces.ed.gov

Retention in Gifted Programs

However high-ability students are identified for special services, they must be able to perform at an advanced level in order to be ready for college at the time of matriculation. This is most likely to happen among students who have had the opportunity for advanced-level work from an early age. Most students in gifted programs are White and middle- or upper-socioeconomic status (see Figure 5.2; Donovan & Cross, 2002; NCES, 2008), so the gifted African American student identified for placement in a special program is likely to be one of few demographically similar students. The potential exists for a culturally based mismatch for African American students attempting to fit into a majority White class. Citing Hale-Benson (1986), Ford and Thomas (1997) suggest that "Black students tend to be field-dependent, visual, and concrete learners, whereas schools teach more often in verbal, abstract, and decontextualized ways" (p. 5). Competition in an advanced class may be uncomfortable for minority students who are unaccustomed to pressure from teachers and peers with competitive goals for performance (Hale-Benson, 1986), but it is important to note that many gifted students feel different from their average ability peers (T. Cross, Coleman, & Stewart, 1995; Robinson, 1996). This differentness is compounded for the African American student in a majority White gifted class (Lee, Olszewski-Kubilius, & Peternal, 2010). Finding intellectual peers can be an affirming experience (Coleman & Cross, 2005), but the feelings of differentness may still exist when those peers are not from the same racial or cultural background (Lee, et al., 2010).

A specific form of cultural mismatch is the "acting White" phenomenon. In their study of Black students' underachievement, Fordham and Ogbu (1986) identified the concept of "acting White" among several of the students they interviewed, who reported being criticized by peers for seemingly rejecting their own culture by pursuing academic (a.k.a., "White") interests. Since the publication of their study, there has been mixed empirical support for this phenomenon. For example, in an analysis of the National Longitudinal Study of Adolescent Health (Add Health) dataset, Fryer and Torelli (2010) found that African American students with a GPA above 3.5 had smaller friendship networks–evidence supporting the social cost of high academic performance. In contrast, Tyson, Darity, and Castellino (2005) found high academic achievement orientations among the 40 African American students in North Carolina secondary schools. A majority of the students interviewed in their qualitative study reported no cultural prohibition against achievement, although this was present in one high school. Wildhagen (2011) found that, not only did the nearly 10,000 African American high school students in the Education Longitudinal Study of 2002 dataset have more positive opinions of school in general than Whites, there was also no evidence that victimization was higher among higher performing African American students. These studies suggest that different communities may respond positively or negatively to African American students who are focused on academic achievement.

Despite its appearance in the literature as a uniquely African American explanation of underachievement, the social rejection that underpins the "acting White" phenomenon is actually a commonplace experience for many high-ability students. Multiple studies have found studious peers are rejected (e.g., Bishop et al., 2004; Schroeder-Davis, 1999; Tannenbaum, 1962), suggesting a more powerful and widespread social proscription against academic pursuits. Whereas Fordham and Ogbu (1986) described "acting White" as peers rejecting academically oriented African American classmates because they were behaving inconsistently with social norms for academic performance, the rejection of peers for their studiousness in the broader community happens when local social norms, irrespective of race, prohibit high academic achievement. Anti-intellectual attitudes can inhibit the possibilities for high-ability African American students if they are insufficiently supported by adults and peers who hold positive attitudes toward academic achievement. Their feelings of differentness may be further validated in an anti-intellectual environment.

African American gifted students may also experience racial prejudice in a gifted classroom (Ford, 2013; Kitano, 2012). The effect of negative stereotypes, regardless of one's belief in them, can impact students' performance. When African American subjects were told that a test diagnosed their intellectual ability, they performed more poorly than when told the test was not for diagnostic purposes (Steele & Aronson, 1995). The same conditions did not affect White subjects' performance. A substantial body of research indicates that this *stereotype threat* has adverse effects on the intellectual performance of African American students (e.g., Inzlicht, & Ben-Zeev, 2003; Steele, Spencer, & Aronson, 2002).

The traditional practices used to identify and serve gifted students have had a negative effect on African American students with academic potential (see Figure 5.2). In fact, gifted education built on the *gifted child model* (Dai, 2010, 2011) has not served the African American community well. In a sad intersection of cultural bias and ignorance about gifted education, African American students tend to be overrepresented in programs for students with disabilities and underrepresented in gifted and talented programs (Donovan & Cross, 2002; NCES, 2008). The cascading effect of missed opportunities begins in the earliest years of schooling (Wyner, Bridgeland, & DiIulio, 2007). This underrepresentation is found at all levels of education, from kindergarten to graduate and professional schools, including among faculty members at higher education institutions (Miller, 2004).

Rectifying this inequitable situation requires a change in the conceptualization of gifted education. The *talent development paradigm* (Dai & Chen, 2013; Subotnik et al., 2011) emphasizes the extensive provision of opportunities to all students, followed by intensive provision of supports to develop talent among those showing potential. Over time and with the right resources, talent is developed among students with the motivation and ability to succeed. This approach requires substantial effort on the part of educators in the early years, when potential must be transformed into achievement. For students from families of economic means, this can be accomplished outside of school. For those who have fewer economic resources, schools will necessarily be a critical part of their development.

Good Ingredients for Rigor Within a Curriculum

According to Nord et al. (2011), NCES data shows that 13% of all high school graduates completed a rigorous academic track in 2009, a significant increase from the 5% rate of completion in 1990. At present, and depending on the source, approximately 6% (Nord et al., 2011) to 8% (Horn & Nuñez, 2000) of African American students are completing rigorous academic tracks in high school. It is encouraging that more students, including African American students, are choosing to complete a rigorous program in high school (Nord et al., 2011). However, the types of schools African American students attend may delimit this opportunity. African American families are likely to live in more segregated neighborhoods that are also more impoverished (Logan, 2011; Patillo, 2003, 2005; Patillo-McCoy, 2000), therefore, African American students from low-income and middle-income families are often enrolled in schools with high rates of poverty in the student body. Neighborhood schools wherein a large number of students are impoverished are characterized by limited, high rigor academic offerings (Galster, Marcotte, Mandell, Wolman, & Augustine, 2007), making it difficult for willing students to pursue a higher academic standard. It is thus not all that surprising that high-ability students from low-income backgrounds are less likely to matriculate into college, attend selective colleges, and pursue graduate degrees (Wyner, et al., 2007).

The college readiness of African American students with even the highest potential will depend upon the opportunities they are afforded in their schooling. African American students with great potential need an appropriate education, one that challenges, stimulates, and potentially facilitates transformation from a novice as a student to an elite as an adult in a talent domain (Lee et al., 2010; Subotnik et al., 2011). Therefore, it is imperative that academic press is an ingredient across the curriculum for all students at all grade levels and is not dependent on an identification process (Rogers, 2007).

Numerous studies have established that a rigorous academic track in high school is one of the best preparatory tools available for success in college and beyond (e.g., Horn & Kojaku, 2001; Horn & Nuñez, 2000; Wyner et al., 2007), with one example of rigorous academic preparation encompassing Algebra I in middle school; four years of English; three years of a foreign language; three years of science, with science encompassing biology, physics, and chemistry; four years of math, with students completing pre-Calculus, three years of social studies; and at least one honors/AP course (Horn & Nuñez, 2000). A curriculum of this nature has the potential to overcome several correlates to low success in college, including an impoverished background and poor scores on standardized tests (Horn & Kojaku, 2001). Along with disciplinary breadth, practitioners of gifted education are in agreement with practitioners of general education when they stipulate that a rigorous curriculum is also challenging; driven by meaningful outcomes, thus enhancing authenticity; and accommodates student differences (Hockett, 2009). Such a curriculum is only possible with deliberate attention to its development.

Challenge in the Curriculum

Because many educators may underestimate what students can successfully master, the basis for stimulating a highly able student, particularly a student not so identified, is querying and upending personal assumptions about developmental appropriateness and, instead, investigating what works for an individual student (Gibson & Mitchell, 2005; Hocket, 2009). A challenging curriculum encompasses going more in-depth, enhancing breadth, building in complexity and interdisciplinary connections, developing conceptual lesson plans, varying pacing based on need, and using real problems as the spring board (Hocket, 2009). In addition to these curricular adjustments, consistent, and potentially daily challenge in the talent area is recommended and is supported by gains in learning that exceed typical yearly growth (Rogers, 2007; Wallace, 2005). Consistent challenge in a talent domain has the added benefit of enhancing motivation and self-efficacy (Lee, et al., 2010; Rogers, 2007).

Gifted education theorists advocate for several best practices when considering the ingredients of a challenging curriculum for high-ability youth. Acceleration in pacing and with advanced content has the strongest research base establishing effectiveness, with researchers examining the impact of this approach over several decades (VanTassel-Baska & Brown, 2007). Acceleration comes in a number of guises, but is broadly defined as fast-paced delivery of content, early entrance to school at differing levels, and grade skipping. Examples of grade acceleration include skipping one to several grades, grade telescoping (completing three to four years of content in two to three years), testing out of classes, and early admission to college (Rogers, 2007).

Subject-level acceleration involves using higher level content, with students accessing this content either through participating in one or more classes above grade level or being taught with material that is above grade level (Southern & Jones, 2004).

Highlighting two forms of acceleration, fast-paced delivery of content, or grade telescoping, can be a successful strategy with high-ability learners. For example, the Study for Mathematically Precocious Youth's (SMPY) 30-year research base consistently shows that gifted students can learn two years, worth of math content in one year. Students who successfully navigate grade telescoping need less practice to gain mastery and are able to demonstrate mastery on standardized tests (Rogers, 2007). Curriculum compacting, another form of acceleration, can also be beneficial for disseminating content in a way that appropriately challenges students. With curriculum compaction, a student is pre-assessed to determine mastery. Replacement work of advanced content is provided when mastery of basic precepts for the learning objective is demonstrated. Curriculum compaction has resulted in advanced knowledge gain and does not impair a students' knowledge base (Reis et al., 1993; Rogers, 2007).

In light of concerns that acceleration might lead to emotional distress, Rogers (2007) reports that subject-level acceleration approaches have shown not only positive academic growth but also no report of heightened likelihood of psychological distress, especially when acceleration involves a mentoring relationship, subject acceleration, advanced placement, or IB programs. Academic gains were especially strong in science and math. Grade acceleration has also resulted in both positive academic gains and small positive impacts on affective characteristics like motivation and self-esteem (Rogers, 2007).

Authenticity in the Curriculum

Authenticity in curriculum can be captured by hewing more closely to the activities of experts in a field of study, using and solving problems reflective of real issues in the discipline, using processes and products from the field, and integrating across disciplines. This type of curriculum should enhance relevancy for students and could potentially result in outcomes that are meaningful. Outcomes that manifest authenticity could also include deep learning and developing expertise, with expertise development considered talent development by gifted education practitioners (Hocket, 2009).

One approach to instituting authenticity in the curriculum is integrating research opportunities into lesson planning. Affording students the chance to engage in research is considered a best practice in gifted education, because it provides for independent practice (Subotnik et al., 2011) and builds in meaningful outcomes (Hockett, 2009; VanTassel-Baska & Brown, 2007). The benefits of research are also highlighted in the literature on students of color and science, technology, engineering, and math (STEM) collegiate experiences.

When examining predictors of success in STEM degree programs, a requisite for developing an affiliation with a STEM area are research experiences (Carlone & Johnson, 2007 Eagan, Hurtado, Chang, Garcia, Herrera, & Garibay, 2004), with research experiences and upper level math and science courses at the high school level serving as important ingredients for developing an interest in a STEM career (Hurtado, Newman, Tran, & Chang, 2010). Several studies exploring the impact of research on undergraduate students of color have demonstrated that research experiences can help students identify a clearer connection between their preparatory classes and careers in science, encourage better time management skills, and are related to higher graduation rates with STEM degrees and higher entrance rates into STEM graduate programs (Barlow & Villarejo, 2004; Slovacek, Whittinghill, Flenoury, & Wiseman, 2012). Odds are better for African American students to sustain interest in STEM coursework if they have the opportunity to engage in research early (Hurtado et al, 2010). Understanding that the quality of the research experience is an important factor for sustaining a student through additional training at the graduate level and/or an eventual career (Barlow & Villarejo, 2004; Carlone & Johnson, 2008), research experiences are also important to developing an identity as a scientist (Carlone & Johnson, 2008).

Accommodating Student Differences in the Curriculum

Finally, a rigorous curriculum should accommodate student differences and be flexible. Not all students will thrive with a curriculum that is accelerated or delivered at a fast pace, even if pre-assessment shows they are capable of managing such an approach. As well, not all students welcome daily or consistent challenge. Curriculum guided by flexibility and acceptance of student difference may include pretesting to find out where coursework should begin and could also include variability in pacing (slower or faster depending on the need), the ability to make choices, and the ability to be independent (Hocket, 2009). Curricula guided by these principles acknowledge that all students are individuals with talent, with such talent needing to be identified and developed (Rogers, 2007; Subotnik et al., 2011). With the needs of the individual serving as the foundation, educators can facilitate a menu of options that best meet the needs of the student and stem from what the student feels she can handle. The child determines what is appropriate and is ultimately the one in control based on what is approached and avoided (Ziegler & Phillipson, 2012).

Possible Selves as a Framework for Psychosocial Coaching

Gifted Education as Part of a System of Support

A student of high ability will not only need a curriculum of appropriate rigor. Rather, Ziegler and Phillipson (2012) argue that the education of highly able youth is part of a system of supports, with the educative process embedded within a cultural context. They posit that this system is comprised of the total body of actions a person can take, or the actions repertoire; goals; the environment; and subjective action space, or a person's ability to make decisions relative to perception of how potential actions, the environment, and goals interact to proscribe possibilities. To facilitate talent development, gifted programming must act on these components as a unit. These arguments are in keeping with Bronfenbrenner's (1994) ecological model of child development.

An example of talent development as a holistic enterprise that is comprised of systems is demonstrated in Griffin, Allen, Kimura-Walsh, and Yamamura's (2007) study contrasting the college preparatory experience of African American students attending a medical magnet high school and a nonmagnet high school in California. The schools were located in urban, low-income communities (approximately 30% of the students attending both schools were participating in the free/reduced lunch program) and the graduation rate for both high schools was over 90%. The magnet school had a more robust college preparatory culture, including a larger selection of AP courses (21 courses vs. 9 courses at the nonmagnet school). As a likely consequence, all students attending the medical magnet school at graduation had met admission requirements for the University of California (UC) and California State University (CSU) systems, as compared to the 8% rate for the nonmagnet school.

The students at the medical magnet school had applied to attend the school, and parents were supportive of this more rigorous path. As with the nonmagnet school, the college counselors were overextended, and the students of the magnet school were very aware of the insufficiency of the college preparatory counseling offered. However, the students attending the magnet school were able to draw more effectively on their parents, siblings, and peers as sources of information about the college process. The admissions counselors from University of California, California State University, and other universities were very aware that these students had agreed to a more rigorous academic track, so visits from universities were numerous — so numerous that students were becoming expert in identifying clear admittance criteria and could complain about the lack of specific entry information from a representative from Princeton University (Griffin et al., 2007).

Psychosocial Coaching

Because the education of children does not occur in an emotional vacuum, talent development will also depend upon systematic psychosocial coaching (Subotnik et al., 2011), with emphasis on helping young people see the path between academic tasks in school and possible selves of the future. The literature base exploring the psychology of high-ability students is healthy, with researchers identifying psychological processes such as perfectionism (e.g., Schuler, 2000), compromising social coping strategies (e.g., T. Cross & Swiatek, 2009), entity versus incremental beliefs about intelligence (e.g., Ablard & Mills, 1996), stereotype threat (e.g., Inzlicht & Ben-Zeev, 2003), and underachievement (Ford, 1996) as possible barriers to achievement. A possible underlying theme for these areas of study is the potential struggle a young person experiences harnessing his or her motivation (Subotnik, et al., 2011; Miller & Brickman, 2004). Yeager and Walton (2011) argue that social psychological interventions that target areas like motivation have the important benefit of releasing students to fully engage in learning opportunities offered in their schooling contexts.

As the Griffin et al. (2007) study demonstrates, family and other knowledgeable others who are important to the child are also key in helping a young person understand what opportunities are actually available for them to credibly pursue, as well as how to pursue them (Miller and Brickman, 2004; Ziegler & Phillipson, 2012). So, a child is likely to be able to master the path to becoming a concert pianist if a parent is also a musician (Ziegler & Phillipson, 2012). In the same way, families that are stymied from identifying and living into their potential are potent examples for their children (Fordham, 1996; Kao, 2000). Though late adolescence is generally a time when people craft ambitious possibilities for themselves (S. Cross & Markus, 1991), many African Americans may be unable to translate these aspirations into outcomes like graduation from high school (Oyserman, Johnson, & James, 2011), college (Horn & Kojaku, 2001), and graduate programs (Eagan et al., 2004), in part because the path to these outcomes are murky or unknown. Thus, our job as counselors and educators is helping young people problem-solve well enough to find answers about the steps to realizing success in a talent domain (Miller & Brickman, 2004).

Possible Selves as Framework for Psychosocial Coaching

The theory development of possible selves could serve as an important framework for psychosocial coaching with high-ability youth. Markus and Nurius (1986) define possible selves as future selves that are expected, hoped for, and feared. These future selves are more than aspirations. Instead, they are "vivid images of the self attaining a future state" (Oyserman et al., 2011, p. 475).

Possible selves are components of a working self-concept, or a self-concept that is temporal and can be destabilized. A working self-concept feeds a stable sense of self in part through the negotiation of possible and negative feedback about potential selves (Markus & Nurius, 1986).

Possible selves are identity based (Dunkel, 2000; Vignoles, Manzi, Regalia, Jemmolo, & Scabini, 2008). As such, constraints to the identities young people claim can also serve to restrain possible selves, especially in light of known life events for important people like family, peers, and friends (Kao, 2000). For example, it will be difficult for an African American female to see a potential self as a chemist as credible in light of stories of racism and sexism pushing her mother away from a science career when she was younger. Therefore, children will need help sustaining possible selves that are nonconventional, with one source of support potentially being recognized from important others like teachers, family, and professionals in the talent domain (Carlone & Johnson, 2007; Frazier, 2012).

The importance of recognition is highlighted in Carlone and Johnson's (2007) study exploring the experience of 15 women of color who were successful in creating science identities. They developed three profiles to help explain the results: (1) the research scientist identity, (2) the altruistic scientist identity, and (3) the disrupted scientist identity. The research scientists were fully welcomed into the science community by their colleagues and professors, and were recognized as good students with something important to contribute. The altruistic scientists were more concerned with being recognized by other important people –family, their church members, and people they hoped to serve. They were in science because of the good it could do for people.

The women with disrupted science identities felt they encountered situations and people who were unfriendly and sometimes hostile and were thus withheld from recognition from influential others that mattered to them. For example, one woman, who was squeamish about killing an animal with her bare hands as part of her responsibilities, was encouraged to change majors and was then fired from her job as a laboratory technician. Importantly, this student was one of the best students in her class and was pushed out of this opportunity (Carlone & Johnson, 2007).

All of the women remained committed to a science identity, and the women with altruistic and disrupted identities were successful in identifying other sources of supports for their potential selves as scientists. Furthermore, the women in the study were aware of the components of the path needed to develop as scientists and were regulated enough to follow the path. In light of all of the women remaining committed to a science identity, one critical implication of Carlone and Johnson's (2007) study is the power of personal agency, especially in light of racism and/or sexism one might confront.

Cross and Markus (1991) demonstrated that there is a readjustment in possible selves over time that is reflective of the success and failures one has experienced. The grandiose aims of youth are modulated and possible selves are scaled back. Miller and Brickman (2004) argue "anticipated future outcomes are an important self-regulatory factor in human functioning. Future goals influence self-regulation through their role in the planning of a path of proximal subgoals leading to future goal attainment" (p. 23). The linchpin between proximal subgoals and possible selves of the future is the instrumentality of current activity.

Oyserman et al. (2011) found that children living in poorer neighborhoods were likely to have school-aimed possible selves. In fact, the poorer the neighborhood, the more focused children were on school. Aspirations are thus not the place where one should expect to see the impact of disadvantage. Instead, it is the creation of strategies to realize their aspirations that could suffer, with the potential being that low-income youth are not sure how to make some of their aspirations reality. In support of this hypothesis, Oyserman et al. found that children from poorer neighborhoods and poorer families have a harder time creating strategies that support academic possible selves, possible selves aimed at academic performance, and possible selves that pursue teacher engagement.

The inability to activate the motivational chain between current activity, subgoals, and future selves is connected to failures to develop possible selves, concrete strategies to realize these possible selves, and an awareness of the instrumentality of current action (Miller & Brickman, 2004). So, a further benefit to the possible selves framework is the connection between future selves and the selves of the moment through the development of actionable, concrete steps (Oyserman et al., 2011; Oyserman, Bybee, & Terry, 2006). To facilitate talent development in a domain, children must understand what the path entails and plan accordingly (Miller & Brickman, 2004). This process can occur through knowledgeable others and fact-finding. Children must believe they have the ability to realize their possible selves, and they must work through value systems that could be at odds with the possible selves they envision (Miller & Brickman, 2004). This process requires the participation of the child, the family, peers, and the educational culture.

Oyersman and her colleagues (Oyersman et al., 2006; Oyserman, Gant, & Ager, 1995; Oyserman, Terry, & Bybee, 2002) have investigated this motivational chain as an intervention in several studies with low-income youth who are predominately African American, with the intent being enhanced academic achievement. In particular, the studies addressed the importance of identifying role models congruent with possible selves as good students, balance (i.e., hoped-for selves and feared selves in the academic domain), the development of plausible strategies to realize academic possible selves, the construction of a community of students that values the academic possible selves the students created, and confronting stereotypes. Possible selves in these studies were selves of the next year. Several of the outcomes from these studies were long term (2 years), with students having higher GPAs, fewer absences, greater self-regulation, less disruptive behavior, greater school bonding, and greater concern about doing well in school following the intervention. Oyserman notes, "when social context is limiting and group membership functions to subtly or not so subtly shape the selves one 'tries on' in the process of adolescent development, we propose that by conceptualizing oneself as a group member, becoming aware of stereotypes and limitations, and developing a perspective of oneself as succeeding as a group member, allows a way out" (Oyserman et al, 1995, p. 1230).

CONCLUSION

A search of Google will produce quite a few examples of talented African American children and young adults pursuing passions and on the trajectory to being contributors and potential elites in their fields. Some talents that children pursue can only be developed outside of school settings, and parents and other knowledgeable mentors are essential to continued growth. Other talents can only grow in school settings, with the educational gestalt being the foundation for development. In all cases, talent grows in the face of rigor. Students must also have the opportunity to engage in authentic work guided by key questions from academic disciplines and that accommodates a child's strengths and weaknesses. Likewise, as part of this process, psychosocial coaching is recommended, as a family member, friend, or teacher is helping an African American young person move past internal and external barriers. Motivation is connected to an understanding of the path that leads to a future self as well as the willingness to walk that path. Parents, teachers, and the child can lay the path together, setting a series of subgoals that depend upon the instrumentality of current action. Educational curriculum and sensitive, timely counseling are key to unleashing the "goodness and genius" (Marshall, 2014) of our children.

NOTE

1. All names are pseudonyms.

REFERENCES

Ablard, K. E., & Mills C. J. (1996). Implicit theories of intelligence and self-perceptions of academically talented adolescents and children. *Journal of Youth and Adolescence, 25*(2). 137–148. doi:10.1007/BF01537340

Barlow, A. E. L., & Villarejo, M. (2004). Making a difference for minorities: Evaluation of an educational enrichment program. *Journal of Research in Science Teaching, 41*(9), 861–881. doi:10.1002/tea.20029

Bishop, J. H., Bishop, M., Bishop, M., Gelbwasser, L., Green, S., Peterson, E., ... & Zuckerman, A. (2004). Why we harass nerds and freaks: A formal theory of student culture and norms. *Journal of School Health, 74*(7), 235–251. doi:10.1111/j.1746–1561.2004.tb08280.x

Bloom, B. (1985). *Developing talent in young people.* New York, NY: Ballantine. doi:10.2307/3396580

Bronfenbrenner, U. (1994). Ecological models of human development. *International Encyclopedia of Education* (Vol. 3, 2nd ed.). Oxford, UK: Elsevier.

Carlone, H. B., & Johnson, A. (2007). Understanding the science experiences of successful women of color: Science identity as an analytic lens. *Journal of Research in Science Teaching, 44*(8), 1187–1218. doi:10.1002/tea.20237

Coleman, L. J., & Cross, T. L. (2005). *Being gifted in school: An introduction to development, guidance, and teaching* (2nd ed.). Waco, TX: Prufrock Press.

Cross, S., & Markus, H. (1991). Possible selves across the life span. *Human Development, 34,* 230–255. doi:10.1159/000277058

Cross, T. L., & Coleman, L. J. (2005). School-based conception of giftedness. In R. J. Sternberg & J. E. Davidson (Eds.), *Conceptions of giftedness* (2nd ed., pp. 52–63). Cambridge, England: Cambridge University Press. doi:10.1017/CBO9780511610455.005

Cross, T. L., Coleman, L. J., & Stewart, R. A. (1995). Psychosocial diversity of gifted adolescents: An exploration of the stigma of the giftedness paradigm. *Roeper Review, 17,* 181–185. doi:10.1080/02783199509553655

Cross, T. L., & Swiatek, M. L. (2009). Social coping among academically gifted adolescents in a residential setting: A longitudinal study. *Gifted Child Quarterly, 53*(1), 25–33. doi:10.1177/0016986208326554

Dai, D. Y. (2010). *The nature and nurture of giftedness: A new framework for understanding gifted education.* New York, NY: Teachers College Press.

Dai, D. Y. (2011). Hopeless anarchy or saving pluralism? Reflections on our field in response to Ambrose, VanTassel-Baska, Coleman, and Cross. *Journal for the Education of the Gifted, 34,* 705–730. doi:10.1177/0162353211416437

Dai, D. Y., & Chen, F. (2013). Three paradigms of gifted education: In search of conceptual clarity in research and practice. *Gifted Child Quarterly, 57,* 151–168. doi:10.1177/0016986213490020

Donovan, M. S., & Cross, C. T. (2002). *Minority students in special and gifted education.* Washington, DC: National Academy Press.

Dunkel, C. S. (2000). Possible selves as a mechanism for identity exploration. *Journal of Adolescence, 23,* 519–529. doi:10.1006/jado.2000.0340

Eagan, M. K., Hurtado, S. H., Chang, M. J., Garcia, G. A., Herrera, F. A., & Garibay, J. C. (2004). Making a difference in science education: The impact of undergraduate research programs. *American Educational Research Journal, 50*(4), 683–713. doi:10.3102/0002831213482038

Feldman, D. H. (with Goldsmith, L. T.). (1991). *Nature's gambit: Child prodigies and the development of human potential.* New York, NY: Teachers College Press. (Original work published 1986)

Ford, D. Y. (2003). Two other wrongs don't make a right: Sacrificing the needs of diverse students does not solve gifted education's unresolved problems. *Journal for the Education of the Gifted, 26*(4), 283–291.

Ford, D. Y. (1996). *Reversing underachievement among gifted black students: Promising practices and programs.* New York, NY: Teacher College Press.

Ford, D. Y. (2013). Gifted underrepresentation and prejudice—learning from Allport and Merton. *Gifted Child Today, 36*, 62–67. doi:10.1177/1076217512465285

Ford, D. Y., Harris, J., III, Tyson, C. A., & Trotman, M. F. (2002). Beyond deficit thinking: Providing access for gifted African American students. *Roper Review, 24*(2), 52–58. doi: 10.1080/02783190209554129

Ford, D. Y., Grantham, T. C., & Whiting, G. W. (2008). Culturally and linguistically diverse students in gifted education: Recruitment and retention issues. *Exceptional Children, 74*, 289–308.

Ford, D. Y., & Thomas, A. (1997). Underachievement among gifted minority students: Problems and promises. ERIC Digest, #E544.

Fordham, S. (1996). *Blacked out: Dilemmas of race, identity, and success at Capital High.* Chicago, IL: The University of Chicago Press.

Fordham, S., & Ogbu, J. (1986). Black students' school success: Coping with the "burden of 'acting White.'" *The Urban Review, 18*, 176–206. doi: 10.1007/bf01112192

Frazier, A. D. (2012). The possible selves of high-ability African American males attending a residential academy for highly able youth. *Journal for the Education of the Gifted, 35* (4), 366–390. doi:10.1177/0162353212461565

Elhoweris, H., Mutua, K., Alsheikh, N., & Holloway, P. (2005). Effect of children's ethnicity on teachers' referral and recommendation decisions in gifted and talented programs. *Remedial and Special Education, 26*, 25–31. doi: 10.1177/07419325050260010401

Fryer, R. G., & Torelli, P. (2010). An empirical analysis of "acting White". *Journal of Public Economics, 94*, 380–396. doi:10.1016/j.jpubeco.2009.10.011

Galster, G., Marcotte, D. E., Mandell, M., Wolman, H., & Augustine, N. (2007). The influence of neighborhood poverty during childhood on fertility, education, and earnings outcomes. *Housing Studies, 22*(5), 723–751. doi:10.1080/02673030701474669

Gibson, K.L., & Mitchell, L.M. (2005). Critical curriculum components in programs for young gifted learners. *International Education Journal, 6*(2), 164–169.

Griffin, K. A., Allen, W. R., Kimura-Walsh, E., Yamamura, E. K. (2007). Those who left, those who stayed: Exploring the educational opportunities of high-achieving Black and Latina/o students at magnet and nonmagnet Los Angeles high schools (2001–2001). *Educational Studies, 42*(3), 229–247. doi:10.1080/00131940701632662

Hale-Benson, J. (1986). *Black children: Their roots, culture, and learning styles* (2nd ed.). Baltimore, MD: Johns Hopkins University Press.

Harden, K. P., Turkheimer, E., & Loehlin, J. C. (2007). Genotype by environment interaction in adolescents' cognitive aptitude. *Behavior Genetics, 37*(2), 273–283. doi:10.1007/s10519–006-9113–4

Hocket, J. A. (2009). Curriculum for highly able learners that conforms to general education and gifted education quality indicators. *Journal for the Education of the Gifted, 32*(3), 394–440.

Horn, L., & Kojaku, L. (2001). *High school academic curriculum and the persistence path through college* (NCES 2001–163). Retrieved from http://nces.ed.gov/pubs2001/2001163.pdf

Horn, L., & Nuñez, A. (2000). *Mapping the road to college: First-Generation students' math track, planning strategies, and context of support* (NCES 2000–153). Retrieved from http://nces.ed.gov/pubs2000/2000153.pdf

Hunsaker, S. L., Findley, V. S., & Frank, E. L. (1997). An analysis of teacher nominations and student performance in gifted programs. *Gifted Child Quarterly, 41*(2), 19–24. doi:10.1177/001698629704100203

Hurtado, S., Newman, C. B., Tran, M. C., & Chang, M. J. (2010). Improving the rate of success for underrepresented racial minorities in STEM fields: Insights from a national project. *New Directions for Institutional Research, 148*, 5–15. doi:10.1002/ir.357

Inzlicht, M., & Ben-Zeev, T. (2003). Do high-achieving female students underperform in private? The implications of threatening environments on intellectual processing. *Journal of Educational Psychology, 95*(4), 796–805. doi:10.1037/0022–0663.95.4.796

Kao, G. (2000). Group images and possible selves among adolescents: Linking stereotypes to expectations by race and ethnicity. *Sociological Forums, 15*(3), 407–430.

Kitano, M. (2012). Social-emotional needs of gifted students of color. In T. L. Cross & J. R. Cross (Eds.), *Handbook for counselors serving students with gifts and talents* (pp. 209–226). Waco, TX: Prufrock Press.

Klawans, H. L. (1996, September 29). Why Michael Jordan couldn't hit: Think it's never too late to learn? Think again. *Chicago Tribune.* Retrieved from http://articles.chicagotribune.com/1996–09-29/features/9609290323_1_fans-brain-skills

Lee, S.-Y., & Olszewski-Kubilius, P., Peternel, G. (2010). The efficacy of academic acceleration for gifted minority students. *Gifted Child Quarterly, 54*, 189–208. doi:10.1177/0016986210369256

Logan, J. R. (2011). *Separate and unequal: The neighborhood gap for Blacks, Hispanics, and Asians in metropolitan America.* Rhode Island: US2010 Project, Brown University.

Markus, H., & Nurius, P. (1986). Possible selves. *American Psychologist, 41*(9), 954–969. doi:10.1037/0003–066x.41.9.954

Marland, S. P., Jr. (1972). *Education of the gifted and talented: Report to the Congress of the United States by the U.S. Commissioner of Education.* Washington, DC: Government Printing Office.

Marshall, S. P. (2014). *About the book, "The Power to Transform"*. Retrieved from http://www.stephaniepacemarshall.com/aboutbook.html

McBee, M. T. (2006). A descriptive analysis of referral sources for gifted identification screening by race and socioeconomic status. *Journal of Secondary Gifted Education, 2*, 103–111.

McBee, M. T. (2010). Examining the probability of identification for gifted programs for students in Georgia elementary schools: A multilevel path analysis study. *Gifted Child Quarterly, 54*, 283–297. doi:10.1177/0016986210377927

Miller, L. S. (2004). *Promoting sustained growth in the representation of African Americans, Latinos, and Native Americans among top students in the United States at all levels of the education system*. Storrs, CT: National Research Center on the Gifted and Talented.

Miller, R. B., & Brickman, S. J. (2004). A model of future-oriented motivation and self-regulation. *Educational Psychology Review, 16*(1), 9–33. doi:10.1023/b:edpr.0000012343.96370.39

Murnane, R. J., Willett, J. B., Duhaldeborde, Y., & Tyler, J. H. (2000). How important are the cognitive skills of teenagers in predicting subsequent earnings? *Journal of Policy Analysis and Management, 19*, 547–568.

National Association for Gifted Children. (2009). *Myths about gifted students*. Retrieved from http://www.nagc.org/resources-publications/resources/myths-about-gifted-students

National Association for Gifted Children. (2006). *Position statement: Early childhood*. Retrieved from http://www.nagc.org/sites/default/files/Position%20Statement/Early%20Childhood%20Position%20Statement.pdf

National Association for Gifted Children. (2013). *2012–2013 State of the nation: Work yet to be done*. Washington, DC: Author.

National Association for Gifted Children. (2014). *National standards for gifted and talented education*. Retrieved from http://www.nagc.org

National Center for Education Statistics. (2008). *Digest of education statistics*. Retrieved from http://nces.ed.gov/

Nord, C., Roey, S., Perkins, R., Lyons, M., Lemanski, N., Brown, J., & Schuknecht, J. (2011). *The Nation's report card: America's high school graduates* (NCES 2011–462). U.S. Department of Education, National Center for Education Statistics. Washington, DC: Government Printing Office. doi:10.1037/e550322011–001

Olszewski-Kubilius, P., Lee, S., Ngoi, M., & Ngoi, D. (2004). Addressing the achievement gap between minority and nonminority children by increasing access to gifted programs. *Journal for the Education of the Gifted, 28*, 127–158.

Oyersman, D., Bybee, D., & Terry, K. (2006). Possible selves and academic outcomes: How and when possible selves impel action. *Journal of Personality and Social Psychology, 91*(1), 188–204. doi:10.1037/0022–3514.91.1.188

Oyserman, D., Gant, L., & Ager, J. (1995). A socially contextualized model for African American identity: Possible selves and school persistence. *Journal of Personality and Social Psychology, 69* (6), 1216–1232. doi:10.1037//0022–3514.69.6.1216

Oyserman, D., Johnson, E., & James, L. (2011). Seeing the destination but not the path: Effects of socioeconomic disadvantage on school-focused possible self content and linked behavioral strategies. *Self and Identity, 10*, 474–492. doi:10.10 80/15298868.2010.487651

Oyserman, D., Terry, K., & Bybee, D. (2002). A possible selves intervention to enhance school involvement. *Journal of Adolescence, 25*, 313–326. doi:10.1006/jado.2002.0474

Patillo, M. (2003). Extending the boundaries and definition of the ghetto. *Ethnic and Racial Studies, 26*(6), 1046–1057. doi:10.1080/0141987032000132487

Patillo, M. (2005). Black middle-class neighborhoods. *The Annual Review of Sociology, 31*, 305–329. doi:10.1146/annurev.soc.29.010202.095956

Patillo-McCoy, M. (2000). The limits of out-migration of the Black middle class. *Journal of Urban Affairs, 22*(3), 225–241. doi:10.1111/0735–2166.00054

Phillips, M., Crouse, J., & Ralph, J. (1998). Does the black-white test score gap widen after children enter school? In C. Jencks & M. Phillips (Eds.), *The black-white test score gap* (pp. 229–272). Washington, DC: Brookings Institution.

Reis, S. M., Westberg, K. L., Kulikowich, J., Caillard, F., Hébert, T., Plucker, J., ... Smist, J. M. (1993). *Why not let high ability students start school in January? The curriculum compacting study* (Research Monograph 93106). Storrs: University of Connecticut, The National Research Center for the Gifted and Talented.

Robinson, N. (1996). Counseling agendas for gifted young people: A commentary. *Journal for the Education of the Gifted, 20*, 128–137.

Rogers, K. B. (2007). Lessons learned about educating the gifted and talented: A synthesis of the research on education practice. *Gifted Child Quarterly, 51*(4), 382–396. doi:10.1177/0016986207306324

Schroeder-Davis, S. J. (1999). Brains, brawn, or beauty: Adolescent attitudes toward three superlatives. *Journal of Secondary Gifted Education, 10*, 134–147.

Schuler, P. A. (2000). Perfectionism and gifted adolescents. *Journal of Advanced Academics, 11*(4), 183–196.

Slovacek, S., Whittinghill, J., Flenoury, L., & Wiseman, D. (2012). Promoting minority success in the sciences: The Minority Opportunities in Research programs at CSULA. *Journal of Research in Science Teaching, 49*(2), 199–217. doi:10.1002/tea.20451

Southern, W., & Jones, E. (2004). *Types of acceleration*. Retrieved from the Davidson Institute for Talent Development website: http://www.davidsongifted.org/db/Articles_id_10313.aspx

Steele, C. M., & Aronson, J. (1995). Stereotype threat and the intellectual test performance of African Americans. *Journal of Personality and Social Psychology, 69*, 797–811. doi:10.1037//0022–3514.69.5.797

Steele, C. M., Spencer, S., & Aronson, J. (2002). Contending with group image: The psychology of stereotype and social identity threat. In M. Zanna (Ed.), *Advances in experimental social psychology* (pp. 379–440). San Diego, CA: Academic Press. doi:10.1016/s0065–2601(02)80009–0

Subotnik, R. F., Olszewski-Kubilius, P., & Worrell, F. C. (2011). Rethinking giftedness and gifted education: A proposed direction forward based on psychological science. *Psychological Science in the Public Interest, 12*(1), 3–54. doi:10.1177/1529100611418056

Tannenbaum, A. J. (1962). *Adolescent attitude toward academic brilliance*. New York, NY: Bureau of Publications, Teachers College, Columbia University.

Turkheimer, E., Haley, A., Waldon M., d'Onofrio, B., & Gottesman, I. I. (2003). Socioeconomic status modifies heritability of IQ in young children. *Psychological Science, 14*(6), 623–628. doi:10.1046/j.0956–7976.2003.psci_1475.x

Tyson, K., Darity, W., & Castellino, D. R. (2005). It's not "a Black thing": Understanding the burden of acting White and other dilemmas of high achievement. *American Sociological Review, 70*(4), 582–605. doi:10.1177/000312240507000403

U.S. Department of Education, Office of Educational Research and Improvement. (1993). *National excellence: A case for developing America's talent*. Washington, DC: Government Printing Office.

Valencia, R. R., & Suzuki, L. A. (2001). *Intelligence testing and minority students: Foundations, performance factors and assessment issues*. Thousand Oaks, CA: Sage. doi:10.4135/9781452231860

Vanneman, A., Hamilton, L., Anderson, J. B., & Rahman, T. (2009). *Achievement gaps: How Black and White students in public schools perform in mathematics and reading on the National Assessment of Educational Progress* (NCES 2009–455). Retrieved from http://nces.ed.gov/nationsreportcard/pdf/studies/2009455.pdf

VanTassel-Baska, J., & Brown, E. F. (2007). Toward best practice: An analysis of the efficacy of curriculum models in gifted education. *The Gifted Child Quarterly, 51*(4), 342–358. doi:10.1177/0016986207306323

VanTassel-Baska, J., & Stambaugh, T. (Eds.). (2007). *Overlooked gems: A national perspective on low-income promising learners*. Washington, DC: National Association of Gifted Children.

Vignoles, V., Manzi, C., Regalia, C., Jemmolo, S., & Scabini, E. (2008). Identity motives underlying desired and feared possible future selves. *Journal of Personality, 76*(5), 1165–1200. doi:10.1111/j.1467–6494.2008.00518.x

Wallace, P. (2005). Distance education for gifted students: Leveraging technology to expand academic options. *High Ability Studies, 16*(1), 77–86. doi:10.1080/13598130500115288

Wildhagen, T. (2011). Testing the "acting White" hypothesis: A popular explanation runs out of empirical steam. *The Journal of Negro Education, 80*, 445–463.

Wyner, J. S., Bridgeland, J. M., & DiIulio, J. J., Jr. (2007). *Achievement trap: How America is failing millions of high-achieving students from low-income families*. Lansdowne, VA: Jack Kent Cooke Foundation Civic Enterprises.

Yeager, D. S., & Walton, G. M. (2011). Social-psychological interventions in education: They're not magic. *Review of Educational Research, 81*(2), 267–301. doi:10.3102/0034654311405999

Ziegler, A., & Phillipson, S. N. (2012). Towards a systemic theory of gifted education. *High Ability Studies, 23*(1), 3–30. doi:10.1080/13598139.2012.679085

Chapter 6

Rigor, Course Choice, and Educational Excellence

Positioning African American Students for Future Success

D'Jalon J. Jackson

Over the past fifty years, higher education has undergone vast transformations to meet the needs of a diversified society (Altbach, Reisberg & Rumbley, 2009). As the United States strives to remain globally competitive, increasing the number of degrees earned is imperative to success (Engle & Tinto, 2008). This undeniably includes addressing and amending the disparity in degrees earned between White students and minority students, specifically African Americans. Naturally, in order to improve the number of degrees obtained by African Americans, access to institutions of higher education must first be ensured.

The struggle to gain access has been a lengthy journey for African Americans; one deeply embedded in racism and discrimination. Auspiciously, legislation such as the landmark 1954 case, *Brown v. Board of Education* of Topeka, Kansas and the Civil Rights Act of 1964 have served to protect and aid in enrollment efforts (e.g. affirmative action), which have grown tremendously (Harvey, 2005). These efforts, nonetheless, have been overshadowed by inequality in regard to the success of African American students in relation to their White counterparts. Success in the context of this chapter is defined as the attainment of a degree. Roderick, Nagaoka, and Coca (2009) contended that to close the achievement gap, emphasis should shift toward increasing the likelihood of degree attainment rather than solely focusing on increasing enrollment. To increase the number of students who experience success, the playing field must be leveled to guarantee that college retention and success, not just college admission, is achievable for all students.

INDIVIDUAL AND SOCIETAL EFFECTS OF HIGHER EDUCATION

College success is an investment that benefits all. From an individualistic perspective, students with a college degree earn on average, higher income than those without a degree. Baum, Ma, and Payea (2013) released the *Education Pays* report, which provides substantial statistical evidence on the benefits of higher education. The report found that "median earnings of Bachelor's degree recipients with no advanced degree working full time in 2011 were $56,500, $21,100 more than median earnings of high school graduates" (p. 5). Consequently, those individuals with Bachelor degrees earned 65% more over their lifetimes than those with only high school diplomas (Baum, Ma, & Payea, 2013). Moreover, those employed without a college degree have been impacted more harshly in the recent economic downturn than those who attended college. Four out of every five jobs lost in the recession were held by workers with no postsecondary education experience (Zaback, Carlson, & Crellin, 2012).

From a collectivist standpoint, higher education infuses social and economic systems and provides a positive impact on these systems. According to Baum, Ma, and Payea (2013), the benefits of higher education for the public good can be observed nationally through increases in tax revenues that contribute to public programs such as parks, road infrastructure and other resources. This increase in revenue coincides with a subsequent decline in public expenditures in the form of government payout to support citizens financially through entitlement programs; indeed, in most cases, higher education allows citizens to give back to their communities and to live financially independent.

An example of public expenditure being affected by higher education is relayed by Baum, Ma, and Payea (2013) who stated that in 2011, 12% of high school graduates aged 25 and older resided in households dependent upon Supplemental Nutritional Assistance Program (SNAP) benefits, while only 2% of those who earned a bachelor's degree or higher in the equivalent age range relied on the program. The authors of the report noted that there was a similar pattern followed for the National School Lunch Program. The percentages of high school graduates aged 25 and older living in households that participate in the free and reduced school lunch program were six times higher than those households with at least a bachelor's degree.

In 2013 the *American Community Survey Briefs* (ACSB) released statistical information gathered from 2007 to 2011 on poverty rates for selected racial groups within the United States. Among these groups the ACSB found that the groups with the highest poverty rates were American Indians and Alaska Natives at 27%, and Blacks or African Americans, with a much denser nationwide population, at 25.8 % (Macartney, Bishaw, & Fontenot,

2013). The national poverty rate for Whites, however, was 11.6%. In fact, in most states, as well as the District of Columbia, Whites accounted for less than 14% of those living in poverty. Concurrently, for the Black population, 43 states and the District of Columbia had poverty rates of 20.0 percent or higher. Iowa, Maine, Mississippi, and Wisconsin all had rates above 35.0 percent for the Black population (Macartney, Bishaw, & Fontenot, 2013).

It is apparent that there is an unequal distribution of poverty among Whites and African Americans in this country, which, among other factors, can be directly correlated to the disparity in percentages of postsecondary degrees obtained between the two groups. In the 2012 *Digest of Education Statistics*, Snyder and Dillow (2013) reported that from 2010 to 2011, 13.9% of African American students received an Associate's Degree and 10.4% received a Bachelor's Degree. Although over thirty years of progress can be observed in degree attainment of African Americans, this growth pales in comparison to the percentages of Associate's and Bachelor's Degrees obtained by White students. During the equivalent time period, 65.3% of White students received an Associate's Degree, while 71.1% received a Bachelor's degree. These massive differences of 51.4% and 60.7% for Associate's and Bachelor's degrees earned between African Americans and Whites may help illuminate the reasons why poverty rates are higher in African American communities. Baum, Ma, and Payea (2013) concluded that postsecondary education is crucial because it serves as the vehicle affording the individualistic and collectivistic transcending of socioeconomic, health, wellness and civic statuses. The ability to achieve equity in these areas through degree attainment serves as the explanation for why increasing college success among African Americans is vital. With the many benefits of degree attainment outlined, inquiry emerges regarding why more African Americans are not entering postsecondary education and matriculating successfully. The answer is likely twofold: (1) they are underprepared academically, and (2) lack sufficient access to career and college information at an early age. These issues are explored in the remainder of this chapter.

MEANINGFUL CAREER EXPLORATION: ACCESS, EXPOSURE, AND ASSESSMENT

An essential component of college preparation that should permeate through every level of learning throughout K-12 education is the development of career readiness for students.

Though often overshadowed by academics, Brown and Trusty (2005) noted that career and academic development are integrated constructs. It is likely that if career readiness is achieved upon institutional access, academic buy-in will occur as a by-product; students will feel equipped and empowered to make wise decisions, including those related to college and major choice. This discernment promotes investment in career development, thus propelling students toward career satisfaction and possibly aiding in academic success and retention efforts. The concept of buy-in is critical for African American students. As access into higher education institutions for African Americans has increased, a disproportionate representation of these students among the ranks of first-generation students has followed suit. Taking into account how impactful parental education and career choice can be on a student's career trajectory (Signer & Saldana, 2001), it is important to be cognizant of the multifarious elements that career development for African Americans entail, as they might be less likely to see career readiness modeled in their environments.

Gottfredson's Theory of Circumscription and Compromise

Research informs that students begin to impose self-limits on the careers they believe are achievable as early as elementary school (Curry & Milsom, 2013; Wood & Kaszubowski, 2008). Without sound career development being implemented that is gender and racially relational, African American students can be additionally affected by this phenomenon. In alignment with child development approaches, career theorist Linda Gottfredson (1981) utilized her theory of Circumscription and Compromise to explain how career development is cultivated throughout childhood and adolescence. Using four theoretical stages as constructs, she enlightened upon why students self-limit their career choices (i.e., circumscription) and make accommodations for those that are perceived to be most attainable, regardless of compatibility (i.e., compromise) (Curry and & Milsom, 2013). Gottfredson's theory is ideal in explaining the process by which children and adolescents utilize their developing self-concept to make long-lasting occupational choices and why career readiness should begin as early as possible.

Throughout the four stages, Gottfredson succinctly outlines when awareness of social constructs occur. During the first stage, *Orientation to Size and Power*, children aged 3–5 begin to develop self-concept as they are able to visualize themselves in adult roles. Upon commencement of the second stage, *Orientation to Sex Roles,* 6–8-year-old children begin to explore careers outside their home environments. For African American students this period is critical, as this is when they become increasingly aware of race as part of their personal identities. African American students who live in communities with lower percentages of degree attainment and higher poverty rates may witness a lack of variety in the career fields of those who share the same racial background as them (Witherspoon & Speight, 2007). During these two crucial stages, developmentally appropriate career curriculum can be utilized, such as introducing students to community partners that are African American (Curry & Milsom, 2013). Utilizing inclusive strategies aids in bringing awareness to careers these students may not be exposed to, thus serving to combat circumscription and compromise.

Adolescents develop a consciousness of the connection between social and economic status and academic ability in Gottfredson's third stage, *Orientation to Social Valuation*. Typically occurring throughout late elementary school and middle school, in this stage students assess their own standings by these constructs, and incorporate them into their self-concept. Whether African American students are surrounded by majority or minority populations, at this stage they are able to compare and contrast their home environments to outside influences, including peers, and are cognizant of differentiations based on race. The realization of these differences leads students to create a *Zone of Acceptable Alternatives* which consists of careers that have not been ruled out up to this point. Particularly, the mention of circumscription based on factors of social status, interests and abilities serves as the primary reason why the implementation of career readiness is crucial in elementary schooling and should pervade throughout secondary schooling. Since these factors can be directly related to students' experiences as African Americans, Gottfredson's Theory of Circumscription and Compromise is ideal when illustrating why waiting until secondary schools to engage students in career development is problematic (Gottfredson, 1981; Curry & Milsom, 2013).

During Gottfredson's final stage, *Orientation to Unique Self*, adolescents are able to clearly communicate their career goals (Curry & Milsom, 2013). Ideally, these aspirations will be reflective of extensive career development throughout elementary and middle school, and leading up to high school. Unfortunately, however, research shows that K-12 career intervention is rare in schools and is even less likely to be experienced by African American students (Wood & Kaszubowski, 2008). It is in the best interest of students that school stakeholders (i.e., parents, teachers, school counselors, administrators, community members) are aware of the pertinence of career readiness for students and subsequently engage in preventive measures to impede circumscription and compromise. Furthermore, if career readiness is advocated for African American students, an increase in the number of occupations achievable to these students most likely would be observed, which could directly affect future college success.

ROLE OF SCHOOL COUNSELOR

Within the school environment, the school counselor is arguably the most essential stakeholder as it relates to career and college readiness.

By profession, school counselors serve as advocates for students; they provide students with the knowledge and skills they need to be successful and facilitate efforts toward success. Furthermore, effective school counselors are expected to foster not only students' academic and personal/social growth, but career growth as well (ASCA, 2012). In this vein, school counselors use curriculum and developmentally appropriate assessments to help students discover how their personal interests and abilities can lead to career satisfaction.

In regard to responsibility, the school counselor serves as what Young (1983) describes an "explicit influence" on the career readiness of students. This influence occurs at the school microsystemic level and pertains to the promotion of career development through activities such as individual and group career counseling, school wide career programs, and the implementation of career-focused curriculum (Curry & Milsom, 2013). Concurrently, school counselors implicitly influence school microsystems as well by indirectly impacting career readiness efforts for students. These efforts include ensuring that career elements are integrated into educational curriculum as well as providing access to diverse courses and extracurricular opportunities that promote the exploration of interests (Curry & Milsom, 2013).

Signer and Saldana (2001) utilize Conroy (2000)'s research in their article in the *Race, Gender & Class* Journal, which makes the following suggestions:

> (a) job awareness and exploration should begin earlier than the typical 9th and 10th grade programs, (b) there should be a regularly planned course of study about labor market trends, (c) students should develop and maintain a career development portfolio to critically evaluate themselves in terms of how they match specific occupations under exploration, and (d) course offerings should reflect the idea of post-secondary preparatory instead of college preparatory versus vocational tracts with an increase in the mathematics, technology, and science requirements for vocational students. (p. 31)

Through implementing these suggestions, school counselors and other school stakeholders assist students to ensure that career and college readiness benchmarks are achieved upon high school graduation.

Additionally, school counselors serve as a liaison not only between teachers and students or administrators and students, but also between students and their parents. Effective school leaders understand that parental involvement is vital to student success. School counselors may serve as a direct point of contact to parents, especially parents of first-generation students, and provide information to parents that allow them to facilitate career and college readiness with their children.

Whether, explicitly or implicitly, school counselors can be extremely influential for African American students who are less likely to receive college and career support elsewhere. Engel (2007) concluded that for first generation students, collegiate aspirations are influenced by the sponsorship they receive from those significant in their life, including school counselors and teachers (Engel, 2007). However, Engle (2007) also notes that in reality, these students are less likely to be championed by stakeholders, who have lower expectations of these students despite their competence, to pursue and achieve success. For this reason it is vital for school counselors to receive rigorous graduate training in multicultural counseling, as well as college and career readiness, and continue to engage in professional development that is culturally competent. These elements promote cultural awareness that can be applied when advocating for African American students.

Time constraints also may prevent school counselors from effectively catering to students' college and career readiness needs. Based on American School Counselor Association (ASCA) recommendations, a counselor to student ratio should not exceed 1:250. In reality however, most states average a ratio of 1:513 and in large cities a counselor to student ratio of 1:740 or higher can be observed (Tierney, Corwin & Coylar, 2003). Moreover, school counselors spend less time than recommended by ASCA in direct service to students (Tierney, Colyar & Corwin, 2005). In schools that serve communities with higher poverty rates, the school counselor may be responsible for other duties outside of counseling students including testing, scheduling, discipline, etc. due to lack of staff and budgetary constraints. These added duties coupled with an overloaded counselor to student ratio leaves little time for direct service, especially regarding college and career counseling (Tierney, Corwin & Coylar, 2005). This is problematic considering that African American students, who are more likely to be first-generation students, are more dependent upon school counselors and other school stake holders to provide college and career knowledge that may be less accessible to them. Without support, students are less likely to obtain the resources needed to effectively navigate the college decision-making process and are at risk to be unsuccessful once enrolled (Roderick, Coca & Nagaoka, 2011). If degree attainment is not achieved, these students will parent first-generation students who are likely to share the same disadvantages and fate unless interventions are put in place to halt this disparity. The ability to break this cycle partly lies upon all educators who should aid in ensuring that all students are college and career ready (Curry & Milsom, 2013). Specifically, it is imperative that school counselors, who serve as social change agents, continue to advocate for and bring awareness to the influence their profession has on this nation's future.

The impact that school counselors can have on closing the gap for disadvantaged students by promoting career and college success has garnered increased national attention. The First Lady of The United States, Michelle Obama, is a proponent of the school counseling profession and sees school counselors as valuable stakeholders to propel her Reach Higher Initiative.

Reach Higher encourages students to pursue higher education and aligns with President Barack Obama's appeal for the United States to regain standing as the producer of the highest percentage of college graduates globally by 2020 (ASCA, 2014; Roderick, Coca & Nagaoka, 2011). It is through efforts such as these that the meaningful work that school counselors engage in is recognized and the school counseling profession is spotlighted.

ACADEMIC ADVISEMENT AND COURSE CHOICE

College preparation efforts should not be strictly reserved for the realm of secondary education, but should also be considered even before a student enters primary schooling. This ideology is especially true for African American students. Researchers have found that African American children enter elementary school with less skill and knowledge than White children and continue to perform lower throughout their educational career on standardized tests and in courses (Lleras, 2008). Though this information is nationally recognized and has resulted in the creation and implementation of government programs such as Head Start, these programs have had little lasting value on educational performance of African American students (Garces, Thomas & Currie, 2000). As students matriculate through elementary and middle school to high school, this gap in achievement typically continues to widen, especially if the school attended has a high concentration of minority students. According to Fuligni and Hardway (2004), secondary schools that effectively champion academic achievement, graduation efforts, and college preparation share a commonality of experienced teachers, a supportive and constructive school climate, and a rigorous curriculum complete with college preparatory courses. In high schools that serve dense populations of African American students, these qualities are less likely to be observed which further impedes the educational success of disadvantaged students.

African American students and their parents believe that academic achievement is important. Unless aware of this fact, school stakeholders may misinterpret underachievement or misbehavior as a lack of concern for education. Additionally, environmental obstacles that African American students may face in addition to their development as adolescents (i.e., poverty, violence and racial discrimination) should also be taken into account when considering the achievement of these students (Cunningham & Swanson, 2010). Academic advisement is vital to college readiness and should also occur early on for African American students.

As students approach middle school, college preparation is no longer a faraway notion, but a present reality. Optimistically, students have received sound instruction in elementary school that has helped them to master foundational concepts. It is typically in middle school that students are able to take courses that directly impact their high school course offerings, allowing them to get ahead or on track to take rigorous courses. One of the best examples of this is math courses offered in middle school. Algebra I serves as the prerequisite to more rigorous courses such as Advanced Math and Calculus. It is ideal for students to take this course in middle school (typically in eighth grade) so that they can take advantage of advanced rigorous courses offered in high school. This may help to position students to gain college credit while still in high school and provides exposure to high level concepts which will aid them in college coursework. First-generation students, which we have discussed earlier in this chapter as being largely African American, are less likely to take Algebra, even when qualified. One reason for this is availability. Engle (2007) noted that for over one-fifth of these students algebra was not offered to them as eighth graders. Moreover, African American students who are similar to their White counterparts, whether in socioeconomic status or performance level, are already prone to falling behind them in math achievement during middle and high school. This may be attributed to the correlation between low academic achievement and educational settings that are highly populated with minorities, which African Americans are likely to attend (Phillips, Crouse, et al., 1998; Lleras, 2008). This is concerning since research shows that success in math and science courses in college greatly depends on performance in the courses in high school (Lleras, 2008). Moreover, Engle (2007) reported that first-generation students who are exposed to a rigorous curriculum containing advanced math have increased chances of attending college. This supports research by Horn and Nunez (2000) who found that first-generation students who take advanced math are more than twice as likely to enroll in a four-year college.

COURSE RIGOR ALIGNED WITH CAREER CHOICE: AP, HONORS, DUAL ENROLLMENT

As students matriculate through middle school to high school, career and college readiness should be occurring simultaneously; students should have an idea of the career path they would like to pursue based on their skills, interests, and abilities and be able to link that career to general academic content. School counselors advocate for students by keeping abreast of career and employment trends, and ensuring that this information is provided to students. One disparity that school counselors should be aware of, as it directly impacts advancement on multiple fronts, is the shortage of African Americans succeeding in the Science, Technology, Engineering and Math (STEM) discipline as well as in the courses that serve as the foundation for this content area. Careers in STEM are key to global advancement for the United States (Chen, 2009). Though high paying, STEM positions are often unfilled due to the scarcity of a qualified workforce (Heinfield, Owens, & Moore, 2008). In 2008–2009, it was reported that 16.1% of college students graduated in a STEM major. Of those students, only 14.9% were African American (NCES, 2011). It is important to note that the lack of African Americans in STEM majors is not an issue to be reserved for discussion at the collegiate level but filters down into elementary, middle and high schooling as well (Heinfield, Owens, & Moore, 2008). The underrepresentation of African American students in STEM could be contributed to low self-efficacy due to stereotype threat (Perna et al., 2009). This perceived academic inability could cause a reluctance to pursue STEM careers due to the rigorous coursework associated with them. Additionally, Curry and Milsom (2013) contended that African American students may not be afforded the same opportunities as their White peers to engage in extracurricular activities that may cultivate their interest in STEM due to financial restraints. The underrepresentation of African Americans in STEM is problematic considering the income and stability these careers provide, among other factors. School personnel should make every effort to introduce and inform African American students to the STEM field as well as the rigorous coursework associated with it, such as physics, calculus and advanced chemistry.

Taking college-level preparatory courses in high school aids students in becoming acclimated to the rigor they will experience in college coursework and fosters success so that students are prepared to excel in careers, such as those in STEM. Research shows that this coursework also serves as an ideal way to better prepare students who do not visualize themselves to have collegiate ability (Hoffman, Vargas & Santos, 2009). Both Advanced Placement (AP) and Dual Enrollment courses are well-known options to experiencing college coursework in high school and have been garnering more attention as the importance of college success becomes apparent nationwide. It is important to note that though taking honors classes does not result in college credit, these courses serve as a sufficient prerequisite to advanced coursework and assists students in becoming ideal candidates for college.

Advanced Placement Courses

According to the College Board (2007), students who take AP courses and receive college credit tend to finish their degrees in four years or less. The College Board, which serves as the entity that collaborates with schools to provide AP exams, advocates that all students have a right to rigorous coursework and those who are willing to accept the challenge should be considered for admission into AP courses (College Board, 2007; 2014). Courses for college credit serve to encourage students of color to attend college by reinforcing the importance of attending college and providing information on careers (Rodriguez, 2000; Moore, & Slate, 2008). As noted by The College Board (2007) Advanced Placement Report to the Nation Equity Policy statement:

> The College Board encourages the elimination of barriers that restrict access to AP courses for students from ethnic, racial, and socioeconomic groups that have been traditionally underrepresented in the AP Program. Schools should make every effort to ensure that their AP classes reflect the diversity of their student population (http://apcentral.collegeboard.com/apc/public/repository/ap07_report_nation.pdf).

The College Board's policy exists because in reality, there is an observable gap in the racial differences between students who take AP coursework. Specifically, African American students are less likely than their White counterparts to enroll in AP courses. Of the students that do enroll in these courses, their percentages are not reflective of their school's racial makeup and they are also less likely to pass their AP exams (VanSciver, 2006; Moore & Slate, 2008). Consequently, these students are less prepared for college than their peers who are exposed to and excel in advanced coursework, which is essential to college and career success (Heinfield, Owens, & Moore, 2008). These findings may further serve to explain why inequity in college degree attainment between African American students and White and Asian/Asian American students exists.

Dual Enrollment Courses

In addition to AP courses, dual enrollment, also known as concurrent enrollment, provides high school students the opportunity to engage in advanced coursework for college credit. Typically, students take advantage of dual enrollment in their junior or senior year and receive both college and high school credit simultaneously for the college course(s) they complete (Hoffman, Vargas & Santos, 2009). There are many advantages for students who choose to dually enroll, and these advantages could serve as the solution to closing the achievement gap as it relates to college success among African American students.

One advantage to dual enrollment is its accessibility to students who are not categorized as high achieving. Lords (2000) contended that students who perform at lower levels are actually capable of higher achievement, yet they might lack the motivation needed because they are disengaged in class or are unable to make the connection between academic performance in school and future success. As dual enrollment expands to students who are middle and low achieving, they too are given the opportunity to experience intense coursework which increases their chances of retention and college success (Hoffman, Vargas & Santos, 2009). Dual enrollment may also provide first-hand experience in navigating a college campus. Becoming familiar with a college campus while still in high school may contribute to students' confidence, thus helping students to see college life as more manageable when they are fully immersed in it.

Dual enrollment also serves to make equitable access to college a reality. Hoffman, Vargas, and Santos (2009) noted that most dual enrollment programs make college courses more affordable to families of high school students by providing reduced or free tuition. In the long run, students can also reduce future tuition costs by taking these courses in high school and gaining credit for them. Also, dual enrollment provides the opportunity for students to take rigorous coursework that might not be available to them within their high school, as is common in schools with dense populations of African Americans. These advantages related to equity can prove to be extremely beneficial to African American students who live in communities with high poverty rates and attend schools with less rigorous curriculum offered.

Community colleges have played a vital role in the success of dual enrollment programs. Kleiner and Lewis (2005) found that of the institutions offering dual enrollment courses, 98% were public two-year institutions, compared to the 77% of public four-year institutions offering college credit to high school students. Additionally, Hoffman, Vargas and Santos (2009) note that through their realigned purpose toward high school student outreach, community colleges strive to provide academic and vocational education and support to students. In an effort to create student buy-in, some community colleges eliminate the reapplication process for dual enrollees once their high school requirements are complete. This fosters self-efficacy and provides a seamless transition to higher education for students.

In regard to vocational education, the benefits of dually enrolling in community colleges are substantial. In schools where there is a lack of emphasis placed on technical careers or a lack of resources to provide students with valuable career and technical education, students can supplement their high school curriculum with community college coursework (Karp & Hughes, 2008). Completing a vocational education curriculum can provide students with stable careers and sufficient income (Hoffman, Vargas & Santos, 2009). In some states, such as Louisiana, high students are afforded the opportunity to take technical courses in addition to their academic coursework through dual enrollment and partnerships with local companies. These courses provide students with the skills needed to succeed in technical fields such as welding and electrician training. Upon completion of their two-year training, students are eligible for industry-based certification which provides them with an opportunity for a sustainable and stable career in their chosen field (Sentell, 2013). Thus, it is important for school counselors to also inform students of the benefits of obtaining a technical education so as to promote success to all students, regardless of the scope of the training they choose to engage in.

In concluding their report, Hoffman and colleagues informed that if well designed, college-level coursework in high school can: (1) increase the number of disadvantaged students who are college ready; (2) equip students for postsecondary success by informing them of the tools and knowledge needed to thrive; (3) increase enthusiasm about higher education through free courses; (4) reduce postsecondary costs by condensing years attended; and (5) foster collaboration between K-12 school system and postsecondary institutions to ensure a successful transition to college for students. Thus, the undeniable advantages of taking college-level coursework can serve to be essential and impactful for African American student achievement.

In order for African American students to reap the academic and societal benefits that are associated with rigorous coursework, school stakeholders must first believe that these students have the capability to take such coursework. This belief should propel stakeholders to ensure that challenging courses are afforded to African American students even before they begin high school. To increase participation in collegiate level coursework, the realistic financial and academic benefits of these courses should be articulated to students and parents. Additionally, once enrolled into rigorous coursework in high school, students must also develop self-regulatory skills that will improve their chances at achievement. When this is accomplished, chances for African Americans to attain college success will undoubtedly increase.

HIGH RIGOR AND THE DEVELOPMENT OF SELF-REGULATORY SKILLS: STRESS MANAGEMENT, TIME MANAGEMENT, AND PROGRESS MONITORING

In addition to academic ability, students who seek to reap the benefits of taking advanced coursework in high school must also be emotionally proficient in order to ensure success (Foust, Hertberg-Davis, & Callahan, 2009). Within college courses, students are typically given only one semester to master course content in comparison to the full academic year given to students in high school. Rigorous courses are described as such because of the advanced pace in which challenging concepts are introduced; thus, they prepare students for the intensity they will experience in college. Developing and implementing self-regulatory skills such as those that promote efficient stress management, time management and progress monitoring while in high school will benefit African American and other students in the long run as they progress to colleges and universities with hopes of achieving college success.

Stress management, time management and progress monitoring can all be achieved through the act of goal setting. Students should be able to align their goals, such as academic achievement in a course, to the behaviors necessary to accomplish them. Such behaviors may include utilizing a planner to manage assignments, organizing supplies and employing study skills and test-taking strategies (Curry & Milsom, 2013). It may be more difficult, however for African American students to self-regulate due to outside factors such as racial discrimination and poverty, which could add to the stress of rigorous coursework.

Frank Pajares (1996) relays Bandura (1986)'s belief that, "individuals possess a self-system that enables them to exercise a measure of control over their thoughts, feelings, and actions" (p. 3). To efficiently utilize this self-system, one must first believe that they have the competence to carry out the task at hand, which is often referred to as self-efficacy (Zimmerman, 1989). Students who believe that they have the wherewithal to succeed are less likely to give up, even when the task becomes more difficult. Self-efficacy in African American students may be lower based on factors they may observe in their environments, such as violence, poverty and a lack of positive modeling (Curry & Milsom, 2013). Additionally African American students are not as likely as their White counterparts to receive encouragement from teachers and administrators at school, who may view them as deficient (Grantham & Ford, 2003; Ford et al., 2002), or parents, who may not have received academic encouragement themselves and thus are inexperienced in providing it to their students (Engle, 2007). School counselors can help build self-efficacy by facilitating mentoring relationships between African American students and successful individuals who share the same racial background so that students are able to vicariously envision themselves being successful (Curry & Milsom, 2003; Britner & Pajares, 2006). Conducting counseling sessions with students focused on goal setting and developing self-regulatory skills is another way that counselors can foster self-efficacy within African American students.

Scholarship Information, School Choice and Early Admissions

As students enter and matriculate through high school, it is important for them to attain essential knowledge of the college-going process early. As the United States offers abundant possibilities for postsecondary education, students require assistance in navigating these options. Stearns, Potochnick, Moller and Southworth (2010) noted that this assistance may come from school counselors, college preparatory teachers or parents who have obtained higher education.

Because African American students overwhelmingly identify as first-generation students, they are less likely to have highly educated parents, thus this responsibility falls onto school counselors and their collaboration with college preparatory teachers. Such knowledge should be disseminated during sophomore and junior year, rather than waiting until the last semester of senior year when prime opportunities may already have expired.

Scholarship and financial aid information is vital for African American students and parents who might be concerned about college affordability (Berkner & Chavez, 1997; Engle, 2007). There is a plethora of scholarship information available to these students who additionally have opportunities to qualify for certain scholarships based on their racial identity or socioeconomic status. In this same vein, students can qualify for stipends and grants that are merit or need based from state and federal government entities. Students and parents must be aware that the process of obtaining financial aid is competitive, and in most cases, time sensitive. It is especially imperative for school counselors to aid African American students and their parents in navigating the financial aid process. Low-income students might find that the financial aid application process is complicated and difficult to navigate and are therefore less likely to apply early, if at all (Roderick, Coca & Nagaoka, 2011). Additionally, involving parents in this process is pertinent regardless of their educational level, as this increases students' chances of attending college (Engle, 2007). School counselors and teachers can make information accessible to students and parents by sponsoring workshops during accommodating times that focus on the financial aid process. These events allow school counselors to disseminate knowledge that parents of African Americans students may not be privy to (Engle, 2007). Because African American students tend to utilize student loans more than other ethnicities to afford college expenses (Elliott & Nam, 2012), addressing the impactful reality of student loans, credit, and budgeting with African American parents and students is also ideal (Curry & Milsom, 2013).

In addition to insufficient information regarding the financial aid process, African American students may also lack essential knowledge necessary to make an informed decision about which college to attend. African American students are more likely to enroll in colleges and institutions that are two-year or nonselective and less-selective four-year institutions regardless of their qualifications (Engle, 2007; Roderick, Coca & Nagaoka, 2011). Factors such as cost, proximity to home environment and inadequate knowledge of conducting a college search explain these students' choices (Engle, 2007; Roderick, Coca & Nagaoka, 2011). Selectivity is important as graduation rates increase based on the selectivity of the college or university, which is an important factor that African American students should consider when choosing colleges to attend. Considering that the quality of the chosen college is also vitally important and that African American students' may not include this as a factor when making college decisions, school counselors should ensure that students should understand that selectivity is paramount.

School stakeholders can also provide college information to African American students through experiential opportunities, such as college fairs and visits. Opportunities for interaction with faculty, students, staff and alumni through physical campus visits or programs such as college fairs, allows African American students and parents to receive answers about college that can be greatly beneficial (Freeman, 1997). Furthermore, college and university fairs and visits should be of wide variety. School counselors should provide college information to students' that is comprehensive yet culturally reflective. Including Historically Black Colleges and Universities (HBCUs) in the dissemination of college knowledge is imperative, especially for African American students (Curry & Milsom, 2013). These opportunities can occur even as early as elementary and middle school and may make a lasting impression on students to pursue higher education.

Optimistically, utilizing these differing channels of information will help students to narrow down their selections and choose a college or university that best suits them. Once this happens, students should be made aware of the benefits of early decision and early action options. Research shows that African American students are less likely to apply for early decision due to the early binding commitment required by the institution, as it can narrow financial aid opportunities which may be a significant factor to these students (JBHE, 2004). However, early decision could prove to be a worthwhile choice for African American students, as more of these students are selected during early decision than during regular admissions. Early action differs from early decision in that it is nonbinding, yet students still receive an early response to their application. This option is especially ideal for students who are interested in obtaining school specific scholarships. Knowledge of these possibilities should be presented to these students who otherwise may be unfamiliar with their options. According to the *Journal of Blacks in Higher Education* (2004) early decision is popular among those who identify as legacy students who have had family members as alumni of the institution of interest. Because the doors to most higher education institutions remained closed to African Americans for many years, current students are less likely to have family members who attended these institutions, and thus may not be familiar with the school's early decision and application process. Meanwhile, White students are more likely to have access to information about the early decision process. To combat such inequality, school counselors must make an active effort to provide this advisement to African American students regardless of perceived capability.

SUMMARY

African Americans have been plagued by racial inequality since being transported to the United States (Allen, 2005). Presently, these inequities surface in the form of high poverty rates, low income and employment rates, and underrepresentation in academic achievement arenas. The information presented in this chapter indicates that achieving success through degree attainment can serve to rectify these inequalities and arrest the cyclical impact that the lack of a college degree has on African Americans and society as a whole. If the United States truly wishes to achieve global advancement through educational dominance, it is imperative that achievement gaps be closed and the playing field be leveled for African American students and other minorities. The first step in accomplishing this feat is to ensure that educators are culturally competent so as to promote advocacy and provide equitable service to these students. Additionally school stakeholders must actively champion academic achievement by affording students the opportunity to engage in rigorous curriculum throughout K-12, including Advanced Placement, Honors or Dual Enrollment coursework in high school. These courses will not only academically prepare students for collegiate coursework, but will also assist in the development of self-regulatory skills needed to succeed in higher education. Endorsing career exploration and development throughout every grade level as a means to provide exposure and encourage buy-in is also advantageous to African American students' college success. Finally, providing information and resources so that students and parents can make an informed decision about college selection and the financial aid process is a critical responsibility of educators. By employing these tactics, school counselors and stakeholders equip students to achieve educational excellence and degree attainment, which equates to increased earning potential and quality of life for African Americans, also producing a substantial civic impact. Thus, the acquisition of college success by African Americans not only serves to remedy the disparities they experience, but ultimately positions this nation for success.

REFERENCES

Allen, W. R. (2005). A forward glance in a mirror: Diversity challenged—access, equity, and success in higher education. *Educational Researcher, 34*(7), 18–23. doi: 10.3102/0013189X034007018

Altbach, P. G., Reisberg, L., & Rumbley, L. E. (2009). Trends in global higher education: Tracking an academic revolution. doi:10.1080/00091381003590845

American School Counselor Association. (2012). *The ASCA national model: A framework for school counseling programs*. (3rd ed.). Alexandria, VA: Author. doi:10.1037/e504812012-001

American School Counseling Association. (2014, June 18). First Lady Michelle Obama to speak at ASCA annual conference. Retrieved from

Bandura, A. (1986). *Social foundations of thought and action: A social cognitive theory*. Englewod Clifs, NJ: Prentice Hall.

Baum, S., Ma, J., & Payea, K. (2013). Education pays 2013. *The College Board*.

Belsky, J. (2007). *Experiencing the lifespan*. New York, NY: Worth Publishers.

Berkner, L. and L. Chavez. (1997). *Access to Postsecondary Education for 1992 High School Graduates*. Washington, DC: National Center for Education Statistics.

Black Students Are Beginning to Seize the Early Admission Advantage. (2004). *The Journal of Blacks in Higher Education, 2004*(43), 81–85. doi:10.2307/4133564

Britner, S. L., & Pajares, F. (2006). Sources of science self-efficacy beliefs of middle school students. *Journal of Research in Science Teaching, 43*(5), 485–499. doi:10.1002/tea.20131

Brown, D., & Trusty, J. (2005). *Designing and leading comprehensive school counseling programs: Promoting student competence and meeting student needs*. Brooks/Cole Pub Co. doi:10.5330/PSC.n.2013-16.172

Chen, X. (2009). Students Who Study Science, Technology, Engineering, and Mathematics (STEM) in Postsecondary Education. Stats in Brief. NCES 2009-161. *National Center for Education Statistics*. doi:10.1037/e595112009-001

College Board. (2007). *Advanced placement report to the nation*. Retrieved from http://apcentral.collegeboard.com/apc/public/repository/ap07_report_nation.pdf

College Board. (2014). *The 10th Annual AP report to the nation*. Retrieved from http://apreport.collegeboard.org/

Conroy, C.A. (2000). Influence of gender and program of enrollment on adolescents and teens; Occupational and educational aspirations. *Journal of Vocational and Technical Education, 14*(2), 18–28

Cunningham, M., & Swanson, D. P. (2010). Educational resilience in African American adolescents. *The Journal of Negro Education*, 473–487.

Curry, J., & Amy Milsom, D. (2013). *Career Counseling in P-12 Schools*. Springer Publishing Company.

Elliott, W., & Nam, I. (2012). Direct effects of assets and savings on the college progress of Black young adults. *Educational Evaluation and Policy Analysis, 34*(1), 89–108. doi:10.3102/0162373711425957

Engle, J. (2007). Postsecondary access and success for first-generation college students. *American Academic, 3*(1), 25–48.

Engle, J., & Tinto, V. (2008). Moving Beyond Access: College Success for Low-Income, First Generation Students. *Pell Institute for the Study of Opportunity in Higher Education*.

Ford, D., Harris. J. J., Tyson, C, & Trotman. M. (2002). Beyond deficit thinking: Providing access for gifted African American students. *Roeper Review, 24*(2), 52–58. doi:10.1080/02783190209554129

Foust, R. C., Hertberg-Davis, H., & Callahan, C. M. (2009). Students' Perceptions of the Social/Emotional Implications of Participation in Advanced Placement and International Baccalaureate Programs. Research Monograph Series. RM09238. *National Research Center on the Gifted and Talented*.

Freeman, K. (1997). Increasing African Americans' participation in higher education: African American high-school students' perspectives. *Journal of Higher Education,* 523–550. doi: 10.2307/2959945

Fuligni, A. J., & Hardway, C. (2004). Preparing diverse adolescents for the transition to adulthood. *The Future of Children,* 99–119. doi:10.2307/1602796

Garces, E., Thomas, D., & Currie, J. (2000). *Longer term effects of Head Start* (No. w8054). National Bureau of Economic Research. doi:10.3386/w8054

Gottfredson, L. S. (1981). Circumscription and compromise: A developmental theory of occupational aspirations. *Journal of Counseling psychology, 28*(6), 545. doi:10.1037/0022–0167.28.6.545

Grantham, T. C., & Ford, D. Y. (2003). Beyond self-concept and self-esteem: Racial identity and gifted African American students. *The High School Journal,* 18–29. doi:10.1353/hsj.2003.0016

Harvey, J. C. (2005). Affirmative action and equal opportunity for Blacks in higher education and the university of Michigan cases. *Race, Gender & Class, 12*(3/4), 47–55.

Henfield, M. S., Owens, D., & Moore III, J. L. (2008). Influences on Young Gifted African Americans' School Success: Implications for Elementary School Counselors. *Elementary School Journal, 108*(5), 392–406. doi:10.1086/589469

Hoffman, N., Vargas, J., & Santos, J. (2009). New directions for dual enrollment: Creating stronger pathways from high school through college. *New Directions for Community Colleges, 2009*(145), 43–58. doi:10.1002/cc.354

Horn, L., and A. Nunez. (2000). *Mapping the road to college: First-generation students' math track, planning strategies, and context of support.* Washington, DC: National Center for Education Statistics. doi:10.1037/e430852005–001

Karp, M. M., & Hughes, K. L. (2008). Study: Dual Enrollment Can Benefit a Broad Range of Students. *Techniques: Connecting Education and Careers (J1), 83*(7), 14–17.

Kleiner, B., & Lewis, L. (2005). Dual Enrollment of High School Students at Postsecondary Institutions: 2002-TAB. NCES 2005–008. *National Center for Education Statistics.*

Lleras, C. (2008). Race, racial concentration, and the dynamics of educational inequality across urban and suburban schools. *American Educational Research Journal, 45*(4), 886–912. doi:10.3102/0002831208316323

Lords, E. (2000). New Efforts at Community Colleges Focus on Underachieving Teens. *Chronicle of Higher Education, 46*(43), A45–A46.

Macartney, S., Bishaw, A., & Fontenot, K. (2013). Poverty rates for selected detailed race and hispanic groups by state and place: 2007–2011. *US Department of Commerce, United States Census Bureau: Washington, DC, USA.*

Moore, G. W., & Slate, J. R. (2008). Who's taking the Advanced Placement courses and how are they doing: A statewide two-year study. *The High School Journal, 92*(1), 56–67.

National Center for Education Statistics. (2011). *2008–2009 baccalaureate and beyond longitudinal study (B& B: 08/09).* Washington, DC: U.S. Department of Education.

Pajares, F. (1996). Self-efficacy beliefs in academic settings. *Review of educational research*, *66*(4), 543–578. doi:10.3102/00346543066004543

Perna, L., Lundy-Wagner, V., Drezner, N. D., Gasman, M., Yoon, S., Bose, E., & Gary, S. (2009). The contribution of HBCUs to the preparation of African American women for STEM careers: A case study. *Research in Higher Education*, *50*(1), 1–23.

Phillips, M., Crouse, J., & Ralph, J. (1998). Does the black-white test score gap widen after children enter school? In C. Jencks & M. Phillips (Eds.), *The black-white test score gap* (pp. 229–272). Washington, DC: Brookings Institution.

Roderick, M., Nagaoka, J., & Coca, V. (2009). College readiness for all: The challenge for urban high schools. *The Future of Children*, *19*(1), 185–210. doi:10.1353/foc.0.0024

Roderick, M., Coca, V., & Nagaoka, J. (2011). Potholes on the road to college high school effects in shaping urban students' participation in college application, four-year college enrollment, and college match. *Sociology of Education*, *84*(3), 178–211. doi:10.1177/0038040711411280

Rodriguez, S. (2000). Ordinary winners: A high school community college preparation program. University of California, Los Angeles.

Sentell, W. (2013, October 29). New program offers nontraditional classes. *The Advocate*. Retrieved from http://theadvocate.com/news/7436074–123/new-state-programs-offers-non-traditional

Signer, B., & Saldana, D. (2001). Educational and career aspirations of high school students and race, gender, class differences. *Race, Gender & Class*, 22–34.

Snyder, T. D., & Dillow, S. A. (2013). Digest of Education Statistics, 2012. NCES 2014–015. *National Center for Education Statistics*.

Stearns, E., Potochnick, S., Moller, S., & Southworth, S. (2010). High school course-taking and post-secondary institutional selectivity. *Research in Higher Education*, *51*(4), 366–395. doi:10.1007/s11162–009-9161-8

Tierney, W. G., Colyar, J. E., & Corwin, Z. B. (2003). *Preparing for college: Building expectations, changing Realities*. Los Angeles: Center for Higher Education Policy Analysis, University of Southern California.

Tierney, W. G., Corwin, Z. B., & Colyar, J. E. (Eds.). (2005). *Preparing for college: Nine elements of effective outreach*. SUNY Press.

VanSciver, J. H. (2006). Closing the diversity gap in Advanced Placement course enrollment. *Multicultural Perspectives*, *8*(3), 56–58. doi:10.1207/s15327892mcp0803_10

Witherspoon, K. M., & Speight, S. L. (2007). An exploration of African Americans' interests and self-efficacy beliefs in traditional and nontraditional careers. *Journal of Black Studies*. doi:10.1177/0021934707305396

Wood, C., & Kaszubowski, Y. (2008). The career development needs of rural elementary school students. *The Elementary School Journal*, *108*(5), 431–444. doi:10.1086/589472

Young, R. A. (1983). Career development of adolescents: An ecological perspective. *Journal of Youth and adolescence*, *12*(5), 401–417. doi:10.1007/bf02088723

Zaback, K., Carlson, A., & Crellin, M. (2012). The Economic Benefit of Postsecondary Degrees: A State and National Level Analysis. *State Higher Education Executive Officers.*

Zimmerman, B. J. (1989). A social cognitive view of self-regulated academic learning. *Journal of educational psychology, 81*(3), 329. doi:10.1037//0022–0663.81.3.329

Chapter 7

Supporting the Transition of African American Students with Specific Learning Disabilities into Post-secondary Education

Sharon H. deFur and Elizabeth Auguste

We approach this chapter from a critical social justice context as we have contemplated the overlap of marginalized educational opportunities that have traditionally been inaccessible to people with disabilities as well as to African Americans. So, as you read this chapter, we ask you to begin by reflecting on your personal experiences, biases, and conceptual models regarding young adults who are African American and have goals of a degree(s) beyond high school. Next, add the layer that includes the presence of learning disabilities for these students. Our engagement with the research literature suggests that it is likely that your K-12 or higher education models that include African American youth and young adults with disabilities exist within a historical web of pejorative conceptualizations. As a first step to change the narrative, we urge you to examine the intersection of your personal ablest and racial beliefs. This prework on beliefs can create a space to envision creative strategies that can promote the goal of preparing African American young adults with specific learning disabilities to be college and career ready.

In writing this chapter we acknowledge a significant problem faced in any interpretation of data on students with disabilities, that is, its "messiness." Included in this population are students with physical, learning, and emotional disabilities and students with autism spectrum disorders. Another category that is often included is students with attention deficit disorders and students with specific learning disabilities. Unfortunately, only rarely do researchers distinguish the type of disability they are identifying in their research. This chapter primarily focuses on students with specific learning disabilities (SLD); however, because of the paucity of research exploring this cohort of students, we will also sometimes refer to data that included students with disabilities (SWD) which represents a very diverse group. Likewise, little research has disaggregated students with disabilities by race/ethnicity. We acknowledge a long challenging history of over-identification of African American students with disabilities, including the category of SLD. The most recent U.S. Department of Education (USDOE) report notes that 11.2% of African American students are identified as having a disability. Of this grouping, 42.4% are categorized as having a SLD (USDOE, 2013).

A specific learning disability (SLD) is often referred to as a hidden disability as there are no physical characteristics associated with this diagnosis. Given the definition of SLD, young adults with SLD should be prime candidates for postsecondary education as these individuals have average to above average intellectual ability. However, these students do underachieve in one or more academic area and may have difficulty with processing skills like memory, metacognition, attention, planning, etc. Their strengths and challenges vary. The 2004 Individuals with Disabilities Education Improvement Act (IDEA) defines SLD as:

> A disorder in one or more of the basic psychological processes involved in understanding or in using language, spoken or written, which disorder may manifest itself in the imperfect ability to listen, think, speak, read, write, spell, or do mathematical calculations, including conditions such as perceptual disabilities, brain injury, minimal brain dysfunction, dyslexia, and developmental aphasia. Specific learning disability does not include a learning problem that arises primarily as the result of visual, hearing, or motor disabilities, of intellectual disability, of emotional disturbance, or of environmental, cultural, or economic disadvantage. (IDEA, 2004)

Specific learning disabilities constitute the most commonly identified disability category under IDEA, accounting for 40.7% of all identified school age children and youth (USDOE, 2013). As with many hidden disabilities, males outnumber females by about three to one. In addition, estimates of co-morbidity of SLD with Attention Deficit Hyperactivity Disorder (ADHD) are cited to be as high as 45% of those identified as having a SLD. Young adults with SLD are a heterogeneous group whose needs will vary for support for transitioning to, and matriculating through, postsecondary education.

Policy and Education Reform

Federal and state education policy and initiatives (e.g., Elementary and Secondary Education Act [ESEA]; Individual with Disabilities Education Act [IDEA]; Common Core State Standards [CCSS]) advance the expectation that all youth completing high school will have an equal opportunity to be college and career ready. This includes students with disabilities. Furthermore, disability policies such as the 1990 Americans with Disabilities Act (ADA) and the Rehabilitation Act of 1973 guarantee non-discriminatory access to postsecondary education for students with disabilities who otherwise meet the college entry requirements.

Section 504 of the Rehabilitation Act required postsecondary education institutions to provide reasonable accommodations to students with disabilities to support attendance at postsecondary education institutions. Nonetheless, colleges and university faculty and administrators have been historically reluctant to acquiesce to what is currently expected regarding disability admission and support rights. Retrospectively, the 1980s exampled a civil rights era where people with disabilities demonstrated on behalf of the need for equitable access to employment, education, and independent living opportunities. Although laws had been passed, regulations had yet to be sufficiently developed or regularly enforced at that time. Shattering decades of hiding disability, the passage of the ADA in 1990 broadened the protection of individuals with disabilities' access to all aspects of community life, including postsecondary education.

Paralleling the evolution of the ADA that elevated the focus on the ability of persons who have a disability, IDEA mandated transition planning and services for all students with a disability, including those identified with SLD. By 1997, this law included a specified requirement to outline a course of study that supported school completion as part of the Individualized Education Program (IEP) for secondary school students with disabilities. Undoubtedly prompted by the disability advocacy and self-determination movement of the 1980s, the 1990 IDEA directive transformed the IEP process most significantly by requiring that IEPs for transition-aged students (age 14 or 16, depending on state regulations) involve students in their IEP transition planning meetings. Recognizing the complexity of transitioning from special education to work and to the postsecondary education world required IEP team member involvement extend beyond the school doors. School districts began identifying transition coordinators and establishing interagency teams that often included representatives of college disability coordinators. The gulf between secondary schools and transition planning for admissible students to postsecondary education with disabilities emerged as a critical topic of discussion and research during this era (deFur & Korinek, 2008).

In 1997 and in 2004, the respective reauthorizations of IDEA continued and strengthened transition requirements, targeting IEP transition services that focus on results-oriented outcomes of post-school employment, education, and adult living. Such planning was further strengthened when IDEA required states to collect data and report on state performance indicators such as graduation, state assessment results, measurable transition goals, and postsecondary outcomes in education and employment. Perhaps most influential was the requirement to make these outcomes public by school district as well as for the states.

These re-authorizations emerged during a period of national attention that called for education reforms. For example, the 2004 IDEA re-authorization followed on the heels of the Elementary and Secondary Act (ESEA) reauthorization in 2001, also known over the past decade as the No Child Left Behind (NCLB) Act, and now again referred to as ESEA. These policies brought renewed attention to educational outcomes for African American youth with SLD. Perhaps the lasting imprint of NCLB will be the requirement to evaluate and hold schools, districts, and states accountable for disaggregating data on the academic outcomes of traditionally underperforming subgroups including African American youth with SLD.

Intended outcomes: Equality. Due to policy changes, an increasing number of young adults identified with disabilities identify attending college or university as a primary post high school goal (USDOE, 2013). Encouragingly, the numbers of young adults with varying disabilities successfully matriculating to postsecondary education significantly increased in the past 20 years. Using data from the National Longitudinal Transition Study 2 (NTLS2), Newman et al. (2011a) reported that 26% of young adults with disabilities who had been out of school for eight years had in fact attended four-year colleges at some point in that time period. Moreover, they also estimated that 60% of school leavers who had a disability had enrolled in some type of postsecondary education during that time period. Yet, this rate of participation still falls below that of typical-age peers. Most pertinent to this chapter is that, in spite of progress made for students with disabilities' participation in postsecondary education, the cohort of African American students with disabilities continues to be disproportionately under-represented.

Unintended outcomes: Marginalization. Having a disability or being an ethnic minority such as an African American currently offers discrimination protections, at least theoretically. In reality, a paradoxical relationship exists at the convergence of protections and practices, and is evident in how this relationship contributes to the creation of a hidden curriculum. Being a member of either sub-group historically places an individual in a marginalized cultural grouping with probable pejorative stereotypes (Banks & Hughes, 2013). There is, however, a compounding impact of race plus disability which negatively influences educational expectations of many professionals, both in K-12 and postsecondary education. For African American youth with SLD, this complicated dynamic is often experienced within an inclusive environment where peers, faculty, or employers question competence based on perceived identity stereotypes.

Banks and Hughes (2013) framed this demographic using Du Bois' discussion of double-consciousness as they researched "the precarious intersections of disability, race, and cultural jeopardy" (p. 368). The authors also exposed inherent research bias in the extant literature as they claim past and current literature addresses "critical issues of postsecondary individuals with disabilities [but] ignores the voices of students of color" (p. 370). This unintended backlash of legislation is evident in educational decisions that limit access to, and equality in, advanced academic educational experiences for African American youth with SLD.

Based on interviews with African American college students with disabilities, Banks and Hughes (2013) suggested this double-consciousness also negatively affects students' self-worth and actualizing intellectual potential. These young adults are then faced with the challenge of adopting an identity path that supports a vision of themselves as capable, most often resulting in a rejection of their disability label because of its added burden to their adult psychological identity development.

Factors Impacting Matriculation

High school experiences. Not surprisingly, the National Longitudinal Transition Study-2 (NLTS 2) (Wagner, Newman, Cameto, & Levine, 2005) reported that students with disabilities who participated more in the general curriculum, completed high school, and who were academically better prepared were more likely to participate in postsecondary education. Relevant to this chapter on the intersection of race and disability is that Newman et al. (2011a) did not find *statistical* differences in postsecondary education participation based on race after eight years in the adult world; yet a comparatively smaller percentage of African American young adults with disabilities reported attending college.

Course portfolio. The National Center for Learning Disabilities (NCLD, 2013) reported that some high school IEP teams use a student's IEP goals to set the terms for graduation rather than attending to graduation requirements or matriculation to postsecondary education. This is problematic as the tendency may be to substitute core courses with less rigorous offerings and to provide extensions and exemptions, all practices which negatively impact a student's course portfolio. In addition, grade point average (GPA) correlates with success in college for all students as does completing a more rigorous course of study. Newman et al. (2011b) reported that students with disabilities achieved lower GPAs than the general student population, earned fewer academic credits, and took less rigorous courses of study during high school. Adding to this dilemma, African American students with disabilities earned even fewer academic credits and earned a lower GPA than their White counterparts. They were also more likely to be educated outside of the general education setting and to have failed one or more courses than their White peers with disabilities. Theoretically, African American students with SLD have an IEP team that can address individual needs including planning a course of study to achieve postsecondary education goals. The data seem to suggest that those teams may be missing critical supports for students with SLD to attend college; moreover, the data implies that the IEP team decision making may result in less equitable opportunities for African American youth with SLD. Decisions made in the IEP impact the likelihood of participating in postsecondary education.

Oesterreich and Knight (2008) assert these race disparities can also coexist along a class divide. If African American students are also from a low socioeconomic background, they face substantial financial barriers that limit access to private tutoring and other out-of-school services for standardized test preparation. This potentially affects college admissions assessment performance scores which, in turn, are major determinants for college matriculation.

Tracking. Unfortunately, current educational practices do not support equality in the achievement of postsecondary education goals for all students with disabilities (SWD), as discrepancies in high school experiences and opportunities for students with SWD fall along a race divide. White high school SWD experience higher teacher expectations, better access to general education classes, and are more likely to be on regular diploma tracks than their non-white peers (Banks & Hughes, 2013). This was reported as especially evident in the low enrollment of high school African American SWD in college preparation classes, including advanced placement courses (Schwartz & Washington, 2002).

The deleterious effects of tracking are also made obvious when looking at curricular exposure. Studies conducted by Trainor (2005) and Pellegrino, Sermons, and Shaver (2011) found that academically able African American SWD, when compared to their white counterparts, were more likely to be tracked to vocational pursuits and other alternatives to college preparation diplomas, regardless of student-declared interest in college attendance. According to Trainor (2005):

> Vocational programs that allow for an early release during the school day and an opportunity to earn money seem attractive.... Students need to fully understand the implications of these programs. For example, they need to understand that early release for employment may conflict with their enrollment in college preparatory coursework. To increase their decision-making skills, students must

receive explicit instruction regarding the expected outcomes of vocational and college-preparatory curricular decisions. Similarly, students need to understand the implications of standardized test exemptions and resulting diploma types offered by their districts, so that they can participate in curricular decisions that align with their postsecondary goals. Students with intentions of attending college need to understand that preparatory courses are distinct from vocational programs. (pp. 244–245)

High school completion. Another factor known to impact matriculation for SWD is high school dropout. Consistently, state and national data trends have shown that students with disabilities drop out of school at significantly higher rates than students without disabilities. Non-completers have poorer post-school outcomes in terms of job and education (Newman, 2011a). Students with SLD represent one of the most common disability cohorts to dropout of school (second to students with emotional disabilities). Fortunately, efforts to reduce dropout rates for students with SLD seem to have been successful. Data from 2011 show that the percentage of SLD student dropout nationally was at 19%, down from a national average of 35% in 2002, and graduation with a regular diploma is now at 68% nationwide (NCLD, 2013). While these improvements are cause for celebration, the stark implications are that more than 30% of young adults with SLD are leaving high school without credentials for further education or employment consistent with ability. In some states, more students with SLD leave school by dropping out than leave with a regular diploma. One could posit that having a SLD raises the risk of not gaining critical competencies for a financially viable future.

Nationally, African American students with or without disabilities have experienced a high degree of school dropout with estimates of up to 18% of all African American students dropping out (America's Promise Alliance, 2014; Jones, 2011). Like their White peers, recent reports demonstrate that this statistic had dropped to 8% (Fry, 2014), although 8% dropout still remains an unacceptable number of youth losing options for their future. Pairing SLD with race contributes even more to the risk of interrupting the path to high school completion. In addition, if risk factors such as poverty, homelessness, violence, foster care, etc., are factored in, the potential for school dropout escalates (America's Promise Alliance, 2014). Creating a school environment with holding power for African American students with SLD is paramount to their successful engagement in college or postsecondary education. Relationships and connectedness make the difference.

Family. According to the NCLD (2013), surveys of high school students with SLD and their parents reveal conflicting expectations for college attendance. Reportedly, parents held lower academic expectations for their child's future achievements than students held for themselves. Parental expectations are important because they are associated with both student achievement and post-high school outcomes. As Chapter 10 thoroughly discusses, when African American students are first-generation college students, their families may lack the knowledge the school system expects of them when navigating the college admission process. This educational maze can become even more complicated for African American families of students with SLD. Banks (2014) conducted rich interviews with African American SWD. One participant discussed his parents' surprise at the decision to attend college as they discounted that option due to his disability.

An intersection of race, disability, and socioeconomic status places an additional and substantial financial burden on families. Wagner et al. (2005) found that of the young adults with disabilities who dropped out of college, 28% of them reported financial burdens and the need to find a job as the major factors informing their decision to leave. These effects are even greater when the SWD is a first-generation college student (Lombardi, Murray, & Gerdes, 2012; Oesterreich & Knight, 2008). According to Chen (as cited in Lombardi et al., 2012), "50% of first-generation students come from families with an annual household income of less than $25,000, as compared to 7% among those whose parents earned bachelor's degrees or higher" (p. 812). The difficulties these families experience when looking at financial planning for college expenses is compounded with the financial stress of additional expenses that usually accompany supporting a young adult with a disability (Mamiseishvili & Koch, 2011).

Mamiseishvili and Koch (2011) found that living on campus during the first and second year of college can have a significant positive impact on college completion. López Turley and Wodtke (2010) frame this discussion by comparing the experiences of students living on campus and comparable peers not living on campus. They reported that not living on campus can lead to disengagement which they defined as a "lack of involvement in the myriad academic activities available at postsecondary institutions, such as language clubs, political or environmental groups, professional and pre-professional associations, honor societies, academic workshops or seminars, and formal or informal discussions with faculty members" (p. 507). Their results showed that engagement does impact persistence to graduation, and that these effects do vary by race. They found that African American students living off campus with family members had significantly lower GPAs than comparable students living on campus. When students are from low socioeconomic families, however, boarding costs are a significant challenge and limitation. To combat this limitation, many young adults from low socioeconomic status households choose to enroll in community colleges, an option that negates on-campus living advantages. Adding another layer, Herbert et al. (2014)

found that the majority of SWD live off campus. Paradoxically, the financial decision to live at home so that postsecondary education can actually be a viable option can be in direct conflict with the academic decision to pursue postsecondary education. A limitation of this discussion is also a commentary on the premise of this entire chapter: most often, each identity (learning disability and African American) is treated separately in the literature, again pointing to the paucity of research specifically targeting African American students with SLD.

Family education regarding the college application process, application for financial support, application for disability services, as well as the types of services that a young adult in college might access is important. Many families are not aware of the processes that most institutes of higher education have in place to support and guide students in their postsecondary education. This mission has changed from a decades old model of "in loco parentis" to a model of "student engagement and development." Families may not understand what this means for their African American son or daughter with SLD or how to support their adult child as they navigate the opportunities and risks of postsecondary education. Wallace (2013) highlights that in addition to this limitation of lack of knowledge, there is evidence in the research that shows that when parents of African American high school students (SLD and non-identified) try to get involved in the school process, they are many times trying to address issues of perceived inequalities. In these instances, their voices are marginalized as school faculty see them as disruptive and they are often labeled such and dismissed, as they face what Wallace calls "institutional barriers to participation" (p. 197). One can surmise that this educational and cultural reality African American parents face is one where the expectation for participation is one of conformity and acceptance to the dominant culture, regardless of how this culture "frames" the aptitude, attitude, and academic future of their child. The implications for advocacy during disability-rights conversations with "school experts" are clear if parents feel marginalized when fighting for rights when a confident knowledge base exists. Within this social and cultural dilemma, African American parents of students with disabilities may be perceived as less involved as their white counterparts in any advocacy process within a school system (Lynch & Stein, 1987). Of interest is that much of the literature stereotypically, and with presumed authority but no data, frame this alleged un-involvement as lack of caring. Practitioners must be aware of their own biases that ignore culturally different approaches to parental involvement in education.

Transition planning. In addition to the significant impact of high school experiences on matriculation, transition planning also meaningfully impacts this process. By law, IEP teams must develop postsecondary goals with SWD that include plans for postsecondary education. In addition, the IEP must develop annual measurable goals that facilitate progress toward the long-term outcomes and include a course of study that leads to the realization of these goals. This strategic plan includes the student and family, with a mandate for their input into the process.

The transition plan must be based on assessment data that can guide the decisions the IEP team makes. Career and transition assessments inform students of their own strengths and weaknesses, preferences, and interests (Trainor, Smith, & Kim, 2012). The IEP team may also include adult service agencies that might be paying for, or providing, transition services. Partnering with these agencies can widen the network of support for African American students with SLD (Balcazar et al., 2012). School counselors are not a mandated member of the transition IEP team. This is unfortunate because of the critical role counselors have in helping youth navigate the path to postsecondary education. Within-school collaboration between school counselors and special educators seems critical to developing shared knowledge and resources to benefit African American students with SLD entering college (Kosine, 2007). Many local school districts have an interagency transition task force and in that capacity collaborate with one or more college disability service providers (DSP) as part of systemic planning for postsecondary education. It is not within the scope of responsibilities for college DSP to participate on individual IEP transition teams, although it is very important for the team to understand the role of disability services and share that perspective as part of the transition plan.

Trainor (2005) discusses the importance of the transition planning process to the success rates of students' adaptation to environments outside of high school, and its impact on positive matriculation experiences. She observed that although legislative mandates ensure this process is in place for students, many high school counselors and teachers follow the letter of the law but not the spirit of the law when assisting students and parents in making choices and setting goals. On the other hand, effectively developed transition IEPs offer an opportunity to help African American students with SLD garner social and cultural capital when the IEP includes early work experiences and experiential internships, supports for participating in extracurricular activities to expand social connections, or providing mentorships with young adults with SLD who have successfully attended college (Dunn, Rabren, Taylor, & Dotson, 2012; Trainor et al., 2012). Oesterreich and Knight (2008) defined social capital for students with disabilities, in relation to college, as "the availability of information-sharing networks about college" (p. 301). In the interviews Banks and Hughes (2013) conducted, one African American college student with SLD indicated that neither his teachers nor his parents discussed future plans of attending college, leaving him with a lack of knowledge about available services. Trainor (2005) reiterates that transition planning offers the place and direction for cross-cultural conversations that support African American students with SLD in gaining the necessary information needed to pursue goals of postsecondary education, since this information is not readily available anywhere else.

People with disabilities (including SLD), as well as African Americans, are underrepresented in careers in science, technology, engineering and mathematics (STEM). Dunn et al. (2012) claim that youth with SLD are not encouraged toward STEM careers often because of low expectations or inaccurate perceptions of indolence by their teachers. Furthermore, students with SLD may need differentiated and scaffolded content as well appropriate accommodations. Technology and universal design for learning (UDL) strategies enable students with SLD access to the rigorous content needed for STEM college and career readiness, but UDL strategies are often underemployed in high school classrooms. Critical for African American students with SLD is engaging in postsecondary connecting activities that support transition into high demand courses of study in postsecondary education, like STEM.

Balcazar and colleagues (2012) described a college connecting program that included a four-week summer training institute where participants who had graduated with a standard diploma from an urban high school completed college applications, financial aid applications, and application for vocational rehabilitation services. These students also received career and vocational assessments and engaged in job shadowing related to their interests. In addition, they received tutoring in specific academic areas. Peer support groups were established and follow-up case management was available over the average time of 14 months of engagement in the project. Of the 164 participants, 44.8% were African American; 68% of participants had SLD. Follow-up found that 82% of the program participants were enrolled in postsecondary education as compared to 50% of comparison group members. Only 6% of the program group had dropped out of their college program. College case management included support for the application process as well as support with tutoring, accessing disability services, and assisting with negotiations related to finances and problems with faculty. This provides a good model for how practitioners can take practical and targeted actions to ensure proactive support for African American youth with SLD.

Post-secondary Education

During 2008–09, eighty-eight percent of two-year and four-year degree-granting postsecondary institutions reported enrolling students with disabilities: 85% of these institutions enrolled students with SLD (Raue & Lewis, 2011). These statistics are promising, but the national average of high school students entering a four-year college is about 70%; this figure drops dramatically to 9% for SWD (NLTS-2, 2005). A perhaps serendipitous match of college participation occurs when race is overlaid. Banks (2014) cited research by Henderson that found 72% of freshmen with disabilities in a four-year college were White compared to only 9% who were African American. Adding SLD college attendance narrows the college demographic for SWD who are also African American. Yet another salient gauge that needs to be added to this traditionally two-dimensional perspective of this college-bound population is college completion rates. Follow-up studies found that college degree completion rates for African American students with disabilities is less than half that reported for their White peers with disabilities (Newman et al., 2011a; Wagner et al., 2005).

On the other hand, and of particular interest, is that the percentage of African American SWD enrolling in college is proportionately increasing at a faster rate than their White counterparts, as the NLTS-2 (2005) also reported a 12% increase in college enrollment of African American SWD and only 10% for White SWD. This convergence of narrowing and broadening data, which encouragingly places more African American SWD in college classrooms, allows us to reiterate a concern that college professors and transition counselors become aware of unintentionally pejorative practices and biases that might undermine student success. There is a need to take steps to confront these attitudes and practices to increase the probability that African American students with SLD will successfully complete college programs. The educational system, leaders, and parents need to confront these lower expectations for students with disabilities and for students of color if they are to have an equal chance at realizing all of their potential.

Disability services in college. African American young adults with SLD who attend college and have documented disabilities have protections under the Americans with Disabilities Act and are entitled to reasonable accommodations when requested. Too often there is a mismatch between the level of support of accommodations during the high school years and what is available in the world of college and work. Accommodations must be reasonable to implement as well as must be meaningful for the youth and young adult, helping to level the playing field and reduce the impact of their disability on their performance. Herbert et al. (2014) conducted a survey of students who had received services through a college disability services office. They found that college students with disabilities indicated a desire that disability support offices provide support services in: admissions, academic counseling and support, disability-related counseling, advocacy and liaison services, and information and referral support. Although all office of disability services provided support in accordance with ADA, the degree of services varies between institutions. School counselors and IEP transition teams need to understand what each institution offers so that the IEP transition team that includes students and their families can create a unique plan matching the student's specific needs to the services offered by the college.

Documentation and disclosure. The Association on Higher Education and Disability (AHEAD) offers guidance to disability service providers and transition planning teams on documentation practices that must be followed to allow students with SLD to become eligible for disability services in the college environment. Madaus and Shaw (2006) reported that students identified a lack of access to adequate evaluation documentation of their disability upon entrance into postsecondary institutions. Using institutional reports for review, Raue and Lewis (2011) found that 44% of degree-granting postsecondary institutions in their federal review reportedly accept the IEP or the 504 plan as documentation of a disability, while 80% accept documentation from the rehabilitation services agency evaluation. Clearly, transition planning to college must also include an early identification of the documentation practices of the institutions to which the young adult with SLD is applying.

Although there are undoubtedly assessment and disability definitional barriers to the documentation process, most critical to receiving services is that students with SLD must be willing to disclose their disability and seek out the disability services offered by the college. Applicants do not document a disability on the college application process and there is no IEP in college. Although every postsecondary college and university, public and private, have disability service offices, these offices are under no obligation to seek out young adults with disabilities enrolled in the college. Raue and Lewis (2011) found that 79% of institutions reportedly disseminated materials that informed and encouraged students with disabilities to access disability support services. Most used their websites to distribute information, but only about 25% indicated that their website met accessibility guidelines.

Of significance to professors and counselors, many students with disabilities choose to not disclose their disability or request accommodations (Banks, 2014; Cawthon & Cole, 2010; Herbert et al., 2014; Newman et al., 2011a; Pelligrino et al., 2011; Walker & Test, 2011). Newman et al. (2011a) reported that when asked in follow-up surveys, 63% of all young adults who had received special education in high school claimed not to even have a disability; 69% of graduates with SLD did not consider themselves as having a disability. Only 28% of postsecondary education enrollees who were former special education students informed the college of their disability. Of those who enrolled in postsecondary education and accessed services, only 19% reported receiving accommodations whereas 87% of these students had received accommodations in high school.

A substantial percentage of college success depends on test-taking competencies. Unfortunately, if students do not report a disability they do not receive accommodations that are necessary for accuracy of testing results. Even when students report a disability, the accommodations provided may not always be of the greatest utility. Newman et al. (2011a) found in the follow-up surveys with students that testing accommodations typically included extended time; seldom were there accommodations that modified assignment requirements. Similarly, based on institutional reporting, Raue and Lewis (2011) found additional time to be a predominant accommodation, but the institutions also reported providing classroom note takers, faculty written notes or assignments, help with learning strategies, alternative exam formats, and adaptive equipment and technology. These findings predict academic difficulties for this population of college students not reporting a disability while trying to "keep up" in college classrooms.

Cawthon and Cole (2010) reported that only 32% of students with SLD in college reported any interaction with faculty about their learning disability. Of note, through a review of data on students seeking evaluations for disability documentation purposes, Pelligrino and colleagues (2011) found that African American students were significantly underrepresented in their sample of students who sought disability documentation. Although Pelligrino and colleagues do not offer a rationale for the underrepresentation of African Americans for disability documentation, other authors (Banks, 2014; Banks & Hughes, 2013) reported that African American college students with disabilities articulated concerns of being negatively stereotyped as academically incompetent, and thus chose not to seek disability services. Banks and Hughes (2013) noted as problematic the history of nondisclosure for African American SWD, citing that such actions can limit the opportunities for postsecondary disability or administrative support.

Furthermore, many students who discussed their learning disability with typical mentors (teachers, faculty, peers, and family) reported often being chastised or questioned by them. Such responses lead to even less inclination to disclose a learning disability (Banks, 2014; Banks & Hughes, 2013; Durodoye, Combs, & Bryant, 2004). Banks (2014) suggested that the "confluence of competing identities thwarted the desire to request accommodations" within the university setting (p. 32). These findings strengthen the argument that accommodations must be person-centered and proven effective; that is, the young adult needs personal proof that using one or more accommodation legitimately enables him or her to demonstrate competence. Lacking that verification, the need to belong, be safe socially, and create distance between themselves and the negative stereotypes they have often seen superimposed on their self-identity significantly outweigh the need to be academically successful.

Self-Determination: Supporting African Americans with SLD Attending College

Herbert et al. (2014) claimed that many students with disabilities enroll in college without understanding their disability, how to communicate their needs, and they lack skill in making connections between their actions and outcomes. Essentially, these reflect sub-skills of the construct of self-determination (Field & Hoffman, 2012; Trainor, et al. 2012; Walker & Test, 2011). Of note, Banks (2014) suggested that African American young adults with disabilities come to college with a myriad of understanding of disability services or self-determination skills, and are even less prepared than their White peers to access needed disability services. Though some of these skills are introduced in high school, they are tailored to that particular environment. Although there are some generalization across settings, developing personal self-determination skills is not ever a one-time event for any human. We encourage you, then, to view this process of supporting self-determination for students with SLD (including those who are African American) as iterative and environmentally laden. For teaching or counseling support purposes, we should view the development of this critical transition skill as a descant for typical adolescent and young adult development.

Knowledge of self and of the environment. By choosing not to identify themselves and register with the office of disability services, African America students with a SLD immediately place themselves at an academic disadvantage. From a self-determination perspective, this begs the question as to whether these young adults chose to change their disability identity to avoid stigma as a young adult or whether they truly did not understand the nature of their learning disability. In all likelihood, it is a combination of both concerns, as they may be able to describe their weaknesses in general terms, but without sufficient career assessment may not truly understand their individual needs and preferences. Many college-aged African American young adults with SLD claim a lack of awareness of the accommodation opportunities; they also describe being unprepared for the college environment (Banks, 2014; Banks & Hughes, 2013).

Connectedness and relationships consistently emerge as critical features for K-12 education or postsecondary education that support any student who grapples with a perceived marginalized identity (America's Promise Alliance, 2014). Transition education that bridges K-12 schools and colleges must work with African American students with SLD, their families (as appropriate), and their mentors in education to incorporate their disability identity as part of the student's individuality separate from race, gender, or socioeconomic status. Concomitantly, it is critical to create an environment that celebrates the potential for postsecondary education involvement for African American youth with SLD. Understanding one's strengths, weaknesses, preferences, or interests is paramount for self-determination.

Self-advocacy. Asking for help is not something that any person does readily. Think about the last time you, as a privileged adult reading this book, asked for help. How hard was it for you? What concerns did you have? On the other hand, too often when we need help or support, even as adults we wonder why other significant adults (friends, spouses, family, teachers, etc.) are not offering the help we need, or why we would even need to ask! This human nature paradox applies to all people, including those with disabilities. It is not terribly surprising that proud African American young adults with SLD choose to not ask for help upon entering the college environment when society views getting help as a sign of weakness. For those with ability or racial privilege, it is somewhat hypocritical to expect a different social reaction from our young, African American students with disabilities. In all honesty, when entering a new environment, we might all want a chance to re-invent ourselves and prove our worth without revealing past histories.

Nonetheless, it is critical that we teach these youth and young adults how and when to seek support in college as a preventive step to facilitate success. Walker and Test (2011) demonstrated that when taught self-advocacy skills, African American college students with SLD can both learn new skills and generalize skills to collaborate with faculty and to maximize their learning outcomes. This should start in high school. High school educators and counselors must prepare and encourage African American youth with SLD to lead their own IEP meetings. The practice of active participation promotes the development of critical self-determination skills and accumulation of experience, prior to college, in the advocacy process, and can be critical to academic success (Banks, 2014). Of even more targeted importance, cultural conversations regarding the intersection of race and disability must be negotiated openly and honestly in high school if the student is expected to engage in self-advocacy.

Jones (2011) identified literature that confirmed African American students developed individual resiliency when provided with affirming racial and disability supportive mentors or images; such resiliency can foster self-advocacy skills. Teaching students how to communicate assertively both verbally and non-verbally, yet not aggressively, supports successful outcomes of self-advocacy. Interestingly, even when made aware of support options, some African American young adults with disabilities continue to resist the help available (Banks, 2014), speaking to the complexities of these issues. To be an effective advocate for this demography, then, a piece-meal approach cannot be taken. The process must be comprehensive and iterative. As many of the pieces of this "affirmative puzzle" need to be in place for support systems to be effective in helping African American young adults with SLD discern the relationship between their career goals and the supports that can help them attain those goals.

Goal setting, planning, and taking action. This process of helping youth with disabilities to set goals, define a plan, and act on that plan results in positive change (Wehmeyer & Field, 2007). Many young adults encounter challenges related to goal setting, planning, and acting as they begin college and independent living. These typical developmental characteristics are compounded by the presence of an SLD, where there are often disability-related challenges in metacognition and problem solving. Goal setting, planning, and taking action can be taught to students with SLD as important transition skills and should be a critical curricular focus for African American youth and young adults with SLD. Likewise, supports at the college level that promote the ongoing development of these important life skills are warranted.

Adjusting based on actions. Perhaps one of the biggest life lessons for any human comes from being able to reframe long-term and short-term goals or actions based on the feedback received. For college students this may come in the form of mid-term or final grades, instructor feedback, peer response and reaction, or meeting steps toward the college course of study. Gerber, Reiff, and Ginsberg (1994) identified the act of reframing as a key action of successful adults with learning disabilities. Jones (2011) spoke to the development of resiliency and persistence as important personal characteristics to develop support for African American youth with disabilities. Grit is another term coined as critical to perseverance through difficult circumstances and, when coupled with passion, is a path to achieving long-term goals (Duckworth, Peterson, Matthews, & Kelly, 2007). Duckworth and colleagues claim that having "grit" has more influence on achievement than intellectual ability or talent alone.

So, in reality, given the environment of colleges and universities and cultural contexts, African American students with SLD probably need even more grit (determination and passion), resiliency supports (a person or place to bounce back with), and re-framing abilities (adjusting expectations based on data) than White students who may have SLD (although these are needed skills by all SWD). The quest remains on how to best coach students in developing these skills; undoubtedly this minimally requires collaboration between all parties involved in this complex process.

Next Steps

As we think of the discomfort, awkwardness, and desire to fit in that is part of the socialization process ALL students face, we need to be more intentional in our efforts for African American students with SLD who in reality face a triple threat. The question then becomes, how can we remove the institutional barriers that exist so that we can level the playing field for students struggling with these identity issues? The main issue seems to be the necessity of building a bridge between high schools and colleges for African American students with SLD. Education of, and cooperation between, high school counselors, college disability service providers, the student, and families seem to be main pillars supporting movement across this divide. As practitioners, we can start this process in-house between high school counselors and college personnel. Relationships and connectedness are expected of us also: we too should seek out the help and support of each other. It is interesting to note that most college orientations today include very comprehensive discussions of the supports nonidentified students would need to make this transition easier in whole group sessions, and also include breakout sessions for parents discussing special concerns athletes may face, international students may face, or even on joining a sorority or fraternity. Why not include as part of the whole group presentation, alongside discussions of support services for the general student population, an explicit description of services available for SWD? This can serve a dual purpose: the conversation normalizes the need for assistance while at the same time abolishing an unspoken message of unimportance within the institution's culture. Why not include breakout sessions for parents of SWD? The opportunities for networking, information sharing, and parental support groups embedded in these sessions are rich and untapped.

As K-16 education professionals, opportunity is knocking on your door asking you to help propel postsecondary education progress for African American young adults with SLD. In addition to asking the questions of how your role can aid these youth in applying for and entering postsecondary education, you need to also ask about what is needed to help these young adults complete their postsecondary education. Undoubtedly, these include academic support, peer support, mentoring support, and possibly financial support. Helping students find positive connections, social safety, and feelings of belonging in the postsecondary community creates holding power. Helping young adults in the college setting continue to hone their self-determination skills and develop social and cultural capital will create their own personal commitment to a successful future.

REFERENCES

America's Promise Alliance. (2014). *Don't call them dropouts–The experiences of young people who leave school before graduation.* Center for Promise, Tufts University.

Americans with Disabilities Act of 1990, 42 U.S.C. 12101 *et seq.*

Balcazar, F. E., Taylor-Ritzler, T., Dimpfl, S., Portillo-Pena, N., Guzman, A., Schiff, R., & Morvay, M. (2012). Improving the transition outcomes of low-income minority youth with disabilities. *Exceptionality, 20*, 114–132. doi:10.1080/09362 835.2012.670599

Banks, J. (2014). Barriers and supports to postsecondary transition: Case studies of African American students with disabilities. *Remedial and Special Education, 35*(1), 28–39. doi:10.1177/0741932513512209

Banks, J., & Hughes, M. S. (2013). Double consciousness: Postsecondary experiences of African American males with disabilities. *The Journal of Negro Education, 82*(4), 368–381. doi:10.7709/jnegroeducation.82.4.0368

Cawthon, S. W., & Cole, E. V. (2010). Postsecondary students who have a learning disability: Student perspectives on accommodations access and obstacles. *Journal of Postsecondary Education and Disability, 23*(2), 112–128.

deFur, S. H., & Korinek, L. (2008). The evolution toward lifelong learning as a critical transition outcome. *Exceptionality, 16*, 178–191. doi:10.1080/09362830802412158

Duckworth, A., Peterson, C., Matthews, M. D., & Kelly, D. R. (2007). Grit: Perseverance and passion for long-term goals. *Journal of Personality and Social Psychology, 92*(6), 1087–1101. doi:10.1037/0022–3514.92.6.1087

Dunn, C., Rabren, K. S., Taylor, S. L., & Dotson, C. K. (2012). Assisting students with high-incidence disabilities to pursue careers in science, technology, engineering, and mathematics. *Intervention in School and Clinic, 48*(1), 47–54. doi:10.1177/1053451212443151

Durodoye, B. A., Combes, B. H., & Bryant, R. M. (2004). Counselor intervention in the post-secondary planning of African American students with learning disabilities. *Professional School Counseling, 7*(3), 133–140.

Field, S. L., & Hoffman, A. S. (2012). Fostering self-determination through building productive relationships in the classroom. *Intervention in School and Clinic, 48*(1), 6–14. doi:10.1177/1053451212443150

Fry, R. (2014, October 2). Re: U.S. high school drop-out rate reaches record low, driven by improvements among Hispanics, Blacks [Electronic mailing list message]. Retrieved from http://www.pewresearch.org/fact-tank/2014/10/02/u-s-high-school-dropout-rate-reaches-record-low-driven-by-improvements-among-hispanics-blacks/

Gerber, P., Reiff, H., & Ginsberg, R. (1994). Critical incidents of highly successful adults with learning disabilities. *Journal of Vocational Rehabilitation, 4*(2), 105–112.

Herbert, J. T., Hong, B. S. S., Byun, S., Welsh, W., Kurz, C. A., & Atkinson, H. A. (2014). Persistence and graduation of college students seeking disability support services. *Journal of Rehabilitation, 80*(1), 22–32.

Individuals with Disabilities Education Improvement Act of 2004 (IDEA), 20 U.S.C. § 1401 [2004], 20 C.F.R. § 300.8[c][10].

Jones, V. L. (2011). Resiliency instructional tactics: African American students with learning disabilities. *Intervention in School and Clinic, 46*(4), 235–239. doi:10.1177/1053451210389032

Kosine, N. R. (2007). Preparing students with learning disabilities for post-secondary education: What the research literature tells us about transition programs. *Journal of Special Education Leadership, 20*, 93–104.

Lombardi, A. R., Murray, C., & Gerdes, H. (2012). Academic performance of first-generation college students with disabilities. *Journal of College Student Development, 53*(6), 811–826.

López Turley, R. N., & Wodtke, G. (2010). College residence and academic performance: Who benefits from living on campus? *Urban Education, 45*(4), 506–532. doi:10.1177/0042085910372351

Lynch, E. W., & Stein, R. (1987). Parent participation by ethnicity: A comparison of Hispanic, Black, and Anglo families. *Exceptional Children, 54*, 105–111.

Madaus, J. W., & Shaw, S. F. (2006). Disability services in postsecondary education: Impact of IDEA 2004. *Journal of Developmental Education, 30*(1), 12–21.

Mamiseishvili, K., & Koch, L. C. (2011). First-to-second-year persistence of students with disabilities in postsecondary institutions in the United States. *Rehabilitation Counseling Bulletin, 54*(2), 93–105. doi:10.1177/0034355210382580

National Center for Learning Disabilities. (2013). *Diplomas at risk: A critical look at the graduation rate of students with learning disabilities*. New York, NY: Author.

Newman, L., Wagner, M., Knokey, A. M., Marder, C., Nagle, K., Shaver, D., … Schwarting, M. (2011a). *The post-high school outcomes of young adults with disabilities up to 8 years after high school. A report from the national longitudinal transition study-2 (NLTS2)*. (NCSER 2011–3005). Menlo Park, CA: SRI International.

Newman, L., Wagner, M., Huang, T., Shaver, D., Knokey, A.-M., Yu, J., … Cameto, R. (2011b). *Secondary school programs and performance of students with disabilities. A special topic report of findings from the national longitudinal transition study-2 (NLTS2)*. (NCSER 2012–3000). U.S. Department of Education. Washington, DC: National Center for Special Education Research.

Oesterreich, H. A., & Knight, M. G. (2008). Facilitating transitions to college for students with disabilities from culturally and linguistically diverse backgrounds. *Intervention in School and Clinic, 43*(5), 300–304. doi:10.1177/1053451208314733

Pellegrino, A. M., Sermons, B. M., & Shaver, G. W. (2011). Disproportionality among postsecondary students seeking evaluation to document disabilities. *Disability Studies Quarterly, 31*(2). Retrieved from www.dsq-sds.org/article/view/1588/1556

Raue, K., & Lewis, L. (2011). *Students with disabilities at degree-granting postsecondary institutions* (NCES 2011–018). U.S. Department of Education, National Center for Education Statistics. Washington, DC: U.S. Government Printing Office.

Rehabilitation Act of 1973, Section 504 Regulations, 34 C.F.R. §104.1 *et seq*.

Schwartz, R. A., & Washington, C. M. (2002). Predicting academic performance and retention among African American freshmen men. *NASPA Journal, 39*(4), 354–370.

Trainor, A. A. (2005). Self-determination perceptions and behaviors of diverse students with LD during the transition planning process. *Journal of Learning Disabilities, 38*, 233–249. doi:10.1177/00222194050380030501

Trainor, A. A., Smith, S. A., & Kim, S. (2012). Four supportive pillars in career exploration and development for adolescents with LD and EBD. Intervention in School and Clinic, 48(1), 15–21. doi:10.1177/1053451212443129

U.S. Department of Education, Office of Special Education Programs. (2013). *35th annual report to congress on the implementation of the individuals with disabilities education act, 2013*. Retrieved from http://www.ed.gov/about/reports/annual/osep.

Wagner, M., Newman, L., Cameto, R., & Levine, P. (2005). *Changes over time in the early postschool outcomes of youth with disabilities. A report of findings from the national longitudinal transition study (NLTS) and the national longitudinal transition study-2 (NLTS2)*. Retrieved from http://files.eric.ed.gov/fulltext/ED494920.pdf

Walker, A. R., & Test, D. W. (2011). Using a self-advocacy intervention on African American college students' ability to request academic accommodations. *Learning Disabilities Research & Practice, 26*(3), 134–144. doi:10.1111/j.1540-5826.2011.00333.x

Wallace, M. (2013). High school teachers and African American parents: A (not so) collaborative effort to increase student success. *The High School Journal, 96*(3), 195–208. doi:10.1353/hsj.2013.0008

Wehmeyer, M. L., & Field. S. L. (2007). *Self-determination: Instructional and assessment strategies*. Thousand Oaks, CA: Corwin Press.

Chapter 8

African Americans Students and Financial Literacy

M. Ann Shillingford, Brian Kooyman, and S. Kent Butler

Writing this chapter on financial literacy of African Americans reminds me (first author) of a conversation that I once had with an elementary school student about his plans for his newly acquired birthday money. Julian, an African American 4th grader, explained that he planned on going to GameStop to purchase the newest Wii games. When I asked whether he would save any of his money he exclaimed that he did not have enough to save if he was to buy the games that he needed. From there I led him into a conversation about wants and needs and the necessity of saving for the future. Although I did not win that battle, my hope was that I made an impression on him about securing his financial future. So as with the case of Julian, this chapter is about preparing African American students for real-world financial experiences.

Whether you are an African American college student, a school counselor assisting students with career preparedness or a college administrator developing policies to support the success of African American students, our hope is that you understand the financial preparedness of African American peoples especially as they compare to the majority population. Along with that understanding, a purposeful willingness to help make long-term systemic changes that will potentially fill the unfortunate gaps in financial literacy for this population.

In 2014, Prudential Financial reported results of their *African American Financial Experience* survey proffering encouraging statistics on the financial statuses of African Americans. The researchers described increased levels of financial confidence and affluence among African Americans with top priorities including reducing debt, saving for retirement, and securing funds for future emergencies. Even so, significant monetary obstacles were noted that still impacted the long-term success of this population. However, before illuminating these hurdles, it is essential to highlight a few of the positive aspects stemming from the Prudential Financial report. For instance, nearly half of the African Americans surveyed shared that financially they were better situated than they were five years ago, indicating a rising generational trend. Even more encouraging, 30% of the African Americans surveyed (as compared to 21% of the general population) reported optimism about making pertinent financial decisions. Other factors that appear to influence African Americans financial confidence included household income, healthcare costs, reducing debt, and planning for their dependents' financial future. Based on these findings, African Americans are more assured about certain aspects of their finances; however, it is important to recognize that debilitating obstacles still exist. African American median household savings register around $40,000, which often is inclusive of retirement accounts. Sadly, this figure is at least $57,000 lower than the financial security accumulated by the general population at $97, 000. Postsecondary education costs find many African American college students twice as likely to consume student loan liability then their educated counterparts. In fact, African American students are more likely to have student loan, credit card, and other personal debt obligations. From these statistics one might deduce that although improvements have been made in terms of the financial buoyancy of African Americans, a significant gap in orientation of future financial success remains for this population.

THE DEBT CRISIS

The only man who sticks closer to you in adversity than a friend is a creditor.

—*Author Unknown*

Debt is not isolated to the African American population. Curry and Milsom (2013) noted that Americans are in chronic debt, much of which was exacerbated by the economic crisis formed by the housing bubble burst in 2008. Debt amassed by the general U.S. populations to over 800,000 foreclosed homes in the United States (Veiga, 2012), over $1.5 million bankruptcy cases (Dugas, 2010), and an average household credit card of $6,500. Although the recent financial crisis may be to blame for an overwhelming amount of this debt, caution abounds as to what extent the U.S. populace as a whole is capable of planning for their economic future. In essence, with planning and the necessary financial literacy skills, much of the crisis for many individuals and families might be avoidable.

Although debt is not isolated to African Americans, special consideration of African American population(s) can provide tailored interventions geared toward improving a person's knowledge of financial management. Financial literacy can be described as an efficacy related to financial management, including the competencies of savings, retirement funding, mortgages, investments, and college funds (Williams, Grizzell, Burrell, & Still, 2011). Financial literacy and general efficacy are closely tied to the problem of debt accrual within the African American population. Efficacy, an individual's personal sense of competency, is an issue that differentiates the African American population, as African Americans tend to demonstrate lower efficacy when compared to other populations (Oyserman, Ager, & Gant, 1995). Family is demonstrated to play a large role in financial literacy and efficacy transmission, acting as a backdrop for all future financial behaviors (Williams et al., 2011). The aforementioned is of particular significance to the African American identity. African Americans report maintaining identities that favor a community life, strong ties to family, and support from other members of the community that may be seen as family (Oyserman et. al., 1995). Connectedness is a value within the African American population, one that seemingly is transmitted from one generation to the next. The central role of the family within the African American identity demonstrates its potency within an African American individual's life. The family acts as a major conduit for efficacy development for the African American individual, playing a central role in the development of aspirations and skills adopted by the population (Oyserman et. al., 1995).

With the family playing an important role within the identity development of the African American population, the focus shifts to the family to understand what knowledge and skill deficits are leading to African American debt accrual. Efficacy and financial literacy play a large role in debt management behaviors. This lack of efficacy and knowledge surrounding finances can ultimately lead to a diminished capacity for managing debt, potentially resulting in harmful financial circumstances (Williams's et. al., 2011). Of note is the condition of overwhelming debt, which happens to be a critical concern for the African American population. For example, instances of foreclosure during the period 2005–2009 were higher African Americans compared to all other populations (Williams et. al., 2011). African Americans also carry significantly higher student loan debt when compared to Whites, with 25 percent of African American college students carrying student loan debt, compared to 20 percent of whites (Jackson, Reynolds, 2013). Along with higher rates of student loan debt, African Americans maintain higher rates of loan default when compared to Whites (Jackson, et. al., 2013). Loan default can diminish the attainment of goals for African Americans. Fair Isaac Corporation (FICO) credit scores are lowered as the result of default, along with possible wage garnishment and withheld tax refunds (Jackson et al., 2013). Unfortunately, loan default is not an unlikely scenario for African Americans. When compared to Whites, African Americans have fewer resources to manage their finances, leading to a greater likelihood for default when faced with a financial crisis (Jackson et. al., 2013).

Debt accrual and the mismanagement of that debt is likely indicative of a lack of financial efficacy and literacy. The family is central in the transmission of information related to financial management. With money mismanagement demonstrated to be a pervasive problem for African Americans, it becomes clear that the family unit is failing to provide necessary financial skills. The deficit of financial knowledge transmission within the African American population may be tied to African American identity, which may find the normative Eurocentric values of independence, success, and achievement of finances and income difficult to attain (Oyserman, 1995). Racism likely plays a role in the failure to adopt normative values, as the African American population may feel they are not able to achieve the successes enjoyed by Whites. The experience of being ostracized from the normative population in terms of financial capital likely results in a lack of participation in financial skills training, or the potential devaluing of knowledge related to financial management. For example, saving for college, saving for retirement, and developing an investment portfolio all necessitate that a family has enough money to pay their necessary expenses first (i.e., housing, food, transportation, clothing, medical care). Historically, many African Americans have been in labor force jobs where they have been underpaid and have not had the opportunity to save money and develop the previously mentioned skill sets. Thus, teaching these skills intergenerationally was also not possible.

The perception of being ostracized may also influence career decision making for African Americans. African Americans are less likely to complete college when compared to Whites, requiring significant financial loans. College completion for African Americans highly correlates to the amount of loans African Americans accrue (Jackson et. al., 2013). Even with loans, African Americans still maintain a higher level of drop out when compared to their White counterparts, dropping out of college with massive student loans. The channels that are meant to benefit the attainment possibilities for the African American population are riddled with challenges that may not exist for other populations. With the African American identity potentially failing to transmit important financial skills, along with perceptions of imminent failure, efficacy development programs for the African American population need to be tailored. The uniqueness of the population demands creative thinking and resourcing as a means of improving financial literacy and efficacy within the population. Fortunately, resources do exist that can benefit African Americans and can be uniquely applied to meet the needs of the population.

COLLEGE: CONQUERING THE FINANCIAL HURTLES

In building the foundation for financial literacy and efficacy of African American students, it is important to begin the education process at an early age. By 10th grade, it is critical that students have a working knowledge of financial support services available for college success. Considering the historical patterns of money mismanagement as a family unit, African American high school students in particular should be enlightened about college financial opportunities. In fact, there are several financial prospects available: grants and scholarships, work-study programs, and student loans. Students need to know that financial supports may come in several different forms (a) U.S. federal government, (b) state government, (c) prospective colleges, and/or (d) nonprofit or private organizations (Federal Student Aid, 2014).

Grants

There are multiple grant opportunities that are available. One, example the Pell grant, is based on a federally funded program specifically developed to support low-income undergraduate and certain postbaccalaureate students. The U.S. Department of Education (2014) specifies that qualification for the Pell grant is based on criterion such as "the student's expected family contribution (EFC); the cost of attendance (as determined by the institution); the student's enrollment status (full-time or part-time); and whether the student attends for a full academic year or less (para 2)."

African American and Hispanic students who have received the Pell grant (up to $5500 per year) have shown significant academic success including higher grade point averages and degree completion compared to their peers not receiving the Pell grant. Dervarics (2012) noted that the Pell grant has been instrumental in supporting African American students' pursuit of degrees in STEM programs. Considering the occupational and financial implications from completing a STEM program (see Chapter 4), the positive connection between Pell grant attainment and STEM enrollment is encouraging. Dervarics also indicated that regardless of the prominence of the Pell grant in influencing academic success in higher education, many low-income students do not take advantage of this program. School counselors have a significant role to play when it comes to increasing student awareness of the Pell grant and similarly functioning programs.

The Teacher Education Assistance for College and Higher Education (TEACH) grant is available to students focused on pursuing careers as educators. According to the Office of Federal Student Aid (FSA; 2014), this grant promises up to $4000 a year to students who qualify and agree to serve:

1. At an elementary or secondary school that serves low-income families
2. For at least four complete academic years within eight years after completing the course of study for which they received the grant.
3. In a high needs fields (bilingual education, foreign language, mathematics, reading specialist, science, and special education).

Any student interested in a TEACH grant should approach the college of choice to find out if that institution is a TEACH partner.

Scholarships

According to the FSA and the U.S. Department of Education, there are thousands of scholarships available to students. Students may qualify for scholarships based on academic performance, athletic ability, and many other factors. Other scholarships are merit based which means that they are restricted to students who meet and exceed particular standards set by the organization giving the scholarship. There are also scholarships based on family involvement with the military. The Reserve Officer's Training Corps (ROTC) scholarships are awarded based on merit rather than financial need (FSA, 2014). There are Army ROTC scholarships and AIR Force ROTC scholarships available, which may be of particular interest to students pursuing foreign language and technical degrees. The Navy also offers two-or four-year ROTC scholarships options with the opportunity to join the Navy, Marines, or Navy Nursing Corp. Finally, the Marine Officer NROTC scholarship program which actually pays for the entire college experience with the option for added scholarship monies if students choose to attend a Historically Black College or University (HBCU). African American students may also explore scholarship options from organizations such as the Anheuser-Busch Legions or the Crown Scholarship program which offers up to $5000; the Marcia Silverman Minority Student award ($5000); Development Fund for Black Students in Science and technology ($2000); Minority Scholarship Award for Incoming College Freshmen ($1000), and many, many more promising educational opportunities.

Work-Study Programs

The U.S. Department of Education (2014) work-study programs provide *"funds for part-time employment to help needy students to finance the costs of postsecondary education"* (para. 1). The FSA (2014) provides an overview of the program:

1. It provides part-time employment for students enrolled in school.

2. It's available to undergraduate, graduate, and professional students with financial need.
3. It's available to full-time or part-time students.
4. It's administered by schools participating in the Federal Work-Study Program.

Jobs may be either on campus or at private not for profit organizations. The FSA highlighted that the jobs should be relevant to students' course of study.

Loans

Students are able to choose between two federal loan options, the William D. Ford Federal Direct Loan (Direct Loan) program and the Federal Perkins Loan Program.

Federal Perkins Loan. The Federal Perkins Loan is made to undergraduate and graduate students based on extreme financial need at an interest rate of 5%. Unlike other loans which will be discussed shortly, the college or university is the lender of the loan not the federal government. The FSA (2014) explained that not all colleges participate in the Perkins Loan Program and so students with plans to attend certain colleges and are in financial need should discover before applying about the availability of the program.

William D. Ford Federal Direct Loan (Direct Loan) Program. The William D. Ford Federal Direct Loan (Direct Loan) Program otherwise referred as the Direct Loan program is available in four different categories: (1) direct subsidized loans, (2) direct unsubsidized loans, (3) direct PLUS loans, and (4) direct consolidation loans. The direct subsidized loans are based on students' financial need and are available to eligible undergraduate students to defray the cost of higher education. African American students who can show financial need may be eligible for these direct loans. However, students should be informed of the stipulations involved such as the school (college) will determine the amount student may borrow; the U.S. Department of Education will cover the interest on the Direct loan while the student is (a) attending college at least part time; (b) for the first six months after leaving college; and (c) during a period of postponement of the loan payments, often called a period of deferment.

Unlike the direct subsidized loans, the unsubsidized loans are also available to graduate students even if the student does not have financial need.

So, African American students who may not necessarily have financial need could potentially qualify for this Direct Unsubsidized Loan. Students applying for this unsubsidized loan should pay close attention to the specifics of this loan program as unlike the subsidized loan, those receiving the Direct Unsubsidized loan are expected to pay the interest on the loans during the borrowing period (FSA, 2014). FSA states that unpaid interest will be accrued and added to the principal on the loan.

Direct PLUS loans are available to graduate students who are enrolled at least part-time in a degree-seeking program or the parent of an undergraduate student in similar education program. Students and parents who qualify for the Direct PLUS loans are those with favorable credit history and receive loans that will cover the maximum amount of the student's attendance expenses (minus other financial aid supports). For families or parents with unfavorable credit history, a third party with favorable credit may be utilized in the application process (FSA, 2014). Bottom line, African American students with acceptable credit as well as families with good credit history may be eligible for this loan program.

Lastly, the Direct Consolidation Loan allows students to consolidate, that is, combine all of their loans. The advantage to this approach is indeed that the student will only have one loan for which they are responsible for paying back over a particular length of time. However, although this loan option may seem to lessen the students' financial responsibilities, there are also disadvantages such as having larger principal and potentially higher interest rates, potentially losing out on loan cancellation opportunities for certain loans, and losing discounted interest rate options offered by particular lenders. African American students interested in this loan option should weigh the pros and cons before following this pathway.

Navigating with Support

Several opportunities for financial aid have been highlighted including grants, scholarship, work-study programs, and various loans. These financial opportunities all come with advantages and disadvantages and may be confusing for students and families to navigate which options may be most appropriate. Additionally, African American students, such as those whom are First-Generation, may not have the family support or knowledge base to traverse through the complexities of the financial aid system. School counselors and college counselors should take an active role in providing African American students and their families with the information that they need to make more informed decisions about their academic pursuits and its overall impact on their financial and academic future.

MANAGING FINANCES: THE ULTIMATE PLAN

In the following section, we propose strategies that school counselors and college counselors may operationalize in preparing African American students financially for college life. Bearing in mind the importance of family engagement in the decision-making process of African Americans, it would be most advantageous for school and college professionals to include or at best introduce families to the following strategies.

Additional Financial Strategies

Below are a few additional strategies that we believe will be beneficial to African American students and their families in promoting financial literacy.

1. Begin the financial training early. Students as young as elementary age should be taught to understand the importance of planning for the future. Classroom guidance lessons in primary and secondary schools may be helpful. Financial workshops for high school students and their parents are strongly recommended. If a school counselor is not prepared to give financial advice, these authors encourage partnering with a local credit union to provide a guest speaker who can demonstrate what a family budget is, how to have a weekly family budget meeting, how to determine how much to save for college, and the different types of accounts available.
2. Explore career and higher education options. As discussed earlier, not all colleges and universities participate in certain financial aid programs. Therefore, it would be beneficial to determine whether the potential college's financial program meets the student's needs.
3. Determine financial need. This could be accomplished by introducing students and families to the Free Application for Federal Student Aid (FAFSA) process. This may often be a daunting task for students therefore, intentional time set aside for this process over the course of the high school experience may be necessary.
4. Apply to college. This process will include the student having some idea of a career path and having explored colleges where the intended program of study is taught. The student is also aware of their financial need and has identified a college that participates in a financial aid program for which they are qualified.
5. Determine and apply for financial aid. Student and families should be supported in identifying suitable grants, scholarships, and/or loans based on their financial needs. It will be extremely important to educate students and families on the expectations for certain loans including interests,

principal, repayment options, and consequences for divergence from these long-term expectations.
6. Create a Budget. The following section provides a comprehensive approach to assisting African American students in developing a budget for college.

Creating a Budget

A most significant factor in supporting African American students in college financial success is assisting them in creating and understanding a budget. At the high school level, school counselors can develop and implement workshops for students and their families on budgeting; local credit union professionals can play an integral part of this process by sharing with students how economic bartering works. For example, a local credit union could discuss with students what it is like to deposit money and then accrue interest over time; what it means to withdraw money and the consequences (fees) associated with this action. This professional can also lead students in discussion and demonstration of applying for a loan and what that entails. Additionally, school counselors can develop summer orientation programs whereby college counselors and current college students can share the processes and expectations of college life and what it means to be on your own financially. Envision African American high school students who may be excited about attending college based on the experiences of others within their community. However, there are often gaps in these exciting stories about the autonomous nature of higher education(e.g., frat parties) and the expectations of being responsible adults (e.g., paying your bills). Summer orientation programs that provide students with the realities of the day-to-day world of college life may be most advantageous to students developing awareness of the comprehensive nature of college including financial responsibility.

Another avenue of support that can and should be provided to African American students is training sessions specifically on developing a budget for college. According to Lending Tree, one of the biggest financial downfalls for college students is getting into the habit of unnecessary spending particularly on items such as drinks and food. Another pitfall noted is credit card debt. The idea of purchasing items and paying later may sound extremely exciting but the reality, often unrealized by these students, is that there are credit card fees involved that may significantly impact their future credit history. There are several websites online that provides guidelines for developing a budget. In the next section, we will explore steps that can be taken in training African American students in understanding and developing effective budgets.

Step One: Duration of the budget. How much time will the budget address? Students should be assisted in developing a financial budget, which could potentially cover a month, semester, or entire academic year. We suggest examining the student's level of maturity and experience with financial responsibility in order to determine the best course for the initial budget. For instance a freshman who has never had a job may need to work with a short-term budget (month) that may be more manageable. Once duration has been determined, the next step should be reviewing the student's income.

Step Two: Total income. How much money does the student have with which to work? Will the student be receiving financial aid? If financial aid will be secured, how frequently will it be received by the student? Will that money be deposited in a lump sum or will proportional deposits be made to the student? Will parents be assisting with financial support? If so, how much will the parents contribute and how frequent. If the student is working or plans on securing a job during college, how much money could they potentially earn and how frequent will payments be made to the student? These questions are extremely important in understanding when monies will be available to the student so that expenses can be addressed in a timely manner. Consider the following illustration:

> James has just graduated from high school and has been working at the nearby amusement park for the past two years. He plans to continue working while attending college. At his job, he makes $800 per month after taxes. He has been able to save $750 over the past two years. Additionally, he received $200 as graduation presents. His family has already promised to deposit $150 per month into his bank account. So far, per month, James has a total income of $1900. He recently found out that he has been approved for the Pell grant from which he will receive $5500 for the academic year ($5500/10 months = $550 per month). James can now safely say that his total income will be approximately $2450.00 per month ($550 + 1900). A counselor working with James on developing his budget for his first semester (approximately 4 months) would multiply his monthly income by four to determine a total income for the Fall semester of $9,800 ($2450 X 4). James now has an idea of how much money he will have available for that first semester.

Step Three: Calculate expenses. So we now have an idea as to how much money the student could potentially be securing to cover financial expenses. Next are the expenses. What will the students expenditures entail per semester? Per academic year? The student's budget should include all expenses such as utilities, car maintenance, gas, food, insurance, laundry and toiletries, entertainment, rent, books, cell phone, and all other fixed and variable expenses. Students should be taught to weigh these expenses versus their income to determine what items are truly necessary and if they are going to be financially able to maintain all expenditures. The following table provides an indication of possible expenses for a college student.

Table 8.1 Possible Expenses for College Student

Fixed Expenses: Minor changes in amount with specific due dates	Variable Expenses
Tuition and related fees	Clothing
Student Insurance	Food (eating out and dining in, groceries)
Car payment (if applicable)	Car maintenance
Room and Board (on-campus residents)	Recreation (movies, parties, sporting events)
Cable bill	Personal expenses (hair, nails, laundry)
Cell phone bill	Health care (medications)
Textbooks	Club fees (gym membership)
Parking fees	

Step Four: Prioritize expenses. After reviewing the student's income and expenses for the semester, does the student have enough money secured to cover all expenses? What might be some expenses that may need to be eliminated? Counselors can certainly assist students in identifying items on the budget that either needs to be removed or modified. For example, reviewing cell phone bills and maybe switching to a more reasonably priced carrier or plan; buying groceries instead of dining out; using student gym membership at the college which may be free to students instead of a private gym. This process of prioritizing should be completed in the hopes of educating students on financial responsibility and creating a path for long-term financial wellness.

FINANCIAL READINESS

Financial solvency, the ability to pay off debts and have cash to pay for future needs, is a goal every person should strive to uphold. African Americans, in order to move ahead and maintain their financial future, need to do it from a position of power. The control comes with full knowledge and understanding of how finances work. Measures are needed like the ones suggested here to enlighten and empower the African American community on all things financial.

Having a firm grasp on one's finances will only help to define and secure their financial future. School counselors, advisors, college counselors, and financial aid staff are in a great position to begin this education process. Community forums and guidance lessons could do wonders in ensuring that African Americans are well versed in how to navigate their best interests from financial literacy to financial freedom. The challenge lies in the giving and accepting of pertinent information that serves to support a change in philosophy that lends to an equitable opportunity for financial solvency.

REFERENCES

Prudential Research. (2014). The African American Financial Experience. Retrieved from http://www.prudential.com/media/managed/aa/AAStudy.pdf

Curry, J., & Milsom, A. (2013). *A Practical Approach to K-12 Career Guidance and Counseling in Schools: Developmental and Contextual Considerations.* New York: Springer.

Dervarics, C. (2012). Study: Pell grant makes difference for students of color. *Diverse Issues in Higher Education.* Retrieved from http://diverseeducation.com/article/16865/

Dugas, C. (2010). More consumers file for bankruptcy protection. Retrieved from http://usatoday30.usatoday.com/money/economy/2010-03-03-bankruptcy03_ST_N.htm

Federal Student Aid. (2014). Types of aid. Retrieved from https://studentaid.ed.gov/types

Jackson, B. A., & Reynolds, J. R. (2013). *The price of opportunity: race, student loan debt, and college achievement.* Sociological Inquiry, 83, 335–368, doi:10/1111/soin.12012

Oyserman, D., Ager, J., & Gant, L. (1995). A socially contextualized model of African American identity: possible selves and school persistence. *Journal of Personality and Social Psychology, 69,* 1216–1232.

U.S. Department of Education. (2014). Federal Pell Grant program. Retrieved from http://www2.ed.gov/programs/fpg/index.html

U.S. Department of Education. (2014). Federal Work-Study (FWS) Programs. Retrieved from http://www2.ed.gov/programs/fws/index.html

Veiga, A. (2012). Foreclosure activity January 2012: foreclosure rates edged up indicating rut may be over. Retrieved from http://www.huffingtonpost.com/2012/02/16/foreclosure-activity-january-2012_n_1281381.html

Williams, D., Grizzell, B., Burrell, D. N., Still, A. T. (2011). An applied case study analysis of potential societal importance of financial literacy education for African–American and Latino American adolescents. *The International Journal of Interdisciplinary Social Sciences, 6,* 245–260.

Chapter 9

Employability Skills and Career Development

Ashley Churbock and Lauren Treacy

Work is a major and vital part of life that allows for both monetary gains and personal fulfillment. Work can provide individuals with a sense of purpose and happiness and might lead to greater life satisfaction. According to Kuchinke (2013), work might also allow for a wide range of human experiences that can vary greatly and have either a positive or negative impact on individuals. Furthermore, work allows for personal growth and development and may provide individuals with a sense of self and purpose. Due to the importance of work, not only for the individual but also for the global economy, it is crucial that contemporary workers have adequate training, skills, and knowledge to ensure that they are prepared to meet the demands of the current workforce.

There is a growing emphasis on improving employability skills and career development for high school students entering postsecondary education and training. Adequate training in these areas can boost competitiveness in local and global markets and increase overall productivity. In addition, targeting skill needs and shortages, especially among the African American population has become more important in recent years. Krahn, Lowe, and Lehmann (2002) explained that a significant deficiency in employability skills by those entering the workforce are due to insufficient training in high school and a lack of awareness of the skills needed to be successful in today's workforce.

Skill deficits and insufficient training is especially observed with African American students who are often exposed to learning environments that provide less opportunities, funding, and resources for students. In 1977, Bourdieu first introduced the idea of cultural capital, which explains how minority groups' attitudes based on barriers to access to social capital, may help or hinder their acceptance into higher social, organizational, or institutional groups (Carter, 2003). Carter contended that schools assist in replicating a class hierarchy through favoring and reinforcing White cultural capital. Evidence for this concept may be found in the statistics surrounding higher African American dropout rates and lower academic achievement than their White counterparts (Davis, Ajzen, Saunders, & Williams, 2002). Furthermore, this factor may play a large role in the employment disparity between Whites and African Americans. Currently, the unemployment rate for Whites is 4.6 percent compared to 10.9 percent for African Americans (Bureau of Labor Statistics, 2014). Lack of preparedness among African American students, coupled with increased pressure to stay ahead in the global marketplace, is evidence that significant improvements in education, training, and skill building are critical to meet current societal demands.

WORKFORCE TRENDS

Kuchinke (2013) noted that

> in the context of the rapidly evolving and postmodern movement, education is viewed as one of the most important forces in civil society to advance democratic ideals, foster civic engagement, and promote opportunities for individuals, societies, and ultimately the global community (p. 203).

In order for continued workforce growth and competitiveness, a variety of educational opportunities must be available to guarantee divergent and extensive training to meet the workforce needs of society. Furthermore, vocational education provides an opportunity for individuals to gain invaluable experience while improving employability and applicable workforce knowledge (Gray & Herr, 1998).

History of Career and Technical Education

Career and Technical Education, or CTE, has shown a continuous evolution that has produced noteworthy outcomes for overall human growth and productivity. CTE can be traced as far back as the Stone Age where fire building, weapon sculpting, and hunting were skills necessary for maintaining and survival purposes. Egyptians developed hieroglyphics, a form of picture writing, which paved the way for two types of schools: (1) schools that solely focused on reading and writing, and (2) skill-based apprenticeships with a skilled scribe (Wang & King, 2009). This division of schools depicts an earlier form of CTE and the recognition that skill acquisition was important in fostering societal growth. Other societies, such as the Ancient Jewish culture, also recognized the necessity for all individuals to be trained with a skill and emphasized the importance of education to contribute to society in a meaningful and productive way (Wang & King, 2009). According to Roberts (as cited in Wang & King, 2009), Greeks and Romans supported the idea of experiential learning.

In the nineteenth century, private trade schools became popular as schools specialized in one of three areas: (1) trade training, (2) trade training and general education, and (3) schools with apprenticeships that offered trade and general education (Gordon, 2014). In addition to trade schools, vocational preparatory programs within private business schools were created to bolster the increasingly successful business world (Gordon, 2014). Under the public sector, manual training, commercial training, domestic science, and agriculture programs were a major development of this time. According to Gordon (2014), these programs merged into one and created vocational education, which supported the idea of intentional goal setting and skill building.

In more recent times, CTE was considered to be a response to social problems caused by industrialization following the Civil War. According to Cohen and Besharov (2002), some educators began to back and support skill-based education as an exclusive form of education for the newly freed African-American population in the South. This particular education was designed to provide African Americans with an educational opportunity and was viewed within the context that African Americans were second-class citizens. The reason CTE was seen as a second-class option, particularly under the Tuskegee Institute model of education, is that academics were not a primary focus of training, hard labor was.

Subsequent gains in CTE as a viable training option for all students developed significantly under Major Dennis Mobley, secretary of the Association for Career and Technical Education (ACTE), who served a fifteen-year term. In 1962, he promoted the concept that vocational education should be for everyone (Gordon, 2014). Mobley's principles were founded on the core values that had emerged in the vocational education movement:

> These principles focused on society's obligation to youth and adults to provide for their occupational well-being as a part of their total education; a recognition of the changing nature of the nation's workforce; a commitment to continued professionalization of vocation education; and a belief that the greatest asset of America was not its tremendous wealth but its ability to use effectively the enormous resources of its people (as cited in Gordon, 2014, p. 49).

In addition, Mobley's philosophy guided his work in the field. His philosophy consisted of 5 major points: (1) Career and Technical Education must be a part of the overall education program; (2) Career and Technical Education must be available to all races/ethnicities, genders, and regardless of one's socioeconomic status; (3) Career and Technical Education must be a concern to all; (4) professionalization and professional organizations of Career and Technical Education must continue; and (5) youth groups and organizations must be considered a vital part of the career and education program (Gordon, 2004). Mobley's philosophy, values, and mission continue to guide and transform CTE and serves as a strong foundation for current educators, law makers, and stakeholders.

Mobley's contributions opened the doors for even more growth and change to CTE. Academic deficits in U.S. schools led to a multitude of legislative changes to education practices and policies. *A Nation at Risk* (1984) was published by the Commission on Education Excellence and demanded more rigorous academic standards in elementary and secondary schools and raised graduation standards across the nation (Cohen & Besharov, 2002). Incidentally, this decreased CTE enrollment for the next twenty years as President Clinton pushed for higher enrollment in college and universities.

The U.S. Department of Education released a report on the National Assessment of Vocational Education (NAVE) in 1994. Specifically, this report noted grave concern for the state of CTE because it was predominately utilized by those who were economically disadvantaged or disabled (Cohen & Besharov, 2002). The writers also expressed concerns about the quality of vocational education, citing deficits in teacher education and training, lack of academic rigor and a lack of adequate requirements for program completion (Cohen & Besharov, 2002). The report stressed a more broad approach to Career and Technical Education in order to prepare students for furthering their postsecondary education at two or four-year institutions. Advocates of CTE were outraged by the U.S. Department of Education's report and pushed for more rigorous training and academic standards. These concerns were echoed in the Perkins Acts of 1990 and 1998, which emphasized program improvement, standards, and academics (Cohen & Besharov, 2002). Furthermore, the American Vocational Association changed its name to the Association for Career and Technical Education to defuse the stigma of vocational training, which was rooted in providing educational opportunities to African Americans after the Civil War.

In 1994, Congress passed the School to Work Opportunities Act in support of Career and Technical Educational advancements. The purpose of this legislation was to focus on students who were choosing not to attend college upon graduation from high school by promoting postsecondary transitions to technical training or the workforce. According to Cohen and Besharov (2002), the U.S. Congress became interested in the European apprenticeship system and sought to model such practices in the United States. This led to an increase in government funds for schools to provide instruction around career majors, vocational and work-based instruction, and matching students with real-world work experience.

Although the School to Work Opportunities Act focused on noncollege bound students, it was also used by federal education administration to stress the importance that CTE be available for all students regardless of their postgraduation plan. This dual focus resulted in diffusion and a lack of clarity about the intended learning outcomes associated with such programs, resulting in local entities offering more general CTE programming than specific and tailored opportunities that may have better served the noncollege bound students (Cohen & Besharov, 2002). Cohen and Besharov noted "this created a whole new system rather than strengthening CTE—and then by emphasizing services for the broad student population, rather than those who are not college-bound—Congress and the nation's schools missed an opportunity to help noncollege youth find their place in a changing economy" (p. 17).

CTE has continuously evolved and supported the growth of humanity throughout centuries and was created through trial and error and extensive changes. As discussed, workforce trends are influenced by demographic trends, technological advancements, and economic globalization. These factors are constantly influencing the workforce that will continue to shape work and training in the United States (Karoly et al., 2004). According to Wang and King (2009) these changes are giving way to more self-directed and lifelong learners who must be prepared for rapid and fluctuating changes to meet current demands and expectations of workers. Therefore, policy makers and educators must consider current developments and modify programming and curricula to fit the needs of today's workforce demands and learn from the prior mistakes and missed opportunities that have been destructive to CTE in the past to ensure future success.

REDEFINING CAREER AND TECHNICAL EDUCATION IN THE TWENTY-FIRST CENTURY

In 1990, the federal government defined Career and Technical Education as preparation for those occupations that did not require baccalaureate or advanced degrees. According to Gordon (2014), although the legal definition has not changed since 1990, the Career and Technical Education field has changed dramatically; in particular,

> Thousands of high schools and community colleges have developed new courses of study that prepare students for work as well as for further education, including four-year college or university. Tech Prep, career academies, industry majors, youth apprenticeships, and other innovations have demonstrated the possibility of combining preparation for both college and careers (p. 22).

These improvements to the field have promoted funding and credibility for CTE. As funding continues to grow in support of such training, it may also encourage state and federal legislation to adopt a new definition, as well as guide state and local practice (Gordon, 2014).

When thinking about the progression of CTE, it is important that educators become more collaborative. Gordon (2014) notes that changes to the statutory definition of career and technical education should enhance collaboration among all educators, vocational and nonvocational, to better prepare students for both work and for further education. In a National Educational Longitudinal Study, it was found that of the 63 percent of students who enroll in college only about half of those students graduate with a college degree (Cohen & Besharov, 2002). These statistics demonstrate that a large portion of graduating high school students are underprepared and are in need of remedial, corrective, or additional education before entering a college or university setting. Thus, it would be suspected that Career and Technical Education would be an important step in helping some students in preparing for work or as a stepping stone to furthering their postsecondary education.

In 2010, considerable stakeholders gathered to discuss the revitalization of the Career and Technical Education field to ensure the highest quality preparation and training for the future workforce, as well as to remain viable in the global market (Gordon, 2014). Gordon also mentioned the National Association of State Directors of Career Technical Education Consortium (NASDCTEC) which emphasizes the importance of valuing individualized talents, learning styles, and innovation that can be found within Career and Technical Education. NASDCTEC established the following core principles to guide their values and mission surrounding CTE: (1) CTE is critical to ensuring that the United States leads in global competitiveness; (2) CTE is delivered through comprehensive programs of study aligned to the National Career Clusters framework; (3) CTE prepares students to succeed in furthering their education and careers; (4) CTE actively partners with employers to design and provide high-quality, dynamic programs (e. g., selected internship programs for students, externships for teachers/faculty, and apprenticeships including registered apprenticeships); (5) CTE is a results-driven system that demonstrates a positive return on investments. Along with these five principles, NASDCTEC emphasizes that working collaboratively to stay abreast of changes to the workforce and adapting programs to fit the needs of the market is a consistent objective (Folkers, 2011 as cited in Gordon, 2014).

The Importance of Career and Technical Education

With the evolution of CTE over the years, high school students are consistently being lectured on the importance of going to college, particularly four-year institutions, upon graduation. Typically the fastest growing occupations are those that require a college degree, although, the careers with high vacancy rates often do not need postsecondary training (Cohen & Besharov, 2002). A further look into these discrepancies often reveal a significant amount of jobs unfilled due to a lack of trained and skilled workers. According to Carnevale, Smith, Gulish, and Beach (2012), health-care jobs are expected to increase by 30% by 2020. Additionally, health-care and health-care support occupations are estimated to experience 5.6 million health-care job vacancies between 2010 and 2020 (Carnevale et al, 2012). These occupations may require some technical training or employability skills, but do not necessarily require four-year college degrees.

An increase in college graduates who are returning to school to enter associate's degree programs, certificate programs, and community colleges has been a growing trend as graduates recognize the trends in workforce needs (Cohen & Besharov, 2002). Consequently, jobs that require less education often result in lower annual income and may be a large deterrent for some students who are weighing their postsecondary options. However, the Bureau of Labor Statistics provides numerous examples of occupations that earn within the top half of the earnings distribution and do not require a four-year college degree including: nurses (registered and licensed practical), computer support specialists, welders, and first-line supervisors in various fields such as construction (Cohen & Besharov, 2002). Indeed, 37 percent of individuals who have completed and earned certificates in their particular career field earn as much or even more than workers with an Associate's degree and 24 percent more than the median male with a Bachelor's degree (Carnevale, Rose, & Hanson, 2012). Therefore, higher income distribution is not solely isolated to college-educated workers. In fact, utilizing more cost-effective programs and training like CTE to reach career goals may result in less financial aid assistance and loan repayment.

Collaboration Among Stakeholders in CTE

To begin developing a comprehensive and inclusive Career and Technical Education program, the United States needs to involve all stakeholders in the process. Also, considering that currently there is not a widely accepted definition when we talk about employability skills, the United States needs a definition of the mission of CTE programs that includes all stakeholder expectations and expertise. Stakeholders are not participating in and/or knowledgeable about all steps of a CTE program. In order to implement this type of stakeholder participation there must first be consensus on who the integral stakeholders to this process actually are. Teachers, school counselors, parents, students, employers, and community members all represent necessary parties to include in developing a career and technical education program.

The largest stakeholder group that has increased in recent years has been employers and those in the business community. Employers are directly affected by the knowledge, or lack of knowledge, that novice workers possess as they enter the workforce; so it makes sense that they have an instrumental voice in developing and partnering with vocational education. McDaniel and Miskel (2002, p. 325) paint the following rationale for business involvement in education in the USA:

> First, corporate executives claimed to be important stakeholders in education because the schools directly affected their operations. Their employees, as products of these schools, too often lacked adequate preparation, cost the companies vast amounts of money for retraining and reduced the companies' ability to compete in a global economy built on knowledge and technical skills. Second, with programs such as school-to-work initiatives, business leaders observed that they also were directly involved in educational practice. Third, they believed that they could assist the schools by providing expertise in areas such as motivation and measuring performance, managing finances and managing change .... (as cited in Hayward, 2004, p. 4)

Currently, although school boards, administrators, and school personnel are developing CTE programs in schools, employers often believe that school systems are not adequately preparing students for the actual workplace. If employers are noticing a gap in employability skills, then schools and businesses need to work together to fill this educational gap. CTE programs are providing a disservice to students by not bridging the gap between classroom learning and actual skills needed in the workplace.

Another important group that has often been disregarded in the conversation around vocational education has been community members and community programs. In a study of 17 high school principals, results found that only 3 of 17 high schools had developed partnerships with their local businesses and social service communities (Lewis & Sanders, 2005). Principals often cited time constraints and lack of support for partnerships as reasons they have not been successful in the past. Schools that had developed school-community partnerships did so because they wanted to improve student academic and personal success, enhance school quality, and support community development (Lewis & Sanders, 2005). In terms of sustaining community partnerships, one principal mentioned constant communication as a necessary aspect (Lewis & Sanders, 2005, p. 10). It is important to note that the National Network of Partnership Schools discovered that high schools versus middle and elementary schools reported greater obstacles in developing partnerships (Lewis & Sanders, 2005, p. 2). This seems counterintuitive as high schools are the last institution to develop students, academic and career skills before they enter college and/or the workforce. To make school-community partnerships successful and long term, school and community leadership have to continue maintaining communication. These partnerships need to develop at the elementary level but must be sustained throughout high school so as to maximize student success. Continued communication among all stakeholders through PK-12 grades allows for revision and assessment about the effectiveness of partnerships and ensures the best impact is being made for students' vocational education.

The Role of Employability Skills in Career and Technical Education

The federal government has shed light on the growing importance of college and career readiness. Pertinent stakeholders expect graduating high school students to not only be intelligent, but also college and career ready (Greenstein, 2012). The twenty-first century worker is expected to enter the workforce trained and knowledgeable while remaining competitive and abreast of the evolving expectations of the global market. Essentially, workers must have the employability skills that are demanded by the competitive global market, which are more than merely academically rooted. According to Greenstein (2012), additional benchmarks of college and career readiness include:

1. Developing a plan for personal and professional growth;
2. Using models of short- and long-term planning in relationship to life and professional roles;
3. Applying skills, knowledge, dispositions, and capacities to personal and professional roles;
4. Recognizing that success comes from hard work and perseverance;
5. Taking personal responsibility for goal achievement;
6. Managing short- and long-term projects;
7. Adapting to the changing landscape of daily life, school, and workplace;
8. Demonstrating a commitment to development of mastery and ongoing learning;
9. Contributing to and supporting others in meaningful productivity;
10. Working to overcome obstacles and develop expertise; and
11. Committing to continuous change and growth (p. 158).

CTE may address these benchmarks, as well as other skills such as academic skills, computer skills, and basic work behavior (Cohen & Besharov, 2002). Cohen and Besharov noted that CTE may provide disengaged students with the opportunity to acquire much needed skills and training.

Career and Technical Education also links student goals with curricula that directly meet these goals. As a result, students are more likely to see the relevance of their education and their practical use. Therefore, CTE can be viewed as a career-oriented approach and may "clarify the connection between schooling and careers for young people who presently see no reason to do well in school" (Cohen & Besharov, 2002, p. 12). Essentially, CTE focuses heavily on employability skills that directly impact students' ability to be successful and productive workers in their chosen field. Regardless of a student's postsecondary route, employability skills are required abilities that all workers must possess to be adequate, competent, and accomplished in today's workforce.

Best Practices for Teaching Employability Skills

One of the most successful programs currently in the United States is career academies. Career academies are one of the oldest and most successful career preparatory programs in the United States. Thorough research studies have shown their effectiveness specifically in addressing low-performing students.

Two career academy themes are small learning communities and partnerships with local employers (Association for Career and Technical Education, 2009). The small learning communities in career academies place students in cohorts who take classes together for two years, the courses are taught by a team of teachers that specialize in different disciplines. For example, students in a construction academy could create cement in their chemistry class to learn about its properties or design bridges to learn physics principles (Association for Career and Technical Education, 2009, p. 4). By building this sense of community, students are able to develop meaningful relationships with their peers. Positive peer relationships help anchor students within the school community and prevent drop-out while concomitantly promoting a safe and productive learning environment. One participant in a career academy noted,

> You have your own little group- it's like being in a sport, except with education. You have your own little community that everybody looks after you and they all know, kind of what you're going through, 'cause you all take the same classes … you're not alone. (Cox & Fletcher, 2012, p. 11)

This sense of belonging and support can foster success for students participating in career academies. This is especially true for African American students, who place great value and importance in community (Jackson, 2005).

Career Academies also focus on partnerships with community groups. As discussed earlier, there is a gap in CTE programs when collaboration with various stakeholders is not implemented. Career Academies fill this void by including local employers and colleges to provide additional or absent resources within the high school. These resources serve to increase student motivation and achievement (Cox & Fletcher, 2012). All of this integration and collaboration provides a true personalized learning environment for students. Cox and Fletcher also surmised that Career Academies allow for various learning modalities, as well as the added experience of work-based learning, job shadowing, and career exploration.

Data and research supports the idea that Career Academies positively impact students' future career experiences. A study by the Manpower Demonstration Research Center (MDRC) employed a longitudinal design for evaluating the effectiveness of Career Academies. The results demonstrated that academy students earned an average 11 percent salary increase per year over noncareer academy students. These earning increases occurred after more than 90 percent of academy students graduated from high school. What is most important to note is that the most concentrated results were noticed in at risk populations (The Role of Career Academies, 2009). These profound results support the use and effectiveness of comprehensive vocational preparation programs like Career Academies. These schools have continued to improve with time and become more inclusive of the business community while also maintaining their academic rigor for students. It would be beneficial for CTE programs implemented in a public or private high school environment to try and mirror some of the aspects of a Career Academy.

Classroom learning is very important and provides knowledge of employment skills and the job market. However, applicable skills need to be developed in a hands-on environment where adolescents can physically practice what they learn in class. The lack of hands-on practice is evident if you examine the current state of CTE programs where many students are not even getting basic vocational skills in the classroom. There is an argument that the youth of today is missing practice and acquisition of integral employability skills. Zimmer-Gembeck and Mortimer (2006) explained that by working in a part-time job, adolescents have the "opportunity for skill development as they learn to deal with supervisors, handle money, follow directions, and conduct tasks, all of which become increasingly routinized as more work experience is acquired" (p. 548). By working entry-level jobs, adolescents can be challenged while enhancing their skills in a low-stress environment where mistakes and learning can take place without extreme or negative consequences.

Student Employment

Student employment is a common but controversial best practice to help teach employability skills. Student employment is similar to a career academy in that experience on a variety of job-related skills is gained usually during the school day. How this works is that the student actually leaves school for a percent of the day and reports to work where they earn an income in lieu of taking courses. The job can be in a variety of places from a fast food restaurant to a retail store. Unlike a career academy though, a high school student who is employed often has more responsibilities and therefore the potential for consequences based on performance. A student who is employed through a business has to abide by company policy and specific rules relevant to that industry. Even though student employment seems like a concrete way to gain job-related skills, the effectiveness and impact of high school student employment and future career experience yields a large amount of conflicting research. Zimmer-Gembeck & Mortimer (2006) discussed that adolescent employment, when related to academic goals can form necessary skills for future work careers. Work for high school students can be seen as providing supplemental skills to what is already being taught in the classroom. However, there must be an intentional opportunity for the students to integrate what they are learning in school about employment and career development with the actual expectations of the day-to-day work they are performing at their job sites. This means there must be institutional oversight and some instructional planning as well.

The Youth Development Study (YDS; 2003) assessed parents' opinion of their own adolescent work experience. Parents cited "responsibility, confidence, commitment to work, time management, interpersonal skills, feelings of self-worth, faith in abilities, and identification of work preferences and job-related skills" (Zimmer-Gembeck & Mortimer, 2006, p. 540). The YDS also noted a correlation between adolescents' reports of higher-quality work experiences and positive emotional ties with parents, intrinsic and extrinsic occupational values, and more control over their lives. These skills could be deemed as professionalism skills that are integral to securing employment but oftentimes very hard to articulate in CTE programs. Looking at the positive attributes adolescents place on their work experience, it is evident that the important aspect of self-efficacy is also being cultivated.

One of the biggest contentions about employment during high school is its effect on early development of teenage independence, deviant behavior, decreased academic performance, and lack of preparation for careers versus jobs. The YDS (2003) determined that it was a curvilinear relationship with students who didn't work or those who worked many hours having lower academic achievement, versus students who worked a moderate amount of hours (around 10 hours) (Zimmer-Gembeck & Mortimer, 2006). A study done by Leventhal et al. (2001) looked at low-income African American youths in Baltimore and showed that "stable employment at the ages of 16–17 enhanced young men's chances of attending college" (Zimmer-Gembeck &

Mortimer, 2006, p. 545). These statistics lends support to the idea that early employment can positively affect academic achievement and future school aspirations. This information provides insight that could be used to advocate for the inclusion of work programs within a school system, or a business-school relationship where school administrators and employers work together to place students in entry-level jobs that will positively build their work experience.

School Counselors' Role in Teaching Employability Skills

One of the greatest advocates for employability and professional skill development are school counselors. School counselors are charged with developing curriculum, leading school administrators in implementation of employability skills, and creating unique ways of infusing career development in the classroom. As previously stated, career and technical education has not been at the forefront of the U.S. educational system. There is immense focus on academic and personal/social development within our school systems but often not enough emphasis is placed on career development. Since school counselors are inherently tasked with providing students with the opportunity to cultivate employability and professionalism skills, it makes sense that these school officials are the stewards of a career development program within the education system (Grothaus & Schellenberg, 2011).

School counselors can develop employability skills several ways: develop and implement a school-wide career curriculum and lesson plans that can be infused in the standard school curriculum, create presentations for students and teachers alike, and broker outside business or community agencies to educate the school on various college and career topics. However, since there is little agreement on what exactly are employability skills and little consensus on a complete definition of professionalism, a disconnect is evident at the school level. Counselors can alleviate this confusion through surveys and assessments that gauge the students' preexisting knowledge of employability and professionalism.

Looking specifically at concrete employability skills, school counselors can develop an assessment that measures tangible skills, such as, literacy, numeracy, and technology skills. Under these three broad measures would be more defined skills such as: (a) job searching, (b) self-management, (c) understanding written instructions, (d) spoken communication, (e) written communication, (f) positive attitude, (g) managing information, (h) working with numbers, (i) problem solving, (j) reliability, (k) adaptability, (l) customer care, (m) work safety, (n) work effectively with others (Employability Skills Scan, 2011). Although this is not an extensive list of employability skills, it does highlight those skills that are integral to the development of future career experiences, such as, first job, internships, and career-based programs and classes.

The Employability Skills Scan (2011) assessment breaks down the above-mentioned categories into even more specific subsets of skills. For example, an item from the assessment "Job Searching" is defined as "Can you write your own resume and cover letter? Can you use the internet to search for jobs?" Students rate their confidence using a measurement, such as a Likert scale, which allows counselors to further assess career development needs by either aggregation or disaggregation methods. Using this type of methodology allows school counselors to implement school-wide, grade-specific, small group, or individual interventions targeting increased experience and knowledge of employability skills. A self-assessment can even be tailored to assess knowledge after application of several career-targeted interventions. By using this tool, school counselors can assess their own effectiveness to ensure their programs are as effective as possible.

Tailoring Employability Skills for African American Students

It is one challenge to implement career and technical education programs and lessons in a school system but another challenge is added when you address diverse students. Unlike their peers, minority students are often misrepresented and have historically been underserved in the public school system. Vocational competence is especially important for these students as studies show that they are less prepared for future employment as their more advantaged peers. Another aspect that affects minority students' vocational success is the theory of circumscription and compromise developed by Educational Psychologist, Linda Gottfredson (1981). This theory explains how students will select out of career avenues they feel they are ill prepared for and/or that are not deemed acceptable for them by society. This circumscription and compromise is often based along gender, ethnicity, and socioeconomic status. For example, an African American student from an urban public school might not feel as prepared or qualified to pursue a career as an engineer when compared to affluent Caucasian peers who attend a private school. This process of circumscription and compromise will often lead students to less fulfilling and challenging career paths as a result.

A major role of school counselors is to advocate for ethnically diverse students and to work toward filling the achievement gap that is widespread throughout the United States. One way to close the achievement gap is to provide culturally sensitive career and technical education programs within the school system. Counselors need to be cognizant of cultural biases and provide inclusive language that appeal to students from all cultural backgrounds. Being competent about cultural nuances and applying this knowledge to the development of CTE programs will greatly increase the effectiveness of school counselors when dealing with diverse student populations.

Cultural awareness and inclusivity is paramount when advocating for African American students who have historically been at the receiving end of discrimination and prejudice. To successfully advocate for African American students, school counselors can lead school administrators in inclusive and culturally sensitive practices. One method of inclusivity is called *standards blending*, an approach that takes the knowledge and experiences of students and multicultural individuals into consideration when lesson planning for CTE programs (Grothaus & Schellenberg, 2011). *Standards blending* is a technique used to bridge a gap between students' lives outside of the classroom and instruction within the classroom. Grothaus and Schellenberg (2011) analyzed the effectiveness of standards blending on counselor career competencies and language arts curriculum and found that this approach opened "meaningful dialog about the cultural interpretation of behavior between school counselors and teachers." Understanding the phenomenological differences among cultural groups and working toward a common understanding is central to any practice targeting ethnically diverse individuals.

Researchers link a standards blending approach to "development of background knowledge, intrinsic interest, and higher order intelligence, and to greater academic achievement and a heightened motivation toward learning" (Grothaus & Schellenberg, 2011, p. 2). From this information, culturally valued skills and activity integration in a CTE program would positively benefit student results. This collaborative approach allows more investment from integral stakeholders, which will increase the effectiveness of a CTE program. A standards blending approach could be implemented in a school system after assessment of students' employability skills is measured. This approach is also responsive and data driven to provide maximum career and technical education knowledge for a diverse student population.

Jackson (2005) called for a more individualized approach when working with ethnic minorities; specifically African American students. In her work she lists several concrete ways that school personnel can foster growth and learning with ethnically diverse student populations. These include: (1) cultural understanding among teachers in regard to their diverse student population, (2) School leaders constantly challenging ingrained misperceptions about ethnically diverse student populations, and (3) Understanding the profound impact of culture on a student's learning. Seeking to understand (which is an important counseling tenet), combatting prejudice, and integrating culturally relevant practices into CTE will create a supportive environment where students from all backgrounds can learn. Jackson then goes even further in her analysis to talk specifically about themes relevant to African American students that can be integrated into school curriculum.

There are nine African cultural themes to be cognizant of:

1. Spirituality—Spirituality is based on the belief that all elements in the universe are of one substance (Spirit) and that all forms of matter, animate or inanimate, are merely different manifestations of the Godforce (Spirit).
2. Resilience—Resilience is the conscious need to bounce back from disappointment and disaster, and to have the tools of humor and joy to renew life's energy.
3. Humanism—Humanism describes the African view of the whole world as vitalistic (alive), and this vitalism is grounded in a sense of goodness.
4. Communalism-Communalism denotes awareness of the interdependence of people.
5. Orality and Verbal Expressiveness—Orality and verbal expression refers to the special importance attached to knowledge that is passed on through word of mouth and the cultivation of oral virtuosity.
6. Realness—Realness refers to the need to face life the way it is, without pretense.
7. Personal Style and Uniqueness—Personal style and uniqueness refers to the cultivation of a unique or distinctive personality or essence, and putting one's own brand on an activity.
8. Emotional Vitality—Emotional vitality expresses a sense of aliveness, animation, and openness conveyed in the language, oral literature, song, dance, body language, folk poetry, and expressive thought.
9. Musicality/Rhythm—Musicality or rhythm demonstrates the connectedness of movement, music, dance, percussiveness, and rhythm, personified through the musical beat (p. 207).

This is a great starting point where school leadership teams (specifically school counselors) can glean information about the African American culture. Using this information as a guide, content pertaining to these nine themes can be infused in career and technical education programs. Specific lesson plans, presentations, and conversations targeting employability skills and professionalism can all be tailored using these nine themes. In addition, employability skills and professionalism can become more culturally inclusive and gain the attention and motivation of African American students. These students will become more invested and, therefore, more dedicated to work within a program that appeals and respects their cultural backgrounds. Bridging the gap between current CTE practices and cultural practices will benefit the students, the effectiveness of the CTE program, and the community and business community at large.

THE FUTURE OF CAREER AND TECHNICAL EDUCATION

The history and current state of career development is filled with progress but also gaps in research and development. Through the evolution of Career and Technical Education, more collaboration between school boards and the business community is evident. As a nation, creating and implementing programs and techniques to educate students, it is crucial to consider the various aspects that influence student employability skills and professionalism in the workplace. Educational programs often disregard the many levels and systems that affect student outcomes and their influence on career development. Being cognizant of the potential positive and negative influences of all levels and systems will provide a more inclusive and, therefore, influential impact when administering CTE programs. This is especially relevant for historically underserved and underrepresented students, such as the African American population in the United States.

As the Career and Technical Education field continues to grow and change, it is important for policy makers, stake holders, parents, and students to keep abreast of the opportunities available and the educational path that best suits individual students' needs. Shifts in demographics, technological advancements, and globalization factors also play a major role in the workforce. As the twenty-first century continues to see major changes to the economy and supply and demands shift, students must be aware of the expectations of employers, how their minority status may affect their attitudes and perceptions about work and career-related opportunities, and what educational programs can best highlight, support, and boost their academic achievement. Career and Technical Education can offer best practices, real-world experiences, and the prospect of gaining more than just academic skills. Focusing and mastering a particular trade, vocation, or skill can be a major advantage to workers of today and lead to various career-related opportunities, job stability, and job growth.

REFERENCES

American School Counseling Association. (2014). *About ASCA.* Retrieved from www.schoolcounselor.org

Autor, D. H., Levy, F., & Murnane, R. (2000). Upstairs, downstairs: Computer-skill complementarity and computer-labor substitution on two floors of a large bank (Working Paper No. 7890). Retrieved from http://academic.engr.arizona.edu/vjohnson/RandCorp21stCenturyWorkforceReport.pdf

Carnevale, A. P., Rose, S. J., & Hanson, A. R. (2012). *Certificates: Gateway to gainful employment and college degrees.* Georgetown University, Center on Education and the Workforce. Available from http://cew.georgetown.edu/certificates

Carnevale, A. P., Smith, N., Gulish, A., & Beach, B. H. (2012). *Healthcare*. Georgetown University, Center on Education and the Workforce. Available from http://cew.georgetown.edu/healthcare

Carter, R. T. (2003). Becoming racially and culturally competent: The racial-cultural counseling laboratory. *Journal of Multicultural Counseling and Development, 31*. 20–30. doi:10.1002/j.2161–1912.2003.tb00527.x

Cohen, M., & Besharov, D. J. (2002). *The role of career and technical education: Implications for the federal government*. ERIC Clearinghouse.

Cox, E. D., & Fletcher, E. C. (2012). Exploring the Meaning African American Students Ascribe to Their Participation in High School Career Academies and the Challenges They Experience. *The High School Journal*, 4–18. Retrieved from http://web.a.ebscohost.com.libezp.lib.lsu.edu/ehost/detail/detail?vid=18&sid=6205ce8c-6a4a-4fdd-9d58-e64f91f26afe%40sessionmgr4003&hid=4107&bdata=JnNpdGU9ZWhvc3QtbGl2ZSZzY29wZT1zaXRl#db=a9h&AN=87646413

Davis, L. E., Ajzen, I., Saunders, J., & Williams, T. (2002). The decision of African American students to complete high school: An application of the theory of planned behavior. *Journal of Educational Psychology, 94*(4), 810–819. doi: 10.1037//0022-0663.94.4.810

Eck, A. (1993). Job-related education and training: Their impact on earnings. *Monthly Labor Review, 116*(10). Retrieved from www.bls.gov/opub/mlr/1993/10/art2full.pdf

Gordon, H. R. D., (2014). *The history and growth of career and technical education in america* (4th ed.). Long Grove, IL: Waveland Press, Inc.

Gray, K. L., & Herr, E. L. (1998). *Workforce education*. Boston, MA: Allyn and Bacon.

Greenstein, L. (2012). *Assessing 21st century skills: A guide to evaluating mastery and authentic learning*. Thousand Oaks: CA: Corwin.

Grothaus, T. & Schellenberg, R. (2011). Using culturally competent responsive services to improve student achievement and behavior. *Professional School Counseling, 14*(3), 222–230. Retrieved from http://web.a.ebscohost.com.libezp.lib.lsu.edu/ehost/command/detail?vid=6&sid=6205ce8c-6a4a-4fdd-9d58-e64f91f26afe%40sessionmgr4003&hid=4107&bdata=JnNpdGU9ZWhvc3QtbGl2ZSZzY29wZT1zaXRl#db=a9h&AN=58646974

Hayward, G. (2004). Foreword: A century of vocationalism. *Oxford Review of Education, 30*(1), 3–12. doi:10.1080/0305498042000190032

Jackson, Y. (2005). Unlocking the potential of african american students: Keys to reversing underachievement. *Theory into Practice, 44*(3), 203–210. Required from http://www.jstor.org/stable/3496999

Johnston, W. B. & Packer, A. E. (1987). Workforce 2000: *Work and workers of the twenty-first century*. Indianapolis, IN: Hudson Institute.

Judy, R. W., & D'Amico, C. (1997). Workforce 2020: *Work and the workers in the 21st century*. Indianapolis, IN: Hudson Institute.

Karoly, L. A., Panis, C. A., United, S., Rand, C., & Labor and Population, P. (2004). *The 21st century at work: Forces shaping the future workforce and workplace in the united states*. Santa Monica, CA: RAND.

Kirschenman, J., & Neckerman, K. M. (1991). "We'd love to hire then but ...": The meaning of race for employers. In Jencks, C., & Peterson, P. E. (Eds.), *The urban underclass* (p. 203–234). Washington, D.C.: The Brookings Institute.

Krahn, H. Lowe, G. S., & Lehmann W. Acquisition of employability skills by high school students. *Canadian Public Policy, 28*(2). 275–296.

Kuchinke, K. P. (2013). Education for work: A review essay of historical, cross-cultural, and disciplinary perspectives on vocational Education. *Educational Theory, 63*(2), 203–220. doi:10.1111/edth.12018

Lewis, K. C. & Sanders M. G. (2005). Building bridges toward excellence: Community involvement in high schools. *High School Journal*, 1–9. Retrieved from http://web.a.ebscohost.com.libezp.lib.lsu.edu/ehost/resultsadvanced?sid=6205ce8c-6a4a-4fdd-9d58-e64f91f26afe%40sessionmgr4003&vid=28&hid=4107&bquery=Building+Bridges+Toward+Excellence%3a+Community+Involvement+%22in%22+High+Schools&bdata=JmRiPWE5aCZ0eXBlPTEmc2l0ZT1laG9zdC1saXZlJn Njb3BlPXNpdGU%3d

Lipman, P. (2004). *High stakes education: Inequality, globalization, and urban school reform.* New York, NY: RoutledgeFalmer. doi:10.1177/0042085907300434

McLaren, P. (1999). Traumatizing capital: Oppositional pedagogies in the age of consent. In Lipman, P., *High stakes education: Inequality, globalization, and urban school reform* (p. 5–22). Lanham, MD: Rowan & Littlefield.

Mortimer, J. T., & Zimmer-Gembeck, M. J. (2006). Adolescent work, vocational development, and education. *Review of Educational Research, 76*(4), 537–566. Retrieved from http://www.jstor.org/stable/4124414

Nall, H. (1997). Vocational education and the african american experience: An historical and philosophical perspective. *Journal of Intergroup Relations, 24*(3), 26–48.

Options 2 Workplace Learning. (2011). *Employability skills scan.* Retrieved from http://archive.excellencegateway.org.uk/media/Skills%20for%20Life%20Support%20Programme/WBL._Options_2._Employability_and_LLN_Skills_Scan.doc

The Role of Career Academies in Education Improvement. (2009). *ACTE Issue Brief,* 1–7.

United States Department of Education, National Center for Education Statistics. (2011). *Projections of education statistics in 2020* [Data file]. Retrieved from http://nces.ed.gov/programs/projections/projections2020/sec5c.asp

United States Department of Education, National Center for Education Statistics. (2013). *Digest of education statistics* [Data file]. Retrieved from http://nces.ed.gov/fastfacts/display.asp?id=98

United Stated Department of Labor, Bureau of Labor and Statistics. (2014). *Employment status of the civilian population by race, sex, and age.* Retrieved from http://www.bls.gov/news.release/empsit.t02.htm

Wang, V. X., & King, K. P. (2009). *Building workforce competencies in career and technical education.* Charlotte, NC: Information Age Pub, 2009. eBook Academic Collection (EBSCOhost), EBSCO*host* (accessed August 3, 2014).

Chapter 10

African American First-Generation College Students

Cyrus Williams, Michael T. Garrett, and Eric Brown

Although numerous retention models, interventions, activities, and best practices have been developed, little has changed in terms of actual college student persistence and attrition rates (Tinto, 2007). According to Bradburn (2002), approximately one-fifth of all students entering four-year institutions depart without completing their degree. This problem of high college attrition rates has the potential to increase because of the ever-increasing number of first-generation college students attending postsecondary institutions (Hsiao, 1992; Pascarella, Palmer, Moye, & Pierson, 2001).

First-generation college students have a higher attrition rate at the Bachelor's, Master's, and doctoral levels, when compared to their higher socio-economic status peers (Macy, 1999; Coffman, 2011; Majer, 2009). These statistics are more disturbing due the fact that first-generation college students represent a significant number (approximately 25%) of all college-going students; yet, only approximately 25% of first-generation students complete their Bachelor's degree (Ecklund, 2013; Horn & Nunez, 2000; Chen & Carroll, 2005). Although there are many commonalities among first-generation college students, they do not represent a homogeneous group. These students come from different economic backgrounds; they live in rural, suburban, and urban settings, represent different ethnicities, and have different academic preparation and cultural backgrounds. They are more likely to be from an ethnic minority group than their peers (Bui, 2002). Black and Hispanic students are more often first-generation college students than Whites or Asians (Fischer, 2007). One subgroup of first-generation college students is African American, first-generation college students. These students have to contend with all of the factors with which first-generation college students are challenged and must additionally deal with the significant cultural, financial, social, and academic integration issues that come along with being an ethnic minority college student. Consequently, African American first-generation college students' transition to college is not just an academic or social issue; this transition requires a significant cultural adjustment. These adjustments further affect this student population's ability to socially integrate, persevere through college, and cope with the added stress to their relationships with their families, friends, and community of origin.

This chapter is meant to provide information concerning first-generation African American students' struggles as they enter and seek to persist in college. Specifically, this chapter will provide (a) details concerning the college participation, access, and academic preparation of African American first-generation college students; (b) an understanding of the ways that race and campus climate play a part in the retention and graduation of this population; (c) a cultural perspective on these students' strengths and leadership qualities; (d) culturally informed counseling theories and retention activities; and (e) overall implications for college administrators.

AFRICAN AMERICAN FIRST-GENERATION COLLEGE STUDENTS

It is difficult to clearly define first-generation college students. They have been defined primarily as students who are the first in their immediate family to attend college. Other definitions describe this population as students whose parents did not graduate from a four-year institution. Still others define this population more strictly, stating that these students are the first in their family to pursue higher education (Saenz & Barrera, 2007). No matter how you define or describe this college student population, they are more likely to be minority and come from lower socioeconomic backgrounds (Bui, 2002). Additionally, they begin college with less information, poorer academic preparation, and lower critical-thinking skills prior to attending college (Dennis, Phinney & Chuateco, 2005; Warburton, Bugarin, Nunez, & Carroll, 2001; Reid & Moore, 2008; Engle, Bermeo & O'Brien, 2006). In past decades, the focus has been squarely on increasing access to higher education for this college attending population. Today, because of the many grassroots community and federally funded programs created to prepare, enroll, and graduate particularly ethnic minority and low-income students from college, access is no longer the emphasis. Today, much of the attention has turned to developing ways for retaining and graduating this population.

There have been many studies that provide information regarding these students' lack of academic preparation. Generally, the results of these studies conclude that this population of college students is less likely to follow a rigorous high school curriculum or take calculus prior to attending college, and are more likely to have lower SAT and ACT scores (Choy, 2001), creating a challenge from the outset. It has also been shown that first-generation college students also receive less academic and emotional support from their families in planning and preparing for college (Choy, 2001; Saenz & Barrera, 2007). As compared to their peers, first-generation college students have lower enrollment rates, lower levels of academic and social integration, lower grade point averages, and lower retention and graduation rates (Chen, & Carroll, 2005; Ishitani, 2006). Consequently, there are substantial inequities among college students' educational attainment when compared to race and income (Gladieux & Swail, 1999). As a result, generational status is synonymous with leaving a four-year institution before the second year (Choy, 2001).

Studies designed to address the nonacademic factors that contribute to the low graduation rates of first-generation students conclude that they have lower college aspirations, conflicting obligations, false or misguided college expectations, and lack of support from friends, family, and community (Hsiao, 1992). Additional studies indicate that these students worry about financial aid and balancing the demands of their community of origin with their new college community (Bui, 2002; Logan, 2007). Finally, first-generation college students possess unique stressors, such as feelings of inner conflict, guilt, and betrayal (Hsiao, 1992). These interpersonal fears and anxieties, coupled with their lack of academic preparation, are intensified because first-generation college students have less knowledge about what is expected of them when they attend college (Kuh, Kinzie, Buckley, Bridges, & Hayek, 2006).

Researchers found that students with pessimistic expectations about being involved on campus academically and socially were more likely to have a difficult time adjusting to college than students who were more optimistic in regard to their social and academic expectations (Jackson, Pancer, Pratt, & Hunsberger, 2000; Smith & Wertlieb, 2005). For African American first-generation college students, not only are their expectations not aligned, these students have limited or no expectations concerning their academic or social involvement on campus. Braxton, Vesper, and Hossler (1995) report that when students' college experiences and expectations are not appropriately aligned with reality, and they are engaged in activities that disconnect them from the college campus, they are more likely to be dissatisfied with their college experience, which consequently effects their ability to persist in their studies and successfully graduate (Braxton, Vesper, & Hossler, 1995). While not all first-generation students report that generational status is an issue, there are many students who state that their college experience is different from the mainstream experience (Bergerson, 2007). For example, when these students attend predominately white institutions (PWIs) they often feel like foreigners on campus and report feelings of disconnection from the majority group (Coffman, 2011). Additionally, the students feel less prepared for college and are more likely to take remedial class work part-time and attend college part-time (Warburton, Burgaarin, Nunex & Carroll, 2001; Reid & Moore, 2008). Furthermore, when these students attend college they feel overwhelmed (Hertel, 2002), because they are tasked to negotiate between two very different cultures, and thus, realize stress as a result (Miville & Constantine, 2006). This stress, and feelings of being overwhelmed, is centered on negotiating the two competing cultures that they have to contend with; each of these cultures have different values, rules, and expectations (Housel & Harvey, 2011). It is critical that college administrators understand these students' expectations because expectations influence subsequent results, such as academic achievement (i.e., grades), persistence, and educational outcomes (Ewell & Jones, 1996; Kuh, 1999; Kuh, Gonyea & Williams, 2005).

Race, Climate, and Engagement

It has been theorized that a contributing factor to the different experiences African American first-generation versus continuing generations face is that often these students are minorities on college campuses and the faculty and staff are predominately White and not familiar with the unique challenges with which these students contend (Douglas, 1998). This kind of environment may be perceived by African American students as unwelcoming, hostile, and even threatening; as a result they feel marginalized and consider themselves outsiders (Oldfielf, 2007; Allen, 1991, 1996; D'Souza, 1992; Hurtado, 1992; Malaney & Shively, 1995). These cultural and environmental factors are regularly overlooked by college administrators, even though research studies indicate that when African American students experience warmer institutional climates, they experience greater satisfaction with college and are more likely to persist through graduation (Kuh, Schuh, Whitt & Associates, 1991; MacKay & Kuh, 1994).

The fact that first-generation African American students experience discomfort on campus may also explain why they are often less social, have fewer friends, feel lonelier, and participate less in extracurricular activities (Pounds, 2004). Each of these factors is associated with persistence and graduation (Tinto, 1998). Additionally, this student population is less likely to form relationships with and conduct research with faculty, which again, is correlated with academic success and retention for minority students (Schweitzer, Griffen, Ancis & Thomas, 1999). This perception of not connecting or trusting goes beyond faculty. Stage and Hamrick (1994) found that many African American students perceive academic support and developmental services to be uninviting and inaccessible. Campus climate, race, and the lack of interpersonal relationships with staff and faculty may explain why African American first-generation college students report having lower levels of institutional commitment, which is defined as students' level of desire to complete a degree (Baker & Siryk, 1989; Bean, 1980; Terenzini, Lorang & Pascraella, 1981).

Cultural Strengths

Although there is empirical evidence indicating that first-generation college students experience significant disadvantages when attending college (Baum & Payea, 2004), there is little research exploring the strengths, skills, and abilities of this college population (Pratt & Skaggs, 1989; Prospero &Vohra-Gupta, 2007). Being unaware or viewing this population as not possessing skills and abilities may result in a distorted view of these students. Accordingly, administrators, faculty, and student service personnel may take the position that these students do not possess strengths and come to the conclusion that their job is to address the deficiencies of these students. Adopting this type of perspective does not acknowledge the cultural strengths that these students indeed possess. Ultimately, the resulting deficit view of this population hampers the ability of those interested in helping this population persist and graduate.

African American first-generation college students should not be viewed as lacking educational capital, nor should they be perceived as possessing nascent skills that need to be coached out of them. Instead, they should be viewed as possessing real attributes, strengths, and skills that need to be adjusted and transitioned to fit this new system called higher education. A culturally sensitive administrator, counselor, or faculty member can help these students recognize and transfer skills to their new and often unfamiliar environment.

In order to recognize the strengths in first-generation college students, one must first understand, deconstruct, and then reconstruct their own personal knowledge of capital and strengths as well as recognize the needed strengths and resources to persist and graduate from college. *Capital* is a set of assets capable of generating future benefits for some individuals (Lackmann, 1978). There are different types of capital or assets that are needed in different aspects or life roles. *Social capital* is defined as advantages derived by individuals from their membership in particular networks (Bourdieu, 1986). Though social capital is a neutral resource it must be acquired through networks that may not be available to all individuals and segments of society. This capital can be used to build up individuals and communities or it can be used to marginalize or alienate certain segments of society. A more modern definition of this term is the ability to seek support from the community to supplement resources needed in your family.

Cultural capital is a resource that focuses on verbal facility, general cultural awareness, educational and scientific knowledge as well as educational credentials and information about the school system. This type of capital centers around social mobilization, examples of cultural capital include educational attainment such as degrees and certifications, and other forms of skills and knowledge that allow you to gain economic advantages in society. The acquisition of this type of capital is acquired in early childhood; therefore, parents must first know and then pass on this information to their children or use other members of the family or community or hire individuals to dispense this power resource into their children (Bourdieu & Passeron, 1990). This capital is not economic although it leads to financial gain, it is transmitted from upper- and middle-class parents to their children in order to sustain generational class status (Ishitani, 2006; DeBerard et al., 2004). *Economic capital* is the root of the acquisition of all capital. *Economic capital* may be defined as money and property, without which it is difficult to acquire the aforementioned forms of capital. In regard to first-generation college students, it is clear that the vast majority of this population does not possess economic capital and this deficiency significantly impairs their ability to both matriculate and persist in higher education. However, a few of these students do possess capital, strengths, and assets that allow them not only to survive but also to flourish in our society.

STRENGTHS AND LEADERSHIP QUALITIES OF AFRICAN AMERICAN COLLEGE STUDENTS

African American first-generation college students have to overcome many hurdles, both academically and personally, to gain admittance to and persist in college. These strengths are steeped in their culture and the systems that they have had to manage and overcome. For most people, it is difficult to articulate the strengths that African American first-generation college students possess. Yosso (2005) identified strengths of individuals from low-income communities that are often undervalued or unacknowledged in middle-class institutions like higher education (Cooper, Liou & Antrop-González, 2010). These four strengths include aspirational capital, family, social and navigational capital, and resistance capital.

The first strength is *aspirational capital*. Like most students, African American first-generation college students are motivated and have high aspiration; what is different about this population is that often their primary motivation is getting a job so they can help their families and communities (Bui, 2002). Though this motivation is acknowledged and celebrated, these students are often asked to adjust their collectivistic motivation. Students are asked to adjust because the majority of research indicates intrinsic, *not* extrinsic motivation is associated with attending classes regularly, remaining in school, and achieving higher academic performance (Dohn, 1992; Rumberger et al., 1990). Helping one's family is a very extrinsic goal and stands in contradiction to the literature that intrinsic motivation is correlated with lower anxiety, higher course retention rates, and higher attainment of performance goals (Black & Deci 2000; Forteir, Vallerand, & Guay, 1995). Vallerand and Bissonnette (1992) found that college students with extrinsic reasons for attending school were much more likely to drop out of school, as compared to students who reported that they were attending school for intrinsic reasons. The research conducted especially with African American first-generation college students states that motivation is neither purely internal nor external; rather, it is a multidimensional construct for this college-going population (Hwang, Echols, & Vrongistinos, 2002). A culturally sensitive staff that recognizes and encourages a collectivistic worldview and empowers students to focus on both sets of motivation (intrinsic and extrinsic) may allow these students to persist toward graduation (Prospero, Russell, & Vohra-Gupta, 2012).

The second strength identified by Yosso (2005) is *family*. The family and communities from which these students originate are often erroneously viewed as detrimental to their success. The knowledge of violence, drugs and lack of education of parents may lead individuals to believe that these students do not have the support and the academic capital needed to succeed in higher education. As such, college administrators may encourage African American college students to distance themselves from their community, friends, and family, which can create additional stress and angst for this population, especially given the context of a college climate that is viewed as hostile and unwelcoming. This viewpoint is very common, but contrary to research which found that there are no generational differences in the level of support for college students (Purswell, Yazedjian & Toews, 2008). The differences are the types of support and the amount of supportive resources that are available. For most first-generation college students, their parents and supporters provide encouragement and motivation. Although students with parents who have graduated from college receive detailed instruction concerning academia, these parents are also involved in helping to select a college as well as provide specific skills such as time management, study skills, and other resources that will allow them to be successful in college (Purswell, Yazedjian & Toews, 2008). It is very important for first-generation college students to be able to manage both the encouraging and discouraging parts of family and community as opposed to distancing themselves from home and culture. Empowering these students to return to their collectivist communities and seek out mentors, agencies and communities that can provide them with the information that they may require to be successful is critical to their success in higher education. Examples of these resources may be a community family who has a child in college, a church that has college preparation opportunities, or a high school counselor that they trust and can mentor them when they return to their community.

The third strength is *social and navigational capital*. First-generation African American students are often very proficient at negotiating systems and institutions; specifically, as a result of their early and often frequent knowledge and exposure to bureaucracies, they are highly skilled and able to identify, understand, and figure out the rules of an organization. Once these students gain the basic understanding of an institution, including its rules, norms, and policies, they will be able to do exactly what they have always done, which is ascertain what they need and where they need to go in order to be successful (Cooper, Liou & Antrop-González, 2010).

The fourth strength identified by Yosso (2005) is *resistance capital*. This is a strength that is very much misunderstood by individuals not familiar with African Americans. Often this strength is used to survive in new environments like college campuses. As such, African American students may deliberately be off-putting, appear aloof, adamant, and difficult (Hall, 2009). These survival mechanisms may be unsettling for college administration and faculty who are not aware of this protective activity; it is important for them to understand that this resistance occurs when these students are unsure and uncomfortable. An in-class example of resistance capital is when a student continues to not follow assignment directions after being provided with feedback. This may be perceived as a student being obstinate and uncooperative, when in fact it is an inappropriate display of power and control on behalf of the student. In actuality the student may not understand the directions and requirements and does not know how to or want to engage faculty. As such, the student completes the assignment as best they can until they can figure out what they are supposed to be doing. This is why it is so important for faculty to engage this population early on and intentionally build a relationship with first-generation college students. This should be done despite the appearance that these students are resistant. These students have to feel that the faculty cares, the campus climate is inviting, and the faculty and staff are culturally alert and willing to allow these students to express their skills in a culturally relevant manner.

Leadership Skills

Yosso's (2005) cultural strengths, detailed above, are consistent with the five leadership categories that include (1) cognitive abilities; (2) personality; (3) motivation; (4) social appraisal and interpersonal skills; and (5) problem-solving skills, identified by Zaccaro, Kemp, and Bader (2004). In other words, many first-generation African American students come into the college or university environment with the skills needed to be a quality leader. Therefore, not only is it important for faculty and staff to recognize the cultural skills and attributes these students possess, it is also important for these students to be encouraged and provided with opportunities to use these skills as leaders on campus. This is important because possessing leadership qualities or the characteristics to become a leader is an asset to college students and is associated with interpersonal skill development (Logue, Hutchens, & Hector, 2005), which is a critical ability for this particular student population to exercise. Additionally, serving as a leader on campus allows these students to recognize and appreciate their cultural strength and may help them feel less alienated, be more likely to engage in the college community, and to interact with faculty and staff.

CULTURALLY SENSITIVE THEORIES FOR ACADEMIC RETENTION AND PERSISTENCE

As indicated above, many of the struggles with which these students are challenged in university settings can be attributed to the cultural distance that exists between the academic institutions represented by staff and students' expectations and needs. One reason for this disconnect may be that higher education institutions are organized around middle- to upper-middle class cultural assumptions. One of these cultural assumptions based out of the presumption of American rugged individualism is that a student should be able to find their own way and succeed on their own through hard work and dedication. However, Relational Cultural Theory (RCT) (Miller, 1976) stands in direct opposition to this stated or more often subtle assumption that one should be self-sufficient. This perspective (RCT) can provide college staff with a meaningful theoretical framework from which to work with all college students and can be especially helpful in fostering academic and social growth for African American first-generation students.

As a primary concept in RCT, the central relational paradox states that people yearn to participate in connections with others and that we all have an internal drive toward relationships where we desire acceptance. The paradox enters when we come to believe that there are things about us that are unacceptable or unlovable, leading us to hide these things and keep them out of our relationships, resulting in a lack of authenticity. Consequently, the connections we make with others may not end up being as fulfilling and validating as they otherwise could be if we allowed ourselves to participate in them more fully, mutually, and authentically (Comstock, 2005; Comstock, Hammer, Strentzsch, Cannon, Parsons, & Salazar, 2008; Miller, 1986).

In the context of RCT, understanding African American first-generation college students' practice of disconnecting should be viewed as a coping style that has worked for them in the past. In other words, isolating and being resistant may have worked in other settings as a coping mechanism. Viewing students' present behavior as a failed solution may not be helpful in assisting this population. These students are indeed trying to use their strengths and knowledge, but need more information and connection in order to figure this new system out and adapt to an unfamiliar environment.

RCT emphasizes growth fostering relationships while recognizing that in developing relationships there will be conflict and misunderstandings. It is important that we resist moving aside to protect ourselves and avoid uncomfortable situations. When we seek to connect and understand, the relationships are enhanced and clarity increases as the relationship continues (Miller, 1976). RCT can do much to inform between faculty/staff and students. It is important that students' experience a sense of being valued by the college community. Jean Baker Miller (2008) states that personal change is inevitable; the question is whether or not change, in the case of the students' development, will go in a positive or negative direction. Change that moves in a direction of positive growth will result in meaningful connections between students' and their new environment.

It is critical for college staff to realize that first-generation college students may use what is known in RCT as strategies of disconnection, where students emotionally distance themselves from the college community, staff, and peers as a coping mechanism. This strategy can be classified as a first-order change, which is a class of solutions that do not change a problem or make a problem worse; it is simply a strategy that has protected their sense of identity in the past (Fraser, 1995). Therefore, it may be important for college administrators to help these students become aware that although this strategy may have worked for them in the past, serving as a way for them to maintain control and avoid being hurt if they did not succeed, it may hinder their academic progress. This serves as one example of how building meaningful, authentic, connections requires interventions that help students connect with others, while still maintaining a sense of who they are within those relationships (Hartling, 2008).

Logotherapy is another theory that may help this unique student population resolve and make meaning out of the complex trauma that they may have had to endure prior to arriving on campus. This complex trauma is the result of inequalities in terms of social, economic, physical and mental health services that some of them may have experienced while living in poverty. Generally speaking, these students may have been witnesses to disproportionately high levels of violence, addiction, death, racism and discrimination as a result of their socioeconomic status (Lott, 2003; Pieterse, Carter, Evans & Walter, 2010). When they arrive on campus, the expectation is that these students will be able to set all of those issues aside, taking advantage of the opportunity with which they have been provided in order to become the first in their families and sometimes in their communities to earn a college degree.

Using the tenants of Logotherapy may allow these students to understand and make meaning of the pressure of their present situation, past experiences, and future possibilities (Tate, Williams, Harden, 2011). First-generation African American college students are in a new environment they have not experienced nor do they understand this new bureaucracy and system, and thus, are searching for solutions and meaning. Logotherapy assumes that the search for meaning is a primary human motivation (Frankl, 1955/2006) and therefore, may allow college student personnel to focus on providing students with ways to overcome challenges and flourish, and in the meantime, make meaning of their past and present situations.

Another important factor to consider is that African American first-generation college students experience guilt and anxiety associated with surviving their surroundings. These thoughts and behaviors are consistent with the term "survivor guilt." Although this term is frequently associated with individuals, families, and communities who survive catastrophic incidents and situations such as earthquakes, physical and sexual assault, war or other forms of large-scale violence, survivor guilt can also apply to individuals living in poverty. Many African American first-generation college students lack financial resources, and experience violence, experience psychological distress, and experience racism, and discrimination as they grow and develop (Barry, Hudley, Kelly & Cho, 2009). This more clinical definition of survivor guilt manifests itself with increased levels of worry, depression, and anxiety, as well as shame and isolation because they are in a better position than others in their family and communities. Often these feelings of shame and guilt caused by being in college and seeking an opportunity to achieve impacts all aspects of students' well-being (O'Connor & Berry, 1996; O'Connor, Berry, Weiss, Schweitzer & Sevier 2000). Viewing the experience of first-generation college students through the lens of survivor guilt can help administrators understand these students more deeply at a cultural level.

CULTURALLY SENSITIVE ACADEMIC RETENTION AND PERSISTENCE INTERVENTIONS

There are a number of examples of retention activities that address the cultural, interpersonal, and environmental issues with which this college-going population are challenged as they matriculate in college. It is important that a collaborative partnership between counselors, student services, residential housing staff, and especially faculty be fostered in order to successfully create and implement these interventions and ensure that they are successful. Several interventions will be discussed here including gender-specific support groups, focus groups, advocacy, Socratic dialogue, and intrusive advising.

Gender-Specific Support Groups

Facilitating support groups and theme-based psychoeducational groups that address issues such as racial and gender identity, self-concept, dealing with racial microaggressions, and coping with an unwelcoming environment has been shown to be effective interventions to help African American students in their transition to college (Rosales & Person; 2003; Schwitzer, Griffin, Ancis, & Thomas, 1999). The male to female disparity on college campuses in general is a topic that can be problematic when working with this population. Oftentimes, practitioners notice that there are significantly less African American males on campus and focus a lot of time and resources on male students to the detriment of African American females. As a result, practitioners come to view African American college students as "sexually monolithic" (Morse, 1982, p. 2); in other words, African American female college students are perceived to have the same problems, needs, and experiences as African American and White males, as well as White females. Consequently, even though women enter higher education in significant numbers, they continue to experience gender bias (Lohfink & Paulsen, 2005). Thus, it is important for practitioners to appreciate the needs of African American males without neglecting the needs of African American females. One way to address this issue is to offer and encourage African American female participation in personal counseling and support groups as soon as they matriculate on campus.

Focus Groups

Facilitating focus groups has been successful in helping students of color express feelings about colleges' unwelcoming environments (Feintuch, 2010). It is vital for experienced and culturally aware college administrators and counselors to serve as group facilitators of these groups. To be effective, these groups should be made up of students from first year through fourth year students. Students who are just a few years further along in their academic experience can both empathize with the current struggles of first-generation freshman, as well as be present models of student success despite the struggles, even going so far as to mentor the newer students.

Advocacy

From a more systemic perspective, Worthington, Hart, and Khairallah (2010) discussed the role of college staff as diversity change agents in higher education through the ability for "creating, redesigning, operating, reconfiguring, or transforming an institution, organization, or system" (p. 566). The emphasis for agents of change then becomes that of working collectively in the university setting to change oppressive social environments and identify systemic or contextual sources of problems and effective methods for resolving them (Worthington et al., 2010). Because these students often perceive themselves as being marginalized on college campuses it is especially important for all members of the campus community be cognizant of the challenges that these students experience on campus, and initiate policies and interventions to aid them as they matriculate toward graduation.

Socratic Dialogue

Getting to know African American first-generation college students may be the key to their success in college. An understanding of their culture, environment, thoughts, values, struggles, and beliefs is critical to the well-being of students. Socratic dialogue is an intervention that is consistent with Logotherapy discussed earlier in this chapter, in which individuals, through dialogue, are able to gain greater awareness and understanding of African American first-generation college students' worldview. Schulenberg, Hutzell, Nassif, and Rogina, (2008) stated that Socratic dialogue is a technique where one asks questions to facilitate deeper understanding of students' feelings; for this population, a faculty member may want to discuss with students the tension between their past and their future and how that affects their present. Additional questions may focus on survivor guilt, as well as students' strengths and attributes. The goal is to help students become reflective of their situation, thoughts, and behaviors, as well as to help the student seek out life meanings, expectations, and clarify available choices (Schulenberg et al., 2008, p. 451). These conversations are very important for students who are living in two cultures and experiencing pressure to join or return from each of these cultures.

Intrusive Advising

Intrusive advising, although sounding unpleasant, is consistent with Relational Cultural Therapy (RCT). This intervention asks staff to be intentional about their contact with students. The goal of the contacts is to convey that students are important and matter; indeed, this may be something that first-generation African American students want, but may not know how to get. Being intrusive and intentional is consistent with the literature on student retention stating that contact with faculty, staff, or administrators is a crucial factor in students' decision to persist and remain in college (Heisserer & Parette, 2002). African American first-generation college students are high-risk students; therefore, it is imperative that faculty, staff, and fellow students be deliberate and thoughtful about the needs and desires of this student population.

An example of an intrusive advising opportunity is when staff proactively contact and meet with first-generation college students after midterms exams. Oftentimes, these students have been working the best that they can and this is the first real feedback that they have received from their faculty. If these students have not done well at the midterm mark they do not know what to do other than try harder to do better next time. These students do not realize that they have options that may mitigate this issue. For instance, they may need to be encouraged to seek more academic assistance or be encouraged to talk to the faculty. More drastic options, however appropriate, may be to drop or withdraw from the class. Frequently, these students do not know of these options or they feel that their financial aid or housing may be affected so they will remain in the class even though the chance of their success is significantly diminished. An intrusive advisor would be able to meet with this population and provide them with sound advice and provide them with the resources they need to be successful, as opposed to this population continuing to try to figure how to fix the problem which may lead them to failing out of school.

TRIO Programs

Assisting first-generation college students in the acquisition of the capital discussed earlier is critical to increasing the amount of students who persist in college and graduate. The federal TRIO programs have been working with low-income and first-generation college students since the late 1960s. The three original federally funded TRIO programs are Upward Bound, Student Support Services and Talent Search. One of the major requirements to receive a grant for one of these programs is that two-thirds of the population served be from low-income families and neither parent graduated from college. Since its inception the family of TRIO programs has expanded to include Upward Bound Math/Science, Educational Opportunity Centers (COE) and the Ronald McNair Post Baccalaureate Achievement Program (U.S. Department of Education, TRIO). These programs focus on providing students with the resources and capital needed to persist in and succeed in college. The interventions used include academic assistance, identifying financial assistance for college, cultural and enrichment activities, college visits, assistance in filling out applications and financial aid documents, and, facilitating psychoeducational programs for parents and the community concerning enrolling and persisting in college. Additionally, program participants have access to community role models, professionals and experiences that allow them to learn and understand the capital needed to be successful in college. These programs and activities are offered from middle school, through high school and college, and even aids students in attending graduate level education.

CONCLUSION

In order to positively affect the low retention rates of first-generation African American college students, it is critical that college administrators understand these students' experiences within their cultural context (Fries-Britt & Turner, 2002). Although there is no simple solution to the academic, interpersonal, and cultural issues with which these students are saddled as they enter college, it is important that all college student personnel, including administrators, faculty, staff, and college counselors, strive to embrace more holistic retention programs that consider the complexities of these individuals and the unique cultural contexts from which they come. It is vital that faculty and staff endeavor to discover the cultural and academic strengths and appreciate the resilience that they possess, and then help build upon this for the benefit of the students and institution (Helms & Cook, 1999).

REFERENCES

Allen, W. R., & Haniff, N. Z. (1991). Race, gender, and academic performance in U.S. higher education. In W. R. Allen & E. G. Epps (Eds.), *College in Black and White: African American students in predominantly White and in historically Black public universities* (SUNY Series: Frontiers in Education, pp. 95–109). Albany: State University of New York Press

Barry, L. M., Hudley, C., Kelly, M., & Cho, S. (2009). Differences in self-reported disclosure of college experiences by first-generation college student status. *Adolescence, 44,* 55–68.

Baker, R. W. & Siryk, B. (1989). *Student adaptation to college questionnaire manual.* Los Angeles: Western Psychological Services.

Baum, S., & Payea, K. (2004). *Education pays 2004: The benefits of higher education for individuals and society.* Washington, DC: The College Board.

Bean, J. P. (1980). Dropouts and turnover: The synthesis and test of a causal model of student attrition. *Research in Higher Education, 12,* 155–187.

Bergerson, A. A. (2007). Exploring the impact of social class on adjustment to college: Anna's story. *International Journal of Qualitative Studies in Education, 20*(1), 99–119.

Black, A. E., & Deci, E. L. (2000). The effects of instructors' autonomy support and students' autonomous motivation on learning organic chemistry: A self-determination theory perspective. *Science Education, 84,* 740–756

Bourdieu, P. (1986).The forms of capital. In J. G. Richardson (Ed.). *The Handbook of the Theory and Research for the Sociology of Education* (pp. 241–58). New York: Greenwood Press.

Bourdieu, P., & Passeron, J. (1990). *Reproduction in education, society and culture* (2nd ed., Richard. Nice, Trans.). Beverly Hills, CA: Sage Publications. (Original work published 1970).

Bradburn, E. M. (2002). Short-term enrollment in postsecondary education: Student background and institutional differences in reasons for early departure, 1996–98. *Postsecondary Education Descriptive Analysis Reports. National Center for Education Statistics*, Publication No. NCES-2003-153.

Braxton, J. M., Vesper, N., & Hossler, D. (1995). *Expectations for college and student persistence. Research in Higher Education* 36(5) 595–612 doi:10.1007/BF02208833.

Bui, K. V. T. (2002). First generation college students at a four-year university: background characteristics, reasons for pursing higher education, and first-year experiences-statistical data included. *College Student Journal, 36*, 3–11.

Chen, X., & Carroll, C. D. (2005). First-generation students in postsecondary education: A look at their college transcripts. *National Center for Education Statistics*. NCES 2005-17.1.

Choy, S. P. (2001). Students whose parents did not go to college: Postsecondary access, persistence and attainment (NCES 2001-126). Washington, DC: U.S. *Department of Education, National Center for Education Statistics.*

Coffman, S. (2011) A Social Constructionist View of Issues Confronting First-Generation College Students. *New Directions for Teaching and Learning, 127*, 81–90.

Comstock, D. (Ed.). (2005). *Diversity and Development: Critical Contexts that Shape Our Lives and Relationships*. Belmont, CA: Thomson Brooks/Cole.

Cooper, R., Liou, D., & Antrop-González, R. (2010). The relationship between high stakes information and the community cultural wealth model perspective: *Lessons from Milwaukee and beyond. Multicultural Learning and Teaching, 5*(2), 73–94.

D'Souza, D. (1992). *Liberal education: The politics of race and sex on campus*. New York: Vintage Books.

DeBerard, M. S., Julka, D. L., & Spelmans, G. I. (2004). Predictors of academic achievement and retention among college freshmen: A longitudinal study. *College Student Journal, 35*(1), 66–80.

Deci, E. L., & Ryan, R. M. (2000). The "what" and "why" of goal pursuits: Human needs and the self-determination of behavior. *Psychological Inquiry, 11*, 227–268.

Dennis, J. M., Phinney, J. S., & Chuateco, L. I. (2005). The role of motivation, parental support, and peer support in the academic success of ethnic minority first-generation college students. *Journal of College Student Development, 46*(3), 223–236. doi:10.1353/csd.2005.0023.

Dohn, H. (1992). ''Drop out'' in the Danish high school: An investigation of psychological, sociological, and pedagogical factors. *International Review of Education, 37*, 415–428.

Douglas, K. B. (1998) Impressions: African American First-year Students' Perceptions of a Predominantly White University. *Journal of Negro Education, 67*, 4, 416–431.

Ecklund, K. (2013). First-Generation Social and Ethnic Minority Students in Christian Universities: Student Recommendations for Successful Support of Diverse Students. *Christian Higher Education, 12*(3), 159–180.

Engle, J., Bermeo, A., & O'Brien, C. (2006). *Straight from the Source: What Works for First Generation College Students.* Pell Institute for the Study of Opportunity in Higher Education.

Ewell, P. T., & Jones, D. P. (1996). *Indicators of "good practice" in undergraduate education: A handbook for development and implementation.* Boulder, CO: National Center for Higher Education Management Systems.

Feintuch, H. (2010). Keeping Their Distance. *Diverse Issues In Higher Education, 27*(3), 20.

Fischer, M. J. (2007). Settling into campus life: Differences by race/ethnicity in college involvement and outcomes. *The Journal of Higher Education, 78(2)*, 125–161.

Forteir, M. S., Vallerand, R. J., & Guay, F. (1995). Academic motivation and school performance: Toward a structural model. *Contemporary Educational Psychology, 50*, 257–274.

Frankl, V. E. (2006). *Man's search for meaning.* Boston: Beacon Press.

Frankl, V. E. (1955). *The doctor and the soul: From psychotherapy to Logotherapy.* New York: Vintage Books.

Fraser, J. Scott. (1995). Process, Problems, and Solutions in Brief Therapy. *Journal of Marital and Family Therapy, 21*, 265–279.

Fries-Britt, S. L., & Turner, B. (2002). Uneven stories: The experiences of successful Black collegians at a historically Black and a traditionally White campus. *The Review of Higher Education, 25*, 315–330.

Gladieux, L. E., & Swail, W. S. (1999). Financial aid is not enough: Improving the odds for minority and low-income students. In J. King (Ed.), *Financing a college education: How it works, how it's changing*, (177–197). Phoenix, AZ: Oryx Press and ACE.

Heisserer, D. L. & Parette, P. (2002). Advising at-risk students in college and university settings. *College student journal, 36*(1), 69–84.

Hertel, J. (2002). College student generational status: Similarities, differences, and factors in college adjustment. *The Psychological Record, 52*, 3–18.

Horn, L., & Nunez, A. (2000, March). *Mapping the road to college: First-generation students' math track, planning strategies, and context of support.* (NCES 2000–153). Washington, DC: National Center for Education Statistics, U.S. Department of Education.

Housel, T. H., & Harvey, V. L. (2011, Fall). Introduction: Shall we gather in the classroom. *New Directions for Teaching and Learning, 127*, 5–10.

Hsiao, K. P. (1992). *First-generation college students.* ERIC Digest, ED351079.

Hurtado, S. (1992). The campus racial climate: Contexts of conflict. *Journal of Higher Education, 63*, 539–569.

Hwang, Y. S., Echols, C., & Vrongistinos, K. (2002). Multidimensional academic motivation of high achieving African-American students. *College Student Journal, 36(4),* 544–554.

Ishitani, T. T. (2006). Studying attrition and degree completion behavior among first-generation college students in the United States. *Journal of Higher Education, 77*(5), 861–865.

Jackson, L., Pancer, S., Pratt, M., & Hunsberger, B. (2000). Great expectations: The relation between expectancies and adjustment during the transition to university. *Journal of Applied Social Psychology, 30*(10), 2100–2125. doi:10.1111/j.15591816.2000.tb02427.x.

Kuh, G. D. (1999). Setting the bar high to promote student learning. In G. S. Blimling, E. J. Whitt and Associates, *Good practice in student affairs: Principles to foster student learning* (pp. 67–90). San Francisco: Jossey-Bass.

Kuh, G. D., Gonyea, R. M., & Williams, J. M. (2005). What students expect from college and what they get. In T. Miller, B. Bender, J. Schuh and Associates, *Promoting reasonable expectations: Aligning student and institutional thinking about the college experience.* San Francisco: Jossey-Bass/National Association of Student Personnel Administrators.

Kuh, G. D., Kinzie, J., Buckley, J. A., Bridges, B. K., & Hayek, J. C. (2006). *What matters to student success: A review of the literature.* Commissioned Report for the National Symposium on Postsecondary Student Success: Spearheading a Dialog on Student Success. Retrieved from http://nces.ed.gov/npec/pdf/kuh_team_report.pdf

Kuh, G. D., Schuh, J. H., Whitt, E. J., & Associates. (1991). *Involving colleges: Encouraging student learning and personal development through out-of-class experiences.* San Francisco, CA: Jossey-Bass.

Lackmann, L. M. (1978). *Capital and its structure.* Kansas City: Sheed Andrews and McNeel.

Logan, J. Q. (2007). Psychosocial influences on college attendance among first and continuing generation college students. *Dissertation Abstracts International, 68* (4), 2713.

Logue, C, Hutchens, T., & Hector, M. (2005). Student leadership: A phenomenological exploration of postsecondary experiences. *Journal of College Student Development, 46A,* 393–408.

Lohfink, M. M., & Paulsen, M. B. (2005). Comparing the determinants of persistence for first generation and continuing-generation students. *Journal of College Students, 46,* (4), 409–428. doi:10.1353/csd.2005.0040.

Lott, B. (2003). Violence in low-income neighborhoods in the United States: Do we care? *Journal of Aggression, Maltreatment & Trauma, 8*(4), 1–15. doi:10.1300/J146v008n04_01

MacKay, K. A., & Kuh, G. D. (1994). A comparison of student effort and educational gains of White and African-American students at predominantly White colleges and universities. *Journal of College Student Development, 35,* 217–223.

Macy, B. (1999). Scaling the ivory tower: The enduring importance of need-based aid. *College Board Review,* (188), 2–7, 29–30.

Malaney, G., D. & Shively M. (1995). Academic and Social Expectations and Experiences of First-Year Students of Color." *NASPA Journal 33, 1*, 3–18.

Majer, J. M. (2009). Self-efficacy and academic success among ethnically diverse first-generation community college students. *Journal of Diversity in Higher Education, 2*(4), 243–250. doi:10.1037/a0017852

Miller, J. B. (1976). *Toward a new psychology of women*. Boston: Beacon Press.

Miller, J. B. (1986). *Toward a new psychology of women*. Boston: Beacon.

Miville, M. L., & Constantine, M. G. (2006). Sociocultural predictors of psychological help-seeking attitudes and behaviors among Mexican American college students. *Cultural Diversity and Ethnic Minority Psychology, 12*, 420–432.

Morse, C. (1982). College yearbook pictures: More females smile than males. *Journal of Psychology, 110*, 3–6.

O'Connor, L., & Berry, J. (1996). *Control mastery research: Empirical studies of guilt*. Retrieved from http://www.behavior.net/forums/archives/clinicalcase/1998.harold/2_5–9.htm.

O'Connor, L., Berry, J., Weiss, J., Schweitzer, D., & Sevier, M. (2000). Survivor guilt, submissive behaviour and evolutionary theory: The down-side of winning in social comparison. *British Journal of Medical Psychology, 73*, 519–530. doi:10.1348/000711200160705

Oldfield, K. (2007). Humble and hopeful: Welcoming first-generation poor and working-class students to college. *About Campus, 11*(6), 2–12.

Pascarella, E., Palmer, B., Moye, M., & Pierson, C. (2001). Do diversity experiences influence the development of critical thinking? *Journal of College Student Development, 42*, 257–291.

Pieterse, A. L., Carter, R. T., Evans, S. E., & Walter, R. A. (2010). An exploratory examination of the relationship between racial/ethnic dis- crimination, racial climate, and trauma-related symptoms in a college student population. *Journal of Counseling Psychology, 57*, 255–263. doi:10.1037/a0020040

Pounds, A. W. (2004). Augustine Pounds. In L. E. Wolf-Wendel, S. B. Trombly, K. N. Tuttle, K. Ward, & J. L. Gaston-Gayles (Eds.), *Reflecting back, looking forward: Civil rights and student affairs* (pp. 475–492). National Association of Student Personnel Administration.

Pratt, P. A, & Skaggs, C. T. (1989). First generation college students: Are they at greater risk for attrition than their peers? *Research in Rural Education, 6*(2), 31–34.

Prospero, M., & Vohra-Gupta, S. (2007). First generation college students: Motivation, integration, and academic achievement. *Community College Journal of Research and Practice, 31*, 963–975.

Purswell, K. E., Yazedjian, A., & Toews, M. L. (2008). Students' intentions and social support as predictors of self-reported academic behaviors: A comparison of first- and continuing-generation college students. *Journal of College Student Retention: Research, Theory & Practice, 10*(2), 191–206.

Reid, M. J. & Moore III. J. (2008). College readiness and academic preparation for postsecondary education: Oral histories of first-generation urban college students. *Urban Education 43*(2), 240–261.

Rosales, A. M. & Person, D. R. (2003, Winter). Programming needs and student services for African American women. In M. F. Howard-Hamilton (Ed.), *New directions for student services. Meeting the needs of African American women* (Vol. 104, pp. 53–66). San Francisco: Jossey-Bass.

Rumberger, R. W., Ghatak, R., Poulos, G., Ritter, P. L., & Dornbusch, S. M. (1990). Family influences on dropout behavior in one California high school. *Sociology of Education, 63,* 283–299.

Saenz, V. B. & Barrera, D. S. (2007). What we can learn from UCLA's "First in My Family" data. *Recruitment & Retention, 21,* 9, 1–4.

Schulenberg, S. E., Hutzell, R. R., Nassif, C., Rogina, J. M. (2008). Logotherapy for Clinical Practice. *Psychotherapy Theory, Research, Practice, Training, 45,* 447–463. doi:10.1037/a0014331

Schwitzer, A. M., Griffin, O. T., Ancis, J. R., & Thomas, C. R. (1999). Social adjustment experiences of African American college students. *Journal of Counseling and Development, 77,* 189–197.

Smith, J. S., & Wertlieb, E. C. (2005). Do first-year college students' expectations align with their first-year experiences? *NASPA Journal, 42*(2), 153–175.

Stage, F. K., & Hamrick, F. A. (1994). Diversity issues: Fostering campus wide development of multiculturalism. *Journal of College Student Development, 35,* 331–336.

Tate, K. A., Williams, C., & Harden, D. (2013). Finding purpose in pain: Using Logotherapy as a method for addressing survivor guilt in first generation college students. *Journal of College Counseling, 16,* 79–92.

Terenzini, P. T., Lorang, W. G, & Pascarella, E. T. (1981). Predicting freshman persistence and voluntary dropout decisions: A replication. *Research in Higher Education. 15,* 108–127.

Tinto, V. (1998). College as communities: Taking the research on student persistence seriously. *Review of Higher Education, 21,* 167–178.

Tinto, V. (2007). Research and practice of student retention: What's next? *Journal of Student Retention, 81(1),* 1–19. doi:10.1.1.133.2661.

Vallerand, R. J., & Bissonnette, R. (1992). Intrinsic, extrinsic, and motivational styles as predictors of behavior: A prospective study. *Journal of Personality, 60,* 599–620.

Warburton, E. C., Bugarin, R., Nuñez, A.-M., & Carroll, C. D. (2001). *Bridging the gap: Academic preparation and postsecondary success of first-generation students.* (Statistical Analysis Report; NCES 2001–153). Washington, DC: U.S. Department of Education, National Center for Education Statistics.

Warburton, E. C, Bugarin, R., & Nunez, A. (2001). Bridging the gap: Academic preparation and postsecondary success of first-generation students. *Education Statistics Quarterly, 3*(3), 73–77.

Worthington, R. L., Hart, J., & Khairallah, T. S. (2010). Counselors as diversity change agents in higher education. In J. G. Ponterotto, J. M. Casas, L. A. Suzuki, & C. M. Alexander (Eds), *Handbook of Multicultural Counseling* (3rd ed., pp. 563–576). Thousand Oaks, CA: Sage.

Yosso, T. J. (2005). Whose culture has capital? A critical race theory discussion of community cultural wealth. *Race, Ethnicity, and Education, 8*(1), 69–91.

Chapter 11

Historically Black Colleges and Universities

Relevance in Modern Education

J. Richelle Joe and Pamela N. Harris

> "Education is for improving the lives of others and for leaving your community and world better than what you found it."
>
> —Marian Wright Edelman

Historically, access to education for African Americans has been viewed as a means by which liberation could be attained. Having often been denied access to formal education in the antebellum period, the Black[1] community took advantage of the freedoms that followed the Civil War to collaboratively establish institutions that would provide for the basic, secondary, and higher education needs of its members. As such, the roots of Historically Black Colleges and Universities (HBCUs) are grounded firmly in the cultural values of a people that have long been committed to the collectivist notion encapsulated in the Edelman quote above. These institutions have afforded educational opportunities to "the least of these" (Esters & Strayhorn, 2013, p. 126), and they continue to provide supportive, challenging academic environments in which African American students can engage in intellectual and personal exploration. HBCUs remain a viable and relevant college option for students from a variety of backgrounds seeking access to higher education.

THE PAST AND PRESENT OF HBCUS

Prior to the Civil War, only three HBCUs existed in the country, namely Cheyney University, Lincoln University, and Wilberforce University (Jewell, 2002). Following the Civil War, HBCUs emerged in multiple regions of the country, including the South, as a confluence of constitutional amendments, federal legislation, and financial endowments that made organized education possible for Black Americans. Scholars have described the founding of these institutions as the establishment of a social contract between Americans of African descent and the society in which they lived (Brown & Davis, 2001). Through this social contract—the effort to fulfill the "good of society" (Brown & Davis, 2001, p. 34), African Americans have aspired to upward mobility through vocational and liberal arts training at universities such as Tuskegee, Howard, Xavier, and Spelman.

Yet, HBCUs have not served as solely a means to individual liberation. Rather, HBCUs "have been called to preserve a culture, prosper a community, equip a new generation of leaders and model what is best about America" (Allen, Jewell, Griffin, & Wolf, 2007, p. 263–264). Often supported in tangible and intangible ways by Black religious communities, HBCUs have provided an atmosphere within which African American culture could be shared, affirmed, and transferred to the next generation (Albritton, 2012). Paul Quinn College, Spelman College, Virginia Union University, Morehouse College, Xavier University as well as other HBCUs trace their financial and cultural origins to faith groups, thus grounding the institutions in the Black spirituality of various Christian denominations (Hawkins, 2012). HBCUs have birthed social and political activism through the development of leaders and organizations like the Student Non-violent Coordinating Committee (Allen et al., 2007), and protest movements such as the sit-ins in Greensboro, North Carolina. Committed to transforming social stratification perpetuated by legal statutes and social customs in the antebellum period, HBCUs pioneered efforts to diversify higher education:

> From the time of their founding and well into their histories, the student bodies at many Black colleges have been diverse to at least some degree and open to all despite their existence within a segregated social order that vigorously sought to preserve a racial hierarchy. (Jewell, 2002, p. 12)

This diversity continues, as HBCUs remain relevant higher education options for ethnic minority students, especially those who identify as African American or Hispanic (Flores & Park, 2013).

Presently, 105 HBCUs, as defined by the *Higher Education Act of 1965*, exist in the United States (United Negro College Fund, Inc. [UNCF], 2014). Although social, cultural, and legal changes within the country since 1865 have impacted the ebb and flow of student enrollment in HBCUs (Palmer, 2013), nearly 20% of African Americans earn undergraduate degrees from these institutions which comprise only 3% of the nation's institutions of higher learning (UNCF, 2014). Landmark court cases and legislation have desegregated higher education, resulting in challenges to the existence and funding of HBCUs (Albritton, 2012) in what is presumed to be a postracial

America. These challenges notwithstanding, HBCUs remain "a touchstone for the Black community" (Allen et al., 2007, p. 264) and a vehicle to empowerment for African American students seeking access to higher education.

CHOOSING A DIFFERENT WORLD

Rarely is the choice to attend a particular college or university made with ease. Multiple factors impact college choice, including familial, financial, and career considerations that can be influenced by access to information and personal characteristics. Additionally, the complexities of college choice for African American students are impacted by the question of whether or not to attend an HBCU. Because HBCUs remain a viable choice for higher education, college bound students might weigh the unique history and culture of HBCUs when determining where they would like to spend the next four to six years of their lives. In particular, students might consider the ways in which HBCUs welcome and nurture through a system of *othermothering* (Hirt, Amelink, & McFeeters, 2008) evident in the experiences and relationships available to students on campus. The main components of *othermothering*–ethic of care, cultural advancement, and institutional guardianship–characterize the atmosphere of HBCUs broadly as well as the instructional methods and interactional patterns specifically distinguishing HBCUs from other institutions of higher learning.

Different World ... Same Family

Since their inception, HBCUs have been distinctly different from historically white institutions (HWIs)[2] in terms of their collective mission, their composition, and the atmosphere on their campuses. Common elements of university life aside, HBCUs offer unique opportunities for engagement within a cultural milieu found in few other places in American society. McCarther, Davis, and Caruthers (2012) illuminated this point in their exploration of the meaning that Homecoming holds for graduates of Lincoln University in Missouri. Founded directly following the end of the Civil War and funded initially by donations of colored infantry units (McCarther, Davis, & Caruthers, 2012), Lincoln University continues to attract its graduates year after year to participate in Homecoming traditions that date back to the mid-1930s. Homecoming is a family affair, as graduates connect and re-connect with old classmates that feel like brothers and sisters.

Yet, it is not Homecoming itself that draws them back; rather graduates have described the *institutional caring* provided by their alma mater as the cord that binds them to the "Black Harvard west of the Mississippi"

(McCarther et al., 2012, p. 15). HBCUs are institutions wherein college-bound African American students can expect to be both challenged and supported by faculty and administrators in an engagement that embodies an ethic of care (Esters & Strayhorn, 2013; Hirt et al., 2008). This engagement is a moral and professional responsibility intended to facilitate racial uplift and cultural advancement: "Relationships stem from a genuine culturally and morally based desire to retain students so that they may perform to their fullest potential" (Hirt et al., 2008, p. 220). HBCUs have a collective history of being founded for the *people*, and a tradition of serving the underserved, "notably the poor, the rural … first-generation students, international students, undocumented immigrants, and the like" (Esters & Strayhorn, 2013, p. 127).

The notion of institutional caring, or an ethic of care transmitted within the context of relationships between students and institutional representatives, distinguishes the world in which African American students find themselves when matriculating through an HBCU. Although selective in their admissions criteria, HBCUs maintain a commitment to providing opportunities rather than restricting students' options. Hence, there is intentionality to their selection process coupled with institutional efforts to remediate and connect with students to promote retention (Albritton, 2012; Hirt et al., 2008). Generally, these connections are genuine manifestations of the ethic of care, and seem to take on filial characteristics such that "the HBCU is an extension of the Black family" (Douglas, 2012, p. 392). Given the institutional caring evident at HBCUs, it is not surprising that African American students at HBCUs report higher levels of academic involvement than those at HWIs, as well as higher satisfaction with their college experience (Outcalt & Skewes-Cox, 2002). For African American students who need or want this type of engagement, namely first-generation students and students who have experienced familial or psychosocial challenges, an HBCU might appropriately match their circumstances whereas a HWI might lack the family atmosphere that would promote their retention and academic success.

Sights and Sounds of Blackness

In addition to the family-like atmosphere present at HBCUs, college-bound African American students might be drawn to these campuses as microcosms of Black culture. Researchers have found that there are significant race-related reasons for choosing to attend an HBCU and these reasons correlate with race-related behaviors on campus (Van Camp, Barden, Sloan, & Clarke, 2009; Van Camp, Barden, & Sloan, 2010). Specifically, race self-development and race focus of the institution were cited as factors contributing to the choice of attending an HBCU. The extent to which race is central to students and their racial identity is solidified may contribute to their preference for receiving their education at an HBCU. Students who have had little intragroup contact (i.e., students who have lived in communities and attended schools with few other African Americans) might seek out an HBCU to immerse themselves in a community of students similar to themselves. The Black college experience is likely perceived as an opportunity to pursue race-related behaviors and cultural opportunities for students who view their race as central to their identity.

This is not to say that African American students who attend HWIs are unable to engage in behaviors that reflect their racial identity. To the contrary, as historically white college campuses have diversified over the last several decades, opportunities have emerged for students of all backgrounds to participate in academic and social activities that are grounded in diverse cultures. Multicultural dormitories have emerged on some college campuses, as have fraternities and sororities established by and for Africans Americans. Such opportunities exist on most college campuses; however, HBCUs, with their rich history and tradition, remain a unique prospect for students seeking a racially and culturally rich college experience.

PRESERVING AND TRANSFERRING CULTURE WITHIN THE VILLAGE

Just as many African American students decide to attend an HBCU in order to engage in culturally relevant experiences, HBCUs make concerted efforts to provide an environment within which aspects of African American culture are honored and transmitted generationally. Again, the unique history of HBCUs distinguishes them from HWIs that are unlikely to have the same vested interest in ensuring the continuance of African American culture. HBCUs, however, were founded and financially supported by religious communities and other culturally conscious organizations, such as the Freedman's Bureau (Albritton, 2012; Bettez & Suggs, 2012), that were committed to the advancement of the Black community. HBCUs continue to honor this commitment through the preservation of African American culture in classrooms and interpersonal relationships across their campuses, while also preparing students to pave the way for the next generation of HBCU scholars.

Village Pedagogy

It takes a whole village to raise a child. This African proverb manifests on the campuses of HBCUs where the ethic of care characterizes classrooms and interactions between the student body and faculty. Conceptualizing the

HBCU as a village, Harris (2012) described an environment wherein African American students move from the margin to the center:

> Village pedagogy is the art of instructing in, from, and through a communal environment. Village pedagogy occurs in teaching and learning in community that enhances campus living and classroom learning for many who attend HBCUs.... Through the HBCU village, African Americans are able to advance through education and not have to acquiesce to alienation, instructional subordination, and systematic marginalization. (pp. 335–336)

African American students expect stress to be higher at HWIs (Yarbrough & Brown, 2012), likely due to concerns about such alienation and marginalization. Hence, the value of the HBCU village is the leveling of the playing field in respect to these concerns. With Black culture and community at the center of HBCUs, there are myriad opportunities for cultural advancement and social replication (Hirt et al., 2008). In fact, socialization at HBCUs has been negatively correlated with depressive symptoms (Laurence, Williams, & Eiland, 2009); that is, students with less social support were more likely to experience depressive symptoms and high stress levels. Supportive relationships with both faculty and peers are also associated with higher levels of satisfaction, and an increased sense of belonging (Strayhorn, 2008). Thus, the impact of the village is threefold, in that it encourages student success and peer support while also teaching and transferring a culture to the next generation.

The HBCU village may also serve as a means to resist dominant culture ideologies that contradict traditionally held values of the Black community. Douglas (2012) found that students at HBCUs, particularly males, reported that attending an HBCU provided "spiritual and cultural grounding" (p. 392) during a formative time. Although not intended to take on the role of the Black church, HBCUs offer spiritual restoration reminiscent of the faith communities so integral to their founding. Whereas spirituality is often a coping mechanism for African American students at HWIs (Weddle-West, Hagan, & Norwood, 2013), it may serve a different purpose for students at HBCUs where the atmosphere is rich with cultural traditions intended to be replicated. Douglas (2012) also found that HBCUs combat notions of materialism through their commitment to community service reflected in their mission statements and graduation requirements (Albritton, 2012). Students at both Oakwood University and Winston-Salem State University live by the mantra *Enter to Learn, Depart to Serve*. Similar mottos at other HBCUs include *Think, Work, Serve* at Tennessee State University, *Culture for Service* at Clark College, and *Truth and Service* at Howard University (Douglas, 2012). Outreach and service to the community connect HBCUs to their historical foundations (Esters & Strayhorn, 2013) and serve to uplift and empower those within the African American community.

Building the Village Through Instruction

In addition to interpersonal relationships that form outside of the classroom, instructional style and techniques contribute to the village feel of HBCUs. Researchers have found that particular types of engagement exist within the space designated for instruction that have the effect of contributing to the village pedagogy and transmitting historical and cultural values across generational lines. Rucker and Gendrin (2003) explored ethnic identification and student learning at HBCUs as a function of verbal and nonverbal immediacy. The concept of immediacy refers to the closeness or distance between individuals that can be communicated in multiple ways and relates to cognitive, affective, and behavioral learning. For African American students at HBCUs, relationships with faculty were mediated by the ethnic identity and perceptions of immediacy within the student-faculty relationship. Students reported a stronger identification with African American instructors than European American instructors with respect to verbal and nonverbal immediacy and Black identity (Rucker & Gendrin, 2003).

This finding is not altogether surprising and may seem intuitive. One might expect that a common racial or ethnic background would facilitate a sense of closeness. Boone (2003), however, described specific instructional methods that facilitate immediacy and build community within classrooms at HBCUs. For instance, instructors at HBCUs may use expressive and culturally meaningful communication styles such as call-response within the educational environment as a means of maintaining and transmitting cultural identity. Call-response communication, a method of vocal exchange between a speaker and an audience, honors African American spirituality, as it has historically been a method of speech used within the Black church (Boone, 2003). Within the classroom, it serves to make content relevant and provide support by building community and strengthening confidence. Moreover, the use of call-response transmits cultural values of both collectivism and individuality:

> It is important to note that both the structuring of the calls and the placement of the responses in this classroom serve as positive reinforcement and support for the members of this community, while at the same time allowing for individual expression. (Boone, 2003, p. 222)

The use of this particular communication and instructional style draws students into the lesson and centers them within the community in a way that validates their individual heritage as well as that of the university.

Guided reflection has also proven to be beneficial at these institutions. Lupinski, Jenkins, Beard, and Jones (2012) examined reflective instructional practices at an HBCU teaching program where instructors incorporated reflection through activities such as admissions interviews, journaling, and lesson plans. Engaging in these practices not only can potentially increase critical thinking skills in students, but also self-esteem—so much so that the current generation of students can pass these methods on to their future students (Lupinski, Jenkins, Beard, & Jones, 2012).

Additionally, these instructional methods and models of mentorship can extend beyond the village. HBCUs have been so effective in producing successful, Black undergraduates that there has been a shift of viewing these establishments through a deficit lens (Castenell, 2007). HWIs may benefit from adopting the teaching styles and climate of HBCUs to reduce the dropout rates of underrepresented students (Castenell, 2007). Thus, partnerships between HBCUs and HWIs can be beneficial for both institutions: HBCUs can strengthen their programs and continue to build credibility, whereas HWIs can learn new strategies to increase minority student retention (Albritton, 2012).

Leaders of the New School

Taking on leadership roles while in high school is generally a strong predictor of college completion, especially for African American and Latino students (Melguizo, 2010). HBCUs try to encourage continued leadership opportunities, especially in regard to finding suitable role models for faculty and administrative positions. In fact, administrators tend to take on the *othermothering* role in regard to supporting and inspiring the student body, as these habits foster successful relationships and, thus, successful college experiences (Hirt et al., 2008). How successful? HBCUs are responsible for 50% of Black teachers, 60% of Black attorneys, 80% of Black federal judges, and 80% of Black military officers (Henderson, 2001). The leadership at these institutions is just as notable—and the most prominent leadership role on the HBCU campus would be that of the college president.

College presidents in general must have a solid understanding of academics, finances, and effective communication—but this is especially the case at HBCUs where students may be unprepared and funding may be lacking (Nichols, 2004). In order to best meet the needs of the students and faculty, HBCU presidents must be prepared to communicate effectively, and not only preserve the history of HBCUs, but prepare for the future as well. This means taking a firm stance in competing for students and funding (Nichols, 2004). However, this also means to secure the future of the campuses by preparing efficient future college presidents. In a study completed by Freeman and Gasman (2014), three-quarters of the college presidents that were interviewed admitted to grooming individuals to replace them in the future, and a key component in selecting potential leaders was an understanding of the HBCU culture. Yet, only 5% of the participants in the Freeman and Gasman study received their doctorates from an HBCU. Thus, a potential push may take place in training and mentoring more HBCU graduates to take on these presidencies—and the *village* and *othermothering* environments of these institutions appear to be fuel to take on this challenge.

Academic Success at HBCUs

Using Texas as a microcosm of American society, Flores and Park (2013) explored the impact of Minority Serving Institutions (MSIs), including HBCUs, on college enrollment and student outcomes. They found that, although two-year colleges were the first institutions of choice, both African American and Hispanic students were likely to choose an HBCU as the path to higher education. Extrapolating these findings to the rest of the country, the question of academic success arises in terms of the effect HBCUs have on degree completion among African American students. Kim and Conrad's (2006) national study examining the effects of HBCUs on degree completion among African American students at HBCUs and HWIs illuminated the personal and institutional factors that contribute to successful student outcomes. For instance, academic preparation (i.e., good grades) is a powerful predictor of degree completion, as is involvement with faculty research. Regarding the latter factor, Kim and Conrad (2006) found that students at HBCUs reported greater involvement with faculty research than those at HWIs. Despite differences in institutional factors such as resources, there were no significant differences in degree completion rates between students at HBCUs and those at HWIs, leading Kim and Conrad to conclude that "Human factors might be more powerful than money factors" (2006, p. 21).

Academic success is certainly possible for African American students at HWIs, but it likely takes more effort (Reeder & Schmitt, 2013) and necessitates a variety of additional coping strategies, including spirituality (Weddle-West et al., 2013). For female students at HBCUs, gender may complicate the black college experience, especially when women arrive on college campuses with cultural and curricular expectations (Kennedy, 2012). Reflecting on her personal experience, Kennedy (2012) noted the possibility that the exploration of racial oppression at HBCUs can eclipse considerations of gender oppression, challenging the liberation of African American women in an environment historically intended to provide for that liberation.

HBCU'S IMPACT ON STEM

A discussion on the academic success of HBCU students would not be complete without addressing the significant role these institutions play in the advancement of students in the science, technology, engineering, and mathematics (STEM) fields. In fact, HBCUs represent 17 of the top 20 institutions that award Bachelor's degrees to African Americans in these areas (Borden & Brown 2004). Even more impressive, 19.2% of undergraduates at HBCUs pursue studies in STEM (Jackson, 2013), and 12% of Black STEM PhD recipients earned their doctorate degrees from an HBCU (Upton & Tanenbaum, 2014). Furthermore, in 2008, 14.6% of the HBCU degrees awarded to African Americans were in the field of medicine (Noonan, Lindong & Jaitley, 2013). So what is it, necessarily, that draws students to pursue STEM undergraduate degrees at HBCUs? Let's break it down by gender.

Black males have a history of being overrepresented in low ability and special education programs, and underrepresented in gifted and advanced classes (Patton, 1995). Enrollment in STEM courses also follows this pattern. Indeed, Black males commonly do not score well on mathematics achievement tests, and few go on to take advanced-level mathematics courses during their secondary school years (Berry, 2005), let alone at the postsecondary level. This population also has to compete with its female counterparts, as Black females tend to score higher on math and science achievement tests, and are more likely to enroll in higher levels of these courses (Hyde & Linn, 2006; Riegle-Crumb, 2006). With this advancement, Black females are closer to narrowing the achievement gap with White males in regard to STEM success, and are more likely to choose a STEM major than White females (Riegle-Crumb & King, 2010). Where does this leave Black males in regard to STEM? More specifically, what kind of role can HBCUs play in preparing Black males for this demanding field?

First, the good news is that more Black males are enrolling in math college preparatory courses; conversely, the bad news is that this increased enrollment is not apparent in science classes (Lamb, Arceneaux, Cox-Moses, Sweat, & Owens, 2013). More disappointing is that even though Black males are attempting to enroll in these advanced STEM courses at the start of high school, they tend to drop out by graduation (Dalton, Ingels, Downing, and Bozick, 2007; Perie, Moran, and Lutkus 2005). However, the support of parents and school counselors has a great impact on whether Black males will enroll in math and science courses (Lamb et al., 2013), indicating that perhaps continued support might encourage this population to pursue STEM-related studies at the postsecondary level. This is where the supportive environment of the HBCU fits in. The concepts of village pedagogy and *othermothering* were already discussed, and can potentially play an essential role in producing more STEM degree attainment by Black males. Nathan (2008) found that relationships with family and friends increase persistence in college, an extrinsic factor that can be replicated at an HBCU. This replication exists through the support of Black professors and peer groups, as well as the accessibility of mentors—both of which influence academic success of undergraduate Black males (Palmer, Davis, & Maramba, 2010).

Though Black females fare better than their male counterparts in regard to STEM success at the secondary level, the same cannot be said at the postsecondary level. In fact, Black females received only 36% of bachelor's degrees in engineering awarded to Black students in 2001 (National Science Foundation, NSF, 2004), and the same patterns can be found in other STEM fields, aside from biological sciences. However, the exception of this underrepresentation at the postsecondary level is within the HBCU institute. In 2004, 33% of Black females attending HBCUs were awarded STEM-related bachelor's degrees, compared to only 26% of Black males (Perna et al., 2009). So, how exactly are HBCUs impacting attainment of STEM degrees for Black females?

In a case study of Spelman College's influence on STEM-related degree attainment, participants shared that an emphasis on cooperation versus competitiveness at HBCUs facilitated success in these fields (Perna et al., 2009). Moreover, the accessibility of academic supports and faculty encouragement also left a strong impact. Academic support can come in the guise of consistently relaying information to students about the requirements of obtaining a degree in the STEM field (Jackson, 2013), but also in developing a STEM identity. In a study on HBCUs' impact on Black female community college transfer students pursuing STEM-related degrees, participants shared that the safe environment of HBCUs assisted in developing not only a cultural identity, but also an identity as a student in STEM—a balancing act that made the transition more successful (Jackson, 2013). The importance of a supportive and safe environment was echoed in a study of the undergraduate and graduate experiences of successful Black female mathematicians (Borum & Walker, 2012). Having Black professors as role models, enrolling in smaller classes, and experiencing the nurturing environment of the HBCU were major influences on why the participants went on to pursue doctorate degrees in the STEM fields.

HBCUs' impact on STEM-related success is apparent through their emphases on social integration, cooperation, and consistent encouragement (Upton & Tanenbaum, 2014), but even nurturing institutions need assistance. These establishments make up only three percent of all institutions that grant undergraduate degrees, yet award one in five African American students bachelor's degrees (Owens, Shelton, Bloom, & Kenyatta Cavil, 2012). However, 88% of students that receive their STEM-related undergraduate degrees at HBCUs decide to receive their graduate degrees at HWIs (Upton & Tanenbaum, 2014). Success and retention in college, especially in regard to pursuing STEM fields, depends on success and exposure to these fields at the elementary and secondary level (Wright 2011). Thus, HBCUs commonly form partnerships with other organizations to facilitate STEM interest. For instance, Winston-Salem State University (WSSU) has launched the Raising Achievement in Mathematics & Science (RAMS) and Summer Undergraduate Research Experience (SURE) programs to increase interest in STEM academics and careers (Fakayode, Yakubu, Adeyeye, Pollard, & Mohammed, 2014). The purpose of these programs was to increase and retain STEM majors, as well as to encourage participants to matriculate into STEM-related graduate programs. Thus far, WSSU has been able to reach these goals overall. Savannah State University has also implemented a program that was designed to increase the number of African Americans teaching in the area of marine science, both in schools and in informal education centers (Pride & Olsen, 2007). After training science majors to teach geoscience lessons to over 300 children in the community, the program saw an increase of 12% of participants that have pursued teaching careers.

At the national level, the Centers of Research Excellence in Science and Technology (CREST), a program established by the National Science Foundation, supports MSIs by aiding in research capabilities. CREST funds several projects to increase minority STEM interests, including the HBCU Research Infrastructure for Science and Engineering (HBCU-RISE). HBCU-RISE supports the advancement of doctoral science and engineering programs by awarding institutions with plans to expand research capabilities, as well as to produce more doctoral students. The impact HBCUs have on STEM success cannot be ignored; more organizations are recognizing this influence, and doing their part to promote STEM-related career fields to underrepresented populations.

CONSIDERATIONS FOR THE FUTURE OF HBCUS

The purpose of this chapter has been to explore the role that HBCUs play in a modern educational context shaped by discussions of economics, race, and access. Although not intended to be a point-by-point comparison of HBCUs and HWIs, this chapter has explored the unique characteristics of HBCUs that have historically distinguished them from other institutions. In light of what HBCUs have to offer college-bound African American students, there are several implications for the sustained relevance of HBCUs in the future.

The complexities of the college choice process for African American students, described above, shed light upon the ways in which adults supporting these students can contribute to this critical decision-making process.

In determining what might be the right college fit, Black students may benefit from reflecting upon the unique cultural characteristics that they embody and that their schools of interest represent. For instance, do students have a particular commitment to racial uplift and cultural advancement within the Black community? These values of HBCUs (Hirt et al., 2008) may resonate with certain students, but not with others. Moreover, students who identify strongly with their race or ethnicity might find a home at an HBCU that provides many and varied opportunities for race-related behaviors (Van Camp et al., 2009; Van Camp et al., 2010) and facilitates immediacy with African American instructors (Rucker & Gendrin, 2003).

There is no denying that HBCUs do a fine job in providing a sense of belonging to students who may be underrepresented at other institutions. HBCUs offer a cooperative environment—or one in which peers can encourage and mentor each other (Borum & Walker, 2012; Harris, 2012; Perna et al., 2009; Strayhorn, 2008). Additionally, faculty members fully invest in facilitating academic and personal success for their students (Borum & Walker, 2012; Hirt et al., 2008). The next step for HBCUs may involve including more formal leadership opportunities for students. As previously addressed, current HBCU college presidents consider awareness of the HBCU culture an important consideration in grooming future leaders; yet many of these presidents have not attended an HBCU, nor do they have prior higher education experience (Freeman & Gasman, 2014). Thus, prescribed shadowing and mentorship opportunities for those interested in pursuing leadership positions may be beneficial. Leadership training and opportunities are also critical in predicting college completion (Melguizo, 2010), and addressing additional needs of minority students (Castenell, 2007). Furthermore, strong leadership not only on HBCU campuses, but also in other influential areas, can effectively promote the needs of HBCUs and, hopefully, address and meet funding concerns (Freeman & Gasman, 2014; Nichols, 2004). Students that typically attend HBCUs come from disadvantaged backgrounds, so HBCUs need the resources to continue to provide opportunities for these students.

As discussed above, the relevance of HBCUs in the STEM fields can be significant. Researchers frequently discuss how exposure to STEM coursework at the elementary and secondary levels influences whether children go on to pursue these fields in the future (Lamb et al., 2013; Owens et al., 2012; Perna et al., 2009). HBCUs have already partnered with other organizations to increase STEM interests on campus, so exploring partnerships with K-12 schools (similar to Savannah State University's model) may prove beneficial for students at all levels. Additionally, partnerships with HWIs may not only assist in diversifying the student body, but also in improving college completion rates of underrepresented populations (Jackson, 2013). If HWIs adopt characteristics of the *othermothering* approach, educators of all backgrounds may be more effective in working with diverse students (Hirt et al., 2008).

In fact, appealing to a more varied student population, while also maintaining the culture and climate that draws Black students to HBCUs, allows these institutions to be more reflective of our evolving society—and provides students a more realistic portrayal of what to expect in the workforce (Albritton, 2012; Nichols, 2004).

PERSONAL REFLECTIONS ON CHOOSING AN HWI

Though neither has actually attended an HBCU, both authors have personal connections to these institutions. Pamela only applied to three colleges as a high school senior, and was accepted to all three—one of which was an HBCU. As a first-generation college student, Pamela sought advice from teachers and school counselors to help her make her decision. Looking back at that time period now, Pamela realizes that she was steered away from accepting the offer from the HBCU. Her school counselor insisted that enrolling in one of the other two institutions (both of which were HWIs) would expose Pamela to more cultures, and provide more opportunities to network and make connections with individuals that could move her further in her career choices. Whereas Pamela had many culturally distinct classmates and professors, she never quite felt a sense of belonging as an undergraduate. Since no one else in her family had attended college prior to her, she did not have any guidance as to what to expect—and she never felt quite comfortable asking professors, classmates, or advisors for assistance. While she ultimately graduated cum laude, and remained at the institution to pursue graduate studies in counseling, she still ponders on how different her experience might have been had she accepted the offer from the HBCU. She went on to work with individuals who had graduated from HBCUs, and they remained connected to the culture, insisting on using vacation days to visit their alma maters. Pamela never felt the pull to return to hers.

In some ways Richelle's experience is similar to that of Pamela. Reflecting back on her time as a student at an HWI, she recalls connections with few faculty members, none of which were sustained beyond her time at the university. Both of Richelle's parents earned undergraduate degrees from HBCUs, and introduced Richelle to their alma mater early on, largely through the experience of Homecoming similar to that of Lincoln University described above. Richelle maintains a fondness for the HBCU her parents attended as well as HBCUs in general because in her experience, the opportunity that her parents had to attend college was a springboard for her own success. Like Pamela, Richelle applied to three colleges–two of which were HBCUs–and was accepted to all three. Although Richelle also chose to attend an HWI, her decision to do so was somewhat different from Pamela's. For Richelle, attending the HWI to which she was accepted provided the opportunity for her to earn both an undergraduate and graduate degree within a five-year time period. Similar programs were not available at the HBCUs to which she applied. Additionally, the HWI she attended was able to offer her substantial financial support through scholarships and grants. Richelle believes that she benefitted from her experience at the HWI, but wonders what peer and collegial relationships she might have established at an HBCU where she likely would have felt "at home." Additionally, having served as an educator and counselor, Richelle also wonders how she might have personally and professionally benefitted from being in an environment driven by the common mission of *leaving to serve*.

Both Pamela and Richelle were academically successful at HWIs and have gone on to establish significant careers in counseling and education. Their personal stories add to the understanding of the relevance of HBCUs in modern education and illuminate some of the research in the literature on college choice, HBCUs, and HWIs. Both personally and professionally they support the preservation and advancement of HBCUs, acknowledging them as a viable option for college-bound students, whether African American, first-generation, or economically disadvantaged.

NOTES

1. Throughout this chapter, the terms *African American* and *Black* will be used interchangeably to connote individuals of African descent living in the United States. The authors acknowledge that this group is diverse, and that members within it may use different terms when self-identifying their race or ethnicity.

2. In the literature, the terms *Historically White Institution* and *Predominately White Institution* have been used in various instances. The authors have chosen to use the term *Historically White Institution* to reflect the diversity in higher education where some colleges and universities are historically white, but are no longer predominately white.

REFERENCES

Albritton, T. J. (2012). Educating our own: The historical legacy of HBCUs and their relevance for educating a new generation of leaders. *Urban Review, 44*, 311–331. doi:10.1007/s11256–012–0202–9

Allen, W. R., Jewell, J. O., Griffin, K. A., & Wolf, D. S. (2007). Historically black colleges and universities: Honoring the past, engaging the present, touching the future. *Journal of Negro Education, 76*(3), 263–280. doi:10.1353/rhe.2002.0007

Berry, III, R. (2005). Voices of success: Descriptive portraits of two successful African American male middle school mathematics students. *Journal of African American Studies, 8*(4), 46–62. doi:10.1007/s12111-005-1003-y

Bettez, S. C., & Suggs, V. L. (2012). Centering the educational and social significance of HBCUs: A focus on the educational journeys and thoughts of African American scholars. *Urban Review, 44*, 303–310. doi:10.1007/s11256-012-0201-x

Boone, P. R. (2003). When the "Amen Corner" comes to class: An examination of the pedagogical and cultural impact of call-response communication in the black college classroom. *Communication Education, 52*(3/4), 212–229. doi:10.1080/0363452032000156208

Borden, V. M. H., & Brown, P. C. (2004). The top 100: Interpreting the data. *Black Issues in Higher Education, 21*, 1–3.

Borum, V., & Walker, E. (2012). What makes the difference? Black women's undergraduate and graduate experiences in mathematics. *The Journal of Negro Education, 81*(4), 366–378. doi:10.1080/03075070601099473

Brown, II, M. C., & Davis, J. E. (2001). The historically black college as social contract, social capital, and social equalizer. *Peabody Journal of Education, 76*(1), 31–49. doi:10.1207/s15327930pje7601_03

Castenell, Jr., L. (2007). Historically black colleges and universities. In *Still Not Equal: Expanding Educational Opportunity in Society* (pp. 245–257). New York: Peter Lang Publishing, Inc.

Dalton, B., Ingels, S., Downing, J. & Bozick, R. (2007). *Advanced Mathematics and Science Coursetaking in the Spring High School Senior Classes of 1982, 1992, and 2004* (NCES 2007–312). National Center for Education Statistics, Institute of Education Sciences, U.S. Department of Education. Washington, DC.

Douglas, T. M. O. (2012). HBCUs as sites of resistance: The malignity of materialism, Western masculinity, and spiritual malefaction. *Urban Review, 44*, 478–400. doi:10.1007/s11256-012-0198-1

Esters, L. L., & Strayhorn, T. L. (2013). Demystifying the contributions of public land-grant historically black colleges and universities: Voices of HBCU presidents. *Negro Educational Review, 64*(1–4), 119–134.

Fakayode, S., Yakubu, M., Adeyeye, O., Pollard, D., & Mohammed, A. (2014). Promoting undergraduate STEM education at a historically black college and university through research experience. *Journal of Chemical Education, 91*, 662–665. doi:10.1021/ed400482b

Flores, S. M., & Park, T. J. (2013). Race, ethnicity, and college success: Examining the continued significance of the minority-serving institution. *Educational Researcher, 42*(3), 115–128. doi:10.3102/0013189X13478978

Freeman, Jr., S., & Gasman, M. (2014). The characteristics of historically black college and university presidents and their role in grooming the next generation of leaders. *Teachers College Record, 116*, 1–34.

Harris, III, O. D. (2012). From margin to center: Participating in village pedagogy at historically black colleges and universities. *Urban Review, 44*, 332–357. doi:10.1007/s11256–012–0199–0

Hawkins, B. D. (2012). Echoes of faith: Church roots run deep among HBCUs. Retrieved from: http://diverseeducation.com/article/17259/.

Henderson, J. (2001). HBCUs will still have a role to play in the 21st century. *Black Issues in Higher Education, 17*, 128.

Hirt, J. B., Amelink, C. T., & McFeeters, B. B. (2008). A system of othermothering: Student affairs administrators' perceptions of relationships with students at historically black colleges. *NASPA Journal, 45*(2), 210–236. doi:10.2202/1949-6605.1948

Hyde, J., & Linn, M. (2006). Gender similarities in mathematics and science. *Science, 314*(5799), 599–600.

Jackson, D. (2013). A balancing act: Impacting and initiating the success of African American female community college transfer students in STEM into the HBCU environment. *The Journal of Negro Education, 82*(3), 255–271. doi:10.7709/jnegroeducation.82.3.0255

Jewell, J. O. (2002). To set an example: The tradition of diversity at historically black colleges and universities. *Urban Education, 37*(1). 7–21.

Kennedy, J. L. (2012). The HBCU experience: Liberating or not? *Urban Review, 44*, 358–377. doi:10.1007/s11256-012-0200-y

Kim, M. M., & Conrad, C. F. (2006). The impact of historically black colleges and universities on the academic success of African-American students. *Research in Higher Education, 47*(4), 399–427. doi:10.1007/s11162-005-9001-4

Lamb, T., Arceneaux, K., Cox-Moses, L., Sweat, T., & Owens, Jr., E. (2013). Examining factors that impact African American ninth grade male students enrollment in math and science college preparatory courses. *Journal of Technology Integration in the Classroom, 5*(1), 55–62.

Laurence, B., Williams, C., & Eiland, D. (2009). Depressive symptoms, stress, and social support among dental students at a historically black college and university. *Journal of American College Health, 58*(1), 56–63. doi:10.3200/jach.58.1.56–63

Lupinski, K., Jenkins, P., Beard, A., & Jones, L. (2012). Reflective practice in teacher education programs at a HBCU. *Educational Foundations, 26*(3/4), 81–92.

McCarther, s. M., Davis, D. M., & Caruthers, L. (2012). A place called homecoming: Memories of celebration and tradition by successful African-American graduates of Lincoln University in Missouri from 1935 to 1945. *Educational Foundations, summer-fall*, 7–32.

Melguizo, T. (2010). Are students of color more likely to graduate from college if they attend more selective institutions? Evidence from a cohort of recipients and nonrecipients of the Gates Millennium Scholarship Program. *Educational Evaluation and Policy Analysis, 32*(2), 230–248.

Nathan, J. (2008). Black men and success. *National Association of Student Affairs Professionals Journal, 11*, 109–125.

National Science Foundation. (2004). *Women, minorities, and persons with disabilities in science and engineering.* Arlington, VA: National Science Foundation (NSF 04–317).

Nichols, J. (2004). Unique characteristics, leadership styles, and management of historically black colleges and universities. *Innovative Higher Education, 28*(3), 219–229.

Noonan, A., Lindong, I., & Jaitley, V. (2013). The role of historically black colleges and universities in training the health care workforce. *American Journal of Public Health, 103*(3), 412–415. doi:10.2105/ajph.2012.300726

Outcalt, C. L., & Skewes-Cox, T. E. (2002). Involvement, interaction, and satisfaction: The human environment at HBCUs. *Review of Higher Education, 25*(3), 331–347. doi:10.1353/rhe.2002.0015

Owens, E., Shelton, A., Bloom, C., & Kenyatta Cavil, J. (2012). The significance of HBCUs to the production of STEM graduates: Answer the call. *Educational Foundations, 26*(3/4), 33–47.

Palmer, R. (2013). The perceived elimination of Affirmative Action and the strengthening of historically black colleges and universities. *Journal of Black Studies, 40*(4). 762–776. doi: 10.1177/00219347083207

Palmer, R., Davis, R., & Maramba, D. (2010). Role of an HBCU in supporting academic success for underprepared black males. *Negro Educational Review, 61*, 85–106.

Patton, J. (1995). The education of African American males: Frameworks for developing authenticity. *Journal of African American Men, 1*(1), 5–27. doi:10.1007/bf02692089

Perie, M., Moran, R., and Lutkus, A. D. (2005). *NAEP 2004 Trends in Academic Progress: Three Decades of Student Performance in Reading and Mathematics* (NCES 2005–464). National Center for Education Statistics, Institute of Education Sciences, U.S. Department of Education. Washington, DC.

Perna, L., Lundy-Wagner, V., Drezner, N., Gasman, M., Yoon, S., Bose, E., & Gary, S. (2009). The contributions of HBCUs to the preparation of African American women for STEM careers: A case study. *Research in Higher Education, 50*, 1–23.

Pride, C., & Olsen, M. (2007). Enhancing diversity in the geosciences through providing HBCU science majors training in natural history interpretation and teaching experiences in predominantly African-American communities. *Journal of Geoscience Education, 55*(6), 550–559.

Reeder, M. C., & Schmitt, N. (2013). Motivational judgment predictors of African American academic achievement at PWIs and HBCUs. *Journal of College Student Development, 54*(1), 29–42. doi: 10.1353/csd.2013.0006

Riegle-Crumb, C. (2006). The path through math: Course-taking trajectories and student performance at the intersection of gender and race/ethnicity. *American Journal of Education, 113*(1), 101–122. doi:10.1086/506495

Riegle-Crumb, C., & King, B. (2010). Questioning a White male advantage in STEM: Examining disparities in college major by gender and race/ethnicity. *Educational Researcher, 39*(9), 656–664.

Rucker, M. L., & Gendrin, D. M. (2003). The impact of ethnic identification on student learning in the HBCU classroom. *Journal of Instructional Psychology, 30*(3), 207–215. doi:10.1080/08824090209384857

Strayhorn, T. (2008). The role of supportive relationships in facilitating African American males' success in college. *NASPA Journal, 45*(1), 26–48.

United Negro College Fund, Inc. (2014). About HBCUs. Retrieved from http://www.uncf.org/sections/MemberColleges/SS_AboutHBCUs/about.hbcu.asp.

Upton, R., & Tanenbaum, C. (2014, September). The role of historically black colleges and universities as pathway providers: Institutional pathways to the STEM PhD among black students. Retrieved from: http://www.air.org/sites/default/files/

downloads/report/Role%20of%20HBCUs%20in%20STEM%20PhDs%20for%20Black%20Students.pdf

Van Camp, D., Barden, J., & Sloan, L. R. (2010). Predictors of black students' race-related reasons for choosing an HBCU and intentions to engage in racial identity – relevant behaviors. *Journal of Black Psychology, 36*(2), 226–250. doi: 10.1177/0095798409344082

Van Camp, D., Barden J., Sloan, L. R., & Clarke, R. P. (2009). Choosing an HBCU: An opportunity to pursue racial self-development. *The Journal of Negro Education, 78*(4), 457–468.

Weddle-West, K., Hagan, W. J., & Norwood, K. M. (2013). Impact of college environments on spiritual development of African American student. *Journal of College Student Development, 54*(3). 299–314. doi:10.1353/csd.2013.0050

Wright, B. (2011). Valuing the "everyday" practices of African American students K-12 and their engagement in STEM learning: A position. *Journal of Negro Education, 80*(1), 5–11.

Yarbrough, Jr., E. G., & Brown, III, U. J. (2012). Major determinants of school choice: Empirical study. *International Journal of Education Research, 7*(1), 107–119.

Chapter 12

African American Students at PWIs

Natoya Haskins and Brandee Appling

African American undergraduate and graduate students often experience social and academic challenges during their enrollment at Predominately White Institutions (PWIs). Researchers have found that when African Americans attend PWIs they consistently underachieve compared to their White peers, and persistence and retention continue to be a challenge (Haizlip, 2012; Hunn, 2014; Kao, 2011; Rodgers & Summers, 2008; Strayhorn, 2012). In this chapter we will examine the role of *Brown vs. the Board of Education* and other pertinent educational legislation, African American student challenges, the role of racial identity in these students' experiences, and support structures and strategies such as mentoring that students can use to enhance their experiences at PWIs. Specifically, in this chapter we: (1) identify historical and current legislation that currently impacts the educational environment of African American student in higher education; (2) recognize the role racial identity has in African American students' educational success; (3) highlight the challenges that impede the recruitment and retention of African American students at PWIs; and (4) identify the types of support structures that African American students need to be academically, socially, and professionally successful.

INTRODUCTION

African American undergraduate, and particularly graduate students, continue to have differential educational experiences when compared to their White counterparts. Historically, scholars recognized these injustices involved in their educational environment; yet, throughout the last 50 years marginal progress has been made to address these challenges. In particular, scholars need to help African American students combat the difficulties they experience. Educators can support these students by addressing their identity in the classroom and integrating standardized support structures such as mentoring into their educational experiences.

AFRICAN AMERICAN HISTORICAL EDUCATIONAL LEGISLATION

After decades of legislative challenges, in 1954, the *Brown v. Board of Education, Topeka Kansas*, set a precedent and took responsibility for the educational discriminatory practices in the United States in the landmark decision that established that "separate but equal" was unconstitutional. In 1955, legislators devised a schedule to facilitate the desegregation of public schools (*Brown v. Board of Education II*, 1955). However, 10 years subsequent to *Brown*, merely 1.2% of Black students in the 11 states in the south attended desegregated schools (Flemming, 1976).

While public schools were continuing to experience challenges with integration, institutions of higher education were beginning to make some gains. In 1964, the Civil Rights Act was signed into law. This law, specifically addressed universities and colleges and made various forms of discrimination illegal (Civil Rights Act, 1964). Title VI of the Civil Rights Act specified that higher education institutions receiving federal financial assistance could not discriminate on the bases of race, color, or national origin (Civil Rights Act, 1964). Numerous types of discriminatory actions, in the day-to-day operations of colleges and universities, were addressed in this legislation (e.g. recruitment, grading, admissions, financial aid, housing, academic programs, athletics, discipline). Furthermore, Title VII of the Civil Rights Act prohibited discrimination in hiring based on sex, race, color, religion, and national origin, in federal, local, and state government, colleges, labor unions, and other government-funded entities (Civil Rights Act, 1964).

The Office of Civil Rights of the Department of Education established Title VI to necessitate schools and colleges taking affirmative action to mitigate the paramount effects of historical discrimination. They also encouraged "voluntary affirmative action to attain a diverse student body" (Civil Rights Act, 1964). However, in 1996 after many years of controversy, California became the first of eight states to ban affirmative action, whereby African American college applicants have preference based solely on skin color. Nevertheless, nationally, Americans seem to strongly support affirmative action in higher education. In a recent survey, 63% of people said programs aimed to increase the number of Black students on college campuses were needed and positively supported them (Drake, 2014).

Current Status of Historical Educational Legislation: Re-envisioning Brown

Diversifying the landscape of higher education continues to be a topic of discussion, 50 years after the first landmark case in the area of education, current educational conditions of African Americans stands in sharp contrast to what was envisioned and sacrificed for *Brown* (Fine, 2004; Orfield, 2014). With White flight, implementation delays, and various court rulings, the educational experiences of African American students continues to be inferior and less desirable (e.g. poorer facilities; fewer instructional resources; less credentialed teachers) (Taylor, Gilborn, & Ladson-Billings, 2009).

While some equity is visible across the United States, collectively the country's secondary schools and institutions of higher education are just as segregated and unbalanced as they were prior to *Brown* (Fine, 2004; Kozol, 2005; Orfield & Lee, 2006). Furthermore, initial legislation did not address invisible, inequitable structures (Fine, 2004). *Brown* demonstrates how the interests of middle- and upper-class Whites are satisfied, while educational leaders fail to address the needs of African American or other marginalized populations. In retrospect, *Brown* allowed leaders to explore how justice and injustice of racialization in urban education has negatively impacted the Black student in secondary as well as in higher education experiences. In addition, *Brown* in the twenty-first century can give leaders a foundation to understand that "justice for all" was not addressed in 1954 or 1964. Reenvisioning *Brown* today can establish social institutions that meet the unique needs of African American students. This reenvisioning might allow leaders and educators to start examining the justice/injustice that still prevent African American students in higher education from having the same nondiscriminatory educational experience as their White counterparts.

Over the last twenty years, there has been an increase in culturally inclusive curricula in schools of education, particularly in regard to helping higher education students meet the needs of students in k-12 settings (Sue & Sue, 2003). These changes in schools of education have helped to increase students' sensitivity and cultural competence with regard to students of color in elementary and secondary settings (Holcomb-McCoy & Myers 1999). However, researchers have found that preparation programs such as teacher education, higher education administration, and counselor education have fallen short in addressing African Americans student needs

(Daniel, 2007; Hazlip, 2012; Haskins et al., 2013; Seward, 2009; Williams Shealey, 2009).

CHALLENGES FACED BY AFRICAN AMERICAN STUDENTS AT PWIS

Since the 1970s, enrollment of African Americans in higher education has significantly increased. Much of the change in the racial/ethnic distribution of students from 1976 to 2011 can be attributed to rising numbers of individuals in these racial/ethnic groups nationally. During that period, the percentage of Black students rose from 10 percent to 15 percent (National Center for Education Statistics, 2013). Between 2000–01 and 2010–11, the number of Bachelor's degrees awarded increased. In 2010–11, White students earned 69 percent of all Bachelor's degrees awarded (vs. 75 percent in 2000–01), Black students earned 10 percent (vs. 9 percent in 2000–01), Hispanic students earned 9 percent (vs. 6 percent in 2000–01), and Asian/Pacific Islander students earned 7 percent (vs. 6 percent in 2000–01). American Indian/Alaska Native students earned about 1 percent of the degrees in both years. In the 2007–2008 school year, the racial cohorts of Masters of Education Graduates racial cohorts numbered as follows: White 139,909, Black 19,816, Hispanic 12,925, Asian 5,002, and Alaska/Native/American Indian 1,088 (National Center for Education Statistics [NCES], 2013). For doctoral cohorts the corresponding degrees awarded in the field of education were: White 6,172, Black 1,743, Hispanic 593, Asian 326, Alaskan Native 81. While African American students' matriculation and completion rates are on the rise, they continue to have challenges during the college experience.

Overall, African American students attending PWIs are often challenged by feelings of isolation, invisibility, and marginalization from White individuals in the form of racism and microaggressions (Browne, 2013; Browne, Mendenhall, & Lewis, 2012; Nagasawa & Wong 1999; Smith & Moore 2002; Torres, Driscoll, & Burrow, 2010).). Moreover, African American students at PWIs also experience stereotype threat, impostor syndrome, and tokenism. While students at various levels (e.g. undergraduate, masters, doctoral) may have slightly different experiences, the identified challenges cut across both undergraduate and graduate education.

Racism

Racism is as a system that "embodies ignorance, exploitation, and power," which oppresses African-American students based on ethnicity, culture, mannerisms, and color (Marable, 1992, p. 5). Studies conducted at both the undergraduate and graduate levels reveal that African American students continue to experience racism and discrimination at predominantly White colleges and universities (D'Augelli & Hershberger, 1993; Jones, 1999; Nettles, 1990; Ong, Fuller-Rowell, & Burrow, 2009; Patterson-Stewart, Ritchie, & Sanders, 1997; Presley, 1996; Solorzano, Ceja, & Yosso, 2000; Tatum, 1997; Taylor & Anthony, 2001). Pointedly, African American students simultaneously experience systemic, institutional, colorblind, and individual interpersonal racism.

Systemic racism is the foundation of institutional as well as individual racism. It encompasses the prejudicial values entrenched in society that maintains and permits discrimination. Institutional racism is a type of racial discrimination that is intertwined throughout power structures, social arrangements and practices, through which combined events produce the use of race as a way to decide who is rewarded (Darder, 1991). *Institutional racism* is privileged access to information resulting in loss of power and loss of voice for African American students (Lee, 2007). Institutional racism serves to legitimize inequality through the interactions of instructors and students in education (Nunez, 1999). Students may experience this type of racism without realizing it due to how embedded it is in the institution. For example, African American undergraduate applicants standardized test scores may be lower, due to the cultural bias of these testing measures; consequently, African American may have lower admission rates to highly selective universities when compared to their White counterparts. Additionally, this type of institutional racism can also impact funding opportunities, as African American student may not receive competitive institutional scholarships because of their lower standardized test scores.

African American students also experience colorblind racism. *Colorblind racism* negates the significance of race and racism (Bonilla-Silva 2001, 2006). Colorblind racism rationalizes, justifies, and explains racial inequality because of natural cultural limitations (Bonilla-Silva 2006). Consequently, dominant culture inadvertently supports the continuation of racial inequality and discrimination in higher education (Bonilla-Silva 2006). Colorblind racism that African American students experience are encompassed in four frames: *abstract liberalism* (i.e., ignoring institutional and systemic practices that perpetuate African American segregation in higher education) *minimization of racism* (i.e., suggests that discrimination is no longer a factor for African American students), *cultural racism* (i.e., relies on culturally based arguments to justify African American current position in education), and *naturalization* (i.e., allows whites to claim segregation happens naturally because African American students gravitate toward other African American students) (Bonilla-Silva, 2009; Gotanda, 1991).

Individual interpersonal racism is the third but often the most visible type of racism experienced by African American students. Individual interpersonal racism involves interactions between individuals that include discrimination, bias, or prejudice (Krieger, 1999). Further, this form of racism includes maltreatment that is targeted at an individuals' attributes, at least in part, to conscious or unconscious racial/ethnic bias on the part of the offender of the mistreatment. They typically take the form of social isolation, harassment, stigmatization, and unfair treatment (Brondolo et al., 2005; Contrada et al., 2001; Haskins et al., 2013). For example, Teddy, an African American undergraduate student, is a freshman who lives in the dorms. Everyone on his floor gets an invitation to get pizza, however, Teddy nor the other African American student on his hall receive an invitation. This type of interaction could be considered interpersonal racism, as Teddy is socially isolated based on the color of his skin.

Microagressions

Chester Pierce and colleagues first cited the term microaggressions in the 1978, asserting that "The chief vehicle for procrastination behaviors are microaggressions. These are subtle, stunning, often automatic, and non-verbal exchanges which are 'put-downs' of blacks by offenders" (p. 66). Sue extended this definition, stating that "Microaggressions include verbal, behavioral, and environmental exchanges, whether intentional or unintentional, that communicate hostile, derogatory, or racial slights and insults that can negatively impact educational experiences" (Sue, et al., 2007, p. 271). African American students often experience these in the form of microassaults, microinsults, and microinvalidations (Harwood, Huntt, Mendenhall, & Lewis, 2012; Lewis, Mendenhall, Harwood, & Huntt, 2013; McCabe, 2009; Truong, 2012).

Microassaults are verbal or nonverbal behaviors meant to hurt an individual by using avoidant behaviors, name-calling, or discrimination. These are often viewed as old-fashioned racism and are often conscious and intentional (i.e., using language such as "colored," "boy," "ghetto," "Negro"). Microassaults are usually used in private settings where an individual feels comfortable and safe or when they lose control and respond without censure. For example, Alfred, an African American undergrad student, overhears two of his White classmates talking about the diversity in the class, "Are you talking about the negro that was sitting in the back of the class?" The language bothers Alfred and he wonders if the racialized language will have a negative impact on his curricular experience in the class. While this type of slur is derogatory and insensitive, African American students consistently experience these types of microaggressions in the classroom as well as in social interactions with other ethnic groups.

Microinsults involve subtle rude and insensitive communications that belittle an individual's race, culture, or identity. Because of the subtlety of these communications, the perpetrator is often unaware of the insensitivity of their communication. African American students may experience this when their success or failure is measured by their race. For instance, Shelly, an African American doctoral student, is in the process of finding a job after graduation. She is told by her advisor, "You should probably look at applying to smaller teaching focused institutions or look for job announcements that are looking to hire a person of color." Instead of the advisor providing support and finding out the job aspirations of the student, the faculty disempowered and further oppressed the student. This message conveys that African American students are not qualified for rigorous or challenging work experiences and that as an African American you can acquire admittance only through diversity recruitment or targeted hiring.

A *microinvalidation* occurs when one ignores, negates, or refutes the feelings, thoughts, or phenomenological experiences of African Americans. Most Americans possess unexamined bias that can potentially cause African American students to experience discrimination. For example, Joy, an African American Master's student, is engaging in a conversation in a cross-cultural class regarding the differential experiences of people of color, when a White student shares, "I don't look at race or ethnicity, I really try to look at all people the same way because we are the same under our skin." This statement fails to consider the differences in cultural heritage as well as the differences in experiences that make people of color's experiences more challenging due to racism, whiteness, stereotyping, and discriminations.

Stereotype Threat

African American students also experience the effects of stereotype treat (Fischer, 2007; Johnson-Ahorlu, 2013; Massey & Owens, 2014). *Stereotype threat* denotes a threat that impacts academic success, which occurs when a negative stereotype about one's own social group is presented and internalized (Aramovich, 2014; Osborne & Walker, 2006; Steele, 1997). When individuals find themselves in a situation involving a negative stereotype situational pressure occurs (Massey & Owens, 2013). Consequently, African American students can become anxious that they may confirm the stereotype or that someone may judge them by it. As a result, the student has an emotional response that impedes their cognitive ability and academic performance (Massey & Owens, 2013; Schmader, Johns, & Forbes, 2008). In this regard, the negative emotions and thoughts that the African American student experience consume the cognitive functioning needed to perform academically, which may in turn impact test scores and other high-stakes assessments (Fischer, 2007; Huguet & Régner, 2007; Ihme & Moller, 2014; Jordan &

Lovett, 2007; Johnson-Ahorlu, 2013; Massey & Owens, 2013, 2014; Muzzatti & Agnoli, 2007.

Impostor Syndrome

The *impostor phenomenon* is an internal experience of fraudulence regarding one's success (Clance & Imes, 1978) and one's roles (Harvey & Katz, 1985). Clance and Imes first observed this subtle yet persistent emotional distress among individuals that are successful. The cause of this distress stemmed from an inability to internalize their success as legitimate. These individuals believe that they are not what they appear to be. Their success is not the result of their own ability, but rather due to luck or personal charms. Impostors believe that others have overestimated their ability and talents, and they constantly worried about the possibility of someone exposing them as frauds. Additionally, they may have feelings of "phoniness" regarding their looks, social skills, social standing, and roles (Harvey & Katz, 1985). These feelings happen when individuals begin to doubt how well or how sincerely, a personal role was being played, even though they appeared to others to be doing well. These feelings create a cycle, where when the individual encounters a new task they immediately experience worry, doubt, or anxiety. For instance, Ashley, an undergraduate student, is one of three African American students in the university's honors program. Upon admission to the program, she was excited but soon after began to feel as if she would not measure up and that others would soon find out that she was not smart enough to be in the program. To alleviate feelings and thoughts like Ashley's, she may either procrastinate or over prepare and when she does succeed at the new task she feels a sense of accomplishment but then begins to feel "fraudulent" again and the cycle is repeated (Chae, Piedmontg, Estadt & Wicks, 1995).

Whiteness Marginalization

Whiteness constitutes "institutional discourses and exclusionary practices seeking social, cultural, economic and psychic advantage for those bodies racially marked as White" (McDonald, 2009; p. 9). Whiteness is an organizing principle that keeps in place the power or access to power and privilege of White people, but is not necessarily deliberate or the result of the conscious actions of individual White people (Blair, 2008). Whiteness is the invisible norm against which society is measured, by which it is structured and through which it exercises power by dominating and oppressing other races both individually as well as institutionally. Whiteness within universities primarily provides material and psychological entitlements to White students and ignores the needs of African American students (Brodkin, 1999; McIntosh, 1990). For example, Chris, an African American graduate student, is in a multicultural class and the instructor begins their lecture on cross-cultural interactions; however, the lecture primarily focuses on helping the students work with ethnically diverse individuals. Chris leaves feeling like the lecture failed to address his interactions with White individuals and believes he will have to figure it out on his own.

Specifically, Whiteness functions to provide White individuals with: (a) *rights of disposition*, (b) *rights to use and enjoyment*, (c) *reputation and status property*, and (d) *the absolute right to exclude* (Ladson-Billings & Tate, 1995). The *rights of disposition* refer to how Whiteness functions to reward students for conforming to perceived White norms in society, such as dress, speech patterns, language, and knowledge. As this relates to Chris, because he does not conform to society's knowledge regarding cross-cultural interactions, he does not receive the reward of acceptance that comes with embracing White norms. The *rights to use and enjoyment* refer to how Whites can use and enjoy the privileges of Whiteness. Chris' educational experience is not preparing him to effectively interact cross-culturally, thus he does not have the same privileges nor can he enjoy them. *The rights to reputation and status property* refer to the notion that to identify a school or program as non-White in any way is to diminish its reputation or status. While this is not overt in Chris' case but maybe implied that knowledge that helps to improve the experiences of students of color is subordinate. *Absolute right to exclude* depicts the construction of Whiteness in this society, as demonstrated initially by denying Blacks access to adequate educational preparation.

Tokenism

Research consistently indicates that African American students at PWIs experience *tokenism* and often are placed in positions where they are viewed as the representative of their race. The term originated from the work of Kanter in the mid-70s. Her work indicated that students who identify with underrepresented ethnicity or racial groups in educational institutions and other contexts would deal with amplified visibility, stereotyping, and seclusion. Typically, tokenism happens when a marginalized group represents less than 15% of the total student population. In this regard, African American students may feel relegated to the expert of diverse issues, and be summoned to represent multiculturalism in educational groups. It may be easier for African American students, who are tokens, to take on these roles rather than challenge the expectations of their program and/or institution (Kanter, 1977). Further, these students may feel trapped in their role, experience alienation, and perform poorer as their representation declines (Young & James, 2001).

Personal expectations, classmates' accomplishments, and the societal norms for success all have an impact on tokenizing African American students. Differences in support and opportunities for advancement can also reinforce feelings of tokenism. For example, Kayla, an African American graduate student, is selected to participate as the student representative for search committee whose task is to interview faculty that will enhance the diversity of their program. Initially, Kayla is excited but soon feels like she was merely selected because of her race, as the committee does not ask her opinion or include her in discussions. Kayla's experience is just one of many that signify how African American students are often selected to serve on committees, to work in groups, or in professional organizations, not necessarily because of their skills and talents but to merely to have a person of color in the room.

Intersectionality

While the above challenges are difficult for African American students it is also important to note that these challenges are intensified when these students have more than one marginalized identity (Gloria & Pope-Davis, 1997). Scholars specify that *intersectionality* recognizes relational constructs of social inequality, takes into account the multiple and interconnecting impacts of policies and practices on African American students, and acknowledges the historically situated as well as current power structures (Crenshaw, 1995; Hankivsky & Christoffersen, 2008). Researchers indicate that intersectionality plays a significant role in African American students' educational experiences (Collins, 2000; Crenshaw, 1995). Intersectionality results in different systems of privilege and advantage (Anderson & Collins, 2007).

There are four guiding tenets of intersectionality. First and fundamentally, race, gender, class, and sexuality are socially defined categories whose meanings are historically dependent (Zinn & Dill, 1996). Second, intersectionality produces a unique set of experiences that involve more than the sum of their parts and reflect the multiplicative nature of intersecting oppressions (Collins, 2000). Third, multiple identities create both oppression and opportunity (Zinn & Dill, 1996). Consequently, those who benefit from non-marginalized statuses such as Whiteness, maleness, heterosexuality, or upper-class status do not only unwittingly oppress those who do not possess those identities, but also enjoy direct social and material benefits (Collins, 2000).

Fourth, since hierarchies of power are intersecting, it is likely that a person will concurrently receive benefits from particular identities and disadvantages from others. For example, Ella, an African American woman, who also identifies as a lesbian, often experiences racism and homophobia in her interactions with students and faculty. She feels omitted from social interactions with students, and her instructors do not address her cultural needs in the course content. She recently had a conversation with a classmate who said, you are so pretty for an African American, I don't understand why you'd want to be gay." Simultaneously, Ella experienced microagressions regarding her gender, race, and sexual orientation. These combined verbal slights might cause more emotional damage than they are able to individually and cause students to withdraw and seek support from others outside their academic experience.

Socialization

African American students at PWIs have consistently struggled with personal/social issues while in attendance (Ancis, Sedlacek, & Mohr, 2000; Negga, Applewhite, & Livingston, 2007; Tuitt, 2010). Other scholars have found that African American students have vast challenges with their faculty and peers in comparison to their White peers (Kador & Lewis, 2007; Proctor & Truscott, 2012; Felder, Stevenson, & Gasman, 2014). For example, interactions with faculty impact African American students' socialization; students need support from faculty to effectively socialize to the graduate experience (Felder et al., 2014). Additionally, African American students attending PWIs had significantly higher levels of stress then their White peers (Negga, Applewhite, & Livingston, 2007).

The identified challenges prevent African American students from embracing their educational experience in a positive manner. In addition, these difficulties often prevent them from being adequately prepared at the completion of their programs. African American students may not be prepared to work cross-culturally with White individuals, or they may not have advance skills that their White counterparts developed through their interactions with White faculty. These obstacles are often a result of the lack of attention of faculty to the African American student's racial identity.

RACIAL IDENTITY OF AFRICAN AMERICAN STUDENTS AT PWIS

Attrition of African American graduate students at predominantly White institutions (PWIs) is a formidable problem compounded by incidents of oppression and racism. In the midst of navigating and negotiating the daily experiences of graduate education faced by most graduate students, African American graduate students at PWIs must contend with perceived individual and institutional racism manifested in feelings of racialized and cultural isolation (Gildersleeve, Croom, & Vasquez, 2011). Scholars purport that racialization, racism, and cultural isolation are often exhibited by experiences such as being the only African American student in class, expectations to represent the African American race, and lack of cultural and linguistic acceptance and inclusion (Gay, 2004).

The Role of Race in Educational Settings

For African Americans students, race plays a salient role in their socialization process. However, assimilating to the culture, rules, and norms of a PWI is inherent to socialization and touted as necessary for academic success and persistence (Brown et al., 2013; Gay, 2006; Gildersleeve, et al., 2011). Therefore, African American students at PWIs often feel forced to adjust their natural forms of expression and behavior to match that of their educational experiences and White peers thus negating their racial/cultural identity (Elion, Wang, Slaney, & French, 2012; Gildersleeve, et al., 2011; Lewis, Ginsberg, Davies, & Smith, 2004). As a result, they might internalize the negative messages they receive about themselves and their ethnicity from their White faculty, White peers, and society in general (Diller, 2004). These internalized beliefs and attitudes may cause African American students to disengage from the education process, which negatively affects their persistence and retention at PWIs (Rodger & summers, 2008; Thomas et al., 2007). Education is replete with social, cultural, and political elements that influence the academic achievement and racial identity of African American students. Plummer (1997) defined racial identity as, "the developmental process by which a person incorporates race" (p. 81). According to Plummer (1997), establishing a racial identity is a critical part of identity formation for African Americans.

Black Racial Identity Models

Consequently, during the last 50 years 10 theories have been developed or expanded that attempt to capture the identity development experiences of African Americans (Akbar, 1979; Baldwin, 1980, 1984; Cross, 1971, 1978, 1991; Cross & Fhagen-Smith, 1996; Helms, 1984, 1990, 1994, 1995; Jackson, 1975; Jackson & Kirschner, 1973; Kambon, 1992; Myers, 1993; Thomas, 1971). Thomas (1971) was the first to describe the identity development of African Americans. His model included 5-stage process, which focused on the individual evolving from lacking self-worth to embracing self and culture then to "transcendence," they are not bound by conflicts concerning their cultural identities. Cross's (1971, 1991) racial identity development model of nigrescence, one of the most widely cited models of African American identity development, stipulates that for African American adolescents, establishing a racial identity is aligned with creating a personal identity. Cross (1971, 1991) further posits that unlike other ethnic peer groups, African Americans are forced to declare their position on their connection or disconnection with their race under the influence of parents, peer groups, and teachers. In Table 12.1 the stages are outlined. Helms (1984) expanded Cross' 1971 model by focusing on how each stage represents a distinct worldview and the specific strategies African Americans use in these approaches.

Although, the roles of race and self-concept in education are prevalent in literature on African American students, the impact of racial identity on the experiences of African American students attending PWIs is sparse (Cole & Arriola, 2007; Rowley & Moore, 2002). Racial identity is a psychological connection to one's race; therefore, it has a direct correlation to the development of a positive self-concept. W.E.B. Du Bois (1903) describes African Americans' internal struggle with their self-perceptions as both African and American in a White society with two identities. The current literature substantiates Du Bois' perspective as African American students at PWIs often experience this sense of duality with their White peers and in the classroom (Grantham & Ford, 2003).

In their research, Rowley and Moore (2002) present a dichotomized view of the relationship between racial identity and the academic achievement of African American students. According to this view, high-achieving African American students fluctuate between social acceptance of their African American peers and mainstream social and cultural value and norms, thus affecting their socialization process and racial identity development (Rowley & Moore, 2002). The values, behaviors, and norms of White mainstream culture are pervasive at PWIs causing African American students at these institutions to oscillate between the accepted and expected campus culture they have been thrust into and their inherited cultural identity (Thomas et al., 2007). This "warring of two souls" or identity conflict is enhanced on the campus of PWIs as African American students often acknowledge feelings of intense isolation and invisibility among many of their White classmates and White faculty as they repress their racial/cultural identity (Lewis, Ginsberg, Davies, & Smith, 2004). Some scholars assert that the repression of racial/cultural identity among African American students contributes in part to the underachievement and attrition rate of African American students at PWIs (Gay, 2004; Gildersleeve, et al., 2011; Thomas, et al.). Further, some African American students may deemphasize their ability level to protect their self-esteem, as achievement is often associated with acting White in the Black community (Lightsey & Barnes, 2007; Reid, 2013; Thomas, et al., 2007).

Positive Racial Identity

Overall, researchers have found that African American students with a positive racial identity are better adjusted and have a more positive school experience than students struggling with cultural conflict (Rowley & Moore, 2002;

Table 12.1 Cross Nigrescence Model for African American Identity Development

Stage	Description	Example	Needed to Transition to the Next Stage
Pre-Encounter	Black is inferior Internalization of dominant cultural values and belief systems	Alfonzo notes that the he would rather work with the White students, stating "I know they will work hard and do well on the assignment."	An external experience that: • challenges the dominant cultural views • illuminates the role of racism in their life
Encounter	• Pro-Black • Conclude that Whites do not view them as equal • Focus in on their identity	Kelly, who knows that they possess the same skills as their white counterparts, is overlooked for a TA position yet again. They decide to seek out African American professors for opportunities.	A desire to seek out the Black community
Immersion-Emersion	• All-encompassing engagement in the African American community and experience • Seek to improve the current state of the African American community	Carl joins the Black Culture Student Organization and a predominately Black fraternity. He recently, organized a voting campaign to encourage African Americans to vote.	Openness for inclusion of others in the work of advancing African American causes
Internalization	• Establishes relationships with Whites allies • Collaborates with other marginalized groups • Positive racial identity	Owen realizes that other individuals outside of the African American community can enhance their current fundraising efforts; consequently, he reaches out to several white allies.	Begin to identify oppressions that one can address by challenging political and hegemonic structures
Internalization/Commitment	Seeks to challenge and confront systems of oppression	Latrice begins a petition to improve immigration laws and connects with Latino/a student groups to support the efforts	

Grantham & Ford, 2003; Thomas, et al., 2007). Therefore, achieving intraracial social acceptance without denying their high achievement status is an imperative developmental task for African American students at predominantly White institutions. Cultural differences make assimilation into PWIs difficult for many African American students, thereby increasing their desire and need to connect with others who are of similar racial origin (Coleman, 2008; Fhagen-Smith, Vandiver, Worrell, 2010; White & Ali-Khan, 2013). However, the limited number of African American students at PWIs limits their ability to connect and build relationships with other racially similar students (Coleman, 2008; Patton, Bridges, & Flowers, 2011).

In a 2010 study of African American students in counselor education programs the researchers found that the participants had an intense inner determination to have their needs met (Heinfield, Owens, & Witherspoon, 2011). Some of the needs identified by the participants in the Heinfield study reflect their desire to express their racial identity through the collective support of identity-based organizations and the necessity of faculty acknowledging and understanding African American students, preferred methods of communication. Further, other African American students acknowledged their need for racial identity affiliation, a desire for reduction in isolation, same identity peer support, and an acceptance of various types of human agency (Heinfield, et al., 2011).

Addressing the racial identity of African American students might help educators improve the educational experiences of these students and increase overall retention of the population. In addition, racial identify can be the starting point for educators to begin to identity other support structures for African American students that can promote an environment that is more inclusive and supportive of student differences and various educational needs.

ACADEMIC SUPPORT F OR AFRICAN AMERICAN STUDENTS AT PWIS

Support from the college environment is a key factor in the academic success of many African American college students. Support can take the form of learning communities, first-year interest groups, tutoring, mentoring, student orientations, faculty supports, and the development of personal coping skills (Myers, 2003).

Community Engagement

Scholars indicate that African American students need to do more than attend class; they need to be engaged in campus life (Kuh, Cruce, Shoup, Kinzie, & Gonyea, 2008). Successfully engaged students display three characteristics:

(1) action (i.e., participation in the campus community), (2) purpose (i.e., the students have a focus which guides how they interact within the campus and wider community), and (3) cross-institutional collaboration (communicate with individuals in various organizations on the campus). African American students' commitment to their college setting is an indicator of their likelihood to persevere and graduate when compared to individuals who merely attend various events. Consequently, institutions should develop opportunities to engage students that enhance positive actions, motivation, and involvement (Pascarella & Terenzini, 2005). Researchers have found that participating in college-based organizations and leadership aids African American students in their retention and allows them to invest in their personal and social development (Sutton & Kimbrough, 2001; Woodard, Mallory, & De Luca, 2001). Peer and faculty interactions within the college environment are important to African American students' academic success (Locks, Hurtado, Bowman, & Oseguera, 2008; Steele, 1997). For example, Leon, who is a college junior, recently spearheaded a partnership between his fraternity and two other campus organizations. He has also worked with several faculty members to ensure the program will have the support of the college community. This type of peer and faculty interaction demonstrates Leon's investment in the community, which can have a significant impact of his academic performance.

First-year Seminars

First-year seminar experiences include summer orientation seminars, academic seminars and program, program of study or professional-based seminars, study skills programs, as well as those that are a combination of the above (Cuseo, 2009; Padgett, Keup, & Pascarella, 2012; Tobolowsky et al., 2008). These experiences have had a significant impact on African American student retention, persistence to graduation, and academic performance (Barefoot et al., 1998; Fidler & Moore, 1996; Starke, Harth, & Sirianni, 2001; Tinto, 1993). Additionally, the benefits of first-year seminar participation on these key educational outcomes appear to be consistent between African American female and male students regardless of major (Starke et al., 2001; Sidle & McReynolds, 1999).

Peers Supports

Researchers suggested that a relationship exists between African American academic success and peer support (Brittian & Gray, 2014; Haskins et al., 2013; Holland, 2011). Peers should be academically oriented and have the same academic goals. Nagasawa and Wong (1999) identified several ways that African American peer networks can be utilized. These peer networks can help African American students navigate the social and academic systems of college. Additionally, relationship with other African American students can help reinforce strength-based personal characteristics, such as excellence, perseverance, and resilience. These networks can also provide social support to deal with microaggressions (e.g. racism, stereotyping). Furthermore, peer connections can increase ethnic/racial camaraderie and increase personal and communal pride. Peer support can take the form of peer tutoring, peer advisors, and academic coaches.

Peer tutoring

Peer tutoring is the collegial preparation for college teaching, expectations, and requirements (Maxwell, 2001). Peer tutoring is cost effective and beneficial to African American students in both the role of atutor or tutee. African American students who serve as tutors engage in the campus community and may also experience improved academic performance, communication skills, self-confidence and leadership ability (Maxwell, 2001).

Peer advisors and coaches

Scholars suggest that advising in collegiate settings has a significant impact on how African American students perceive the college experience (Kuh et al., 2008). At many universities and colleges, faculty and staff conduct advising of African American students. However, advisement time with staff and faculty might be limited based on the focus of the institution (i.e., research) leaving students to have to figure out important details of the education process such as program of study, course choice and elective information, and how to transition from undergraduate to graduate school. In addition, this process can assist African American students with the socialization process from a student perspective. Furthermore, many African American students desire consistent contact with an advisor and the value of advising can make this an effective support strategy for African American students (Wyckoff, 1999).

Coaching peers has been used outside of higher education to train or offer support for new personnel for decades. Recently, leaders in higher education have begun to identify the value of this practice by assisting African American students with transitions. The coach and the African American student should have a collegial relationship built on trust. Academic coaches can model appropriate behavior related to college norms and academic success for African American students (Cuseo, 2009). They meet several times during the year to examine progress toward academic goals and personal goals.

Faculty Interactions

While scholars over the last 30 years have indicated that faculty interactions are important to the development of college students, faculty interactions are critical for the academic achievement of African American students (Fischer, 2007; Gregory, 2003; Nagda et al., 1998). Pointedly, faculty support is a determining factor in African American students' overall satisfaction; conversely, faculty support is not a significant predictor of success for White students (Delucchi, 1997).

Faculty should provide learning tasks that include opportunities for dialogue. Discussions should allow African American students an opportunity to explore their personal challenges as well as address racialized concerns. Discussions should expand students' knowledge of the curriculum content and help them apply this knowledge to their current setting (Vella, 1994). Faculty should be accessible, show concern, and be committed to providing instruction that not only address professional standards but also integrate contents that reflect African American students' worldview (Taylor, Gillborn, & Ladson-Billings, 2009). Faculty support is positively related to grade point average for African American females (Baker, 2013). Whereas, African American males may benefit academically from mentoring and strength-based approaches (Butler, Evans, Brooks, Williams, & Bailey, 2013).

Summer Transition Programs

African American students who enroll in college bridge or transition programs have higher graduation rates (Douglas & Attewell, 2014). Colleges and universities often provide independent transitions that focus on supporting students of color in their transition to college. Several such programs include the Meyerhoff Summer Bridge, First STEP, New Start Summer Program, and OASIS (Cabrera, Miner, & Milem, 2013; Maton, Pollard, McDougall Weise, & Hrabowski, 2012; Raines, 2012). These programs are designed to help the students enhance college readiness, specifically focusing on academic preparation, financial aid support, community and individual support, as well as micro skills such as organizational skills, leadership skills, and resiliency (Venezia &Jaeger, 2013). Further, these programs help improve African American students' academic skills, orient them to campus life, build their social and cultural capital, and help them begin to look at college with a positive perspective (Stolle-McAllister, 2011).

The federally supported TRIO educational opportunity programs serve to increase both the higher education admission and attendance rates, specifically for students from low-income households and those from ethnically marginalized populations (Cowan Pitre & Pitre, 2009). TRIO includes three programs: Educational Talent Search, Upward Bound, and Student Support Services. TRIO, developed in response to the Economic Opportunity Act of 1964, focused on providing educational equality, using programs that enhance college readiness (Council for Opportunity in Education, 2014).

Currently, there are over 2,700 TRIO Programs nationwide that serve approximately 866,000 low-income Americans between the ages 11 and 27 (Council of Opportunity in Education, 2007). Over 1,000 colleges, university, and community agencies include TRIO programs in the support structures (Council for Opportunity in Education, 2007).

MENTORING AFRICAN AMERICAN STUDENTS

One of the most researched support strategies to support African American success in institutions of higher education is mentoring. While some receive mentoring, most African Americans students have been left out of the mentoring process (Bova, 2000; Dixon-Reeves, 2003; Patton, 2009). This gap is due in part to the racial demographics of mentors available in their settings. Seventy-nine percent of African American undergraduate student, 90% African-American master's students, and 75% of African American doctoral students attend predominantly white universities; only 4% of the faculty are African American (NCES, 2011). Consequently, all faculty need to take on the onus to mentor African American students and not just African American faculty.

Mentoring serves to enhance African American persistence and retention of both men and women (Brown, 2009; Butler et al., 2013; Cuyjet, 2006; Hines, 2009; Patton, 2009). Mentoring is the process of developing an individual professionally and personally (Crawford & Smith, 2005). Crawford and Smith (2005) indicate that a mentor is a person that "affords the protégé with opportunities to learn and practice and to reward him or her so that acquired knowledge, performance, and motivation can increase" (p. 64). Adams (1992) identified two characteristics of effective research mentors: (1) must be able to share time, give guidance, and opportunities for research development and (2) must themselves be published researchers.

Blackwell (1983) asserted that African American women were less likely than African American men to receive mentoring. Twenty years later, researchers indicate that a differential between women and men continues to persist. This may be due to the gender inequalities in the professional communities, in which men continue to receive most of the leadership positions. For this reason, current scholars suggest that on-campus as well as community members should provide encouragement for all African American male and female students (Golde, 2000; Patton & Harper, 2003; Taylor & Antony, 2001). African American students base their persistence and retention in part on the encouragement they receive from African American faculty mentors (Cuyjet, 2006; DeFrietas & Bravo, 2012; Johnson-Bailey, 2004). Non-academic mentoring relationships and experiences (e.g. practical experiences, job shadowing) are also beneficial as they provide social and emotional benefits, such as self-confidence, self-esteem, and motivation (Butler et al., 2013; Patton, 2009).

Mentoring in Higher Education

African American students can engage in two forms of on-campus mentoring: formal and informal. Formal mentoring involves structured campus programming and/or curricular requirements (Cuseo, 2010). Institutions across the country utilize this type of mentoring and it is often provided by campus organization (e.g. diversity and multicultural offices) and academic department; however, most of the mentoring that takes place at the departmental level is peer oriented (Colvin & Ashman, 2010; Cuseo, 2010).

Formal mentoring

Scholars indicate that formal mentoring involves key elements, which include the following (Eby, Rhodes & Allen, 2007; Garvey & Alred, 2003; Grossman & Rhodes, 2002): (a) an agreed-upon definition that the interaction involves a professional and student, (b) the selection of mentors and mentees in a culturally sensitive manner, (c) participation should be optional to the mentor and mentee, (d) the process involves acceptance and support as well as coaching, advocacy, and information giving, (e) objectives of the relationship are clear and understood, (f) the mentoring relationship is valued and supported by the organization or department, and (g) the relationship has a clear impact over time.

Informal mentoring

Informal mentoring, which is far more common in higher education, is a naturally occurring relationship, which often begins in higher education due to the student's regular interactions with the faculty member through research, teaching, or other nontraditional interactions (Coles & Blacknall, 2011; McLearn, Colsanto, & Schoen, 1998). The informal relationship provides both psychosocial (e.g. enhances student wellbeing) and career support (Inzer & Crawford, 2005; Rhodes, Grossman & Resch, 2000). Formal mentoring is different from informal mentoring because, typically, in formal mentorship the organization develops a program and process for mentoring to take place. The relationship is usually short term (one year) formally, with the hope it will develop informally over the long term (Inzer & Crawford, 2005).

Both types of mentoring are essential in creating a supportive educational environment for African American students. They allow these students to enhance their professional preparation as well as provide emotional supports for the racialized experiences involving discrimination and oppression that they experience during their programs.

SUMMARY

This chapter explored how historical legislation has yet to realize the goal of equitable educational experiences for African American students at predominantly white institutions. The numerous challenges and difficulties that African American students continue to experience related to racism, marginalization, and stereotyping are staggering in comparison to their white peers and other ethnic groups. This chapter also detailed the role racial identity has in the educational experiences of African American students. In this regard, support strategies, such as mentoring and peer supports were presented to provide readers with guidance on how to meet the needs of African American students that attend PWIs.

REFERENCES

Adams, H. G. (1992). Mentoring: An essential factor in the doctoral process for minority students. Notre Dame: The GEM Program.

Akbar, N. (1979). African roots of Black personality. In W. D. Smith et al. (Eds.). *Reflections on Black Psychology.* Washington, DC: University Press of America.

Ancis, J. R., Sedlacek, W. E., & Mohr, J. J. (2000). Student perceptions of campus cultural climate by race. *Journal of Counseling & Development, 78,* 180–185.

Anderson, M. L., & Collins, P. H. (2007). Race, *Class, and Gender: An Anthology* (6th ed.), Belmont, CA: Wadsworth Publishing.

Aramovich, N. P. (2014). The effect of stereotype threat on group versus individual performance. *Small Group Research, 45,* 176–197.

Baker, C. N. (2013). Social support and success in higher education: The influence of on-campus support on African American and Latino college students. *Urban Review, 45,* 632–650.

Baldwin, J. A. (1980). The psychology of oppression. In M. K. Assante & A. Vandi (Eds.), *Contemporary Black thought* (pp. 97–109). Beverly Hills, CA: Sage.

Baldwin, J. A. (1984). African self-consciousness and the mental health of African-Americans. *Journal of Black Studies, 15,* 177–194.

Barefoot, B. O., Warnock, C. L., Dickenson, M. P., Richardson, S. E., & Roberts, M. R. (Eds.) (1998). Exploring the evidence: Reporting research on first-year seminars (Vol. II) (Monograph No. 25). Columbia, SC: University of South Carolina, National Resource Center for The First-Year Experience and Students in Transition.

Baum, S. (2013). Where do African American students go to college? *Metrotrends Blog.* Retrieved from http://blog.metrotrends.org/2013/08/african-american-students-college/Black graduate women. *Race Ethnicity and Education, 7*(4), 331–349.

Blackwell, J. E. (1983). *Networking and mentoring: A study of cross-generational experiences of Black graduate and professional schools.* Atlanta, GA: Southern Education Foundation.

Blair, M. (2008). "Whiteness" as institutionalized racism as conspiracy: Understanding the paradigm. *Educational Review, 60(3),* 249–251.
Bonilla-Silva, E. 2001. "Anything but racism: how social scientists limit the significance of racism." *Race and Society 4,* 117–131.
Bonilla-Silva, Eduardo. (2006). *Racism without Racists: Color-Blind Racism and the Persistence of Racial Inequality in the United States.* Rowman & Littlefield.
Bova, B. (2000). Mentoring revisited: The Black woman's experience. *Mentoring & Tutoring, 8*(1), 5–16.
Brittian, A. S., & Gray, D. L. (2014). African American students' perceptions of differential treatment in learning environments: Examining the moderating role of peer support, connection to heritage, and discrimination efficacy. *Journal of Education, 194,* 1–9.
Brodkin, K. (1999). *How Jews Became White Folks and what that Says About Race in America.* New Brunswick, NJ: Rutgers University Press.
Brondolo, E., Thompson, S., Brady, N., Apppel, R., Cassells, A., Tobin, J. N., Sweeney, M. (2005). The relationship of racism to appraisals and coping in a community sample. *Ethnicity & Disease, 15,* S5–16-19.
Brown v. Board of Education of Topeka II, 349 U.S. 294 (1955).
Brown v. Board of Education, 347 U.S. 483 (1954).
Brown, C. L., Love, K. M., Tyler, K. M., Garriot, P. O., Thomas, D., & Roan-Bell, C. (2013). Parental attachment, family communalism, and racial identity among African American college students. *Journal of Multicultural Counseling and Development, 41,* 108–122.
Brown, N. L. (2009). Fusing critical race theory with practice to improve mentorship. *International Forum of Teaching and Studies, 5,* 18–21.
Browne Huntt, M. (2013). Coping with gendered racial microaggressions among Black women college students. Journal of African American Studies, 17, 51073. DOI: 10.1007/s12111–012-9219–0.
Browne, M., Mendenhall, R., & Lewis, J. A. (2012). Racial microaggressions in the residence halls: Experiences of students of color at a predominantly White University. *Journal of Diversity in Higher Education, 5,* 159–173.
Butler, S. K., Evans, M. P., Brooks, M., Williams, C. R., & Bailey, D. F. (2013). Mentoring African American men during their postsecondary and graduate school experiences: Implications for the counseling profession. *Journal of Counseling and Development, 91,* 419–427. DOI: 10.1002/j.1556–6676.2013.00113.x
Cabrera, N. L., Miner, D. D., & Milem, J. F. (2013). Can a summer bridge program impact first-year persistence and performance?: A case study of the New Start Summer Program. *Research in Higher Education.* DOI: 10.1007/s11162–013-9286–7
Chae, J. H., Piedmont, R. L., Estadt, B. K., & Wicks, R. J. (1995). Personological evaluation of Clance's impostor phenomenon scale in a Korean sample. *Journal of Personality Assessment, 65,* 468–485.
Civil Rights Act of 1964 § 7, 42 U.S.C. § 2000e et seq (1964).
Civil Rights Act of 1964, Pub.L. 88–352, 78 Stat. 241 (1964).
Clance, P. R. & S. Imes. 1978. The imposter phenomenon in high achieving women: Dynamics and therapeutic interventions. *Psychotherapy: Theory, Research and Practice* 15: 241–247.

Cole, E. R., & Arriola, K. (2007). Black Students on White Campuses: Toward a Two-Dimensional Model of Black Acculturation. *Journal of Black Psychology, 33*(4), 379–403.

Coleman, L. D. (2008). Experiences of African American Students in a Predominantly White, Two-Year Nursing Program. *ABNF Journal, 19*(1), 8–13.

Coles, A., & Blacknall, T. (2011). The role of mentoring in college access and success. Washington, DC: Institute for Higher Education Policy. Retrieved from http://www.ihep.org/assets/files/publications/m-r/THE_ROLE_OF_MENTORING_IN_ACCESS_AND_SUCCESS_FINAL_Spring_2011.pdf

Collins, K. M. T., Onweugbuzie, A. J., & Jiao, Q. G. (2014). Reading ability as a predictor of African American graduate students' technical writing proficiency in the context of statistics courses. *Journal of Negro Education, 83,* 135–146.

Collins, P. H. (2000). Gender, Black feminism, and Black political economy. *Annals of the American Academy of Political and Social Science, 568.* 41–53.

Colvin, J. W., & Ashman, M. (2010, May). Roles, risks, and benefits of peer mentoring relationships in higher education. *Mentoring & Tutoring: Partnership in Learning, 18*(2), 121–134.

Contrada, R. J., Ashmore, R. D., Gary, M. L., Coups, E., Egeth, J. D., Sewell, A., et al. (2001). Measures of ethnicity-related stress: Psychometric properties, ethnic group differences, and associations with well-being. *Journal of Applied Social Psychology, 31,* 1775–1820.

Council for Opportunity in Education, retrieved www.coenet.us

Cowan Pitre, C. & Pitre, P. (2009). Increasing underrepresented high school students' college transitions and achievements: TRIO educational opportunity programs. *NASSP Bulletin 93,* 96–110.

Cowan Pitre, C., & Pitre, P. (2009). Increasing underrepresented high school students' college transitions and achievements: TRIO educational opportunity programs. *NASSP Bulletin, 93,* 96–110.

Crawford, K., & Smith, D. (2005). The we and the us: Mentoring African American women. *Journal of Black Studies, 36*(1), 52.67.

Crenshaw, K. (1995.) Mapping the Margins: Intersectionality, Identity Politics, and Violence against Women of Color. In Kimberlé Crenshaw *et al.* (eds.). *Critical Race Theory. The Key Writings That Formed the Movement.* New York: The New Press.

Cross, W. (1991). *Shades of Black: Diversity in African American identity.* Philadelphia, PA: Temple University Press.

Cross, W. E., Jr., & Fhagen-Smith, P. (1996). Nigrescence and ego identity development: accounting for differential Black identity patterns. In P. B. Pedersen, J. G. Draguns, W. J. Lonner, & J. E. Trimble (Eds.), *Counseling across cultures* (4th ed., pp. 108–123). Thousand Oaks, CA: Sage.

Cuseo, J. (2010). Peer Power: Empirical evidence for the positive impact of peer interaction, support, and leadership. *E-Source for College Transitions, 7*(4), 4–6.

Cuseo, J. B. (2009). The empirical case for the first-year seminar: Course impact on student retention and academic achievement. E-Source for College Student Transitions, 6(6), 5–7.

Cuyjet, M. J. (Ed.). (2006). African *American men in college.* San Francisco, CA: Jossey-Bass.

D'Augelli, A. R., & Hershberger, S. L. (1993). African American undergraduates on a predominantly White campus: Academic factors, social networks, and campus climate. *Journal of Negro Education, 62*(1), 67–81.

Darder, A. (1991). *Culture and power in the classroom: A Critical foundation for bicultural education.* Westport, CT: Bergin & Garvey.

DeFreitas, S. C., & Bravo, A. (2012). The influence of involvement with faculty and mentoring on the self-efficacy and academic achievement of African American and Latino college students. *Journal of the Scholarship of Teaching and Learning, 12*(4), 1–11.

Delucchi, M. (1997). "Liberal arts" colleges and the myth of uniqueness. Journal of Higher Education, 68, 414–426.

Diller, J. V. (2004). *Cultural diversity: A primer for the human services.* 2nd ed. Belmont, CA: Brooks/Cole-Thomson Learning.

Dixon-Reeves, R. (2003). Mentoring as a precursor to incorporation: An assessment of the mentoring experience of recently minted Ph.D.s. *Journal of Black Studies, 34*(1), 12–27.

Douglas, D., & Attewell, P. (2014). The bridge and the troll underneath: Summer bridge programs and degree completion. *American Journal of Education, 121,* 87–109.

Drake, B. (2014). Public strongly back affirmative action programs on campus. *Pew Research Center.* Retrieved from http://www.pewresearch.org/fact-tank/2014/04/22/public-strongly-backs-affirmative-action-programs-on-campus/

Du Bois, W. E. B. (1903). *The Souls of Black Folk.* University Press John Wilson and Son: Cambridge.

Du Bois, W. E. B. (1989). *The souls of Black folk.* New York: Penguin. Originally published 1903.

Eby, L. T., Rhodes, J. E., & Allen, T. D. (2007). Definition and evolution of mentoring. In T. D. Allen & L. T. Eby (Eds.), The Blackwell handbook of mentoring: A multiple perspectives approach (pp. 7–20). Oxford, England: Blackwell. DOI: 10.1111/b.9781405133739.2007.00002.x

Elion, A. A., Wang, K. T., Slaney, R. B., French, B. H. (2012). Perfectionism in African American student: Relationship to racial identity, GPA, self-esteem, and depression. *Cultural Diversity and Ethnic Minority Psychology, 18,* 118–127.

Feagin, J. R., & Sikes, M. P. (1995). How Black students cope with racism on White campuses. *Journal of Blacks in Higher Education, 8,* 91–97.

Felder, P. P., & Barker, M. J. (2013). Extending Bell's concept of interest convergence: A framework for understanding the African American doctoral student experience. *Internal Journal of Doctoral Studies, 8,* 1–20. Retrieved from http://ijds.org/Volume8/IJDSv8p001–020Felder0384.pdf

Felder, P. P., Stevenson, H. C., & Gasman, M. (2014). Understanding race in doctoral student socialization. *International Journal of doctoral studies, 9,* 21–42.

Fhagen-Smith, P. E., Vandiver, B. J., Worrell, F. C., & Cross, W. E. (2010). (Re)examining racial identity attitude differences across gender, community type, and socioeconomic status among African American college students. *Identity, 10,* 164–180. DOI: 10.1080/15283488.2010.495907.

Fidler, P. P., & Moore, P. S. (1996). A comparison of effects of campus residence and freshman seminar attendance on freshman dropout rates. *Journal of The Freshman Year Experience and Students in Transition, 8*(2), 7–16.

Fine, M. (2004). The power of the Brown v. Board of Education decision: Theorizing threats to sustainability. *American Psychologist, 59,* 502–510. DOI: 10.1037/0003-066X.59.6.502

Fischer, M. J. (2007). Settling into campus life: Differences by race/ethnicity in college involvement and outcomes. *The Journal of Higher Education, 78,* 125–161.

Flemming, A. S. (1976). Fulfilling the letter and spirit of the law: Desegregation of the nation's public schools. Washington, DC: U.S. Commission on Civil Rights.

Garvey, B., & Alred, G. (2003). An introduction to the symposium on mentoring: Issues and prospects. *British Journal of Guidance and Counselling, 31,* 1–9.

Gay, G. (2004). Navigating marginality en route to the professoriate: Graduate students of color learning and living in academia. *International Journal of Qualitative Studies in Education, 17*(2), 265–288.

Gildersleeve, R. E., Croom, N. N., Vasquez, P. L. (2011). "Am I going crazy?!" A critical race analysis of doctoral education. *Equity and Excellence in Education, 44*(1), 93–114.

Gloria, A. M., & Pope-Davis, D. B. (1997). Cultural ambience: The importance of a culturally aware learning environment in the training and education of counselors. In D. B. Pope-Davis & H. L. K. Coleman (Eds.), *Multicultural Counseling Competencies: Assessment, Education and Training, and Supervision* (pp. 242–259). Thousand Oaks, CA: Sage.

Golde, C. M. (2000). Should I stay or should I go? Student descriptions of the doctoral attrition process. *The Review of Higher Education, 23*(2), 199–227.

Gotanda, N. 1991. "A Critique of 'Our Constitution Is Color-Blind.'" *Stanford Law Review. 44*(1), 28–30.

Grantham, T. G., & Ford, D. Y. (2003). Beyond self-concept and self-esteem: Racial identity and gifted African American students. *High School Journal, 87*(1), 18–29.

Gregory, S. T. (2003). Planning for the increasing number of Latino students. *Planning for Higher Education, 31*(4), 13–19.

Grossman, J. B., & Rhodes, J. E. (2002). The test of time: Predictors and effects of duration in youth mentoring. *American Journal of Community Psychology, 30,* 199–219.

Haizlip, B. N. (2012). Addressing the underrepresentation of African-Americans in counseling and psychology program. *College Student Journal, 46,* 214–222.

Hankivsky, O., Christoffersen, A. (2008). Intersectionality and the determinants of health: a Canadian perspective. *Critical Public Health, 18 (3),* 271–283.

Harvey, J. & C. Katz. 1985. *If I'm so successful, why do I feel like a fake? The imposter phenomenon.* New York: St. Martin's.

Harwood, S. A., Hunett, M., Mendenhall, R., & Lewis, J. A. (2012). Racial microaggressions in residence halls: Experiences of students of color at a predominantly White university. *Journal of Diversity in Higher Education, 5,* 159–173.

Haskins, N., Whitfield-Williams, M., Shillingford, M. A., Singh, A., Moxley, R., & Ofauni, C. (2013). The experiences of Black master's counseling students:

A phenomenological injury. *Counselor Education and Supervision, 52,* 162–178. DOI: 10.1002/j.1556–6978.2013.00035.x

Helms, J. E. (1984). Towards a theoretical explanation of effect race on counseling: A black and white model. *Counseling Psychologist, 12,* 153–165.

Helms, J. E. (1990). *Black and White racial identity.* Westport, CT: Greenwood Press.

Helms, J. E. (1994a). Racial identity and career assessment. *Journal of Career Assessment, 2,* 199–209.

Helms, J. E. (1994b). The conceptualization of racial identity and other "racial" constructs. In E. J. Trickett, R. J. Watts, & D. Birman (Eds.), *Human diversity* (pp. 285–311). San Francisco: Jossey-Bass.

Helms, J. E. (1995). An update of Helms's White and people of color racial identity models. In J. G. Ponterotto, J. M. Casas, L. A. Suzuki, & C. M. Alexander (Eds.), *Handbook of multicultural counseling* (pp. 181–198). Thousand Oaks, CA: Sage.

Henfield, M. S., Owens, D., & Witherspoon, S. (2011). African American students in counselor education programs: Perceptions of their experiences. *Counselor Education and Supervision, 50,* 226–242.

Hines, M. T. (2009). Having their say: Black women's lived experience at predominantly White doctoral programs of educational leadership. *National Forum of Educational Administration & Supervision, 26,* 90–121.

Hing, J. (2012). Here's how students of color fit into higher ed's shifting ecosystem. *ColorLines.* Retrieved from http://colorlines.com/archives/2012/07/the_shifting_highereducation_ecosystemand_how students of color fit.html/

Holcomb-McCoy, C., & Myers, J. E. (1999). Multicultural competence and counselor training: A national survey. *Journal of Counseling and Development, 77,* 294–302.

Holland, N. E. (2011). The powers of peers: Influences on postsecondary education planning and experiences of African American students. *Urban Education, 46*(5), 1029–1055.

Huguet, P., & Régner, I. (2007). Stereotype threat among school girls in quasi-ordinary classroom circumstances. *Journal of Educational Psychology, 99,* 545–560.

Hunn, V. (2014). African American students, retention, and team-based learning: A review of the literature and recommendations for retention at Predominately White Institutions. *Journal of Black Studies, 45,* 301–314.

Hurtado, S. (1992). The campus racial climate: Contexts of conflict. *The Journal of Higher Education, 63*(5), 539–569.

Ihme, T. & Möller, J. (2014). "He Who Can, Does; He Who Cannot, Teaches?": Stereotype threat and preservice teachers. *Journal of Educational Psychology,* Advance online publication. Doi: 10.1037/a0037373

Iloh, C., & Toldson, I. A. (2013). Black students in 21st century higher education: A closer look at for-profit and community colleges (Editor's Commentary). *The Journal of Negro Education, 82,* 205–212.

Inzer, L. D. & Crawford, C. B. (2005). A review of formal and informal mentoring: Processes, problems, and design. *Journal of Leadership Education, 4,* 31–50.

Jackson, B. (1975). Black identity development. *Journal of Educational Diversity, 2,* 19–25.

Jackson, G. G., & Kirschner, S. (1973). Racial self-designation and preference for a counselor. *Journal of Counseling Psychology, 20,* 560–564.

Johnson-Ahorlu, R. N. (2013). "Our biggest challenge is stereotypes": Understanding stereotype threat and the academic experiences of African American undergraduate. *The Journal of Negro Education, 82*, 382–392.

Johnson-Bailey, J. (2004). Hitting the proverbial wall: Participation and retention issues for outcomes. *Journal of Higher Education, 78*(2), 125–161.

Jones, S. T. (1999). *A study of how the climate on a predominantly White campus of a state funded public urban institution of higher education effects the persistence of undergraduate African-American females.* (Doctoral Dissertation, State University of New York at Buffalo). Dissertation Abstracts International. 60. (A2866).

Jordan, A. H., & Lovett, B. J. (2007). Stereotype threat and test performance: A primer for school psychologists. *Journal of School Psychology, 45*, 45–59.

Kador, J. & Lewis, C. (2007). The role of mentors/advisors in the doctoral training of African American students at predominately White universities: Implications for doctoral training. *Essays in Education, 19*, 100–118.

Kambon, K. (1992). *The African personality in America: An African-centered framework.* Tallahassee: NUBIAN Nation.

Kanter, R. M. (1977). *Men and Women of the Corporation.* New York: Basic Books.

Kao, G. (2001). Race and ethnic differences in peer influences on educational achievement. In E. Anderson & D. S. Massey (Eds.), Problem of the century: Racial stratification in the US (pp. 437–460). New York: Russell Sage Foundation.

Kozol, J. (2005). *Shame of the nation: The restoration of apartheid in America.* New York, NY: Crown Publishing.

Krieger, N. (1999). Embodying inequality: A review of concepts, measures, and methods for studying health consequences of discrimination. *International Journal of Health Services, 29*, 295–352.

Kuh, G. D., Cruce, T. M., Shoup, R., Kinzie, J., & Gonyea, R. M. (2008). Unmasking the effects of student engagement on first-year college grades and persistence. Journal of Higher Education, 79(5), 540–563.

Kuh, G. D. (1996). Guiding principles for creating seamless learning environments for undergraduates. *Journal of College Student Development, 37*(2), 135–148.

Lee, J. J. (2007). Racism toward international student. *About Campus, 11,* 28–30.

Lewis, C. W., Ginsberg, R., Davies, T., & Smith, K. (2004). The experiences of African American PH.D. students at a predominantly White Carnegie 1 research institution. *College Student Journal, 38*(2), 231–246.

Lewis, J. A., Mendenhall, R., Harwood, S. A., & Browne Huntt, M. (2013). Coping with gendered racial microaggressions among Black women college students. *Journal of African American Studies, 17*(1), 51–73. Doi: 10.1007/s12111-012-9219-0

Lightsey, O. R., & Barnes, P. W. (2007). Discrimination, attributional tendencies, generalized self-efficacy, and assertiveness as predictors of psychological distress among African Americans. *Journal of Black Psychology, 33,* 27–50.

Locks, A. M., Hurtado, S., Bowman, N., & Oseguera, L. (2008). Extending notions of campus climate and diversity to students' transition to college. *Review of Higher Education, 31*(3), 257–285.

Marable, M. (1992). *Black America.* Westfield, NJ: Open Media.

Massey, D.S., & Owens, J. (2014). Mediators of stereotype threat among Black college students. *Ethnic and Racial Studies, 37*, 557–575. DOI: 10.1080/01419870.2013.786110

Maton, K. I., Wimms, H. E., Grant, S. K., Wittig, M. A., Rogers, M. R., Vasquez, M. J. T. (2011). Experiences and perspectives of African American, Latina/o, Asian American, and European American psychology graduate students: A national study. *Cultural Diversity and Ethnic Minority Psychology, 17*(1), 68–78.

Maton, K. I., Pollard, S. A., McDougall Weise, T. V., & Hrabowski, F. A. (2012). Meyerhoff scholars program: A strengths-based, institution-wide approach to increasing diversity in science, technology, engineering, and mathematics. *Mount Sinai Journal of Medicine, 79* (5), 610–623.

Maxwell, M. (2001). "Peer tutoring, an overview: History and research on program effectiveness." *Journal of the National Tutoring Association, 1*(1), 8–16.

McCabe, J. (2009). Racial and gender microaggressions on a predominantly-White campus: Experiences of Black, Latina/o and White undergraduates. *Race, Gender, & Class, 16*, 133–151.

McDonald, M. G. (2009). Dialogues on "Whiteness", leisure, and (anti)racism. *Journal of Leisure Research, 41*(1), 5–21.

McIntosh, P. (1990). White privilege: Unpacking the invisible knapsack. *Independent School, 49*, 31–36.

McLaurin v. Oklahoma State Regents, 339 U.S. 637 (1950).

McLean, K. T., Colasanto, D., and Schoen, C. 1998. Mentoring Makes a Difference: Findings from The Commonwealth Fund 1998 Survey of Adults Mentoring Young People. The Commonwealth Fund. Retrieved from http://www.commonwealthfund.org.

McNeill, B. W., & Hom, K. L., & Perez, J. A. (1995). The training and supervisory needs of racial and ethnic minority students. *Journal of Multicultural Counseling and Development, 23*, 246–258.

Missouri ex rel. Gaines v. Canada, Registrar of the University of Missouri, 305 U.S. 337 (1938).

Muzzatti, B., & Agnoli, F. (2007). Gender and mathematics: Attitudes and stereotype threat susceptibility in Italian children. Developmental Psychology, 43, 747–759.

Myers, L. J. (1993). *Understanding an Afrocentric world view: Introduction to an optimal Psychology* (2nd ed.). Dubuque, IA: Kendall/Hunt.

Myers, R. D. *College Success Programs: Executive Summary.* Washington, D.C.: Pathways to College Network, 2003.

Nagasawa, R., & Wong, P. (1999). A theory of minority students' survival in college. Sociological Inquiry, 69(1), 76–90.

Nagasawa, R., & Wong, P. (1999). A theory of minority students' survival in college. *Sociological Inquiry, 69*(1), 76–90.

Nagda, B. A., Gregerman, S. R., Jonides, J., von Hippel, W., & Lerner, J. S. (1998). Undergraduate student-faculty research partnerships affect student retention. *Review of Higher Education, 22*(1), 55–72.

National Center for Education Statistics (2011). Retrieved from http://nces.ed.gov.

National Center for Education Statistics. (2013). Retrieved from http://nces.ed.gov.
Negga, F., Applewhite, S., & Livingston, I. (2007). African American college students and stress: School racial composition, self-esteem and social support. *College Student Journal, 41*, 823–830.
Negy, C. (1999). A critical examination of selected perspectives in multicultural therapy and psychology. *Psychology: A Journal of Human Behavior, 36*, 2–11.
Nettles, M. T. (1990). Success in doctoral programs: Experiences of minority and White students. *American Journal of Education, 98*(4), 494–522.
Nunez, R. (1999). The validity of LatCrit: History, race, and the education of the Mexicano/Chicano child. *Harvard Latino Law Review, 3,* 1–48.
Ong, A. D., Fuller-Rowell, T., & Burrow, A. L. (2009). Racial discrimination and the stress process. *Journal of Personality & Social Psychology, 96,* 1259–1271.
Onwuegbuzie, A. J., Mayes, E., Arthur, L., Johnson, J., Robinson, V., Ashe, S., Elbedour, S., Collins, K. M. T. (2014). Reading comprehension among African American graduate students. *Journal of Negro Education, 73,* 443–457.
Orfield, G. (2014). Realizing the promise of the civil rights revolution: Challenges and consequences for graduate education. *American Journal of Education, 120* (4), 451–456.
Orfield, G. and Lee, C. (2006). Racial Transformation and the Changing Nature of Segregation. Cambridge, MA: The Civil Rights Project at Harvard University.
Osborne, J. W., & Walker, C. (2006). Stereotype threat, identification with academics, and withdrawal from school: Why the most successful students of colour might be most likely to withdraw. *Educational Psychology, 26,* 563–577.
Padgett, R. D., Keup, J. R., Pascarella, E. T. (2012). The impact of first-year seminars on college students' life-long learning orientations. Journal of Student Affairs Research and Practice, *50*(2), 133–151.
Pascarella, E. T., & Terenzini, P. T. (2005). How College Affects Students, Volume 2, A Third Decade of Research. San Francisco, CA: Jossey-Bass.
Patterson-Stewart, K. E., Ritchie, M. H., & Sanders, E. T. W. (1997). Interpersonal dynamics of African-American persistence in doctoral programs at predominantly White universities. *Journal of College Student Development, 38,* 489–498.
Patton, L. D. (2009). My sister's keeper: A qualitative examination of mentoring experiences among African American women in graduate and professional schools. *Journal of Higher Education, 80,* 510–537.
Patton, L. D., & Harper, S. R. (2003). Mentoring relationships among African American women in graduate and professional schools. In M. F. Howard-Hamilton (Ed.), Meeting the needs of African American women. *New Directions for Student Services,* no. 104, pp. 67–78.
Patton, L. D., Bridges, B. K., & Flowers, L. A. (2011). Effects on Greek affiliation on African American students' engagement: Differences by college racial composition, *College Student Affairs Journal, 29,* 113–123.
Pierce, C., Carew, J., Pierce-Gonzalez, D., & Willis, D. (1978). An experiment in racism: TV commercials. In C. Pierce (Ed.), *Television and education* (pp. 62–88). Beverly Hills, CA: Sage.
Plessy v. Ferguson, 163 U.S. 537 (1896).

Plummer, D. (1997). Racial identity development of African American adolescents. In N. BaNikongo (Ed.), Leading issues in African American studies (pp. 81–88). Durham, NC: Carolina Academic Press.

Proctor, S. L., & Truscott, S. D. (2012). Reasons for African American student attrition from school psychology program, *Journal of School Psychology, 50*, 655–679.

Raines, J. M. (2012). FirstSTEP: A preliminary review of the effects of a summer bridge program on pre-college STEM majors. *Journal of STEM Education, 13*, 22–29.

Reeder, M. C., & Schmitt, N. (2013). Motivational and Judgment Predictors of African American Academic Achievement at PWIs and HBCUs. *Journal Of College Student Development, 54*(1), 29–42.

Reid, K. W. (2013). Understanding the relationships among racial identity, self-efficacy, institutional integration and academic achievement of Black males attending research universities. *Journal of Negro Education, 82*, 75–93.

Rhodes, J. E., Grossman, J. B. & Resch, N. L. 2000. "Agents of Change: Pathways Through Which Mentoring Relationships Influence Adolescents' Academic Adjustment." *Child Development, 71*, 1662–1671.

Rodgers, K. A., & Summers, J. J. (2008). African American students at Predominantly White Institutions: A motivational and self-systems approach to understanding retention. *Educational Psychology Review, 20*, 171–190.

Rowley, S. J., & Moore, J. A. (2002). When who I am impacts how I am represented. *Roeper Review, 24*(2), 63.

Sailes, G. A. (1993). An investigation of Black student attrition at a large, predominantly White, Midwestern university. *The Western Journal of Black Studies, 17*(4), 179–182.

Schmader, T., Johns, M., & Forbes, C. (2008). An integrated process model of stereotype threat on performance. *Psychological Review, 115*, 336–356.

Seward, D. X. (2009). *Understanding Students of Color in Multicultural Counselor Training Courses: A Qualitative Investigation of Student Perspectives.* (Unpublished Doctoral Dissertation). University of Rochester. Retrieved from Dissertations and Theses Database (AAT 3357083).

Sidle, M. W., & McReynolds, J. (1999). The freshman year experience: Student retention and student success. NASPA Journal, *36*(4), 288–300.

Sipuel v. Board of Regents of Univ. of Okla., 332 U.S. 631 (1948).

Smith, S., & Moore, M. (2002). Expectations of campus racial climate and social adjustment among African American college students. In W. Allen, M. Spencer, & C. O'Conner (Eds.), African American education: Race community, inequality, and achievement (pp. 93–118). NY: Elsevier Science Ltd.

Solorzano, D., Ceja, M., & Yosso, T. (2000). Critical Race Theory, racial micro aggressions, and campus racial climate: The experiences of African American college students. *The Journal of Negro Education, 41*, 171–187.

Starke, M. C., Harth, M., and Sirianni, F. (2001). Retention, bonding, and academic achievement: Success of a first-year seminar. *Journal of the First Year Experience 13*(2): 7–35.

Steele, C. M. (1997). A threat in the air: How stereotypes shape intellectual identity and performance. *American Psychologist, 52*(6), 613–629.

Stolle-McAllister, K. S. (2011). The Case for Summer Bridge: Building Social and Cultural Capital for Talented Black STEM Students. *Science Education, 20,* 12–22.

Strayhorn, T. L. (2012). Satisfaction and retention among African American men at two-year community colleges. *Community College Journal of Research and Practice, 36,* 358–375.

Sue, D. W., & Sue, D. (2003). Counseling the culturally diverse: Theory and practice (4th ed.). New York: Wiley.

Sue, D. W., Capodilupo, C. M., Torino, G. C., Bucceri, J. M., Holder, A. M., Nadal, Keven, L., & Esquilin, M. (2007). Racial microaggressions in everyday life. *American Psychologist, 62,* 271–286. DOI: 10.1037/0003-066X.62.4.271

Sutton, E. M., & Kimbrough, W. M. (2001). Trends in Black student involvement. *NASPA Journal, 39,* 30–40.

Sweatt v. Painter, 339 U.S. 629 (1950).

Tatum, B. D. (1997). *Why are all the black kids sitting together in the cafeteria? And other conversations about race.* New York, NY: Basic Books.

Taylor, E., & Anthony, J. S. (2001). Stereotype threat reduction and wise schooling: Towards the successful socialization of African American doctoral students in education. *Journal of Negro Education, 69*(3), 184–198.

Taylor, E., & Anthony, J. S. (2001). Stereotype threat reduction and wise schooling: Towards the successful socialization of African American doctoral students in education. *Journal of Negro Education, 69*(3), 184–198.

Taylor, E., Gillborn, D., & Ladson-Billings, G. (2009). *Foundations of critical race theory in education.* New York, NY: Routledge.

Taylor, E., Gillborn, D., & Ladson-Billings, G. (2009). *Foundations of critical race theory in education.* New York, NY: Routledge.

Thomas, C. W. (1971). *Boys no more.* Beverly Hills, CA: Glencoe Press.

Thomas, S. P., Thompson, C., Pollio, H. R., Greenberg, K., Conwill, W., Sall, A., Klukken, G., Davis, M. W., & Dias-Bowie, Y. (2007). Experiences of struggling African American students at a predominantly White university. *Research in the schools, 14*(2), 1–17.

Tinto, V. (1993). *Leaving college: Rethinking the causes and cures of student attrition.* Chicago; London: University of Chicago Press.

Tobolowsky, B. F., & Associates. (2008). 2006 National Survey of First-Year Seminars: Continuing innovations in the collegiate curriculum (Monograph No. 51). Columbia, SC: University of South Carolina, National Resource Center for The First-Year Experience and Students in Transition.

Torres, L., Driscoll, M. W., & Burrow, A. L. (2010). Racial microaggressions and psychological functioning among highly achieving African-Americans: A mixed-methods approach. *Journal of Social & Clinical Psychology, 29.* 1074–1099. DOI: 10.1521/jscp.2010.29.10.1074.

Truong, K. A., & Museus, S. D. (2012). Racial trauma in doctoral study: An inventory for coping and mediating relationships. *Harvard Educational Review, 82,* 226–254.

Tuitt, F. (2010). Sidelines and separate spaces: Making education anti-racist for students of color. *Race, Ethnicity, and Education, 22,* 246–257.

Vella, J. (1994). Learning to Listen, Learning to Teach, San Francisco: Jossey-Bass
Venezia, A., & Jaeger, L. (2013). Transitions from high school to college. *Future of Children, 23,* 117–136.
White, J. W., & Ali-Khan, C. (2013). The role of Academic discourse in minority students' academic assimilation. American Secondary Education, *42*(1), 24–42.
Williams Shealey, M. (2009). Voices of African American doctoral students in special education: Addressing the shortage in leadership preparation. *Race, Ethnicity, and Education, 12,* 349–361. DOI: 10.1080/13613320903178295
Woodard, D. B. Jr., Mallory, S. L., and De Luca, A. M. (2001). Retention and institutional effort: A self-study framework. *NASPA Journal, 39*(1), 53–83.
Wyckoff, S. C. (1999). The academic advising process in higher education: History, research, and improvement. *Recruitment & Retention in Higher Education, 13*(1), 1–3.
Young, J. L., & James, E. 2001. Token majority: The work attitudes of male flight attendants. *Sex Roles,* 45: 299–320.
Zinn, M. B., & Dill, B. T. (1996). Theorizing difference from multiracial feminism. *Feminist Studies, 22(2),* 321–333.

Chapter 13

Engaging a Discourse of Policy Analysis and Curriculum that Addresses Poverty and Race

Democracy through Collective Impact Models

Jessica Exkano

It is believed that, "Social development and community development are symbiotic processes" (Mohan, 2011, p. 174). A tenet of policy analysis is that human behavior is deliberate, and that to facilitate change, one must also deliberately seek to change peoples' beliefs and attitudes (Bots, 2013). Successful policy analysis designs provide for a diagnostic within a policy context (to determine whose mind needs to change in the interest of the client), and allow for leaders to design communicative interactions that will produce these changes (Bots, 2013). Utilizing tools from policy analysis to bridge the gap from conceptual to practical, the purpose of this chapter is to: (1) define curriculum, (2) reframe curriculum development for low income, African American youth as a social and community development issue through a systems approach, (3) argue that, as do current federal funding patterns for low income youth, after-school programs reflect a certain understanding of curriculum as collaborative and community based, and (4) highlight the Collective Impact Model, a design-oriented collaborative model, which uses systems logic of shared resources between industry partners to tackle complex social issues to show how after-school programs might be better positioned as likely candidates for sustained funding.

CURRICULUM AS DOING VERSUS CURRICULUM AS KNOWING: UNDERSTANDING THE METAPHORS WE LIVE BY

In this section policy context is defined as conceptual orientations of curriculum that manifest themselves materially. In order for the action to be changed, the guiding conceptual orientation must be identified.

Roget's Twenty-First-Century Thesaurus (Kipfer, 1999) provides a starting point for understanding how concepts manifest themselves in very material ways. Each main entry is related to a master concept, the foundational conceptual building blocks from which words derive their meaning. The term curriculum originates from the Latin term *currere*, to run, as in, to run in the course of a race. Interestingly, the term curriculum does not appear as a main entry in the thesaurus, but rather appears as a subentry of the main entry term *course*, a noun defined as a "plan of study" (p. 178). Further, to provide context to curriculum's linguistic roots, *course* is listed under the master concept of "objects used in" Education. Yet, Roget's lists four other main entries for course, each with linguistic roots in different master concepts:

> (1) Course, a noun, "progress, advance" related to the concepts of "progress" States Of Change and "order" as Physical States; (2) Course, a noun, "path, channel" related to the concepts of "object used for" Transportation, and as "water" listed under Geography of the Planet; (3) Course, a noun, length of action, related to the concept of "duration", as a Time Weight and Measure; (4) Course, flow, run, related to the concepts of "moving oneself slowly or quickly" under the action of Motion.

However, curriculum in an American educational context functions under the master concept of *objects used* in education. In this sense, curriculum becomes a passive actor, a mere object, used in the educative process when conceptualized as a noun. A return to the verbal form, *currere*, better suggests action, a curriculum in motion that one runs in the course of life's race.

Running in the course of life's race, however, is a complex concept for impoverished, African American youth. These youth face setbacks that give them unfair disadvantages that follow them as they set off to compete in life's race. For instance, a study of racial gaps in early childhood on the social, emotional, health, and developmental outcomes for African American boys found that as early as 9 months, racial disparities in socio-emotional development emerge and remain among toddlers and pre-school age boys. Additionally, the study found that as early as 24 months cognitive development disparities emerge in African American boys at statistically significant rates (Aratani, Wright, & Cooper, 2011). Further hampering impoverished youth's course of life is the "double jeopardy" impact; third grade reading scores and poverty negatively influence high school graduation rates for Black youth. Specifically, in a longitudinal study, Hernandez reported that

31% of poor African American boys who could not read at the third-grade level failed to graduate (Hernandez, 2012). And yet, this trend in early grade reading nonproficiency for impoverished African Americans is national. The Annie E. Casey Foundation (2013) noted 82 percent of fourth graders from low-income families—and 84 percent of low-income students who attend high-poverty schools—failed to reach the "proficient" level in reading on the National Assessment of Educational Progress (NAEP) in 2011 (p. 2). Poverty and race are strong indicators that running life's course will be much more difficult for youth of color.

The biggest misconception of the relationship between race and poverty owes itself to a fundamental misunderstanding that one causes the other. A basic rule of statistics is that a correlation of events does not equal causation. The implication is to understand that an existing relationship between two things does not implicate one thing as *causing* the other. Correlating statistics should be understood as an increased likelihood of the presence of associated factors for a particular phenomenon. A sophisticated analysis then seeks to determine *how* those factors interact.

Perspectives of Curriculum for Impoverished/African American Youth

That curriculum is conceptualized as a plan of study, related to the master concept of an object used in school, is a fairly recent development. A historical look at public policy suggests conceptions of curriculum guided by the master concept that curriculum actually begins *before* formal schooling. This may make sense when one considers that curriculum might be understood in the Latin sense of the word as a race that is run during the course of life. Thus, from a lifespan perspective, curriculum might be the things one learns in the classroom of one's immediate environment whether it is home, a child care center, church, a homeless shelter, the street or whatever space an individual occupies.

Four main perspectives are used to understand the rationale for the provision of enrichment services for impoverished youth: (1) biological; (2) environmental—home; (3) environmental—school; and (4) environmental—community. The first perspective is a model of genetics which suggests educational traits are biologically inherited, and as such, achievement is a by-product of race (Winfield, 2007). This perspective is faulty and absolves social and political structures of complicity. For instance, the strongest predictor of academic achievement is parental socioeconomic status (NYSED, 2009). Yet, the status alone isn't the determinant of academic achievement as much as the social resources unavailable to low-income families who live in a society which favors middle-class resources (Bourdieu, 1973). In the context of child development then, one study suggests that oftentimes when race,

SES, and demographics are controlled for, no differences exist in academic achievement for African American boys (Aratani et al., 2011). The second perspective focuses on family characteristics, suggesting familial socioeconomic status and other personal characteristics negatively influence achievement (Placier, 1993, 1996). Indeed, one of the earliest reports concerning African American youth is entitled, "Compensatory Education for Cultural Deprivation," where compensatory and cultural deprivation were synonymously interchangeable titles for impoverished African American youth, realized through the sociologically driven research of the 1950s and '60s (NYSED, 2009). Compensatory education, when understood as the historical response to systemic inequity, has always been dictated by an enveloping idea of a student's sociocultural familial characteristics (microlevel) understood as a lived curriculum. The third perspective suggests the structure of the school delimits academic achievement (Whelage & Rutter, 1986), which was a significant advancement from previous constructions of achievement as solely racial, or reflecting of socioeconomic status. This perspective suggests the school cannot effectively meet the needs of an increasingly diverse student population. The fourth perspective incorporates and extends perspectives two and three, in unifying multiple partners, community, educational, and school, in a collaborative process (Afterschool Alliance, 2013). Perspectives one and two operate under the assumption of a deficit view of the actors, while perspective three delimits other contributing factors, and are therefore, unfruitful for this analysis. It is perspective four that is of interest in this chapter.

UNDERSTANDING MULTIPLE DOMAINS OF STUDENT EXPERIENCE

A developmental ecology view suggests child development occurs across multiple embedded contexts (Bronfenbrenner, 1977; Arnold, Lu, & Armstrong, 2012). Specifically, a developmental ecological approach enables an understanding of a child's development as always-already occurring in a nested web of linked contexts: home, neighborhood, policy, and culture. Developmental ecology theory (Bronfenbrenner, 1977) asserts that multiple systems' interaction is necessary for low-income remediation.

UNDERSTANDING THE NEED FOR ENRICHMENT SERVICES: HOW COGNITIVE ORIENTATIONS OF CURRICULUM REFLECT THE TYPES OF SERVICES PROVIDED

When poverty is conflated with race, it disallows for public policy solutions that can benefit an entire population. Poverty and race have been embodied in

Engaging a Discourse of Policy Analysis 263

Child/Home

Neighborhood

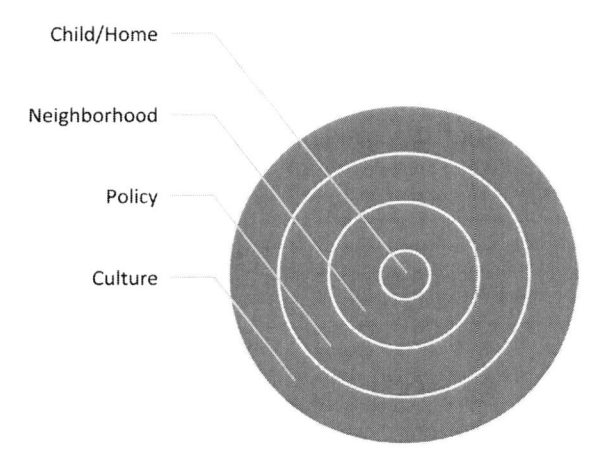

Policy

Culture

Figure 13.1   A Depiction of Urie Bronfenbrenner's Developmental Ecology Model

the concept of the *at risk* youth. Social development and community development must be realized as symbiotic processes as stated earlier in the chapter. To develop community, the old models of poverty as genetic, racialized, family pathology must be reversed. The problem, therefore, is not a question of how to educate at risk youth, but rather, the question is how to consider the topic in a way that benefits many stakeholders in a cost-effective manner? Another question is how to consider at-risk, not in its historical Eugenicist (Winfield, 2007) verbiage as a "pathology" (Placier, 1993, 1996) defined as the science of the causes and effects of diseases, but rather, reframing the topic as a development topic. This can be accomplished when development is understood as identifying and addressing student needs, designing programs, developing policies, and creating environments that encourage positive student growth (Evans, Forney, Guido, Patton, & Renn, 2010). Thus, the narrowly framed, socially stigmatizing problems of race and poverty become essentially reframed as a community development topic.

APPLYING BRONFENBRENNER'S DEVELOPMENTAL ECOLOGY AS A FRAMEWORK FOR UNDERSTANDING YOUTH SYSTEMS INTERACTION

Developmental Psychologist Urie Bronfenbrenner developed a model for understanding the environmental influences affecting child development. These nested contexts (systems), ranging from most influential to least influential on childhood development, include: microsystem, mesosystem, exosystem, and macrosystem.

An ecological developmental approach assumes (a) adolescent development occurs in changing environments, embedded in larger social contexts, over time; (b) solutions should address the interconnections between environments, and allow for innovative restructuring of prevailing systems (Bronfenbrenner, 1977); and (c) a change in one system has ripple-effect implications for other parts of the system (Bess & Dee, 2008). Four environmental contexts conceived of as "nested structures" comprise the settings for developmental interventions (again, referring to Figure 13.1). Identifying the environmental contexts of development allows for locating the needs of students at different levels. Targeted interventions can be addressed once needs have been located. The *Immediate environment (microlevel) of the adolescent* (home, school, after-school program) and the activities, norms, and interpersonal relationships occurring in the immediate environment have the greatest impact on developmental and academic outcomes. *Interrelations between two or more settings* (mesosystem) in which the developing student is involved, such as the relationships between the home and school, or the school and the workplace, comprises the second level at which to provide interventions. Parents of low-income youth face more structural barriers than their high-income peers, including less information, money, and time, which contribute to low levels of parental involvement in college-going decisions (Rowan-Kenyon, Bell, Perna, 2008a). The need for community partners to mitigate the gulf between low-income youth and their families, and to serve as advocates becomes increasingly important (Walpole, 2007). *Social structures (exosystem),* which influence indirectly the immediate settings of students (policies, governmental agencies, distributions of goods and services), provide another level of intervention. For example, social networks can hamper low-income communities' political involvement in neighborhood, community, school enrollment and success in college. Stanton-Salazar (2000) suggests that minority group expectancies of success are relative to actual and perceived access to opportunities in social and educational structures. Negative network orientations (Stanton-Salazar, 2000) and its limitations then can be addressed by community partners through exercises and experiences which enumerate different life roles and choices (Gottfredson, 2004), and enhance social networking capacity. *The culture or overarching pattern* (macrosystem) reflects the belief systems, opportunity structures, and/ or material resources in an environment.

Personal Characteristics of At Risk Youth

The term *at risk* is typically used to identify students who have the propensity to drop out of high school due to academic and social background characteristics (NCES, 1992). At risk youth dropout potentially increases with the presence of multiple indicators (Hammond, Linton, Smink, & Drew, 2007). These indicators typically fall under two categories, behavioral and social/environmental. Behavioral indicators include: (a) students who repeat grades, (b) students with histories of poor math and English grades, (c) students who do little homework; (d) students who often come to class unprepared for classwork, (e) students who often cut class, or are tardy from school; (f) students whose teachers thought they were passive, disruptive, inattentive, or thought they were underachievers; and (g) first-generation students (NCES, 1992; Bergerson, 2010; Bell, Rowan-Kenyon, & Perna, 2009; Rowan-Kenyon, Bell, & Perna, 2008a).

Social/environmental dropout indicators include: (a) students who come from single-parent families, (b) students who frequently changed schools; (c) students whose parents are not actively involved in their school, (d) students whose parents never talk to them about school-related matters, (e) students whose parents hold low expectations about their child's educational attainment; and (f) students from urban schools with large minority populations (NCES, 1992; Bergerson, 2010; Bell, Rowan-Kenyon, & Perna, 2009; Rowan-Kenyon, Bell, & Perna, 2008a). Students whose unique risks make them more susceptible to low college enrollment or dropping out are typically defined as students from families with low incomes, students whose parents did not attend college, or students whose parents work lower-class occupations (Walpole, 2007; Bergerson, 2010). An understanding of the social/environmental and behavioral predictors of at risk dropout culture presents a focalized starting point for targeting and addressing the needs of this population (Hammond, Linton, Smink, & Drew, 2007).

Low Postsecondary Aspirations

According to the NCES (2006) postsecondary aspirations survey, low SES students vary from their high SES counterparts in terms of educational aspirations. Specifically, in 2004, just over half (51%) of high school seniors from low SES backgrounds aspired to attain a bachelors or graduate degree compared to their middle (67%) and high (87%) SES peers' degree aspirations, respectively (NCES, 2006). Further, the study found high school seniors' expectations of graduate school attendance, "were positively related to their academic preparation and experiences, including mathematics course-taking and proficiency, never repeating a grade, and taking college entrance examinations" (NCES, 2006; p. 60), factors which have already been shown to be predictive of dropout culture. While aspirations and actual *outcomes* are two different factors, the research shows that student aspirations are strongly related to the material practices that serve to reify aspirations, highlighting the significance of the role aspirations and experience play in creating a pathway to college (Toldson, Braithwaite, & Rentie, 2009). African American male students aspire to attend college at rates similar to peers in other races. Additionally, African American males' desire to attend college is related to positive academic achievement, positive school experiences, healthy communication with parents, and overall self-efficacy (Toldson et al., 2009). Yet, African American males are not receiving guidance about pathways to college at rates similar to peers of other races. Similarly, African American females fail to have school advocates position them into STEM fields (West-Olatunji et al., 2010).

Self-Esteem

The literature suggests that psychosocial measures of low self-esteem can lead to dropping out. Brown and Rodriguez (2009) found that educational neglect and, socially and intellectually alienated students dropped out of school, highlighting the fact that schooling conditions affect both the psychosocial development of students and subsequent actions such as dropping out. Higher parental involvement is associated with greater levels of self-esteem in adolescents (Bulanda & Majumdar, 2009). However, Gibson (2006) found that relationships with peers, mentors, and specific community groups are related positively to adolescents' self-concept. Myers, Willse, and Villalba (2011) found that wellness factors are predictive of self-esteem in adolescents. Hutz, Martin and Beitel (2007) suggest that a perceived environmental fit (a person's general sense of belongingness within a particular environment) can influence self-esteem in minorities and contribute to lower levels of college environment adjustment. In addition, school-based extracurricular participation can be beneficial to students from different social backgrounds if those activities reflect self-concept and skill sets that remain relevant beyond school (Kort-Butler & Hagewen, 2011). Searcy (2007) suggests that self-esteem is developed through associations, activities, and aurally. According to the literature then, self-esteem is a psychosocial dynamic that can change in accordance to specific social structures and interactions and can influence lifestyle choices.

Mentoring

Mentoring can be beneficial to low SES youth, specifically in terms of increasing prosocial behavior (Toldson et al., 2009) and increasing cultural capital such as social networks (Stanton-Salazar & Spina, 2000). Researchers have shown that resilient youth who overcome at risk backgrounds consistently have mentors (Rhodes & Dubois, 2006). They list the benefits of mentoring: improvements in self-esteem, better interpersonal relationships, greater school connectedness, improved academic performance, and reductions in substance use, violence, and other at-risk behaviors (Rhodes & Dubois, 2006). Hurd and Zimmerman (2010) found low SES students who have a natural mentor to have positive health outcomes in their transitions to adulthood; specifically, they experience less depressive symptoms and less sexual risk behavior over time. They found that natural mentoring relationships contributed to the resilience of low SES African American youth transitioning into adulthood, by moderating the stress associated with the transition to adulthood (Hurd & Zimmerman, 2010). Erickson, McDonald, and Elder (2009) found a strong positive impact of mentoring on high school performance and educational attainment. Moreover, they found that "relatives, friends, teachers, and community-based mentors" contribute to educational success; they also note that youth with more cultural "resources to draw upon" are more likely to engage in mentoring relationships (p. 345). A literature review of over 300 articles on mentoring showed that mentoring provides a host of learning, professional growth, and developmental benefits (Hansford, Ehrich, & Tennent, 2004), however, short-term mentoring has been shown to neither positively nor negatively impact at risk students' behavior (NCEE, 2009). Research suggests that early educational interventions in the lives of at risk youth increase the chances of school completion, decreases juvenile delinquency and school dropout; and is associated with better educational and social outcomes up to age 20 (Reynolds, Temple, Robertson, & Mann, 2001).

Youth Social/Environmental Characteristics

Low income youth are identifiable in the literature by a host of indicators. These indicators include students who come from single-parent families, are over age from their peer group, students who frequently changed schools, students whose parents are not actively involved in their school, students whose parents never talk to them about school-related matters, students whose parents hold low expectations about their child's educational attainment; and students from urban schools with large minority populations (NCES, 1992; Bergerson, 2010; Bell, Rowan-Kenyon, & Perna, 2009; Rowan-Kenyon, Bell, & Perna, 2008b). Students whose unique risks make them more susceptible to low college enrollment, or dropping out, are typically defined as students from families with low incomes, students whose parents did not attend college, or students whose parents work lower class occupations (Walpole, 2007; Bergerson, 2010). An understanding of the social/environmental and behavioral predictors of at risk dropout culture presents a focalized starting point for targeting and addressing the needs of this population (Hammond, Linton, Smink, & Drew, 2007).

Policy Level Environmental Influences

Educational partners are increasingly becoming instrumental in closing the achievement gap for at risk youth. That local educational agencies'(LEA) roles in closing the achievement gap for at risk youth is increasingly known and is part of a growing trend toward the consideration of college and career readiness issues through an ecological framework (Bronfenbrenner, 1977). An ecological framework "captures the complexity of interacting environmental influences" (Arnold, Lu, & Armstrong, 2012, p. 5) on student development that mediate college and career readiness. Federal legislation, such as the enactment of Title IV, Part B of the Elementary and Secondary Education Act, with its development of Twenty-First Century Community Learning Centers, also supports an ecological view. The twenty-first Century program provides students from high-poverty and poorly performing schools, opportunities to receive educational enrichment services and programming through LEAs. The twenty-first CCLC model encompasses before and after school, and summer recess programming. Additionally, the Higher Education Act of 1965, as amended, Title IV, Part A, Subpart 2, Chapter 2, authorized the Gaining Early Awareness and Readiness for Undergraduate Programs (GEAR UP), designed to increase the number of low-income students who are prepared to enter and succeed in postsecondary education. GEAR UP provides six-year grants to starts to serve a cohort of 7th grade students through high school, with newly added funding to provide for the first year of postsecondary education. GEAR UP offers state or partnership grants. Understanding program attributes relative to performance outcomes can illuminate best practices for model LEAs and community partners.

It is important to understand *how* the positive outcomes of effective programs as identified in the literature interact with the personal and social characteristics of at risk youth. Research on afterschool programming shows effective programs are known to have positive impacts on a "range of academic, social, prevention, and other outcomes" (Little, Wimer, & Weiss, p. 1). High-retention programs often foster a sense of community through close bonds with program staff and peers (Deschenes et al., 2010). Successful afterschool programs improve "youths' feelings of self-confidence and self-esteem, school bonding, positive social behaviors, school grades, and achievement" (Durlak & Weissberg, 2007, p. 5), are intentional in relationship building (Birmingham, Pechman, Russell, & Mielke, 2005) and promote positive development settings such as: physical and psychological safety, clear and consistent structure and adult supervision, opportunities to belong, support for efficacy and mattering, and opportunities for skill building (Eccles & Gootman, 2002).

In addition to strong programmatic features, effective programs have certain structural components (Little, Wimer, & Goss, 2008): participants have access to and sustained participation in programs, quality programming allowing for close interaction of participants with program staff, and strong community partnerships. Features of strong partnerships include programs which leverage resources across multiple stakeholders, including families, schools, and communities (Harvard Family Research Project, 2008). Strong partnerships in the school include programs that fostered strong relationships with school staff, principals, and teachers (Intercultural Center for Research in Education, 2005), active participation with school districts, and communication from service providers. Strong partnerships with the community used cross-sector collaboration between schools and community-based providers in facilitating referrals and providing access to academic records (Arbreton, Sheldon, & Herrera, 2005). Regular communication between sponsoring organizations and site managers is another feature of strong partnerships (Birmingham, Pechman, Russell, & Mielke, 2005).

Funding

A major hurdle for programs aiming to provide services for at-risk youth is that no secure funding mechanism exists for these programs. Grant writing at the foundation, state, and federal levels is necessary to meet grantor matching requirements. Additionally, securing federal funding is increasingly contingent upon an organization's ability to have data management capabilities, and program evaluators. The federal government contributes 11% of afterschool costs, while parents typically pay 76% of costs through tuition and fees (After School Alliance, 2009). Indeed, federal funding for after-school programming is increasingly relying upon partnerships between local educational agencies (LEA), institutions of higher education (IHE), and community organizations to provide educational services to at risk youth. Moreover, partnerships applying for federal funding are increasingly required to provide matching funds, not less than 50% of the cost of the program (a dollar-for-dollar match), from State, local, institutional, or private funds (U.S. Department of Education, 2014).

A lack of dedicated funding threatens after-school programming, with its well-documented ability to positively impact the social, personal, and academic achievement of low income, and primarily minority youth. However, a solution-based approach reflecting systems interaction logic exists. The solution aligns multiple agencies working together, while there are more shared resources. While out of school programs yield benefits, a collective impact approach has social mechanisms to effect greater systemic change through shared resources.

COLLECTIVE IMPACT ORGANIZATIONS: COMMUNITY PARTNERSHIPS FOR SOCIAL CHANGE

Social problems are often multifaceted and coexist in a network of other problems. An attempt to redress a social problem such as educational disparity will be less effective without coordinated attempts to address the multiple, interrelated domains contributing to the disparity (Hammond, Linton, Smink, & Drew, 2007; West-Olatunji, Frazier, & Kelley, 2011). Systems theory provides a framework for understanding how sets of components interact with each other, and suggests that a "change in any part of a system has implications for all other parts of the system" (Bess & Dee, 2008, p. 471). These coordinated attempts to address multiple domains reflect the logic of systems theory. The idea of systemic coordination is also reflected in paradigms of model community partnerships (see Figure 13.2).

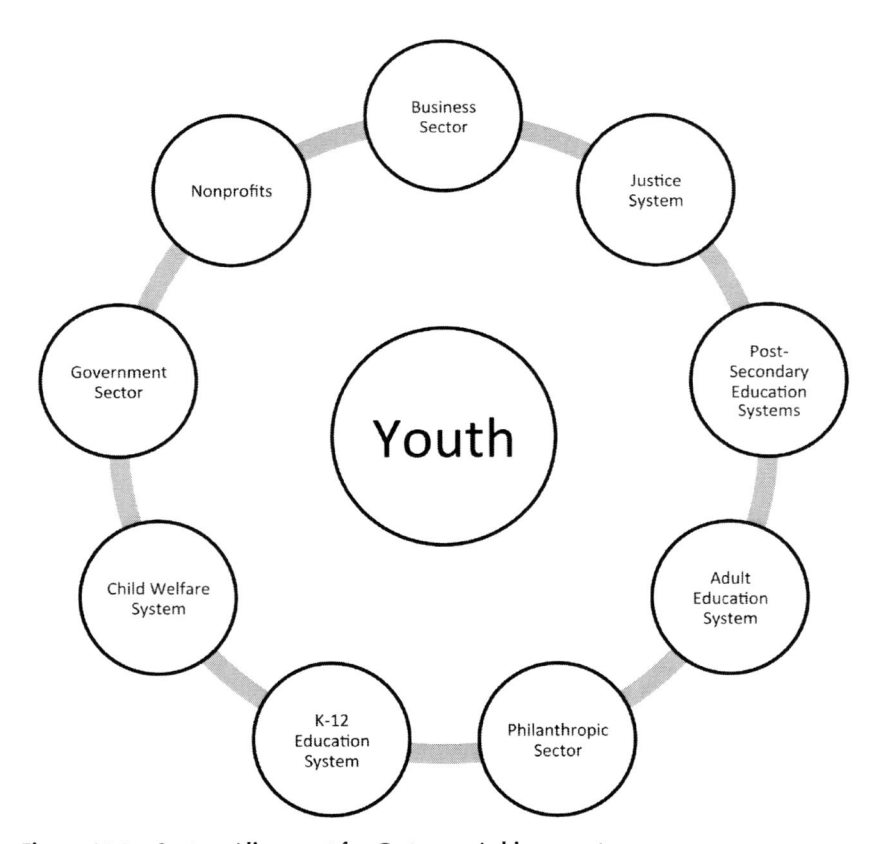

Figure 13.2 System Alignment for Outcome Achievement

Characteristics of Collective Impact Initiatives

One such model community partnership is the Collective Impact collaboration. Introduced in the *Stanford Social Innovation Review* (2011), *collective impact* is defined as the commitment of a group of important actors from different sectors to a common agenda for solving a specific social problem (Kania & Kramer, 2011). Collective impact is not the same as a partnership. Collective impact initiatives are characterized by: a centralized infrastructure, a dedicated staff, a structured process that leads to a common agenda, shared measurement, continuous communication, and mutually reinforcing activities among all participants (Kania & Kramer, 2011; Turner, Merchant, Kania & Martin, 2012). Large-scale change to social problems can be best addressed using a collective impact approach by cross-sector organizations such as nonprofits, governments, business, and the public.

Backbone Support

Central to the idea of a collective impact initiative is the backbone support organization. A separate entity from the participating organizations, the backbone organization is conceptualized as the project management team, characterized by its ability to "plan, manage, and support the initiative through ongoing facilitation, technology and communications support, data collection and reporting, and handling the myriad logistical and administrative details needed for the initiative to function smoothly" (Kania & Kramer, 2011, p. 40). Backbone organizations, in effect, function as change agents who address social problems in a systemic manner utilizing principles of change theory. A theory of change addresses "how a complex change initiative will unfold over time" (Anderson, 2005, p. 1). A theory of change is outcome oriented while offering commentary, providing context, and explaining the processes at each stage in the change process (Annie E. Casey Foundation, 2004). Backbones participate in six common change agent activities, guide vision and strategy, support aligned activities, establish shared measurement practices, build public will, advance policy, and mobilize funding (Turner et al., 2012, p. 1).

The priorities of granting agencies are increasingly aligned with the logic of a collective impact models. The funding pendulum is currently swinging toward LEAs and IHEs who maximize resources through cross-sector collaboration. For instance, the Department of Education's 2014 GEAR UP RFP allocated a Competitive Preference Priority 2 to applicants seeking to combine GEAR UP services with other Federal antipoverty programs in federally designated "Promise Zones" (national areas with persistent pockets of poverty). Promise Zones align the work of multiple, federal programs in high-poverty urban, rural, and tribal communities with substantial needs and strong, evidence-based plans to address those needs. The goals of Promise Zones are creating jobs, increasing economic activity, improving educational opportunities, reducing violent crime, and leveraging private investment (U.S. Department of Education, 2014) This is one example of leveraging resources across sectors, U.S. Departments of Housing and Urban Development, Education, Agriculture, and Justice to apply a community development model which addresses a plethora of social issues.

Again, this historical period is calling for a systems approach to address social problems. The rugged individualist American ethos must give way to the twenty-first century demands of a nation with exceedingly different population characteristics. Federal funding is clearly echoing what scholars know to be true: social development and community development are symbiotic processes (Mohan, 2011). Indeed, Bronfenbrenner postulated that culture influences policy, which in turn influences school and neighborhoods, their effects ultimately trickling down to the level of the student. Collective Impact as a cultural ideal will make our communities stronger, and our kids brighter. The Pathways to Prosperity Project, aptly envisioning the cross-sector collaboration necessary to effect twenty-first century systemic change said,

> Developing a system that provides every young person with high quality pathways to adulthood will require that we make a leap forward in the collective responsibility we assume for the education and training of our young people. While educators will obviously continue to play a central role, meeting the pathways challenge will also require major contributions from the nation's employers and governments. We should begin by articulating a new social compact with America's young people. This compact should spell out what educators, employers and governments will do to provide pathways, and how they will support young people as they navigate them. In addition, it should clarify what we expect from young people. (Symonds, Schwartz, & Ferguson, 2011)

CONCLUSION

The focus of this chapter is the reconceptualization of curriculum development for low income youth as a community development issue, in hopes of engendering sustained funding for after-school programs. In this chapter, the concept of curriculum as something that is active was introduced along with a review of characteristics of low income youth. A systems view of child development, foreshadowing the current trend of funding for programs that incorporate cross-sector partnerships, was described. Also discussed was the context for reconceptualizing curriculum development for youth as social and community development issues, through the argument that conceptual orientations of curriculum (policy) guide educational services provided to students, manifesting themselves materially through funding patterns. Lastly, the Collective Impact model was presented as a starting point for service providers of after-school programming to consider as a structural component of their organizations. The benefits are numerous: shared resources, less financial burden on the service provider, cross-sector collaboration resulting in a holistic model of services to a population who can stand to benefit the most from a community development model.

REFERENCES

After School Alliance. (2009). *Roadmap to Afterschool for All: Examining Current Investments and Mapping Future Needs.*

After School Alliance. (2013, August). *21st century community learning centers: providing afterschool and summer learning supports to communities nationwide.*

Anderson, A. A. (2005). *The Community Builder's Approach to Theory of Change: A Practical Guide to Theory Development.* The Aspen Institute.

Annie E. Casey Foundation. (2004). *Theory of change: A practical tool for action, results, and learning.* Baltimore, MD: Organizational Research Services. Retrieved from http://www.aecf.org/resources/theory-of-change/

Annie E. Casey Foundation. (2013). *early warning confirmed: A research update on third-grade reading*, Executive Summary.

Aratani, Y., Wright, V. R., & Cooper, J. L., (2011). *Racial gaps in early childhood: Socio-emotional health, developmental and educational outcomes among African-American boys.* National Center for Children in Poverty.

Arbreton, A. J. A., Sheldon, J., & Herrera, C. (2005). *Beyond safe havens: A synthesis of research on the Boys & Girls Clubs.* Philadelphia, PA: Public/Private Ventures.

Arnold, K. D., Lu, E., & Armstrong, K. (2012). The ecology of college readiness. *ASHE Higher Education Report, 38*(5).

Bell, A. D., Rowan-Kenyon, H., & Perna, L. W. (2009). College knowledge of 9th and 11th grade students: Variation by school and state context. *The Journal of Higher Education, 80*(6), 663–685.

Bergerson, A. (2010). College choice and access to college: Moving policy, research and practice to the 21st century. *ASHE Higher Education Report, 35*(4), 1–130.

Bess, J. L., & Dee, J. R. (2008). *Understanding college and university organization: Theories for effective policy and practice.* Sterling, VA: Stylus Publishing.

Birmingham, J., Pechman, E. M., Russell, C. A., & Mielke, M. (2005). *Shared Features of High-Performing After-School Programs: A follow-up to the TASC evaluation.* Policy Study Associates, Inc. The After-School Corporation and Southwest Educational Development Laboratory.

Bots, P. W. G. (2013). Designing the policy analysis process. In W. A. H. Thissen & W. E. Walker (Eds.), *Public policy analysis: International series in operations research & management science* (pp. 103–132).

Bourdieu, P. (1973). Cultural reproduction and Social reproduction. In J. Karabel, Halsey & A. H. (Eds.), *Power and Ideology in Education* (pp. 487–511). New York: Oxford University Press.

Bronfenbrenner, U. (1977). Toward an experimental ecology of human development. *American Psychologist, 32*(7), 513–31.

Brown, T. M., & Rodriguez, L. F. (2009). School and the co-construction of a dropout. *International Journal of Qualitative Studies in Education, 22*(2), 221–242.

Bulanda, R. E., & Majumdar, R. E. (2009). Perceived parent-child relationships and adolescent self-esteem. *Journal of Child and Family Studies, 18*, 203–212.

Deschenes, S. N., Arbreton, A., Little, P. M., Herrera, C., Grossman, J. B., Weiss, H. B., Lee, D. (2010). *Engaging Older Youth: Program and city level strategies to support sustained participation in out-of-school time.* Harvard Family Research Project.

Durlak, J. A., & Weissburg, R. P. (2007). *The impact of after-school programs that promote personal and social skills.* Chicago, IL: Collaborative for Academic, Social, and Emotional Learning.

Eccles, J., & Gootman, J. A. (2002). Community programs to promote youth development. Washington, DC: Committee on Community-Level Programs for Youth. Board on Children, Youth, and Families, Commission on Behavioral and Social Sciences Education, National Research Council and Institute of Medicine.

Erickson, L. D., McDonald, S., & Elder, G. H. (2009). Informal mentors and education: Complementary or compensatory resources. *Sociology of Education, 82*, 344–367.

Evans, N. J., Forney, D. S., Guido, F. M., Patton, L. D., & Renn, K. A. (2010). *Student development in college: Theory, research, and practice.* (2nd ed.). San Francisco, CA: Jossey-Bass.

Gibson, D. M., Jefferson, R. N. (2006). The effect of perceived parental involvement and the use of growth-fostering relationships on self-concept in adolescents participating in GEAR UP. *Adolescence, 41*(161), 111–125.

Gottfredson, L. S. (2004). Using Gottfredson's theory of circumscription and compromise in career guidance and counseling.

Hammond, C., Linton, D. Smink, J., & Drew, S. (2007). *Dropout risk factors and exemplary programs.* Clemson, SC: National Dropout Prevention Center, Communities In Schools, Inc.

Hansford, B. C., Ehrich, L. C., & Tennent, L. (2004). Formal mentoring programs in education and other professions: A review of the literature. *Educational Administration Quarterly 40*(4), 518–540.

Harvard Family Research Project. (February 2008). *After school programs in the 21st century: Their potential and what it takes to achieve it.* Issues and Opportunities in Out-of-School Time Evaluation, *10*.

Hernandez, D. J. (2012). *Double jeopardy: How third-grade reading skills and poverty influence high school graduation.* Baltimore, MD: The Annie E. Casey Foundation.

Hurd, N., & Zimmerman, M. (2010). Natural mentors, mental health, and risk behaviors: A longitudinal analysis of African-American adolescents transitioning into adulthood. *American Journal of Community Psychology, 46*, 36–48.

Hutz, A., Martine, W. E., and Beitel, M. (2007). Ethnocultural person-environment fit and college adjustment: Some implications for college counselors. *Journal of College Counseling, 10,* 130–141.

Intercultural Center for Research in Education, & National Institute on Out-of-School Time (2005). *Pathways To Success For Youth: What Works In Afterschool: A Report of the Massachusetts Afterschool Research Study (MARS).* Boston, MA: United Way of Massachusetts Bay.

Kania, J., & Kramer, M. (Winter 2011). *Collective Impact.* Stanford Social Innovation Review. pp. 36–41.

Kipfer, B. A. (Ed.). (1999). *Roget's 21st Century Thesaurus.* (2nd ed.). New York: Dell Publishing.

Kort-Butler, L. A. & Hagewen, K. J. (2011). School-based extracurricular activity involvement and adolescent self-esteem: A growth-curve analysis. *Journal of Youth Adolescence, 40,* 568–581.

Little, P. M. D., Wimer, C., & Weiss, H. B. (2008). After School Programs in the 21st Century: Their potential and what it takes to achieve it. *Issues and Opportunities in Out-Of-School Time Evaluation,* Number 10. Harvard Family Research Project.

Little, P. M. D., Wimer, C., & Goss, C. B. (February 2008). *Issues and opportunities in out-of-school time evaluation.* Cambridge, MA: Harvard Family Research Project.

Mohan, B. (2011). *Development, poverty of culture, and social policy.* New York: Palgrave Macmillan.

Myers, J. E., Willse, J. T., & Villalba, J. A. (2011). Promoting self-esteem in adolescents: The influence of wellness factors. *Journal of Counseling & Development, 89*(1), 28–36.

National Center for Education Evaluation and Regional Assistance, Institute of Education Sciences, U.S. Department of Education. (2009). *Impact Evaluation of the U.S. Department of Education's Student Mentoring Program* (NCEE 2009–4047). Washington, DC.

National Center for Education Statistics. (1992). *National education longitudinal study of 1988: Characteristics of at-risk students in NELS:88,* (NCES 92–042), Washington, DC: U.S. Government Printing Office. Retrieved 12-12-2011 from http://nces.ed.gov/pubsearch.

National Center for Education Statistics. (2006). *The condition of education 2006,* NCES 2006–071, Washington, DC: U.S. Government Printing Office. Retrieved 12-12-2011 from http://nces.ed.gov/pubsearch.

New York State Education Department. (2009). Federal education policy and the states, 1945–2009: A brief synopsis. *States' Impact on Federal Education Policy Project.* Albany, NY: New York State Archives.

Placier, M. L. (1993). The semantics of state policy making: The case of 'at risk'. *Educational Evaluation and Policy Analysis, 15*(4), 380–395.

Placier, M. L. (1996). The cycle of student labels in education: The cases of culturally deprived, disadvantaged, and at risk. *Education Administration Quarterly, 32*(2), 236–270.

Reynolds, A. R., Temple, J. A., Robertson, D. L., & Mann, E. A. (2001). Long-term effects of an early childhood intervention on educational achievement and juvenile arrest: A 15-year follow-up of low-income children in public schools. *Journal of the American Medical Association, 285*(18), 2339–2346.

Rowan-Kenyon, H. T., Bell, A. D., & Perna, L. (2008a). Contextual influences on parental involvement in college going: variations by socioeconomic class. *The Journal of Higher Education, 79*(5), 564–586.

Rowan-Kenyon, H. T., Bell, A., & Perna, L. W. (2008b). How parents shape college opportunity for their children: Variations by socioeconomic status. *Journal of Higher Education, 79,* 564–586.

Rhodes, J. E., & DuBois, D. L. (2006). Understanding and facilitating the youth mentoring movement. *Social Policy Report, 20*(3), 1–20.

Searcy, Y. D. (2007). Placing the horse in front of the wagon: Toward a conceptual understanding of the development of self-esteem in children and adolescents. *Child and Adolescent Social Work, 24*(2), 121–131.

Stanton-Salazar, R. D., Spina, S. U. (2000). The network orientations of highly resilient urban minority youth: A network-analytic account of minority socialization and its educational implications. *The Urban Review, 32*(3), 227–261.

Symonds, W. C., Schwartz, R. B., & Ferguson, R. (February 2011). *Pathways to Prosperity: Meeting the Challenge of Preparing Young Americans for the 21st Century.* Report issued by the Pathways to Prosperity Project, Harvard Graduate School of Education: Pearson Foundation.

Toldson, I. A., Braithwaite, R. L., & Rentie, R. J. (2009). Promoting college aspirations among school-age Black American males. Black American Males in Higher Education: Research, Programs, and Academe, *Diversity in Higher Education, 7,* 117–137.

Turner, S., Merchant, K., Kania, J., & Martin, E. (2012, July 17). *Understanding the value of backbone organizations in collective impact.* http://www.ssireview.org/blog/entry/understanding_the_value_of_backbone_organizations_in_collective_impact_1

U.S. Department of Education, Office of the Under Secretary, Policy and Program Studies Service. (2004). *Early implementation of supplemental educational services under the No Child Left Behind Act: Year one report.* Washington, DC. www.policystudies.com/studies/school/nclb.html

U.S. Department of Education Office of Postsecondary Education. (2014). *FY 2014 Application for grants under the Gaining Early Awareness & Readiness for Undergraduate Programs (GEAR UP) Partnership Grants.* CFDA Number 84.334A. OMB No. 1840–0821.

Walpole, M. (2007). Economically and educationally challenged students in higher education: Access to outcomes [Monograph]. *ASHE Higher Education Report, 33*(3) 1–104.

Wehlage, G. G., & Rutter, R. A. (1986). "Dropping out: How much do schools contribute to the problem?" *Teachers College Record, 87*(3), 374–392.

West-Olatunji, C., Shure, L., Pringle, R., Adams, T., Lewis, D., Cholewa, B., (2010). Exploring How School Counselors Position Low-Income African American Girls as Mathematics and Science Learners. *Professional School Counseling, 13*(3), pp. 184–195.

West-Olatunji, C., Frazier, K. N., Kelly, E. (2011). Wraparound Counseling: An ecosystemic approach to working with economically disadvantaged students in urban school settings. *Journal of Humanistic Counseling*; *50*(2), 222.

Winfield, A. G. (2007). *Eugenics and education in America: Institutionalized racism and the implications of history, ideology, and memory.* New York: Peter Lang.

Chapter 14

African American Males
A Career and College Readiness Crisis
Christopher T. Belser

Despite increases in awareness of the issues facing minority students in primary, secondary, and higher education, African American males continue to fall behind their peers in high school and postsecondary education attainment due to a myriad of social, economic, and institutional barriers (Jackson & Beaudry, 2012; Palmer & Maramba, 2010; Palmer, Moore, Davis, & Hilton, 2010; Toldson & Lewis, 2012). Recent data indicates that African American males have the lowest high school graduation rates in approximately three-fourths of the 50 states and the District of Columbia and have a nationwide graduation rate of 52%; in contrast, the graduation rate for White, non-Latino males is 78% (Jackson & Beaudry, 2012). Although the statement that there are more African American males in prison than college is no longer accurate, African American males are still underrepresented in postsecondary institutions and overrepresented in the criminal justice system (Toldson & Lewis, 2012). Championed by the Obama Administration, *A Blueprint for Reform: The Reauthorization of the Elementary and Secondary Education Act* (2010) highlighted the need for improvements in how elementary and secondary schools promote college and career readiness, identifying this as a key priority for the United States; moreover, this plan identified equity for diverse learners and marginalized minority groups as a salient point within the discussion of college and career readiness (U.S. Department of Education, 2010). Several years later, however, African American males remain significantly behind their peers in educational outcomes.

What, then, is causing this population's struggles comparative to their peers, and what can be done? This chapter addresses both internal and external factors that contribute to the career and college readiness crisis facing African American male students, including the school-to-prison pipeline, stereotype threat, and inequities within education systems. Additionally, this chapter includes steps that educators can take to contend with these identified issues and provides implications for future research.

THE SCHOOL-TO-PRISON PIPELINE

Years of systematic educational exclusion due to both academic underperformance and disciplinary struggles have contributed heavily to the large number of youth (primarily African American males) who enter the court system (Wilson, 2014; Teske, Huff, & Graves, 2013). This phenomenon has become known as the school-to-prison pipeline. In June 2014, African Americans represented approximately 37% of the inmate population in the United States, despite only representing about 12% of the nation's total population (Federal Bureau of Prisons, 2014). Moreover, a 2013 Pew Research Center analysis found that black males had a likelihood of being incarcerated at a rate that is six times higher than that of white males, based on 2010 data (Drake, 2013).

Scholars, researchers, and leaders attribute these racial disparities to a variety of reasons (adaptations to poverty, inconsistencies in law enforcement and sentencing, overemphasis on the Drug War, etc.), and most agree that the United States' trend toward mass incarceration has impacted African Americans—particularly males—at a higher rate than other sub-groups (Conyers, 2013; Alexander, 2011). Conyers (2013) noted that "[a]n African American boy born in 2001 has a 32% chance of serving time in prison at some point in his life" while "a white male born at the same time would have a 6% chance" (p. 378). Additionally, law enforcement agencies have greatly increased efforts to combat the drug war in recent decades, but these policies, when not created and enforced with fidelity, can unfairly and disproportionately affect African Americans. For example, African American adolescents have a likelihood of being incarcerated for a drug charge that is 48 times higher than White adolescents with similar records, and approximately 25% of African American adolescents arrested for drug-related incidents are released with their charges dropped, while the number for white adolescents is closer to half (Bernstein, 2014). Alexander (2011) suggested that extensive media coverage of the raw numbers without discussion of the racial disparities and undertones only promulgates negative racial stereotypes.

Impact on Career Outcomes

For adolescents and adults, arrests and incarcerations can have an extremely negative impact on career outcomes. Natsuaki, Ge, and Wenk (2008) found that adolescent males who were arrested earlier in adolescence rather than later had a higher probability and frequency of additional arrests; their findings also support the idea that high school graduation is a predictor of fewer arrests over the lifespan for early starters and late starters, but they clarified that high school graduation alone is not likely to break the cycle. A longitudinal study conducted by Wiesner, Kim, and Capaldi (2010) revealed a correlation between arrests and poor career outcomes in adulthood in at risk young men, measured in part by the amount of time they were unemployed. They further discussed that these outcomes could be attributed to a number of related factors, including (a) not being hired for a job due to negative findings on a criminal background check, (b) general lack of self-control that may cause one to be fired from a job, (c) less educational attainment resulting in one taking jobs in unstable fields prone to short-term appointments and layoffs, and (d) increased substance use which is correlated to more negative outcomes.

Incarceration and probation also present logistical complications that limit opportunities for adolescents to gain early work life experience. First, adolescents sentenced to juvenile detention centers or similar facilities are limited to the confines of the institution, which may or may not provide options for youth to gain skills for employability. Similarly, adolescents on probation may have curfew and/or travel restrictions that limit one's availability to work. As previously noted, many jobs require either a background check or self-disclosure of arrest history, which will likely lead to these adolescents being passed over for jobs. Whatever the limitation is, gaining work or volunteer experiences during teenage years can help individuals build key soft skills and transferrable technical skills that will benefit them throughout their career. For adolescents involved in the juvenile justice system, denial of these opportunities is just another setback that compounds upon developmental, psychosocial, and sociocultural factors to be discussed in future sections.

AFRICAN AMERICAN MALE DEVELOPMENT

Physical and Cognitive Development

For males, the adolescent years represent a critical period complete with major changes in physical appearance and cognitive functioning. Physically, these years mark the onset of puberty and are a time for physical growth, heightened hormonal activity, and increases in strength. Regarding cognitive development, Piaget (1969) noted the shift during adolescence from *concrete operations* to *formal abstract thought*, which includes several higher-order thinking skills such as projecting into the future, hypothesizing, and understanding others' perspectives. Curry and Milsom (2014) discussed the importance of both physical and cognitive development to career exploration during adolescence, noting that, respectively, one can greatly affect self-concept and self-evaluation, while the other affects conceptualization of careers and approaches to planning for the future. The emphasis on athletics combined with exclusionary educational practices may result in more opportunities that foster physical development rather than cognitive development.

Psychosocial Development

While developmental theorists provide varying models of psychosocial development, adolescent males essentially are seeking answers to the questions *Who am I?* and *Who am I in relation to those around me?* Erikson (1963) described the key task for adolescence as *identity versus role confusion*, which can be characterized by the desire to begin detaching from ones family of origin in an attempt to identify one's place in society. In another model, Steinberg (1993) posited that males become aware of gender and sex roles during the Cognitive Stage (early childhood to pre-adolescence) and that adolescence is marked by the Conformist Stage, during which males are more likely to conform to the social norms of masculinity in attempt to be socially acceptable. Later in adolescence, according to Steinberg's theory, adolescents begin to reconcile their internal values within the context of social pressures.

Acknowledging the effect of social learning, Horne, Jolliff, and Roth (1996) identified five male figures that aid in adolescent males' development, rather than a stage model of development: (a) the nurturer, (b) the role model, (c) the initiator, (d) the mentor, and (d) the elder; they further noted that the absence of one of these models in a young boy's life may have a negative effect on his development. The nurturer role is typically filled by the father or another father figure, such as an uncle, a grandfather, or a family friend. The role model provides an opportunity for "vicarious learning through observation" and can be an individual the young male knows, someone in the community, a figure from popular culture, or even a fictional character (p. 15). Initiators are figures who teach "the importance of teamwork, loyalty, and commitment to the larger group," such as coaches, pastors, and community leaders (p. 15). Mentors and elders both are older, more experienced males who convey wisdom to younger males; elders, though, typically are much older and may have some social standing within a community. This social-learning model, as well as the other models of psychosocial development, will provide further insight into topics discussed later in this chapter.

Racial Identity Development

Erikson (1968) proposed a model for ego identity development that aligns with his earlier work on psychosocial development. In this model, he claimed that during the adolescent years, individuals begin to question and explore their identity in relation to sex roles, the world of work, society, and values systems. Phinney (1989) expanded on Erikson's model in relation to African Americans, noting that African Americans undergo the same tasks but within the context of being African American; this context takes into consideration experiences with and interpretations of past discrimination, institutional racism, and other societal barriers. Subsequent research on this model has shown that individuals may not go through the stages (diffuse, foreclosed, moratorium, and achieved) in a linear order and may move forward or regress (Scottham, Cooke, Sellers, & Ford, 2010). One's racial identity can be shaped by countless factors including family members, mentors, affiliations (including churches and social organizations) and negative or positive racial experiences.

For African American adolescents, much of these identity development processes are related to the context and environment in which individuals live, including home, school, and community (Scottham et al., 2010). For example, the experiences of an African American male who lives in a multiracial middle-class neighborhood and attends a predominantly white school will be significantly different from an African American male who lives in a lower-SES community and attends a predominantly minority school. Brewster and Stephenson (2013) documented the struggles that their son faced as one of the few African Americans in a primarily White private school, noting that while he was seen as an "other" at school, his African American friends in the neighborhood often commented that he acted and talked like a White person; nevertheless, he still faced discrimination in the community based on negative stereotypes of African American male teens. Negative racial experiences, including exposure to overt racism, intentional and unintentional discriminatory practices, and microaggressions, can contribute to feelings of "otherness." These experiences could be as explicit as someone using racial slurs with intent to hurt someone or as inadvertent as a teacher unknowingly communicating lower expectation of minority students. If internalized, they can become enmeshed with one's identity.

Negative stereotypes communicated through mass media also contribute to identity development. The recent shootings of Oscar Grant, Trayvon Martin, and Michael Brown by law enforcement or security officers present a world in which young African American males may be presumed to be threats because of racial stereotypes. After the death of Michael Brown, a *TIME* video report covering the protests in Ferguson, Missouri, displayed a young African American male holding a sign that read, "Am I next?" (Weissman & Levine, 2014). Along the same lines, this author had numerous conversations with students following the death of Trayvon Martin, and his students communicated not only anger with the situation but also fear that they could easily find themselves in a similar situation.

While some African American males may emerge from negative racial situations as leaders for social change, others may respond with hypervigilance and distrust as protective factors. These dichotomous paths can have markedly different results in relation to career development. In the former situation, educators and parents can better serve these students by connecting them with mentors and opportunities to grow social advocacy skills. With the latter situation, educators, especially counselors, will likely need to process the feelings associated with the negative experience. Duncan-Andrade (2007) discussed social justice pedagogy as an avenue for teachers to engage students in critical conversations while promoting "hopeful alternatives to the oppression of poverty, racism, and injustice" (p. 1); he further noted that the school curriculum should address the basic educational skills while also challenging them to adopt a social justice mind-set.

Stereotyping and Stereotype Threat

For African American males, stereotyping is not a new phenomenon. African American males—especially adolescents—are frequently depicted in the media as being hard, unmotivated, violent, disrespectful, and academically deficient. They are portrayed as thugs, druggies, fighters, gang members, and dropouts. Conversely, they are expected to have a higher prowess in athletics, whether or not this is an actual interest to the particular student. Academic institutions created by and designed predominantly for white students are constant reminders for African American males of their "otherness," and in a competitive accountability-driven culture, the pressures of educational benchmarks and standardized tests can invoke a fear of living up to a stereotype.

Steele and Aronson (1995) explored the effects that negative stereotypes about one's race or gender have on one's internal processing. The findings of their studies supported the notion that individuals belonging to populations who are frequently subjected to negative stereotyping (in this case, African Americans) performed lower on academic tasks when their performance on the task would be judged and possibly might confirm the stereotype. Calling this phenomenon *stereotype threat*, Steel and Aronson further noted that their research "[did] not focus on the internalization of inferiority images or their consequences" but rather "on the immediate situational threat that derives from the broad dissemination of negative stereotypes about one's group" (p. 798). The research related to stereotype threat that has been conducted since the original studies in 1995 have primarily examined the effects on academic performance (Johnson-Ahorlu, 2013). Schmader, Johns, and Forbes (2008) generated a model of stereotype threat that integrated cognitive, physiological, and social processes and described the interrelatedness of a variety of factors on the output performance. Additionally, they clarified that while stereotype threat and test anxiety can have similar effects, stereotype threat elicits a negative response during evaluative situations due to one's membership in a negatively stereotyped group, while test anxiety, or performance anxiety, relates more to individual internal processes that occur when presented with an evaluative task. Appel and Kronberger (2012) concluded that stereotype threat could also have a negative effect on knowledge acquisition, which opens the discussion not only to testing situations but also to general learning in the classroom.

In the original study conducted by Steele and Aronson (1995), African American college students scored lower than White students on an academic test when the purpose of the test was described as a diagnostic that would be used to evaluate their performance; African American students in the control group, who were not told the purpose of the test, scored almost even with White students. However, when the test was framed as a challenge instead of as a diagnostic, African Americans' scores were not affected. In a follow-up study, Steele and Aronson found that African American students who were required to indicate their race prior to taking a test scored lower than African American students who were not required to indicate their race. Much of the work conducted by Steele and Aronson focused on college students who already overcame the obstacles in getting to higher education; with that in mind, educators should consider the impact of stereotype threat on African American males in K-12 environments that foster low expectations of postsecondary achievement with this population. Moreover, Logel, Peach, and Spencer (2012) reported that individuals at risk for stereotype threat are likely to avoid the threatening situation altogether, which may account for some African American males' avoidance of challenging academic situations.

AFRICAN AMERICAN MALES AND ATHLETICS

Stereotype threat in African American males has also been examined within the framework of being a student athlete. Martin, Harrison, Stone, and Lawrence (2010) found that African American student-athletes are more likely to experience negative stereotypes than White student-athletes, particularly related to their academic performance and sense of belonging; the participants in their study reported that their athletic ability was not questioned but they had to prove themselves in the classroom, whereas their White classmates were given the "benefit of the doubt" (Martin et al., 2010, p. 138). Stone, Harrison, and Mottley (2012) added that African American student-athletes who are more engaged in their academic endeavors have a higher likelihood of experiencing stereotype threat related to their academic performance if their identity as a student athlete is primed before completing an academic task. Their investigation suggests that those involved in the education process should combat the frequent stereotypes (e.g. dumb jock, slacker, academically disengaged) that are ascribed to student-athletes. Stone, Chalabaev, and Harrison (2012) posited that stereotype threat can begin to affect athletic performance, especially related to the cognitive processes and psychological elements in preparing for athletic events.

African American males grow up in a society that values their athletic abilities more than their academic pursuits. While many African American families have clear, high expectations for academics, athletic abilities are seen as viable ways out of poverty; for example, being on a high school football team ensures that a student stays in school, and getting a basketball scholarship helps pay the high costs of college. One study revealed that young African American males are more likely to be socialized into sports rather than academics for a variety of reasons, including those listed above (Beamon, 2010). Participants in the study reported receiving pressure from their families, their neighborhoods, and the media to enter into athletics, and many also noted that their role models who were not members of their immediate family were predominantly professional athletes. Porter (2012) offered a possible explanation in that African American males may see athletics as an easier route to success than academics, likely due to the media coverage of African American professional athletes. Undeniably, being involved in sports gives African American males more social capital within schools (Scottham, Sellers, & Nguyen, 2008).

The increased emphasis on sports often leads to decreased exposure to nonathletic curricular and extracurricular activities (Beamon, 2010). De-emphasizing academic pursuits for the sake of athletics can deprive students of opportunities to broaden their understanding of the world of work and to develop soft skills and transferrable skills. Additionally, many students who do wish to engage in extracurricular or enrichment activities outside of sports have difficulty juggling the schedule conflicts (i.e., after-school activities overlapping with practice times). Similarly, African American males are at risk for exploitation within the world of competitive sports, where talented males are recruited from low-income neighborhoods and given scholarships to summer sports camps, private high schools, and inter-collegiate athletic programs under the promise of a better education and a way out of poverty (Barlow, 2004; Beamon, 2008; Rheenen & Atwood, 2014). Many student-athletes have reported feeling exploited and noted that sports takes precedence over academics at their respective institutions (Beamon, 2008; Rheenen & Atwood, 2014).

In many conversations the author has had with African American male middle school students, the students discussed being a professional athlete not only as their top career choice but also as one of only a few that they have considered, and in many cases, the only career they have considered. Despite these potential issues, athletics are not an ill-fated pursuit, as being involved in sports can help develop skills of leadership and self-discipline in the presence of quality coaching and mentoring. Additionally, as previously noted, belonging to a sports team can keep a student engaged in school. However, engaged educators should assist students and families in navigating their academic and athletic options and rights.

AFRICAN AMERICAN MALES AND HYPERMASCULINITY

Hypermasculinity in African American males has been studied increasingly in recent years (Cunningham, Swanson, & Hayes, 2013; Porter, 2012; Roberts-Douglass & Curtis-Boles, 2012; Seaton, 2007; Spencer, Fegley, Harpalani, & Seaton, 2004). Spencer et al. (2004) defined hypermasculinity as "the exhibition of stereotypic gendered displays of power and consequent suppression of signs of vulnerability" (p. 234). They further noted that characteristics of hypermasculinity include the belief that violence is a display of masculinity, an exaggerated view of danger as being exciting, and displays of insensitivity and indifference toward women. Numerous environmental factors influence adolescent males' socialization into roles that are considered masculine; Roberts-Douglass and Curtis-Boles (2013) identified several specific male figures who helped foster the development of a masculine identity, including fathers (or other paternal figures), male friends, and male teachers (including coaches and counselors).

The crisis of hypermasculinity in African American males has been attributed to several factors. Cunningham et al. (2013) posited that exaggerated masculinity could be conceptualized as a protective response to perceived threats in society, including school and neighborhood violence. By presenting with a hypermasculine bravado, African American males are less likely to be challenged or threatened. Porter (2012) supported this notion but added that many African American males imitate the actions of athletes and hip-hop stars to gain social capital, as these represent environments where African American males have been publicly successful. The prevalence of absent fathers and/or father figures in the home is another possible explanation, according to Porter; he argued that without positive male role models in the home, adolescent males look to male figures in their environment for examples of what it means to be a man, and today's African American youth hold athletes and performing artists in high regard because of their predominant social status. This last idea relates to the earlier work of Horne, Joliff, and Roth (1996), who noted that the absence of key male figures can negatively impact a child's psychosocial development. Each of these conceptualizations sheds light on the presentation of hypermasculinity in African American males, and it is likely that they all hold merit as an explanation.

Hypermasculine behaviors place African American males at risk for negative outcomes. The prevalence of violent and aggressive behaviors likely explains why the leading cause of death for Black males is homicide (My Brother's Keeper Task Force, 2014). Spencer et al. (2004) discussed distrust as a contributing factor to the presentation of hypermasculinity, and without trust for certain adults in their lives, African American males may not seek assistance when needed (e.g. academic support, advisement, career planning, etc.). Additionally, the outward expression of hypermasculine behaviors combined with negative racial stereotypes causes people to view African American males "through 'adultified' lenses rather than being viewed as youth developing in what are often high-risk contexts" (p. 252). School personnel may be less likely to offer additional support to the males who need it, and employers may view these young men as disrespectful and unemployable; as such, African American males could once again be excluded from opportunities that for academic and career advancement.

INSTITUTIONAL DISCRIMINATION AT SCHOOL

Zero Tolerance Policies

The rise in the number of students—especially African American males—who are being suspended and/or expelled from school has also been documented and studied extensively (Skiba, 2014; Hoffman, 2012; Fowler, 2011). Throughout the 1980s and 1990s, school discipline reforms known as *zero tolerance* policies were enacted, aimed at using pre-determined harsh punishments to counter severe behaviors, such as possessing or using a weapon or drugs; however, these policies have increasingly become more broadly defined to include fights, dress code violations, theft, and numerous other infractions (Hoffman, 2012). On a superficial level, these policies serve to create safer learning environments, but a primary downside is that students who are subject to disciplinary action under these policies are excluded from the learning environment through suspension and expulsion. In reality, zero tolerance policies have had the opposite effect on their intended goal of reducing suspensions and expulsions and have damaged school culture instead (Skiba, 2014). Bernstein (2014) explained:

> For far too many young people of color, coming of age is marked by metal detectors and onsite police officers in their schools, security guards following them in stores, the "gang squad" showing up to break up school yard scuffles, purse clutchers, car-door lockers, and many other signals that they are now old enough to be presumed guilty at a glance (2014, p. 61).

What started as a means of ensuring safety and order has resulted in schools becoming militarized and highly regulated in many cases; furthermore, these practices contribute negatively to the educational achievement gap.

Discipline Versus Punishment

The literature is rife with studies and findings related to the negative effects of zero tolerance policies that are highly punitive, yet these policies are still widely used as the discipline structure in many schools. Though the terms are used interchangeably, researchers, policy makers, and educators should consider the key differences between discipline and punishment. Carlson (2009) defined discipline as "the process of teaching a child the difference between acceptable and unacceptable behavior" (p. 1). She further clarified that punishment, in contrast, is a form of discipline that uses negative consequences for these unacceptable behaviors in attempt to deter them from happening again. Common school disciplinary practices, such as suspension, expulsion, and time out, are forms of punishment, as they involve an adverse consequence to a negative behavior exhibited at school. While these practices do have merits as part of a school discipline policy, they are exclusionary in nature, meaning that students who are prescribed one of these consequences are removed from class time or other activities. When schools employ these exclusionary practices without a restorative or remediation component, students may view the action as a punishment rather than a disciplinary action and, over time, may become disenfranchised with school. As a comparison, if a student incorrectly answers a multistep word problem on a math test, a teacher marking the question wrong and handing back the test paper only indicates to the student that he [the student] calculated the problem incorrectly; however, if the teacher gives the student feedback, allows for reflection, and provides another practice activity, the student stands a greater chance of not making the same mistake again. Restorative discipline and other alternatives to suspension and expulsion will be discussed later in the chapter.

The U.S. Department of Education Office of Civil Rights (2014b) analyzed enrollment and discipline data for approximately 49 million students and discovered that 33% of students receiving one-time out-of-school suspensions, 42% of students receiving multiple out-of-school suspensions, and 34% of students who were expelled were African American, even though African Americans only accounted for 16% of the student population that was examined. More specifically, 20% of African American males received at least one out-of-school suspension, compared to only 6% of White males. The data for preschool discipline is equally if not more alarming; 42% of preschool students suspended only once and 48% of preschool students suspended multiple times were African American, despite African Americans only accounting for 18% of preschool students in the data set. Bowman-Perrott et al. (2011) conducted a longitudinal study that examined outcome data for over 2500 elementary students over six years and found that African Americans, males, and students with disabilities who are excluded for disciplinary reasons (i.e., expelled or suspended) in the first few years of elementary school have a high probability of being excluded again before the completion of elementary school.

These data sets confirm that African American males are being suspended and expelled at higher rates and that when they are suspended or expelled in early grades, their chance of being suspended or expelled again increases. In Caton's (2012) qualitative study of African American males who dropped out of high school, participants noted that intense security measures (e.g. metal detectors, bag searches, security guards, and resource officers) and unsupportive teacher interactions created an environment that was unwelcoming. Additionally, they explained that repeatedly being excluded from class due to disciplinary action (i.e., suspension and expulsion) caused them to fall farther behind academically and that all of these factors contributed to their decision to quit school. In the author's own experiences working with African American males in middle schools, frequent exclusion from classes without a restorative action creates a rift between the student and the teacher and often leads to the student blaming the teacher for failed assignments or drops in grades, especially in cases in which the student believes the removal from the classroom was unjust or unwarranted. This type of toxic relationship can lead to disinvestment in the class, drops in grades, and possible escalation of negative behaviors that earn another removal from class as a way to avoid the teacher.

Overrepresentation in Special Education

The overrepresentation of African American males in special education programs has been widely examined and attributed to a variety of factors (Toldson & Lewis, 2012; Serpell, Hayling, Stevenson, & Kern, 2009; Hosterman, DuPaul, & Jitendra, 2008; Moore, Henfield, & Owens, 2008). Moore et al. (2008) contended that African American males are overdiagnosed with intellectual disabilities, developmental delays, learning disabilities, and emotional/behavior disorders. African American students who live in poor neighborhoods are less likely to attend preschool and more likely to attend schools with high numbers of inexperienced teachers, high teacher absence and turnover, larger class sizes, and limited access to instructional technology and supplemental materials (Ford & Moore, 2013). These factors are outside of the students' control, yet they rob students of opportunities that exist for students in more advantaged schools. Then, students are evaluated based on assessments (often containing a certain level of cultural bias) for which they have not been prepared. African American males in this situation are often socially promoted despite having critical skill deficits (e.g. poor reading comprehension, difficulties with basic math functions, etc.) due to a lack of high-quality instruction. In the author's experiences working in a large urban school district with high student mobility, he encountered numerous African American males who had been promoted through multiple grades even though they consistently failed core classes and performed below grade level in reading comprehension; most had not been offered any type of quality remediation in previous grades to fill the skill gaps, but their teachers wanted to refer them for an evaluation to determine if they qualified for special education. These cases reveal a bigger problem in which educators place the blame on the student (i.e., labeling them with a learning disability) when the student actually has not been adequately taught how to master a specific skill, and unnecessarily adding these students to a special education program dilutes available resources for those who actually need them (see Figure 14.1).

Cultural differences between students and teachers likely affect the lens through which teachers evaluate students. Delpit (2006) explained that teachers are inadequately trained in how to teach African American males, and, therefore, their classes reflect the cultural values of the teacher and not the educational needs of the students. As a result, White teachers often misinterpret the actions and behaviors of African American males, rate their behaviors as more severe (e.g. ADHD rating scales), and judge their academic abilities based on "culture-related movement styles" and speech patterns (Serpell et al., 2009, p. 322). For example, Neal, McCray, Webb-Johnson, and Bridgest (2003) studied middle-school teachers' perceptions of students walking with "a deliberately swaggered or bent posture" referred to as a "stroll" (p. 50); their findings indicated that teachers perceived both African American and White students who walked this way as academically weaker and more likely in need of special education services, despite this having nothing to do with their academic performance. Interestingly, though, White students walking with a stroll were judged more harshly than African American students, which the authors posited is the result of teachers penalizing White students for "acting Black" while expecting this type of behavior from African Americans (p. 55). These discrepancies in how behaviors are interpreted are troubling in themselves, but they can also result in students being unfairly tracked into less rigorous programming or special education.

Dre is a 14-year old African American student in the 7th grade at JFK Middle School. His parents transferred him to this school after feeling he was treated unfairly at his previous school, although Dre tells his classmates that he wanted to be on JFK's winning basketball team. In his first week at JFK, Dre's teachers begin to notice that he is significantly behind in multiple subjects, and he is referred to Ms. Blast, a white female and the school's Reading Specialist, as a possible candidate for JFK's new reading intervention program. Ms. Blast gives Dre the Gates-McGinitie Reading Test, which reveals that his reading comprehension is at a 2nd grade level. A student reading that far below grade level is usually flagged for a special education referral. Enraged by his results, Dre asks to speak to Mr. Todd, the school counselor, who had previously checked in with Dre about being new at the school.

Mr. Todd, a white male, gets more information from Dre about his past history in school. Dre reports that in his elementary and previous middle school, he had two teachers who quit mid-year and had numerous teachers who were new and "didn't know what they were doing." He said his 4th grade teacher, an African American female, was really nice and tutored him after school in reading, but he still was retained because he didn't pass the state test. In 5th grade, he was expelled for pushing a teacher, which he proudly claims he did because she called him slow; he spent the rest of the year in an alternative school and had to repeat the grade. Dre refers to himself as a "beast" at basketball and says that is what will make him rich and famous. He has been on multiple basketball teams in the past and said that several coaches at private high schools have already talked to him about playing for them. Dre knows that being in the reading intervention class will help him keep his grades up so he can be on the basketball team but does not want to be labeled as "special ed."

Within the first few months of school, Dre frequently is removed from class by a disciplinarian because of disruptive behavior and he gets written up three times by his English teacher for disrespect and willful disobedience. His English teacher, Ms. Cain, only sees him one hour per day because he spends the other part of his English-Language Arts block with Ms. Blast. His teachers describe him as unmotivated, rude, and academically deficient, and some have openly stated that they do not like him. Additionally, they say that having him in the reading intervention class is a waste of time and that he should be referred for special education because "kids like him need to be in a self-contained class."

Figure 14.1 Case Study of Dre

> Mr. Todd has been working with Dre on a behavior contract for a few weeks with limited success and offers to help Dre with his reading and writing a few days a week during his English class. Ms. Cain gladly agrees to this arrangement and Ms. Blast helps Mr. Todd identify specific skills to work on. After about a month of receiving additional assistance from Mr. Todd and Ms. Blast, Dre is showing lots of improvement academically, tested almost two grade levels higher on the Gates-McGinitie Reading Test, and is having fewer problems in Ms. Cain's class. Mr. Todd and Dre's teachers meet again and decide to continue with the current intervention model instead of a special education referral; additionally, other teachers agree to offer him one-on-one tutoring after school and during their planning periods.
>
> Consider the following questions:
>
> 1. What messages were Dre's teachers conveying about their belief in his ability to learn?
> 2. How did Dre's past educational experiences shape his current situation?
> 3. What role did athletics play in Dre's life?
> 4. How did the approach taken by Mr. Todd and Ms. Blast benefit Dre more than a special education referral?

Figure 14.1 *(Continued)*

Being in special education does not eliminate the possibility of future success, but it can close many doors. Students in special education are more likely to be tracked into lower-level classes and trade-based classes. The author has also worked with numerous African American males who see their enrollment in special education classes as a label of being "stupid" and, therefore, do not see their futures containing the opportunities that their "regular" education peers have. Students who are involved in special education programs for a number of years may also be placed on a nontraditional diploma track, as in a career diploma or a certificate of achievement; while these may be appropriate for some students, students who have been incorrectly identified as needing special education services have once again been denied an educational opportunity with long-term postsecondary and career consequences.

Underrepresentation in Gifted, Advanced Placement, and Honors

While African American males are overrepresented in special education programs, they tend to be underrepresented in gifted and talented programs, as well as Advanced Placement and honors classes (Jackson & Beaudry, 2012; US Dept. of Education Office of Civil Rights, 2012). African American students account for approximately 10% of the gifted and talented population in the United States despite accounting for almost 20% of students in schools that offer gifted and talented programs (OCR, 2012). This statistic, however, becomes more problematic when broken down by gender and when compared to the larger number of African American students who attend schools that do not offer gifted and talented programs. Ford and Whiting (2010) explained that bias in recruitment and identification is a large contributor to this gap, including lower expectations from teachers and flawed assessment criteria. A study by Hargrove and Seay (2011) revealed that approximately twice as many minority teachers than white teachers identified "[t]eachers' inability to recognize indicators of potential giftedness" as an obstacle for African American male gifted identification (p. 453); moreover, minority teachers identified testing bias and teacher prejudices as barriers at a rate three times higher than white teachers. If the issues of stereotype threat and teacher expectations that were previously discussed are taken into consideration, it is conceivable that many African American males who could otherwise qualify for gifted programs are denied access.

In addition to discriminatory practices, African American males identified feelings of isolation within these programs (i.e., being one of a very small number of African American males) and social messages that being in a gifted program is a form of "acting white," which is seen as counter to their racial and gender identity (Ford & Whiting, 2010; Whiting, 2009). Henfield (2013) noted that not addressing these identity development issues with African American males only contributes to the achievement gap and protects the status quo. Whiting (2009) also indicated that adolescents are driven by role models (good or bad) and that society presents role models to young African American males that do not encourage rigorous academic pursuits. These concepts shed light on why students may not pursue gifted identification or self-remove from gifted programs (see Figure 14.2).

Furthermore, being locked out or opting out of rigorous coursework places African American males at a disadvantage for postsecondary education. These more advanced classes better prepare students for college-level coursework. Moreover, higher education institutions that are highly selective want to see these classes on the transcripts of their potential admits, and when African American males present transcripts devoid of them, they are likely to be passed over for other applicants. This is especially important for students who are interested in science, technology, engineering, and math [STEM] fields need higher-level coursework in high school (Curry & Milsom, 2014).

Thad is an 8th grade African American student at MLK Charter Middle School. Thad has changed schools for three consecutive years, but his mother finally chose to enroll him at MLK because of the school's focus on STEM activities and because he has previously has expressed interest in becoming an engineer. He has always excelled academically and has had great test scores; moreover, he has a bubbly personality and is well liked by his teachers. Although he has never taken advanced classes, Thad qualifies for their magnet program, and he and another student are invited by Mr. Cullen, the Assistant Principal, to participate in math enrichment. MLK is the first school where Thad feels at home, and he has built a fairly large group of friends.

What most students and teachers do not know is that Thad is being raised by a single mother with three other children. She works late a few nights a week and Thad is responsible for making dinner and taking care of his younger siblings. Three months ago, they were evicted from their apartment and have been bouncing around between friends' houses and motels since then. Thad has only confided this to Mr. Cullen and Ms. Triche, MLK's school counselor. Mr. Cullen has been driving Thad home after their math enrichment sessions, and Ms. Triche frequently had to pressure the school's bus company to quickly make changes to Thad's bus route due to his frequent moves.

After winning the regional and state science fair, Mr. Cullen encourages Thad to apply to Learning Academy, the city's most prestigious (and most expensive) high schools. Thad and his mother feel uncomfortable with applying but decide to pursue it anyway. In May, Thad receives a letter from the school indicating that he had been accepted and offering him a full tuition scholarship (valued at $18,000 per year). He and his mom are both thrilled about this and excitedly tell his teachers and Mr. Cullen. Some of his friends are happy for him but say they will miss him next year; other friends joke with him about being "the only black kid at that white school."

Thad confides in Ms. Triche that he is having second thoughts about accepting the offer from Learning Academy. He does not want to leave all the friends he made this school year and says he wants to go to the charter high school where most of them plan to attend. Thad also tells Ms. Triche that he read more about Learning Academy online and looked at pictures on their website. The only other African American students he saw were on the football team, and he worries that he will not fit in since he does not

Figure 14.2   The Case of Thad

play sports. Thad also fears that other students there will make fun of him because his family is poor and basically homeless.

Consider the following questions:

1. What opportunities did MLK provide for him to excel academically?
2. What internal factors affect Thad's high school planning?
3. What external factors affect Thad's high school planning?
4. What struggles might Thad face at Learning Academy and how can you address those as an educator?

Figure 14.2 (*Continued*)

THE ROLE OF EDUCATORS

The focus of the chapter now shifts away from exploring the problems to identifying solutions. Solving the problems facing African American males may seem like a daunting task, but educators, including administrators, counselors, teachers, and researchers, have an ethical imperative to tackle these issues and remove the barriers to academic and career success. The sections that follow highlight five key areas that educators should address in their work: professional advocacy, establishing quality mentorship programming, employing restorative discipline practices, early gifted identification, and contextually appropriate career and college exploration. While some topics may not directly apply to all stakeholders, all education stakeholders should be aware of these areas and their potential.

Professional Advocacy

Most professional codes of ethics include standards related to promoting equity and diversity for all learners. For example, the American School Counselor Association *Ethical Standards* (2010) posit that school counselors "[e]nsure equitable academic, career, post-secondary access and personal/social opportunities for all students through the use of data to help close achievement gaps and opportunity gaps" (Standard A.1.c). Standards such as this one apply to a broad array of learner groups, but bears significance to the African American male population as a call for advocacy. Educators should take into consideration the institutional structures that may unfairly and adversely affect African American males at their schools, such as access to resources, zero tolerance discipline policies, identification procedures for special education, and recruitment procedures for gifted and talented, Advanced Placement (AP), and honors programs.

Educators can begin to identify biases and oversights among school staff as they relate to marginalized students by examining disaggregated school data (e.g. enrollment data, demographic data, and outcome data). As an example, the author once joined a counseling department consisting of two female school counselors, and within a few months, staff members were openly excited about finally having someone to whom they felt comfortable referring their male students. If the other two school counselors had been collecting data about their referrals and counseling interventions, they could have identified an underrepresentation of males being referred for counseling despite high numbers of school discipline issues involved male students. Using this data as an advocacy tool, they could have encouraged the principal to hire a male counselor earlier, marketed their services better to teachers to include male students, or conducted a needs assessment with students to determine what services they felt were needed.

To better enhance educators' abilities to identify these issues, principals, counselors, or independent third parties can conduct faculty in-services related to the intersection of race, gender, and poverty and how teachers can perpetuate the problem. This same conversation could also be conducted through a faculty book study on a text related to the topic (See texts by Lisa Delpit or Ruby Payne as examples). Essentially, every educator who has contact with students needs to become aware of the unintended trickle-down effect that policies and procedures (from the district level to the school level to the classroom level) can have on marginalized students when potential issues of bias are not considered. Eliminating biases and barriers within educational settings and communities can open more doors for successful student outcomes and should aid in shrinking the educational achievement gap.

The My Brother's Keeper initiative (2014) is a collaborative effort of the Obama Administration, community leaders, and philanthropic leaders built around principles of advocacy and social change. The initiative highlights six goals related to males of color and educational outcomes: (a) preparing students to enter school with the necessary skills, (b) getting males to successfully read at their appropriate grade level by third grade, (c) completing high school prepared for a postsecondary option (college or career), (d) finishing some type of postsecondary education and/or training, (e) job attainment, and (f) intervening with community and school violence. This initiative reinforces the idea that college and career readiness is a lifelong process, and as such, educators should be engaged in related advocacy efforts targeting early childhood programs, PK-12 programs, and postsecondary opportunities.

Quality Mentorship

Whiting (2009) discussed the significance of male role models and mentors to African American males. He also posited that while males and females who are not African American "have been able to successfully raise and educate Black males," it is critically important that young African American males have contact with positive adult African American male figures beyond coaches and disciplinarians, such as teachers, mentors, pastors, and counselors (p. 230). This argument aligns with research presented earlier in the chapter that highlights African American males' desire to connect with positive role models and allows them to see adults like them who have been successful in areas other than athletics and entertainment. Grimmett (2010) proposed the *Brothers in Excellence Conceptual Model*, which suggests that empowerment and mentoring must first target identity development and then social development before being able to effectively target career development. With this framework in mind, one can begin to see why simply targeting career development with African American males without addressing identity and social development might be ineffective.

Duncan-Andrade (2009) expressed that educators should strive to provide the best education for their students while placing it in the relevant context of their lives. He additionally identified the instillation of hope in students as crucial but warned that *hokey hope* (merely saying that things will get better), *mythical hope* (saying that things already are better), and *hope deferred* (abstractly blaming hardships on the "system") are counterproductive. Instead, his conceptualization of *critical hope* involves making connections between instructional content and real life, being willing to empathize with students situations and walk their journey with them, and caring deeply enough about students to fight for changes on their behalf.

Numerous models and programs exist with the mission of mentoring African American males. Porter (2012) contended, though, that a mentor/mentee relationship must be built on trust, safety, and mutual respect and should not be entered lightly. With that in mind, rapport building is foundational to establishing a positive relationship with a student. Some adult mentors (e.g. coaches, athletes, and members of African American fraternities) historically possess social capital that can make the rapport building stage easier, but others have to work harder to gain a student's trust. In the author's experience as a White male counselor in a predominantly African American school, he found that African American males responded better to him when he displayed genuine care and concern for their well-being, honored their autonomy in establishing the alliance, and actively listened and learned about their life situations. Additionally, educators who are not African American should remain genuine to their personalities and interests and should not try to adopt personas that they assume students will like (i.e., don't *pretend* to like rap music or basketball just to have talking points); students typically can see through this façade and this will only damage the potential relationship.

Once rapport is established, a mentoring relationship should be future oriented and based on positive role modeling. Moreover, the relationship should not be simply a hangout session or a string of positive affirmations but should challenge and encourage the student to become all that he wants to be. Porter (2012) offered a four-step *CODE* model to fostering a positive mentoring relationship that involves helping African American males:

1. *Connect* to their vision for success
2. *Observe* their shortcomings so they can change
3. *Discipline* themselves to master self—thoughts, attitudes, and behaviors
4. Seek positive *Examples* of success to follow (p. 105).

This model is broad enough to allow for individual differences but captures critical pieces that should exist for successful mentoring. In establishing a vision, the mentor should identify the student's goals and encourage them to reach higher but should avoid pushing the student toward future paths in which they are not interested. Assisting the student in working through shortcomings and becoming self-disciplined should be used as opportunities to build his self-efficacy that may lead to the student strengthening his life goals.

Restorative Discipline

Meyer and Evans (2012) described restorative school discipline as a paradigm shift away from traditional school discipline policies. The underlying tenets of this model indicate that all members of a society (i.e., a school) have value and a right to be included and that steps should be taken to maintain a positive, inclusive school culture. Within a framework of discipline, restorative practices operate as a prevention/intervention model rather than a rules/consequences model. To achieve this, the school first has a responsibility to foster a positive school culture by teaching positive interpersonal skills instead of simply presenting a list of rules. Anyon et al. (2014) identified classroom circles and conferences between victims and offenders as two alternatives to suspension that have shown positive results. These interventions focus less on the punitive action for the offender and focus more on making the situation right and restoring a positive culture. Mullett (2014) further noted that restorative practices give a voice to the victim and foster collaboration and healing over getting even. For the most severe cases of student discipline problems (i.e., the repeat offenders), proponents of restorative discipline recommend individualized interventions, such as personal counseling and behavior planning, much like a Tier 3 approach in Response-to-Intervention programs.

Due to the extreme differences between traditional discipline programs and restorative discipline programs, school leaders should take a careful approach to ensure that every educator in the building is effectively trained in the model and that they are fully invested in the model. This approach cannot work effectively without full support. Following the previously discussed theme of advocacy, school leaders and counselors can engage educators in a dialogue about the relevant research highlighting the racial and gender disparities in existing discipline policies compared to the outcomes of restorative programs. Many teacher education programs train educators on a behavior management model, so a shift to restorative discipline may seem uncomfortable and unnatural; however, this should not be an excuse to abandon this endeavor. In providing rationale for restorative practices, school leaders should reiterate that the goal is not to give students a free pass on negative behavior, but instead to provide more pro-social alternatives to suspension and expulsion that would result in students missing less class time; as a result of being in class more, students have more opportunities to learn and master key academic concepts.

Gifted Identification

Bonner and Jennings (2007) posited that criteria for gifted identification should take into consideration leadership abilities, as well as "unique attributes, learning styles, and cultural backgrounds of African American male students" (p. 33). Recruiting, identifying, and retaining more African American males into gifted programs should help to eliminate some of the feelings of isolation and shame that current African American male have expressed within these programs. A specific area of need is in identifying African American males early in elementary schools, which also necessitates a call for improved access to preschool and school readiness programs that have been linked to higher rates of gifted identification (Winsler, Karkhanis, Kim, & Levitt, 2013). Whiting (2009) also suggested that assisting students in developing a scholar identity (e.g. high self-efficacy, internal locus of control, future orientation, self-awareness, need for achievement, etc.) is critical to retaining African American males in gifted programs. In the end, having more African American males in gifted or accelerated programs can make them more prepared and more competitive for postsecondary education.

Career & College Exploration

For African American males, exploring future options can sometimes seem narrowly focused or even unrealistic based on their internalized societal expectations. Educators play a key role in African American males' career and college exploration processes, as they can begin to instill the value of future planning even in elementary school. Gottfredson (1981) explained that children can begin to eliminate future career options around age four or five based on what they see as possible for someone like them. Many African American males grow up seeing limited views of their career possibilities due to mass media attention on African Americans in sports and entertainment careers, rather than occupations like doctors, lawyers, engineers, and teachers. Teachers and counselors at the elementary level should expose students to a wide array of career role models and provide them opportunities to explore an array of career options to help them solidify their interests and skills.

Early in middle school, educators should assist students in integrating their interests, values, and skills to begin narrowing career options to potential interest areas. Many who have worked with African American males at this stage can attest to the common belief by students that they will be future star professional athletes or award-winning recording artists; while some may have the potential to achieve this dream, the statistics are not working in everyone's favor. At the same time, educators should not serve as "dream squashers" but instead should challenge students to think harder; these conversations and links can help students pinpoint the technical and transferrable skills involved with their dream career and identify related options (e.g. athletic trainer or sound editor). Educators commonly engage males who are interested in sports careers in a conversation about hypothetical injuries, but these conversations, in the author's experience, make the student feel as if they are not being heard. Instead, he would pose the following question to these students: *Since many professional athletes retire by age 35 or 40, what would you plan to do after that?* This question does not squash the dream but gets them thinking about other interests and possibilities (e.g. sports commentating, team management/ownership, coaching, etc.); he would then dialogue with them about the education and training that could support those secondary careers.

Another key focus for middle and high school, especially for African American males, is the logistics of being admitted to postsecondary education. It is critically important for students at this age to understand the costs associated with higher education but also the many resources present to support low-income and minority students, such as grants, scholarships, loans, and tax credits. Highlighting these resources early can prevent students from giving up in early grades simply because of the costs. Likewise, educators should assist students with understanding the timeline and steps required, such as taking the ACT/SAT, completing applications, and completing the FAFSA, and supporting them through the process. African American males may also find it beneficial to learn about on-campus resources, including minority affairs offices, financial aid offices, and student support services, before getting to college to instill that they will not be navigating the process alone.

SUMMARY

This chapter highlighted the specific barriers to career and college readiness facing African American males in today's schools. As racial and gender identity are salient to overall identity development, the author discussed the presentation of hypermasculinity, stereotyping, and stereotype threat as risk factors for success. African American males also face institutional discrimination at school through zero tolerance policies, over-identification in special education, and under-identification in gifted education; these school structures can foster a climate where African American males feel undervalued. Educators are ethically compelled to advocate for social justice in education by identifying and challenging these policies and procedures, and educators can act as critical mentors and role models who can guide students toward future success.

REFERENCES

Alexander, M. (2011). *The new Jim Crow: Mass incarceration in the age of colorblindness*. New York, NY: The New Press.

American School Counselor Association. (2010). *Ethical standards for school counselors*. Retrieved from http://www.schoolcounselor.org/files/EthicalStandards2010.pdf.

Anyon, Y., Jenson, J. M., Altschul, I., Farrar, J., McQueen, J., Greer, E., ... Simmons, J. (2014). The persistent effect of race and the promise of alternatives to suspension in school discipline outcomes. *Children and Youth Services Review*, *44*, 379–386. doi: 10.1016/j.childyouth.2014.06.025

Appel, M., & Kronberger, N. (2012). Stereotypes and the achievement gap: Stereotype threat prior to test taking. *Educational Psychology Review*, *24*, 609–635. doi: 10.1007/s10648-012-9200-4

Barlow, D. (2004). Basketball in the ghetto: Exploitation mistaken for opportunity. *Education Digest*, *70*(1), 63–67.

Beamon, K. K. (2008). "Used goods": Former African American college student athletes' perception of exploitation by Division 1 universities. *Journal of Negro Education*, *77*(4), 352–364.

Beamon, K. K. (2010). Are sports overemphasized in the socialization process of African American males? A qualitative analysis of former collegiate athletes' perception of sport socialization. *Journal of Black Studies*, *41*(2), 281–300. doi: 10.1177/0021934709340873

Bernstein, N. (2014). *Burning down the house: The end of juvenile prison*. New York, NY: The New Press.

Bonner, F. A., & Jennings, M. (2007). Never too young to lead: Gifted African American males in elementary school. *Gifted Child Today*, *30*(2), 30–36. doi: 10.4219/gct-2007-32

Bowman-Perrott, L., Benz, M. R., Hsu, H. Y., Kwok, O. M., Eisterhold, L. A., & Zhang, D. (2011). Patterns and predictors of disciplinary exclusion over time: An analysis of the SEELS national data set. *Journal of Emotional and Behavioral Disorders, 21*(2), 83–96. doi: 10.1177/1063426611407501

Brewster, J., & Stephenson, M. (2013). *Promises kept: Raising black boys to succeed in school and in life.* New York, NY: Spiegel & Grau Trade Paperbacks.

Carlson, K. M. (2009). *What's the difference between discipline and punishment?* Retrieved from Center for Early Education and Development website: http://www.cehd.umn.edu/ceed/publications/questionsaboutkids/disciplineenglish.pdf.

Caton, M. T. (2012). Black male perspectives on their educational experiences in high school. *Urban Education, 47*(6), 1055–1085. doi: 10.1177/0042085912454442

Conyers, J. (2013). The incarceration explosion. *Yale Law & Policy Review, 31*, 377–387.

Cunningham, M., Swanson, D. P., & Hayes, D. M. (2013). School- and community-based associations to hypermasculine attitudes in African American adolescent males. *American Journal of Orthopsychiatry, 83*(2/3), 244–251. doi: 10.1111/ajop.12029

Curry, J., & Milsom, A. (2014). *Career Counseling in P-12 Schools.* New York, NY: Springer Publishing Company.

Delpit, L. (2006). *Other people's children: Cultural conflict in the classroom.* New York, NY: Norton.

Drake, B. (2013). *Incarceration gap widens between whites and blacks.* Retrieved from http://www.pewresearch.org/fact-tank/2013/09/06/incarceration-gap-between-whites-and-blacks-widens/.

Duncan-Andrade, J. M. R. (2007). Developing social justice educators. In G. S. Goodman (Ed.), *Educational psychology: An application of critical constructivism* (pp. 1–11). New York, NY: Peter Lang.

Duncan-Andrade, J. M. R. (2009). Note to educators: Hope required when growing roses in concrete. *Harvard Educational Review, 79*(2), 181–194. Retrieved from http://www.unco.edu/cebs/diversity/pdfs/duncan_note%20to%20educators_%20hope%20required%20when%20growing%20roses%20in%20concrete.pdf

Erikson, E. H. (1963). *Childhood and society* (2nd ed.). New York, NY: Norton.

Erikson, E. H. (1968). *Identity: Youth and crisis.* New York, NY: Norton.

Federal Bureau of Prisons. (2014). *Inmate Race* [Data set]. Retrieved from http://www.bop.gov/about/statistics/statistics_inmate_race.jsp.

Ford, D. Y., & Moore, J. L. (2013). Understanding and reversing underachievement, low achievement, and achievement gaps among high-ability African American males in urban school contexts. *Urban Review, 45*, 399–415. doi:10.1007/s11256-013-0256-3

Ford, D. Y., & Whiting, G. W. (2010). Beyond testing: Social and psychological considerations in recruiting and retaining gifted black students. *Journal for the Education of the Gifted, 34*(1), 131–155. doi: 10.1177/016235321003400106

Fowler, D. (2011). School discipline feeds the "pipeline to prison". *Phi Delta Kappan, 93*(2), 14–19. doi: 10.1177/003172171109300204

Gottfredson, L. S. (1981). Circumscription and compromise: A developmental theory of occupational aspirations. *Journal of Counseling Psychology, 28*(6), 545–579. doi: 10.1037/0022-0167.28.6.545

Grimmett, M. A. (2010). Brothers in excellence: An empowerment model for the career development of African American boys. *Journal of Humanistic Counseling, Education and Development, 49*, 73–83. doi: 10.1002/j.2161-1939.2010.tb00088.x

Hargrove, B. H., & Seay, S. E. (2011). School teacher perceptions of barriers that limit the participation of African American males in public school gifted programs. *Journal for the Education of the Gifted, 34*(3), 434–467. doi: 10.1177/016235321103400304

Henfield, M. S. (2013). Special issue: Meeting the needs of gifted and high-achieving black males in urban schools. *Urban Review, 45*, 395–398. doi: 10.1007/s11256-013-0266-1

Hoffman, S. (2012). Zero benefit: Estimating the effect of zero tolerance discipline policies on racial disparities in school discipline. *Education Policy, 28*(1), 69–95. doi: 10.1177/0895904812453999

Horne, A. M., Jolliff, D. L., & Roth, E. W. (1996). Men mentoring men in groups. In M. P. Andronico (ed.). *Men in groups: Insights, interventions, and psychoeducational work* (pp. 97–112). Washington, DC: American Psychological Association.

Hosterman, S. J., DuPaul, G. J., & Jitendra, A. K. (2008). Teacher ratings of ADHD symptoms in ethnic minority students: Bias or behavioral difference? *School Psychology Quarterly, 23*(3), 418–435. doi: 10.1037/a0012668

Jackson, J., & Beaudry, A. (2012). *The urgency of now*. Retrieved from Schott Foundation for Public Education website: http://blackboysreport.org/urgency-of-now.pdf/.

Johnson-Ahorlu, R. N. (2013). "Our biggest challenge is stereotypes": Understanding stereotype threat and the academic experiences of African American undergraduates. *The Journal of Negro Education, 82*(4), 382–392. Retrieved from http://jeg.sagepub.com/content/34/3/434.full.pdf

Logel, C., Peach, J., & Spencer, S. J. (2012). Threatening gender and race: Different manifestations of stereotype threat. In M. Inzlicht & T. Schmader (Eds.), *Stereotype threat* (pp. 159–172). New York, NY: Oxford University Press.

Martin, B. E., Harrison, C. K., Stone, J., & Lawrence, S. M. (2010). Athletic voices and academic victories: African American male student-athlete experiences in the Pac-Ten. *Journal of Sport and Social Issues, 34*(2), 131–153. doi: 10.1177/0193723510366541

Meyer, L. H., & Evans, I. M. (2012). *The school leader's guide to restorative school discipline*. Thousand Oaks, CA: Corwin.

Moore, J. L., Henfield, M. S., & Owens, D. (2008). African American males in special education: Their attitudes and perceptions toward high school counselors and school counseling services. *American Behavioral Scientist, 51*(7), 907–927. doi: 10.1177/0002764207311997

Mullett, J. H. (2014). Restorative discipline: From getting even to getting well. *Children & Schools, 36*(3), 157–162. doi: 10.1093/cs/cdu011

My Brother's Keeper Task Force. (2014). *Report to the president*. Retrieved from http://www.whitehouse.gov/sites/default/files/docs/053014_mbk_report.pdf.

Natsuaki, M. N., Ge, X., & Wenk, E. (2008). Continuity and changes in the developmental trajectories of criminal career: Examining the roles of timing of first arrest and high school graduation. *Journal of Youth Adolescence, 37,* 431–444. doi: 10.1007/s10964-006-9156-0

Neal, L. I., McCray, A. D., Webb-Johnson, G., and Bridgest, S. T. (2003). The effects of African American movement styles on teachers' perceptions and reactions. *The Journal of Special Education, 37*(1), 49–57.

Palmer, R. T., & Maramba, D. C. (2010). African American male achievement: Using a tenet of Critical Theory to explain the African American male achievement disparity. *Education and Urban Society, 43,* 431–450. doi: 10.1177/0013124510380715

Palmer, R. T., Moore, J. L., Davis, R. J., & Hilton, A. A. (2010). A nation at risk: Increasing college participation and persistence among African American males to stimulate U.S. global competitiveness. *Journal of African American Males in Education, 1*(2), 105–124. Retrieved from http://journalofafricanamericanmales.com/wp-content/uploads/downloads/2010/05/FINAL-PALMER.pdf

Payne, R. (2013). *A framework for understanding poverty: A cognitive approach* (5th ed.). Highlands, TX: aha! Process.

Phinney, J. S. (1989). Stages of ethnic identity development in minority group adolescents. *The Journal of Early Adolescence, 9*(1/2), 34–49. doi: 10.1177/0272431689091004

Piaget, J. (1969). The intellectual development of the adolescent. In G. Caplan & S. Lebovici (Eds.), *Adolescence: Psychosocial perspectives* (pp. 22–26). New York, NY: Basic Books.

Porter, K. T. (2012). *Angry little men: Hypermasculinity, academic disconnect, and mentoring African American males.* Chicago, IL: African American Images.

Roberts-Douglass, K., & Curtis-Boles, H. (2012). Exploring positive masculinity development in African American men: A retrospective study. *Psychology of Men & Masculinity, 14*(1), 7–15. doi: 10.1037/a0029662

Schmader, T., Johns, M., & Forbes, C. (2008). An integrated process model of stereotype threat effects on performance. *Psychological Review, 115*(2), 336–356. doi: 10.1037/0033-295X.115.2.336

Scottham, K. M., Cooke, D. Y., Sellers, R. M., & Ford, K. (2010). Integrating process with content in understanding African American racial identity development. *Self and Identity, 9,* 19–40. doi: 10.1080/15298860802505384

Scottham, K. M., Sellers, R. M., & Nguyen, H. X. (2008). A measure of racial identity in African American adolescents: The development of the Multidimensional Inventory of Black Identity—Teen. *Cultural Diversity and Ethnic Minority Psychology, 14*(4), 297–306. doi: 10.1037/1099-9809.14.4.297

Seaton, G. (2007). Toward a theoretical understanding of hypermasculine coping among urban black adolescent males. *Journal of Human Behavior in the Social Environment, 15*(2/3), 367–390. doi: 10.1300/J137v15n02_21

Serpell, Z., Hayling, C. C., Stevenson, H., & Kern, L. (2009). Cultural considerations in the development of school-based interventions for African American adolescent boys with emotional and behavioral disorders. *The Journal of Negro Education, 78*(3), 321–332. Retrieved from http://www.jstor.org/stable/25608749

Skiba, R. J. (2014). The failure of zero tolerance. *Reclaiming Children and Youth, 22*(4), 27–33. Retrieved from https://reclaimingjournal.com/sites/default/files/journal-article-pdfs/22_4_Skiba.pdf

Spencer, M. B., Fegley, S., Harpalani, V., & Seaton, G. (2004). Understanding hypermasculinity in context: A theory-driven analysis of urban adolescent males' coping responses. *Research in Human Development, 1*(4), 229–257. doi: 10.1207/s15427617rhd0104_2

Steele, C. M., & Aronson, J. (1995). Stereotype threat and the intellectual test performance of African Americans. *Journal of Personality and Social Psychology, 69*(5), 797–811. doi: 10.1037/0022–3514.69.5.797

Steinberg, W. (1993). *Masculinity: Identity, conflict, and transformation*. Boston, MA: Shambhala Publications.

Stone, J., Chalabaev, A., & Harrison, C. (2012). The impact of stereotype threat on performance in sports. In M. Inzlicht & T. Schmader (Eds.), *Stereotype threat: Theory, process, and application* (pp. 217–230). New York, NY: Oxford University Press.

Stone, J., Harrison, C. K., & Mottley, J. (2012). "Don't call me a student-athlete": The effect of identity priming on stereotype threat for academically engaged African American college athletes. *Basic and Applied Social Psychology, 34*, 99–106. doi: 10.1080/01973533.2012.655624

Teske, S. C., Huff, B., & Graves, C. (2013). Collaborative role of courts in promoting outcomes for students: The relationship between arrests, graduation rates, and school safety. *Family Court Review, 51*(3), 418–426. doi: 10.1111/fcre.12038

Toldson, I. A., & Lewis, C. W. (2012). *Challenging the status quo: Academic success among school-age African American males*. Retrieved from: http://www.cbcfinc.org/oUploadedFiles/CTSQ.pdf.

U.S. Department of Education. (2010, March). *A blueprint for reform: The reauthorization of the elementary and secondary education act*. Retrieved from http://www2.ed.gov/policy/elsec/leg/blueprint/publicationtoc.html.

U.S. Department of Education, Office of Civil Rights. (2014). *Data snapshot: School discipline* (Issue Brief No. 1). Retrieved from http://www2.ed.gov/about/offices/list/ocr/docs/crdc-discipline-snapshot.pdf.

U.S. Dept. of Education, Office of Civil Rights. (2012). *Revealing new truths about our nation's schools*. Retrieved from http://www2.ed.gov/about/offices/list/ocr/docs/crdc-2012-data-summary.pdf.

Van Rheenen, D., & Atwood, J. R. (2014). Confirmatory factor analysis of perceived exploitation of college athletes questionnaire. *Journal of College Student Development, 55*(5). doi: 10.1353/csd.2014.0045

Weissman, N. (Producer), & Levine, J. (Producer). (2014). *"Am I next?" Ferguson's protests through the eyes of a teenager*. Retrieved from http://time.com/3126991/ferguson-missouri-protests-michael-brown/.

Whiting, G. (2009). Gifted black males: Understanding and decreasing barriers to achievement and identity. *Roeper Review, 31*, 224–233. doi: 10.1080/02783190903177598

Wiesner, M., Kim, H. K., & Capaldi, D. M. (2010). History of juvenile arrests and vocational career outcomes for at-risk young men. *Journal of Research in Crime and Delinquency, 47*(1), 91–117. doi: 10.1177/0022427809348906.

Wilson, H. (2014). Turning off the school-to-prison pipeline. *Reclaiming Children and Youth*, *23*(1), 49–53. Retrieved from http://web.a.ebscohost.com/ehost/pdfviewer/pdfviewer?sid=043e26c5-1ae4-44ac-ae48-029b7a3a36c1%40sessionmgr4001&vid=1&hid=4209

Winsler, A., Karkhanis, D. G., Kim, Y. K., & Levitt, J. (2013). Being black, male, and gifted in Miami: Prevalence and predictors of placement in elementary school gifted education programs. *Urban Review*, *45*, 416–447. doi: 10/1007/s11256-013-0259-0

Chapter 15

African American Athletes and Higher Education

Linwood Vereen, Nicole R. Hill, and Michelle Lopez

The relationship between African American student-athletes and higher education is one that can be described as disharmonious and tenuous, while simultaneously being replete with opportunity and growth. Enhancing our understanding of African American student-athletes is critical because they represent the largest racially minoritized group in the National Collegiate Athletic Association (NCAA). The literature is fraught with stories outlining the contextual factors that contribute to issues of retention and lack of success of student-athletes (Brooks, Jones, & Burt, 2012; Harper & Harris, 2012; Sellers, Kuperminc, & Damas, 1997), while at the same time outlining the developmental challenges to growth (Singer, 2005) and the creation of a sport and non-sport identity (Beamon, 2012; Clopton, 2010; Harrison, Sailes, Rotich, & Bimper, 2011; Stone, Harrison, & Mottley, 2012). These issues have been compounded by contextual factors such as racialization, racial identity, and explorations of the dynamics that lead to the overall level of resiliency in the face of conflicting outcomes including isolation, marginalization, praise, and adoration.

More recently, there has been an increase in literature concerning the legal aspects of athletic participation; this focus further underscores the fragility of the relationship between African American student-athletes and the academy. This is done as a means of framing an unrealized facet of the relationship that is often overlooked (Donnor, 2005), yet is critical to the understanding of the uniqueness of collegiate life for the African American student-athlete. The compilation of these narratives and the lived experiences of young men and women has been seen through many contextual lenses outlining the developmental challenges of being an African American student-athlete. Over time, this has led to reforms in institutional and systemic practices that do not serve to benefit the African American student-athlete in the same manner as it does for other student-athletes who are not African American. Proposition 48 which was implemented in 1986 and replaced by Proposition 16 in the mid-1990s is one example of a systemic plan that was intended to facilitate academic readiness and positively influence graduation rates, yet the policy has initially struggled to do that. What occurred was that many colleges and universities did not have the infrastructure or resources in place to support the needs of these student-athletes many of whom were from low income households. The impact on entrance into college, eligibility, and matriculation disproportionately impacted poor and low income African Americans in a negative manner. In addition to the above-mentioned incidents, issues related to campus climate (Davis et al., 2004; Griffin, Jayakumar, Jones, & Allen, 2010; Harper, 2009; Harper, 2013; Harper & Hurtado, 2007), faculty relations, expectations for success, and experiences at predominantly White institutions add to the variables impacting the daily experience of African American men and women who attend college as a student-athlete.

The focus of this chapter is African American student-athletes through the lens of Critical Race Theory (CRT) as a means of seeing race and beyond. CRT has grown in its use and application to expand the discourse focused on the reality of the role that race, racism, and power play within education and contemporary society (Donnor, 2005; Ladson-Billings, 1998; Parker & Lynn, 2002; Tate, 1997). In addition, CRT provides an understanding of how university systems can play a role in the perpetuation of discriminatory practices while claiming to provide access, equity, fairness, and opportunity in a space purported to focus on higher learning, education, personal growth and advancement. Donnor (2005) illustrates how interest convergence as a foundation of CRT is a means of enhancing the knowledge of what challenges student-athletes face. Interest convergence not only sheds light on issues of race but enhances its purview through the inclusion of legal contexts and issues that enlighten us to reveal the ways in which those who claim to have the best interest of student-athletes at heart perpetuate barriers to education, access, and opportunity. At the same time, interest convergence can be utilized as a mechanism to face and conceptualize challenges of oppression, bias, lack of fairness, and exclusion faced by student-athletes.

The institutional paradigms that exacerbate racial differences existing within higher education provide the rationale for CRT. CRT has the potential to illuminate where and how dominant cultural mores are pervasive within society and higher education and provide context in how to combat these injustices in a manner that other theories may evade. It is here where CRT provides a contextual lens that demands an evolution in educational practices bringing to the forefront issues of how power, race, and racism stand in way of growth, development, opportunity and access for more African American men and women who attend college on an intercollegiate athletic scholarship.

HIGHER EDUCATION CONTEXTUAL FACTORS IMPACTING AFRICAN AMERICAN ATHLETES

The experiences of African American student-athletes are significantly impacted by a multitude of contextual factors within the higher education environment (Harper, 2013). The well-researched impact of toxic climates on African American students at predominantly White institutions (Davis et al., 2004; Griffin et al., 2010; Harper & Davis, 2012; Harper & Hurtado, 2007; Harper, 2009; Harper, 2013) provides a framework for understanding how student-athletes experience similar challenges and obstacles (Harper & Hurtado, 2007; Harper, 2013). The experience of toxic climates is defined here as the culmination of an educational history that has been inundated with the absence of African American role models, culturally relevant curriculum, and pervasive expectations for poor academic proficiency and performance of African American students (Harper & Harris, 2012). The lens of Critical Race Theory provides focus for this context to better understand the historical backdrop of how students of color have experienced climates that have been found to be unhealthy and unwelcoming at the same time (Donnor, 2005; Ladson-Billings, 1998; Singer, 2005).

In 2012, Snyder and Dillow asserted that 84% of African American undergraduates received their bachelor degrees from predominantly White institutions. This is a significant enrollment shift for African American students in that only 25% of undergraduates were enrolled in predominantly White institutions in the early 1970s. If the institutional profile is comprised of mostly White students, then African American student-athletes encounter a host of challenging environments, exacerbated by what Harper et al. (2011) described as "onlyness" (p. 190). *Onlyness* is the psycho-emotional experience of being the isolated individual experiencing a convergence of factors and being perceived as being a spokesperson for that complexity of experience. The experience of onlyness can be mediated or exacerbated based on the campus climate in which African American student-athletes are situated.

Campus Climate

From the mid-1960s to the present, the experience of African American students at predominantly White institutions has been extensively researched with many scholars identifying isolation, racism, racial microaggressions, and toxic campus climates as continual and pervasive areas of concern (e.g.- Fleming, 1984; Harper, 2013; Kammen, 2009; Sedlacek, 1987; Sellers et al., 1997; Willie & Cunnigen, 1981). Educational attainment has been significantly correlated to higher levels of physical wellness, more resilient mental health, and more economic opportunity and outcomes (Harris, 2014;

Ou & Reynolds, 2008). Academic expectations have been linked consistently with academic performance measures (Charles, Roscigno, & Torres, 2007). Race, gender, and social class converge to impact educational attainments, and when combined with the stereotypes and hostile climate, might have a debilitating impact on academic expectations and performance (Stone, 2012). Consistently hearing a message that you are not prepared or ready for the college academic experience may also negatively impact African American athletes' motivation, self-efficacy, and performance.

Griffin et al. (2010) conducted an analysis of 40 years of data from the University of California-Los Angeles Cooperative Institutional Research Program survey and found that African American undergraduates in 2004 were markedly different than their same race counterparts in the previous 40 years. Specifically, the 2004 cohort of students in the study were from wealthier families, evidenced better academic records, and reported higher levels of confidence about their abilities and skills. Despite this reality, there is an overwhelming stereotype that African American students, especially men, are from poverty-stricken neighborhoods and are poorly prepared to academically manage the expectations of higher education. Harper (2013) asserts that the overrepresentation of African American men in college athletics compounds this stereotype by generating a perception that African American athletes are only at college to advance their sports careers and are not committed to academic learning.

Expectations for Success and Achievement

Student-athletes experience pressures that are different than most college students in that their academic progress is correlated to eligibility based on the National Collegiate Athletic Association (NCAA) standards. Table 15.1 provides a summary of current academic requirements for student-athletes. The correlated expectations for success and achievement for student-athletes might be viewed as contradictory at best. In many instances, success is viewed merely as athletic success which is expected by friends, family, coaches, peers, and the university community at large. The construct of "majoring in eligibility" (Harrison, 2008, p. 50) captures this emphasis on athletic prowess as the benchmark for success (Duderstadt, 2000; Shulman & Bowen, 2001). This is contradicted with expectations for academic success which can be seen as situational and centered on athletic eligibility.

For example, each semester student-athletes must show progress toward degree completion, but the required grade point average (GPA) in the first four semesters falls below what is required for matriculation. Thus, Donnor (2005) argues that the actual requirements for eligibility are below those required for academic success, thereby generating a system that creates and

Table 15.1 NCAA Stipulated Academic Requirements for Student-Athletes

Division I Requirements	Division II Requirements	Division III Requirements*
Completion Percentages • By the end of second year, 40% of coursework for degree must be completed • By end of third year, 60% must be completed • By end of fourth year, 80% must be completed	Completion Benchmarks • 24 hours of degree credit each academic year (of which 6 can be earned in the summer)	Completion Benchmarks • Make satisfactory progress toward degree as defined by institution
Course Load Per Semester • Earn 6 credits	Course Load Per Semester • Earn 6 credits	Not defined
GPA Requirements • 90% of institution's minimum overall GPA necessary to graduate in year 2 • 95% necessary to graduate in year 3 • 100% by year 4	GPA Requirements • 1.8 GPA after 24 semester/36 quarter hours • 1.9 GPA after 48 semester/72 quarter hours • 2.0 GPA after 72 semester/108 quarter hours	GPA Requirements • Maintain good academic standing at institution

Retrieved from http://www.ncaa.org/remaining-eligible-academics on January 15, 2015.
*No stipulated national standards for Division III.

perpetuates attrition. A recent court case provides an example of how the eligibility requirements can generate systemic failures regarding student-athlete success (Donnor, 2005). In *Taylor v. Wake Forest University*, the student-athlete was required to achieve a grade point average (GPA) of 1.35 after the first year, 1.65 after the second year, and 1.85 after the third year. While maintaining athletic eligibility, these GPA requirements would not lead toward graduation within a four- to six-year time span which is expected in today's athletic climate. The specific student-athlete in this case was removed from athletic scholarship when he withdrew from athletic practice to focus on his education (Donnor, 2005). The system's emphasis on academic success did not change because the legal case was settled on the side of the institution, thereby generating a lack of interest convergence as described by Critical Race Theory.

The emphasis on athletics to the detriment of academics has a significant impact on African American athletes. Specifically, the overall graduation rates for African American student-athletes are consistently lower than those of their counterparts who are also student-athletes yet not of color, and for those who are students not participating in intercollegiate athletics. However, an examination of gender provides an even greater concern for consideration. In particular, according to the 2014 *Tides Report*, the gap between African American women and White women student-athletes is closing. Of the teams participating in the NCAA women's basketball tournament, 90% graduated at least 70% of their White student-athletes while 81% graduated at least 70% of their African American women athletes. In stark contrast, of the men's teams participating in the tournament 84% graduated at least 70% of their White male student-athletes while only 44% of teams graduated at least 70% of their African American male student-athletes. One potential explanation for these trends is that the availability of professional opportunities in one's sport after college has been correlated with academic performance. For example, one of the contributing factors for women athletes performing at a higher academic standard and graduating more often than their male counterparts is the dearth of professional opportunities in athletics postcollege. For African American women athletes, their athletic identity, while important, tends to be superseded with an academic identity and a focus on career preparedness (Coakley, 2001). From an advising, mentoring, and coaching framework, women tend to be pushed to focus on their career after athletics and academics, while men tend to be pushed to prioritize and focus on athletics to the potential exclusion of academics and career preparedness.

Recruitment of African American Student-Athletes

Recruitment of student-athletes, especially high profile athletes at high profile institutions, garners much media and popular culture attention each year. Recruitment is a politically and racially charged topic for many in higher education because much of athletics, especially football and basketball, tend to be dominated by highly skilled and talented African American male athletes. The dominance of high profile recruits into athletic programs does not parallel the representation of African American students across other college contexts, thereby generating a racial separation across the campus experience. For example in 2009, African American men composed 55% of teams in revenue-generating sports at Division I programs while only accounting for 4% of full-time college students (Harper, 2012; Harper & Harris, 2012). Race functions as both a context and construct within the recruitment process, especially in situations of high profile athletes (Duderstadt, 2000; Harrison, 2008).

In his qualitative study of 167 college students, Harrison (2008) explored the recruitment process of African American male student-athletes. For the purposes of the study, participants watched a scene from the movie *The Program* and then processed in writing their perceptions. Emergent from his study, Harrison found that both African American ($n = 18$) and White American ($n = 149$) participants perceive the recruitment process as glamorizing athletics and being devoid of an academic or educational focus. Further, participants consistently spoke to the sexualized stereotype of African American males.

Recruitment practices vary considerably based on the gender of the athlete, whether the sport is revenue generating, and the NCAA classification of the institution. The recruitment process, in and of itself, sends an external message that can be viewed negatively by both men and women. Those students who are recruited by colleges and universities that are seen as athletic powers become used to lots of attention from college coaches in the form of letters, emails, texts, and home visits. The volume of attention is much less for those who are recruited to play at schools that hold a lower NCAA division rank. For those students recruited who are then dropped and lose the attention of a major athletic power or those who were rarely, if ever, recruited, the feelings of loss, wondering, and isolation can be difficult to navigate. The recruitment process can be more difficult for students and families who are new to the process and are unaware of the rules. Often, a young person is faced with a life altering decision and does not have the support of relatives who are knowledgeable about the rules of recruitment. The confusion can be compounded when intense community and media pressure are added.

In the case of football and basketball at a major division I institution, it is not uncommon for there to be national media in the gymnasium or library of a high school documenting the announcement of a high profile recruit of where he will be choosing to attend college and play football or basketball. With those being the highest profiled and revenue producing college sports, it stands to reason for many that they should garner the most media attention. This scenario becomes gendered when compared to women's sports. Rarely are the national media present for the verbal commitment and national letter of intent signing of female athletes. The external message that can be negatively internalized by young women is that their athletic accomplishments are second to those of their male counterparts. To exacerbate the external messaging, one need only contemplate the last instance where an athlete who committed and signed to play at a Football Championship Subdivision (FCS) or Division II school had the event documented by the national media. This again sends a strong message to those African American men and women who are not recruited by high profile institutions or high profile athletic programs that could be negatively internalized regarding where we as a society and educational system place our values.

EDUCATIONAL EFFECTS OF AFRICAN AMERICAN ATHLETES

Faculty-Student Relationships

African American student-athletes encounter stereotypes that are situated in racial assumptions as well as in athletic assumptions. Edwards (2000) potently describes African American student-athletes as exposed to three dominant stereotype threats, namely the "dumb jock caricature," "the myth of innate black athletic superiority," and the "blatantly racist stereotype of the dumb Negro" (p. 126). The stigmatized notion of the "dumb jock" influences faculty relationships with African American student-athletes (Stone, 2012). Numerous scholars describe the "dumb jock" stereotype as being correlated to the belief that student-athletes receive privileges for being athletes, are more likely to engage in academic dishonesty, are not prepared for higher education, benefit from lenient evaluation practices, and pursue "easy" classes and majors (Edwards, 1984; Foster, 2009; Stone, 2012). Compared to their White peers, African American student-athletes believe that the "dumb jock" stereotype is more rigidly and pervasively applied to them and that they receive less flexibility from faculty members about the impact of their athletic commitments to their academic attendance and practices (Martin, Harrison, Stone, & Lawrence,2010; Singer, 2005). Athletes have reported that they have overheard faculty explicitly commenting on these negative assumptions in classes. Not only do the negative stereotypes contribute to faculty members being less engaged, more dismissive, and more likely to question a student's veracity, they also prevent African American athletes from being integrated across campus contexts (Harrison, 2008). These negative stereotypes are more problematic for highly motivated students. Specifically, African American athletes who are highly motivated to excel academically are more susceptible to the negative impact of stereotypes related to their athletic identity (Stone, 2012).

At predominantly White institutions, African American athletes encounter the spokesperson expectation from many of their White faculty members (Davis et al., 2004; Harper, 2013; Winkle-Wagner, 2009). Students must navigate the "psychoemotional burden" (Harper et al., 2011, p. 190) of underrepresentation in which they are expected to speak and share their presumed expertise on topics of race and socioeconomic status within classrooms. African American student-athletes must allocate energy and patience in educating White faculty members about the experience of being Black and in disrupting the discourse that permeates predominantly White classrooms. This phenomenon is referred to as *tokenism*.

In addition to the experience of tokenism in the classroom, African American student-athletes are impacted by a pervasive belief that they are not serious about their academic work or committed to pursuing an undergraduate degree. Emergent from this stereotype, White professors are less likely to engage African American students in research opportunities, tend to expect them to perform poorly, and are more likely to identify them as being absent or late from class (Harper, 2009). Within the classroom, African American student-athletes must navigate a dialectic of invisibility and hyper-visibility (Davis et al., 2004; Flowers, 2003; Strayhorn, 2013).

Another systemic issue that influences African American student-athletes is the absence of role models among faculty members and staff who are African American. Harper (2013) analyzed data from the 20 largest public universities in the United States and computed that the ratio of African American undergraduates to African American tenure track faculty member was 32 to 1. When situated at predominantly White institutions, the disparity between groups increases to a ratio of 43 to 1. This ratio is even less positive when situated within African American student-athletes on campuses across the country. The dearth of professional role models negatively impacts African American student-athletes' academic achievement, academic motivation, and career readiness (Flowers, 2003; Strayhorn, 2013). The impact is that African American athletes must work harder, encounter more stress and anxiety to be able to perform in the academic arena (Stone, 2012).

The Benchmark of Attrition: Graduation Rates

Researchers have consistently found that African American men have the lowest college completion rates with approximately 66% of them not finishing within 6 years of starting college (Harper & Harris, 2012). There is a gendered difference with African American women having considerably higher completion rates. Women athletes tend to perform better academically which translates into higher graduation rates when compared to their male counterparts (Meyer, 1990). The college completion data is further complicated for the academic outcomes for African American student-athletes. From 2002 to 2005 graduation data, there was a 13% point difference between African American male student-athletes and student-athletes overall.

Attrition can be understood within the context of environmental, social, and psychological factors (Strayhorn, 2013). Failure to consider and understand all these dimensions will undermine the ability to examine the complexity of variables impacting African American student-athletes' completion rates. Environmental factors include campus climate, burden from family and community of origin, pressures of revenue-generating sport teams including media scrutiny, and potentially competing demands of academic and athletic responsibilities (Flowers, 2003; Strayhorn, 2013). Social factors include African American student-athletes' ability to form positive and affirming relationships with diverse peers, faculty members, coaches, and administrators (Flowers, 2003; Harper, 2006; Strayhorn, 2013). Engagement with campus organizations and events can have a significantly positive impact on attrition rates for African American student-athletes. Finally, academic success and degree completion are influenced by cognitive and behavioral characteristics (Strayhorn, 2013).

One behavioral quality that is garnering more attention in recent literature is the role of grit, or persistence, tenacity, and diligence, in African American student success (Duckworth & Quinn, 2009; Strayhorn, 2013). Strayhorn conducted a study of 140 African American students at predominantly White institutions and examined whether grit contributed incremental predictive variability to academic success. Even though the participants were all male and only 9% identified as student-athletes, the results of Strayhorn's study have implications for African American student-athletes. Specifically, he found that grit did positively correlate to academic success for his participants. Further, Strayhorn determined that after controlling for age, year in school, previous academic achievement, engagement activities, career aspirations, and transfer status, grit predicted higher academic achievement. Achievement, and thus attrition, can then be a factor of effort and talent, thereby providing another avenue through which to support African American student-athletes in attaining their degree and career aspirations.

THE GENDERED LANDSCAPE OF ATHLETICS FOR AFRICAN AMERICAN STUDENTS

African American women student-athletes are impacted by Title IX, federal legislation that was enacted in 1972. Title IX specifically states that: "No person in the United States shall, on the basis of sex, be excluded from participation in, be denied the benefits of, or be subjected to discrimination under any education program or activity receiving federal financial assistance" (U.S. Congress, June 23, 1972). This legislation fundamentally changed the ways in which athletics were regulated at all educational levels and contributed to an unprecedented increase in female sport opportunities. Despite the overall positive impact of Title IX on athletic accessibility and participation, this impact is differentially experienced for African American women. Pickett, Dawkins, and Braddock (2012) found that high schools predominantly attended by African Americans do not offer the same range of sports for women as the high schools populated primarily by Whites. The gap between what is offered and available at the precollege level might have detrimental longitudinal impacts on representation of women student-athletes across racial groups (Bruening, Armstrong, & Pastore, 2005).

As institutions add women's sports, it is critical that the accessibility of African American women student-athletes is assessed in the context of those new sports. For example, some sports such as crew, golf, soccer, or lacrosse do not have a high percentage of African American women involved in them at a precollege level. Failure to address the systemic perspective of how Title IX enforcement practices impact sociocultural groups differentially could have a long-term consequence of denying accessibility of African American women into collegiate-level athletics (Bruening et al., 2005; Pickett et al.,

2012; Sellers et al., 1997). African American women's participation in athletics has been primarily in sports that are the most affordable for individual families and school districts, namely basketball and track and field. Specifically, White women are dominating the participation and engagement in the growth and new sports, such as lacrosse. As Title IX policy has focused on closing the gender gap in athletics, it has failed to address the racial gap in athletics with White women benefitting more collectively at the collegiate level as compared to African American women (Pickett et al., 2012)

Acosta and Carpenter (2014) conducted a thirty-seven year analysis of women in athletics and found that there were approximately 180,000 women college athletes on over 9,000 institutional teams. Despite the substantial increase of women participating in college athletics since the implementation of Title IX in the early 1970s, there is minimal media coverage of female athletes (Daniels, 2012). When women athletes are portrayed in the media, they are often highly sexualized and White (Berry, 2003; Daniels, 2012). When attractiveness is the dominant quality within media portrayals, both men and women athletes in the images are perceived as less competent, less admirable, less powerful, and less strong (Knight & Giuliano, 2001). When women student-athletes are the ones viewing media sexualized portrayals of other women athletes, Daniels (2009) found that they tended to self-objectify and move from an athleticized focus to a physical appearance focus. African American women athletes tend to self-objectify more when viewing sports with players having more muscular physiques such as basketball (Harrison & Fredrickson, 2003). Further, the media's dominant portrayal of White female athletes positions them as the ideal which other women should be striving to attain (Berry, 2003). For the African American student-athlete, these messages can create a challenging context that impacts body image, self-esteem, identity development, and belongingness. Body image, self-objectification, other-objectification, and performance demands contribute to eating disorders and the interrelated health concerns of inadequate energy supply, menstrual disorders, and decreased bone density (Becker, McDaniel, Bull, Powell, & McIntyre, 2013; Manore, Kam, & Loucks, 2007). The consequences are potentially dangerous for the emotional and physical well-being of African American women athletes.

In 2012, Daniels conducted research with 258 girls and 171 college women in which photographs of White female athletes were presented for observation and written reflections. There were three different categories of images used as the intervention in the study, namely performance athlete group, sexualized athlete group, and sexualized model condition. For the college women in the study, 23% were on an organized sports team and only 1% of them identified as African American. Daniels found that the performance-focused images generated comments about sport intensity, role modeling, breaking out of gender expectations, and inspiration, whereas the sexualized athlete images garnered other-objectification and self-objectification and critiques about societal inequities regarding physical appearance. Based on her findings, Daniels demanded that performance-based images of female athletes be more consistently integrated into popular media coverage due to the positive impact on understanding athleticism and developing an instrumental focus on the body. Notable in this study was the minimal number of African American women participants, so it is unclear how sexualization in media and society of female athletes may be impacting African American women student-athletes specifically. More research is needed to understand the intersectionality of gendered, sexual, racial, and athleticized factors on the African American women student-athlete.

Research on the lived experiences of African American women who were student-athletes was completely absent from the professional literature until the late 1990s and early 2000s (Bruening et al., 2005; Sellers et al., 1997). As more scholars have examined the experience of African American women in college athletics, there continues to be a disproportionate focus in the literature on the African American male experience and the experience of athletes involved in high revenue-generating sports, such as football and basketball. African American women have been silenced in the sports literature—"both as researcher and as the researched" (Bruening et al., 2005, p. 85). Sports continue to be dominated by men and by Whites which has profound effects on African American women student-athletes.

The Silencing of African American Women in Sports

African American women student-athletes experience the convergence of multiple identities that are associated with racism, sexism, and potentially classism (Collins, 2000). The intersectionality of identities manifests in oppressions that are concurrently unfolding and compounding each other. Bruening et al. (2005) described silencing in sports from a tri-modal context: (1) absence of opinions and perspectives of African American women student-athletes; (2) dearth of awareness and interest in the experience of African American women student-athletes by administrators, coaches, institutions, and media; and, (3) encountering marginalization based on race and gender. Exploring the interplay of gender and race on the experience of African American student-athletes using Critical Race Theory is essential to provide appropriate support to women, create meaningful and positive collegiate experiences, and eradicate discrimination in athletic departments.

In a recent qualitative study, Bruening et al. examined the lived experiences of 12 African American women athletes at a large NCAA Division I institution. The women in the study spoke about the influence of mass media, the impact of athletic administrators and coaches, and the experience of male student-athletes. For the participants, there are a disproportionate number of African American women student-athletes in basketball and track and field compared to other athletic options, and there is a noticeable absence of media coverage. The participants described the impact of minimal media coverage on providing less role models to youth, decreasing accessibility to sport opportunities, lowered rate of sport participation, and not legitimizing African American women as athletes (Bruening et al., 2005). Regarding support from athletic administrators, the 12 women differed in how supported they felt. Some appreciated the efforts made at the university level, yet these positive perspectives were countered by concerns about a lack of prioritization and valuing of women athletics and an over-emphasis on football to the detriment of other sports.

Coaches, as described by the African American women in Bruening et al.'s (2005) study, had significant impact on the experience and success of the student-athletes. Women articulated how coaches perpetuated a culture endemic with stereotyping, de-valuing, and negative training situations. African American athletes on track and field teams experienced being isolated from their White peers, a reality that was perpetuated by the coaches' lack of effort to integrate the team or to even know the names of the athletes. Coaches also contributed to a gendered experience in the weight room by asking some of the African American women student-athletes to change their attire because they were distracting the male athletes and by requiring them to step aside so the male athletes could use the equipment. The gendered landscape of the weight room was exacerbated by male student-athletes who treated the women in the study as sexual objects as opposed to peers. Because African American women student-athletes' voices have been marginalized and only listened to on the fringe, Bruening et al.'s study provides a critical voicing of the oppressive and negative experiences that some African American women are having from the influences of media, athletic administrators, coaches, and male student-athletes. Race and gender contributed to feelings of powerlessness and objectification, and the absence of role models compounded these experiences of being silenced. Critical examinations of race and gender are necessary to understand and then proficiently support African American women student-athletes.

RELATIONAL CONTEXTUAL FACTORS IMPACTING AFRICAN AMERICAN STUDENT-ATHLETES

Understanding the contextual factors that impact the various relationships of student-athletes is important prior to the development of any support or intervention to assist in overall readiness for the college and university experience. As such, the intersecting relationships of influences such as family, friends, teammates, and coaches are critical to explore. Examining these relationships can situate professionals to be better advocates and supports.

Family and Community of Origin

The family and community of origin can play a critical role in the transition and adjustment to college and university life when savvy regarding the complexity of the terms of an athletic scholarship, degree completion requirements, and the time commitment needed to balance the multiple roles played by the student-athlete. This is offset by the divergent needs for personal growth and identity development experienced by each student-athlete. Family members and community members sometimes warn African American students about the level of racism at predominantly White institutions – such as expectation at the onset of experience on campus contributes to increased levels of dissatisfaction as African American students were already expecting toxicity (Harper, 2013). This is juxtaposed with the message from family and community members that athletics holds the key to success and upward mobility. That message is further confounded when the dialogue of access and opportunity are grounded in a discussion about athletic ability and potential and does not include an equally in-depth dialogue about academic success and achievement aimed at growth and development that will last a lifetime.

While over 98 percent of the student-athletes who engage in intercollegiate athletics actually do not go to a professional career in athletics, this unrealistic dream of a professional sports career lives within many student-athletes, their families, and their communities of origin. According to Harper, Williams, and Blackman (2013), what needs to occur is a deeper understanding of the realities of participation in intercollegiate athletics prior to the beginning of the experience. As such, families and support systems are encouraged to pose a substantive set of questions to coaches, athletic administrators, support staff, and university faculty that include and then go beyond the realm of athletics. For example, a series of questions asking about the graduation rates of male and female student-athletes of color and their postgraduate career choices could provide a better framework for understanding what the developmental and career opportunities are during and after the collegiate experience. In addition, a number of questions about academic expectation, level and type of academic support, emotional and psychosocial support, and faculty engagement on behalf of the student-athlete present a set of questions focused on overall well-being and development. These and other questions expand the cursory set of inquiries about athletic scholarships and the potential for athletic success during and after college. What occurs is a set of critical inquiries focused on the overall growth and development and health and well-being of the student-athlete over the course of the lifespan. Lifespan development must include personal well-being, career readiness, and professional preparedness. This requires a paradigm shift from family, friends, and coaches to focus on career development for the student-athlete toward a set of skills and talents that carry beyond athletic ability. While this notion is not new to the realm of literature focused on the student-athlete, it is rarely, if ever, broached in terms of development over the course of the lifespan.

The emotional and psychosocial toll of "playing for family" is a paradigm that requires more attention when engaging in a dialogue focused on growth and development over the course of the lifespan for African American men and women who attend college on an athletic scholarship. Many are first-generation within their families to attend college or a legacy within their family which creates a separate set of confounding issues. In addition to this, in the event that a student-athlete has parents or siblings who have attended college, a pressure to live up to the family name is experienced potentially leading to identity consolidation concerns. The impact of family and community of origin on the experience, well-being, and academic achievement of African American student-athletes is significant, so professionals in higher education need to consider how to leverage these systems to optimize the support provided to individual athletes.

Peer Relationships

Participating in sports at the collegiate level offers a meaningful set of experiences that are often not available for nonathlete students. Student-athletes are said to benefit from wide recognition and pride of the school community, the celebrity of being student-athletes, and the consequential sense of belongingness to an institution that values them (Melendez, 2008). At the same time, athletes contribute to their institutions by achieving national recognition, which also increases alumni support and attracts new students (Broughton, 2001). For many student-athletes of color, being overtly valued by their institution can be a new experience that reifies and brings closer the notions of opportunity, fame, and millionaire contracts that might have been limited in their immediate contexts of origin. Also, the possibility of becoming an intercollegiate student-athlete presents opportunities for high visibility, travel, leadership development, exempt tuition costs, stipends, academic support, and social and athletic support (Melendez, 2008).

Several studies have addressed African-American athletes' experiences of playing sports for predominantly White institutions (e.g., Beamon, 2008; Harrison, Sailes, Rotich & Bimper, 2011; Melendez, 2008; Singer, 2005; Steinfeldt, England, Stenifeldt & Speight, 2009) and have found similar

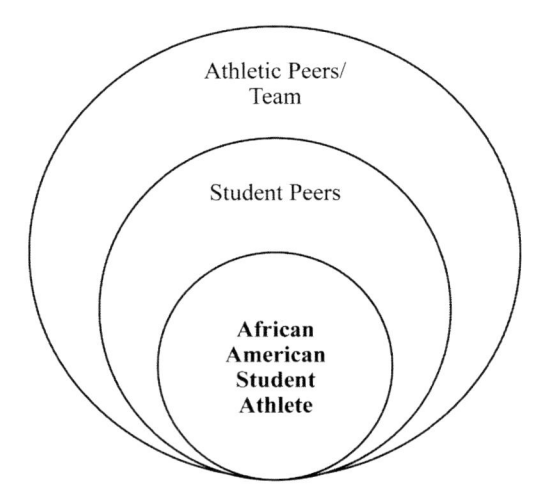

Figure 15.1 Peer-Based Relationships for Student-Athletes. The Figure Represents Peer-Based Psychological Pressures and Opportunities that Define African-American College Athletes' Experience

psychological pressures and opportunities at the level of student-peer interactions and with team members (see Figure 15.1).

Several studies have demonstrated the potentially negative nature of the perceptions of African American athletes by their peers (Harrison et al., 2011; Melendez, 2008; Singer, 2005). In a qualitative study exploring the social experiences of African American football players attending predominantly White institutions, Melendez (2008) found that these students experienced both a lack of understanding by and judgment from their student peers. In this study, student-athletes described being perceived as not prepared, engaged, and valued by their classmates. The African American football players attributed this misperception to the additional flexibility provided to them to meet class and attendance requirements. Further, White students at predominantly White institutions report being disinclined to include their African American peers in group projects due to a pervasive stereotype that the student-athletes are not highly invested in their own education (Charles, Fischer, Mooney, & Massey, 2009; Harper, 2013).

In a quantitative study, Harrison et al. (2011) examined the relationship between race and athletic identity in 109 NCAA Division I African American and White football players. Harrison et al. found significantly higher athletic identity identification in African American student-athletes. African American football players were mainly viewed as athletes, and Harrison et al. attribute this finding to the social construction of negative labels for African

American individuals as dumb athletes who are not serious about their education. Melendez's (2008) and Harrison et al.'s (2011) findings suggest the pervasiveness of negative views among students that target and impact specific identities based on distorted assumptions of capabilities or motivation to academic achievement. Melendez suggested the theme "Stigma" (p. 437) as one of the main themes in his study, which coincides with the discussion around "stereotype" in Harrison's et al. deconstruction of their findings. These findings are contraindicated by the number of peers who cheer the athletic accomplishments of student-athletes, while simultaneously disparaging their academic proficiency and commitment.

In his seminal work entitled *Stigma,* Goffman (1963) describes the identities susceptible to be stigmatized as those who are perceived to have different levels of intellectual or physical ability. Harrison et al. (2011) stressed the relationship between the salience of African American football players' athletic identity and their peers' perceptions of them as incapable of academic excellence. An example is classmates' suspicion of African American student-athletes obtaining A's or passing their courses. Researchers have found that African American student-athletes are viewed in demeaning ways based on their status as athletes and their race, an experience commensurate with Gottman's notion of stigma. Peer stereotypes impact perceived possibilities for interaction and inclusion of African American student-athletes, thereby increasing their sense of being misunderstood or unaccepted in their academic contexts.

Athletic Peer and Team Interactions

African American student-athletes' experiences of being misunderstood and judged have extended to their interactions with peer athletes and coaches. Singer (2005) and Melendez (2008) found that these students felt victims of negative views related to academic competence and capacity by their teammates and coaches. In Melendez's study, these views informed the participant's pervasive view of their White coaches' ideal image of a football player as the "All-American pretty boy" (p. 435) along with the notion of having to work twice as hard to meet the coaches' demands. Therefore, the African American student-athlete is not valued the same.

On the other hand, Melendez' participants recognized overt efforts by coaches to foster a sense of community within the team using the metaphor of the team as family by encouraging dependence among teammates toward the achievement of common goals. Even though the fostering of community among teammates potentially brings many opportunities for all the players, the African American student-athletes experienced the coaches as dismissing racial and ethnic dynamics within the members of the team, thereby silencing and disenfranchising African American student-athletes. The unaddressed nature of cultural tension within the group of players seems to create significant amounts of conflict, misunderstanding, and resentment in the athletes who have minority identities.

THE EMOTIONAL WELL-BEING OF AFRICAN AMERICAN STUDENT-ATHLETE

Goffman (1963) stresses the social and psychological interplay between stigmatized and normal people, and offers a critical examination of societal values and expectations that are played out through both groups' attitudes and behaviors. He proposes different responses from stigmatized individuals. One response is alienation from normative societal views and consequent shame for not meeting that standard which creates the pressure for being/behaving/ looking more "normal." Secondly, stigmatized individuals can also experience pressure to compensate differentness by reaffirming their uniqueness, which in consequence reinforces their differentness and strengthens the assigned stigma.

Alienation and Isolation of African American Athletes

The literature consistently articulates African American student-athletes' experiences of alienation and cultural mistrust. Being an athlete is not necessarily disadvantageous per se, but the unfavorable views associated with being an African American student-athlete might foster the experience of estrangement and subsequent dis-identification with one's institution. The central theme found by Melendez (2008) revolves around these African American student-athletes feeling foreign to their athletic and academic environments, and consequently, developing a sense of mistrust in their immediate contexts and the larger community. The participants in this study mentioned giving up their cultural values and identities, in their attempt to accept and integrate into the mainstream culture at a predominantly White institution. The incongruence between the cultural environment and their own core cultural values in turn increased their level of isolation and misunderstanding. Even though fit and acceptance seem to be critical topics for college students (Broughton, 2001), these developmental tasks are infiltrated by cultural misconceptions that impact African American student-athletes' ability to navigate them (Melendez, 2008). Additionally, African American student-athletes might present higher levels of athletic identity identification as a result of the difficult interplay of their own values and host culture, increasing negative psychological responses, limiting social interactions (Steinfeldt et al., 2009), reinforcing the idea of being singled out because of race (Singer, 2005), experiencing onlyness (Harper, 2013), and perpetuating a cycle of stereotype and isolation for these students (Harrison et al., 2011).

In terms of wellness, Watson and Kissinger (2007) found the greatest levels of wellness in the Social Self domain (Myers & Sweeney, 2005) in nonathlete students. One possible interpretation is the experience of alienation and isolation particularly for African American college student-athletes, which critically and negatively impacts the Social Self domain. Watson and Kissinger (2007) and Amorose, Anderson-Butcher, and Cooper (2009) explain that stringent academic demands and competition schedules increase the psychological demands and pressures for athletes in general. However, according to the previous analysis, it can be added that the multisystemic factors impact African American student-athletes to experience belongingness, friendship and love in their social interactions.

Identity Reaffirmation in African American Athletes

An alternative response to stigma consists of African American athletes responding in ways that stress the uniqueness of their contribution to the institution. In Harrison's et al. (2011) study, the item "Sport is the only important thing in my life" modestly discriminated between White and African American's athletic identity strength. According to these authors, increased athletic identity development in African American student-athletes dissuades academic achievement, which also represents a disadvantage for their professional future and career outlook if their aspirations of becoming professional players are not met. According to Goffman (1963), identity reaffirmation places student-athletes in a double stigmatization risk because if they are not able to maintain the initial status (as an athlete in this case,) then they might also face negative views for not accomplishing the first goal. In the case of African American student-athletes, not entering professional athletics or attaining the sizeable salaries of professional athletes can represent an extra reason to be negatively viewed in a number of contexts. The possibilities of being negatively viewed by peers and the larger community increase when African American student-athletes experience emotional vulnerability and need to seek out professional help (Broughton, 2001; Steinfeldt et al., 2009). Even though the stigma toward help-seeking is moderated by gender (Steinfeldt et al., 2011), this might represent increased levels of anxiety, emotional tension, pressures to succeed that can remain unaddressed in many of the African American student-athletes.

Moreover, Watson and Kissinger (2007) found that athletes also scored lower on Essential Self in terms of wellness (Myers & Sweeney, 2005) compared to nonstudent athletes. The wellness factor related to the sense of meaning and purpose in life, the excessive demands of intercollegiate athletic participation can significantly impact athletes' possibilities for intrapersonal and interpersonal self-exploration. Watson and Kissinger attributed this low score to the notion of identity foreclosure, explaining that athletes over-identify with their athletic identity, not promoting other academic, social, personal, and cultural identities.

Harrison et al. (2011) attributed identity foreclosure to the excessive contextual demands for athletic achievement placed on African American student-athletes, which is reinforced by "coaches and sport administrators whose jobs are based on winning" (p. 99). Such a paradigm contributes to African American athletes considering sports "the only important thing in my life." Even though Harrison's et al. study only included males in their sample, Johnson et al. (2004) and Becker et al. (2013) emphasize lower self-esteem, higher body dissatisfaction, and disturbed eating behaviors in African American female student-athletes compared to males. Independent of the response from the stigmatized person, Goffman (1963) emphasized the psychological cost of realizing and negotiating the social reality, which fosters negative experiences of anger, isolation, and shame. African American athletes might further react to their experiences by joining others who share the same reality, and coping with their inner experiences through self-support and supporting others.

EXPLOITATION OF AFRICAN AMERICAN ATHLETES

Fifty years ago, Goffman (1963) explained how societal negative views are transmitted through generations, converting stigmatized individuals to passive entities that receive what non-stigmatized individuals assign to them, specifically social degradation and lack of voice. However, more contemporary approaches to social issues and systems of production take a more critical stance, and explain economic dynamics and inequalities that consider the multiplicity of social markers as well as individuals' transgressive power (Erevelles, 2011; Hawkins, 2010; Samuels, 2014). The more recent literature is organized around Erevelles' (2011) Historical Materialism as an analytical framework for the experiences of exploitation of African American student-athletes at predominantly White institutions. The dialects shaping this analysis are visible versus invisible, deserving versus unworthy, and assets versus commodities.

Visible vs. Invisible

Across the literature, African American student-athletes' visibility in media and institutional communications undeniably provide salience to their athletic identities. From National Signing Day to athletic seasons in schools, African

American student-athletes are exhibited and celebrated as valued members of the school community (Morris & Adeyemo, 2012). However, the high visibility resulting from public display and emphasis in their athletic role is mainly related to their perceived profitability rather than expectations for academic success (Beamon, 2008). This perpetuates Critical Race Theory's notion of how the lack of interest convergence creates stagnation and exploitation (Donnor, 2005).

For Erevelles (2011), social markers of race, gender, and disability are socially produced by violence and colonialism, and its social, economic and political expressions. According to this, the state has no material or moral obligations to individuals that do not belong to the mainstream racial group, as they are considered inferior citizens. From this point of view, people of color, non-Americans, undocumented, Native Americans, impoverished, women, and disabled individuals have been historically considered inferior or second-class citizens.

Harrison et al. (2011) and Beamon (2008) have emphasized the secondary nature of academic experiences in African American student-athletes. Specifically, the need for superior athletes that can maintain team performance levels and generate revenue can cause institutions to disregard athletes' educational needs by creating pressures to win even at the expense of educational attainment. Despite the societal myth of African American athletes of having "made it" through athletics, scholars argue that they are actually being exploited by being prohibited from attaining a meaningful education and expanded professional and career skills during their student-athlete experiences (Harris, 2014). African American student-athletes often experience difficulties in balancing their athletic, academic, and social roles, often giving more prominence to the athletic demands (Beamon, 2008). From this critical point of view, African American student-athletes are considered second-class students. This is substantiated by the stereotype threat literature capturing faculty and peer perceptions of insufficient academic seriousness and preparedness (Edwards, 2000; Stone, 2012).

Deserving vs. Unworthy

Being considered athletes first and students second (Beamon, 2008), many participants in Harrison et al.'s (2011) and Melendez's (2008) studies described their peers' perception of them as not being interested in academics or unintelligent, therefore, non-deserving of academic support. In Melendez's study (2008), the participants expressed being immersed in a foreign world that is incongruent with their cultural beliefs, and being perceived as being in school only because they play, not because of intellectual abilities. These perceptions are usually paired with notions of benevolence and opportunity that are provided to minority students to hopefully make a (economic) change in their lives and their communities. However, African American student-athletes have to "pay" for these enticing opportunities by "selling out" their identities (Harrison et al., 2011), experiencing increasing athletic demands through the institutional pressures to win (Melendez, 2008), and also sacrificing their opportunity to receive life-changing educational experiences that prepare them for the life after the field (Beamon, 2008).

Erevelles (2011) articulates collective fantasies of altruism and kindness toward oppressed groups and the intention to help these individuals through social initiatives or life changing opportunities. However, moral and emotional gaps create room for the detachment between the oppressed or victim and our contribution in generating and perpetuating systems of oppression. These fantasies of kindness and compassion to vulnerable others serve as a façade for institutionalized structural violence, fostering people's unawareness of the political dimension. Farmer, Nizeye, Stulack, and Keshavjee (2006) described structural violence as economic, political, legal, religious and cultural structures that prevent individuals from living free lives and reaching their full potential and portray them in an ordinary way that makes them invisible to others' perception. Examples of structural violence include lack of access to economic, educational, health care, language, and legal resources and political power within the oppressive apparatus. When applied to collegiate sports, revenue-generating institutions may exert excessive pressures to win and neglect their educational responsibility toward African American student-athletes, leaving them unprepared to join the work force, and most importantly, taking away their opportunity for a meaningful career alternative to sports (Beamon, 2008).

Assets vs. Commodities

Erevelles (2011) describes the historical material view of individuals in terms of the level of productivity in their lives. Certain groups are considered a burden for society given their lack of productivity and are, therefore, not deserving the full consideration of citizenship. Extrapolating to the athletic world, those who get injured, lose eligibility to keep their athletic performance level, to maintain their scholarships, and consequently do not meet the standard of productivity within the industry (Beamon, 2008). Moreover, the amount of African American student-athletes who achieve successful positions within professional arenas is minimal compared to the amount of African American athletes receiving scholarships and enrolling in colleges each year (Harrison et al., 2011; Melendez, 2008). Given the high number of student-athletes who play at the college level but do not become professional players, these athletes' lives become commodities, which are highly replaceable and expendable in the process of winning games and championships.

Moreover, given the minority status and cultural disadvantages of African American athletes, these student-athletes usually experience increased difficulties to understand, voice, and advocate for their educational needs (Beamon, 2008; Melendez, 2008), thereby making sports their only viable future (Morris & Adeyemo, 2012). This racialized view of disposable lives responds to cultural dominant narratives of who matters and the correlated discriminatory practices intended to protect and privilege certain groups only (Erevelles, 2011).

CRITICAL RACE THEORY AND AFRICAN AMERICAN ATHLETES

According to Ladson-Billings (1998) and Singer (2005), CRT is an epistemological structure allowing for the challenge of hegemonic paradigms through the use of race as the lens to envision and then deconstruct the challenges faced by people who are not White. These challenges are brought forth due to the lack of convergence of interests of the dominant culture and the use of power to marginalize differing peoples. Critical Race Theory goes on to identify that until the interests of the dominant society are served, evolution and change are slow and methodical at best. Additionally, CRT provides recognition for the lack of active transparency that perpetuates racism and racialization fostering the marginalization of those who are not White and serving to block change to the overall structure of power within the Unites States. Singer (2005) outlines through Tate (1997) that CRT views race and racism as being grounded in the fabric of the United States represented within systemic structures. These structures include educational, social, media, legal, political, and sport systems. As such, any critical discussion of evolution or systemic change requires a focus on race as this is an organizing principle. Additionally, CRT recognizes that policy set out to advance access and opportunity for marginalized persons may in fact restrict access.

CRT provides us a critical lens to view the psychological, psychosocial, physiological, historical, institutional, and legal injustices that impact the agency and being of African American student-athletes. Trahan and Lemberger-Truelove (2014) point out that absence of race as a leading consideration in the discussion and attempts to remedy the educational experience for student-athletes removes the core of experiences of racialization and subjugation for marginalized student-athletes. Further, they argue that the promulgation of the code will not be experienced as personally meaningful to a professional or client who has been racialized and subjugated. According to Trahan and Lemberger-Truelove (2014), the psyche of current U.S. society is fraught with racial bias ground in societal norms of the White collective. The authors go on to point out that in order for a just society to be possible, action-oriented steps must be taken to address and advocate for the reform of practices (in this case educational and legal) that are bound by the norms of a dominant culture.

According to Harrison et al. (2011), many young African Americans view athletics as the door to success replacing education as the perceived road to personal growth, upward mobility, and economic opportunity. What has been missing is a contextual lens such as critical race theory with which to explore this phenomena. Across the history of higher education in this nation race, power and institutional influence have impacted opportunity and access for young African American men and women.

Thinking forward, CRT allows for the narratives of those marginalized persons to aid in the development of reparations to oppressive systems (Singer, 2005). In the case of African American student-athletes, this would allow for the voices of past and present students to aid in the development and implementation of systemic change that helps evolve their existence in the university setting. The narratives of women have the ability to expound on the marginalization that has occurred historically through omission, oppression, and lack of equal access to educational opportunity. These narratives can pave the way to seeing how legal mandates such as Title IX, while put in place to combat oppression, can actually contribute to perpetuating oppression.

In the case of African American men, CRT can shed light on the marginalization due to consistently lower graduation rates of African American males as compared to their White counterparts and their female peers. CRT aids in empowerment through the development and implementation of active efforts to combat this phenomena. One example is the outward effort of some institutions to commit to actions that will increase the graduation rates of African American men who compete in intercollegiate athletics through systemic programming geared towards change. Implications for college and career readiness must be grounded in the recognition that policy makers must be leveraged to provide pressure on institutions, thereby creating interest convergence.

IMPLICATIONS FOR COLLEGE AND CAREER READINESS

Implications for college and career readiness for African American athletes are grounded in environmental, social, and psychological factors. Harper (2012) outlines an anti-deficit achievement model that encompasses three pipeline points of precollege orientation and preparedness, college success, and postcollege achievement. The anti-deficit achievement framework channels the influence of family, K-12 schools, college preparation resources, college class experiences, college engagement activities, peers, faculty members, graduate school, and career to examine how African American student-athletes can be successful in college and in career. At the environmental level, educational systems, policymakers, and career profiles must be critically examined and engaged to evoke change (Harper & Harris, 2012). Some specific recommendations include:

1. Institutions should actively and continually examine how they are explicitly or implicitly excluding student-athletes (Stone, 2012).
2. NCAA should take a leadership role in developing policy that engenders counternarratives to combat the "dumb jock" ideology (Stone, 2012).
3. Critically examine the way language shapes experience. Even the use of the term "student-athlete" has been highly criticized by some scholars because they believe that it perpetuates negative stereotypes, situates academics and athletics as oppositional identities, and generates threat cues that prime administrators, coaches, faculty members, and peers to assume a reductionistic stance in relationship to athletes (Katz, 2008; Staurowsky & Sack, 2005; Stone, 2012).
4. Credit generating courses focused on the transition into campus life and the multifaceted expectations of being a student-athlete (Harper & Harris, 2012). Brooks et al. (2012) recommend that institutions develop pre-college initiatives that also focus on campus adjustment and academic enrichment.
5. Given the inequities across racial lines for student outcomes in revenue-generating sports, Harris and Harper (2012) challenge the NCAA to increase transparency of graduation rates at the institutional level and develop a regulation banning postseason play for institutions that would be enacted based on low graduation rates across racial groups.
6. Develop systemic initiatives to pursue "near completers," namely African American student-athletes who were close to finishing their degrees or accrued enough credits to earn an Associate's degree, with the intent of an attainable and feasible plan for completion (Harris & Harper, 2012).
7. Active and dedicated commitment to recruiting and retaining African American faculty and staff (Brooks, Jones, & Burt, 2012). Having role models promotes academic engagement, hopefulness, and grit.
8. Title IX needs to be interpreted within a context that recognizes the intersectionality of race and gender in college athletics (Pickett et al., 2012). Systemic review of how growth sports are available and accessible across communities needs to occur.
9. At the institutional program level, the role of grit in predicting academic success even beyond college readiness indices should be recognized and channeled to cultivate skills associated with grit, namely time management, persistence, regulation of energy across time, and creative problem solving (Strayhorn, 2013).

Recommendations for college and career readiness at the social level for African American student-athletes emerge from the awareness of how familial factors, peers, and faculty members influence individual student-athlete's experience of felt belonging, engagement, and support. Attrition has been successfully negated through harnessing the power of forming positive and affirming relationships. Recommendations from the social level include:

1. Coaches, faculty members, and staff need to openly and explicitly inform, discuss, and process stereotype threats with student-athletes (Stone, 2012).
2. Student organizations can provide a safe and non-threatening way to support African American student-athletes (Harper & Harris, 2012). Student-athletes must be actively encouraged and supported to participate in such out-of-class engagement activities.
3. There are many barriers to student-athletes seeking counseling when needed (Lopez & Levy, 2013). Athletic departments, coaches, and staff can reduce those barriers by advocating for the importance of mental well-being, building relationships with counseling center staff to strategize how to overcome issues of time availability and potential lack of confidentiality in seeking services.
4. Beginning experiences really provide a foundation for how African American student-athletes adjust to new athletic requirements (more media scrutiny, more advanced competition, higher stakes for athletic performance), new academic demands (more reading, different methods for participation, time demands, writing requirements), and different interpersonal realities (potentially away from family and community of origin, living on their own). Faculty members and administrators need to intentionally shape early experiences in the classroom, with faculty, peers to be empowering and success-building (Stone, 2012).
5. Faculty members need to increase their consciousness about the assumptions they hold regarding African American student-athletes and how this can create a hostile classroom environment and bias in grading.
6. Family members need to be provided with resources about navigating the recruitment process so that questions regarding education and academic attainment can be included at the same level of emphasis as questions about the team and athletic department (Harper et al., 2013).

Psychological factors relate to the cognitive and behavioral qualities that can be strengthened to increase college success and career readiness. Specific recommendations include:

1. Strayhorn (2013) asserts that intentionally harnessing and encouraging grit with African American student-athletes can translate into more academic

achievement and lower levels of attrition. Academic advisors, family members, tutors, coaches, faculty members, and other support people could actively emphasize persistence, perseverance, and hard work in the face of obstacles as well as the traditional benchmarks of grades and academic scores.
2. Addressing gender-specific mental health factors is an important implication for college success and career readiness. African American women student-athletes would benefit from programming focused on their emotional health, eating health, body image, navigating both sexist and racist situations in athletic and academic arenas, navigating both sexist and racist situations in athletic and academic arenas, and empowering their voices. The research consistently suggests that African American men student-athletes need increased professional development experiences centered around financial skills, professional skill development, grit and self-expectancy for success, and navigating racism in athletics and on campus.

Professionals engaged in higher education, providing support and encouragement to African American student-athletes must develop a systemic framework for understanding the complexity of dynamics impacting college readiness and career preparedness. Implementing an anti-deficit model that identifies and leverages growth and support strategies across the three pipeline points of precollege orientation and preparedness, college success, and postcollege achievement (Harper, 2012) will be critical if we are to make advances in how we nurture, encourage, and develop young African American men and women who are student-athletes. Focusing on environmental, social, and psychological factors, like those identified above, is necessary to ensure the well-being, emotionally, socially, mentally, and physically, of African American student-athletes. Policymakers, institutional leadership, coaching and athletic staff, college advisors, counselors, faculty members, communities, and families must collaborate and converge their interests to better serve the needs and opportunities for African American student-athletes.

REFERENCES

Acosta, R. V., & Carpenter, J. (2014). Women in intercollegiate sports: A longitudinal, national study thirty seven year update. Retrieved from http://www.acosta-carpenter.org/

Amorose, A. J., Anderson-Butcher, D., & Cooper, J. (2009). Predicting changes in athletes' wellbeing from changes in need satisfaction over the course of a competitive season. *Research Quarterly for Exercise and Sport, 80*(2), 386–392. doi:10.1080/02701367.2009.10599575

Beamon, K. (2008). "Used goods": former African American college student athletes' perception of exploitation by division I universities. *The Journal of Negro Education, 77*(4), 352–364.

Beamon, K. (2012). I'm a baller: Athletic identity foreclosure among African American former student-athletes. *Journal of African American Studies, 16,* 195–208. doi:10.1007/s12111–012-9211–8

Becker, C. B., McDaniel, L., Bull, S., Powell, M., & McIntyre, K. (2013). Can we reduce eating disorder risk factors in female college athletes? A randomized exploratory investigation of two peer-led interventions. *Body Image, 9,* 31–42. doi:10.1016/j.bodyim.2011.09.005

Berry, G. L. (2003). Developing children and multicultural attitudes: The systemic psychosocial influences of television portrayals in multimedia society. *Cultural Diversity and Ethnic Minority Psychology, 9,* 360–366. doi:10.1037/1099–9809.9.4.360

Brooks, M., Jones, C., & Burt, I. (2012). Are African-American male undergraduate retention programs successful? An evaluation of an undergraduate African-American male retention program. *Journal of African American Studies, 17,* 206–221. doi:10.1007/s12111–012-92332

Broughton, E. (2001). Counseling and support services for college student athletes. Presented at American College Personnel Association.

Bruening, J. E., Armstrong, K. L., & Pastore, D. L. (2005). Listening to the voices: The experiences of African American female student-athletes. *Research Quarterly for Exercise and Sport, 76,* 82–100. doi:10.1080/02701367.2005.10599264

Charles, C. Z., Fischer, M. J., Mooney, M. A., & Massey, D. S. (2009). *Taming the river: Negotiating the academic, financial, and social currents in selective colleges and universities.* Princeton, N.J.: Princeton University Press. doi:10.1515/9781400830053

Charles, C., Roscigno, V., & Torres, K. (2007). Racial inequality and college attendance: The mediating role of parental investments. *Social Science Research, 36,* 329–352. doi:10.1016/j.ssresearch.2006.02.004

Clopton, A. W. (2011). Using identities to explore social capitol differences among white and African American student-athletes. *Journal of African American Studies, 15,* 58–73. doi:10.1007/s12111–010-9121–6

Coakley, J. J. (2009). *Sport in society: Issues and controversies.* Boston, MA: McGraw-Hill.

Collins, P. H. (2000). *Black feminist thought: Knowledge, consciousness, and the politics of empowermen*t. New York: Routledge. doi:10.4324/9780203900055

Daniels, E. A. (2009). Sex objects, athletes, and sexy athletes: How media representations of women can impact adolescent girls and young women. *Journal of Adolescent Research, 24,* 399–422. doi:10.1177/0743558409336748.

Daniels, E. A. (2012). Sexy versus strong: What girls and women think of female athletes. *Journal of Applied Developmental Psychology, 22,* 79–90. doi:10.1016/j.appdev.2011.12.002

Davis, M., Dias-Bowie, Y., Greenberg, K., Klukken, G., Pollio, H. R., Thomas, S. P., & Thompson, C. L. (2004). A fly in the buttermilk: Descriptions of university life by successful undergraduate students at a predominantly White Southeastern university. *Journal of Higher Education, 74,* 420–445. doi:10.1353/jhe.2004.0018

Donnor, J. K. (2005). Towards an interest convergence in the education of African American football student athletes in major college sports. *Race, Ethnicity, and Education, 8*, 45–67. doi:10.1080/13613320520003 4099

Duckworth, A. L., & Quinn, P. D. (2009). Development and validation of the short grit scale (Grit-S). *Journal of Personality Assessment, 91*, 166–174. doi:10.1080/00223890802634290

Duderstadt, J. J. (2000). *Intercollegiate athletics and the American university: A university president's perspective*. Ann Arbor, MI: The University of Michigan Press

Edwards, H. (1984). The Black dumb jock: An American sports tragedy. *The College Board Review, 131*, 8–13.

Edwards, H. (2000). Crisis on the eve of black athletes. *Society, 37*, 9–13. doi:10.1007/bf02686167

Erevelles, N. (2011). *Disability and Difference in Global Contexts. Enabling a Transformative Body Politic*. New York, NY: Palgrave MacMillan. doi:10.1057/9781137001184

Farmer, P. E., Nizeye, B., Stulac, S., & Keshavjee, S. (2006). Structural violence and clinical medicine. *PLoS Medicine, October, 3*(10), 1686–1691. doi:10.1371/journal.pmed.0030449

Fleming, J. (1984). *Blacks in college: A comparative study of students' success in Black and in White institutions*. San Francisco, CA: Jossey-Bass.

Flowers, L. A. (2003). Effects of college racial composition on African American students' interactions with faculty. *College Student Affairs Journal, 23*, 54–63.

Foster, F. (2009). When eligibility is over. Diverse Issues in Higher Education.

Goffman, E. (1963). Stigma. Notes on the Management of Spoiled Identity. New York, NY: Simon & Schuster.

Griffin, K. A., Jayakumar, U. M., Jones, M. M., & Allen, W. R. (2010). Ebony in the ivory tower: Examining trends in the socioeconomic status, achievement, and self-concept of Black male freshmen. *Equity & Excellence in Education, 43*, 232–248. doi:10.1080/10665681003704915

Harper, S. R. (2006). Enhancing African American male student outcomes through leadership and active involvement. In M. J. Cuyjet and Associates (Eds.), *African American men in college* (pp. 68–94). San Francisco, CA: Jossey Bass.

Harper, S. R. (2009). Niggers no more: A critical race counternarrative on Black male student achievement at predominantly White colleges and universities. *International Journal of Qualitative Studies in Education, 22*, 697–712. doi:10.1080/09518390903333889

Harper, S. R. (2012). *Black male student success in higher education: A report from the National Black Male College Achievement Study*. Philadelphia, PA: University of Pennsylvania.

Harper, S. R. (2012). *Black men students in public higher education: A 50-state report card*. Washington, D.C.: Congressional Black Caucus Foundation.

Harper, S. R. (2013). Am I my brother's teacher? Black undergraduates, racial socialization, and peer pedagogies in predominantly White postsecondary contexts. *Review of Research in Education, 37*, 183–211. doi:10.3102/0091732x12471300

Harper, S. R., & Davis, C. H. F. (2012). They (don't) care about education: A counter-narrative on Black male students' responses to inequitable schooling. *Educational Foundations*, 103–120.

Harper, S. R., & Harris. F. (2012). *Men of color: A role for policymakers in improving the status of Black male students in U.S. higher education*. Washington, D.C.: Institute for Higher Education Policy.

Harper, S. R., Williams, C. D., & Blackman, H. W. (2013). Black male student-athletes and racial inequalities in NCAA Division I college sports. Philadelphia: University of Pennsylvania, Center for the Study of Race and Equity in Education.

Harper, S. R., Davis, R. J., Jones, D. E., McGowan, B. L., Ingram, T. N., & Platt, C. S. (2011). Race and racism in the experiences of Black male resident assistants at predominantly White universities. *Journal of College Student Development, 52*, 180–200. doi:10.1353/csd.2011.0025

Harper, S. R., & Hurtado, S. (2007). Nine themes in campus racial climates and implications for institutional transformation. In S. R. Harper & L. D. Patton (Eds.), *Responding to the realities of race on campus* (pp. 7–24). San Francisco, CA: Jossey-Bass.

Harris, P. C. (2014). The sports participation effect of educational attainment of Black males. *Education and Urban Society, 46*, 507–521. doi: 10.1177/0013124512446219

Harrison, C. K. (2008). "Athleticated" versus Educated: A qualitative investigation of campus perceptions, recruiting and African American male student-athletes. *Challenge, 14*, 39–60.

Harrison, K., & Fredrickson, B. L. (2003). Women's sports media, self-objectification, and mental health in Black and White adolescent females. *Journal of Communication, 53*, 216–232. doi:10.1111/j.1460–2466.2003.tb02587.x

Harrison, L., Sailes, G., Rotich, W. K., & Bimper, A. Y. (2011). Living the dream or awakening from the nightmare: Race and athletic identity. *Race Ethnicity and Education, 14*, 1, 91–103. doi:10.1080/13613324.2011.531982

Hawkins, B. (2010). *The New Plantation: Black Athletes, College Sports, and Predominantly White NCAA Institutions*. New York: Palgrave MacMillan. doi:10.1057/9780230105539

Johnson, J., Crosby, R., Engel, S., Mitchell, E., Powers, P., Wittrock, D., & Wonderlich, S. (2004). Gender, ethnicity, self-esteem, and disordered eating among college athletes. *Eating Behaviors, 5*, 147–156. doi:10.1016/j.eatbeh.2004.01.004

Kammen, C. (2009). *Part and apart: The black experience at Cornell*. Ithaca, NY: Cornell University Libraries.

Knight, J. L., & Giuliano, T. A. (2001). He's a Laker; she's a looker: The consequences of gender-stereotypical portrayals of male and female athletes by the print media. *Sex Roles, 45*, 217–229. doi:10.1023/A:1013553811620

Ladson-Billings, G. (1998). Just what is critical race theory and what's it doing in a nice field like education? *Qualitative Studies in Education, 11*, 7–24. doi:10.1080/095183998236863

Lopez, R. L., & Levy, J. J. (2013). Student athletes' perceived barriers to and preferences for seeking counseling. *Journal of College Counseling, 16*, 19–31. doi: 10.1002/j.2161–1882.2013.00024.x

Manore, M. M., Kam, L. C., Loucks, A. B. (2007). The female athlete triad: Components, nutrition issues, and health consequences. *Journal of Sports Sciences, 25*, S61–S71. doi:10.1080/02640410701607320

Martin, B. E., Harrison, C. K., Stone, J., & Lawrence, S. M. (2010). Athletic voices and academic victories: African American male student-athletes academic experiences in the Pac-Ten. *Journal of Sport and Sociological Issues, 131*, 131–152. doi:10.1177/0193723510366541

Melendez, M. (2008). Black football players on a predominantly white college campus: psychosocial and emotional realities of the black college athlete experience. *Journal of Black Psychology, 3*(4), 423–451. doi:10.1177/0095798408319874

Meyer, B. B. (1990). From idealism to actualization: The academic performance of female college athletes. *Sociology of Sport Journal, 7*, 44–57.

Morris, J., & Adeyemo, A. (2012). Touchdowns and honor societies, expanding the focus of black male excellence. *Phi Delta Kappan, 93*(5) 28–32. doi:10.1177/003172171209300507

Myers, J. E., & Sweeney, T. J. (2005). The indivisible self: An evidenced-based model of wellness. *Journal of Individual Psychology, 61*, 269–279.

Ou, S., & Reynolds, A. (2008). Predictors of educational attainment in the Chicago longitudinal study. *School Psychology Quarterly, 23*, 199–229. doi:10.1037/1045-3830.23.2.199

Parker, L., & Lynn, M. (2002). What's race got to do with it? Critical race theory's conflicts with and connections to qualitative research methodology and epistemology. *Qualitative Inquiry, 8*, 7–22. doi:10.1177/107780040200800102

Pickett, M. W., Dawkins, M. P., & Braddock, J. H. (2012). Race and gender equity in sports: Have White and African American females benefitted equally from Title IX? *American Behavioral Scientist, 56*, 1581–1603. doi:10.1177/00002764212458282

Shulman, J. L., & Bowen, W. G. (2001). *College sports and educational values: The game of life*. Princeton, NJ: Princeton University Press.

Sedlacek, W. E. (1987). Black students on White campuses: 20 years of research. *Journal of College Student Personnel, 28*, 484–495.

Sellers, R. M., Kuperminc, G. P., & Damas, A. (1997). The college life experiences of African American women athletes. *American Journal of Community Psychology, 25*, 699–720. doi:10.1023/a:1024691002055

Singer, J. N. (2005). Understanding racism through the eyes of African American male student athletes. *Race and Ethnicity in Education, 8*, 365–386. doi:10.1080/13613320500323963

Snyder, T. D., & Dillow, S. A. (2012). *Digest of educational statistics, 2011*. Washington, D.C.: National Center for Education Statistics.

Stone, J. (2012). A hidden toxicity in the term "student-athlete": Stereotype threat for athletes in the college classroom. *Wake Forest Journal of Law & Policy, 2*, 179–197.

Stone, J., Harrison, C. K., & Mottley, J. (2012). "Don't call me a student-athlete": The effect of identity priming on stereotype threat for academically engaged African American college athletes. *Basic and Applied Social Psychology, 34*, 99–106. doi:10.1080/0973533.2012.655624

Steinfeldt, J. A., Stenifeldt, M. C., England, B., & Speight, Q. L. (2009). Gender role conflict and stigma toward help-seeking among college football players. *Psychology of Men and Masculinity, 10*(4), 261–272. doi:10.1037/a0017223

Strayhorn, T. L. (2013). What role does grit play in the academic success of Black male collegians at predominantly White institutions? *Journal of African American Studies*. doi: 10.1007/s12111–012-9243–0

Tate, W. (1997). Critical race theory and education: History, theory, and implications. In M. Apple (Ed.), *Review of research in education* (pp. 191–243). Washington, D. C.: American Educational Research Association.

Trahan, D. P., & Lemberger-Truelove, M. E. (2014). Critical race theory as a decisional framework for the ethical counseling of African American clients. *Counseling and Values, 59,* 112–124. doi:10.1002/j.2161–007X.2014.00045

Watson, J. C. & Kissinger, D. B. (2007). Athletic participation and wellness: Implications for Counseling college student-athletes. *Journal of College Counseling, 10*, 153–162. doi:10.1002/j.2161–1882.2007.tb00015.x

Willie, C. V., & Cunnigen, D. (1981). Black students in higher education: A review of studies. *Annual Review of Sociology, 7*, 177–198. doi:10.1146/annurev.so.07.080181.001141

Winkler-Wagner, R. (2009). *The unchosen one: Race, gender, and identity among Black women in college*. Baltimore, MD: John Hopkins University Press.

Chapter 16

African American Students Navigating Higher Education Through a Wellness Approach

M. Ann Shillingford and Amy Williams

"If you neglect to recharge a battery, it dies. And if you run full speed ahead without stopping for water, you lose momentum to finish the race."

—Oprah Winfrey

As you begin to read this chapter, think about a time when you felt off balance; your personal life seemed to be off kilter; work life was less than optimal; and something just did not seem right. Was there something that you were doing wrong or was it things and people around you that were interrupting your equilibrium? If you have ever felt that way, which we all have at some point, we can imagine that you were concerned about your well-being and took steps to align your "yin and yang." What if we told you that there is an actual term used to describe this sense of wholeness that you desire? That delineation of wholeness refers to wellness. Wellness has become a regular focus and fixture within scholarly literature, the media, and everyday life.

What exactly is wellness and what gives this term such power to make a difference in the lives of individuals? Myers, Sweeney, and Witmer (2000) defined wellness as "a way of life oriented towards optimal health and well-being, in which body, mind, and spirit are integrated by the individual to live life more fully within the human and natural community" (p. 252). Wellness has been associated with positive work satisfaction, work performance, and quality of life (Lawson & Myers, 2011). Higher levels of burnout indicated lower wellness engagement. Additionally, Roach and Young (2007) associated wellness with graduate students' level of support and professional performance. What may be inferred from these statements is that developing a more holistic way of life where body, mind, and spirit are connected involves fostering a successful balance between professional and personal lifestyles.

That is, being well, through practicing a holistic approach to well-being, promotes a more gratifying existence. In this chapter, you will find (a) an introduction to models of wellness, (b) an exploration of wellness practices as they relate to college success, (c) discussion on the challenges faced by African American students, and (d) wellness implications for African American students as they prepare for, and navigate through, college life.

Models of Wellness

In the following section, we discuss models of wellness. If you will, consider these models as a navigational system in understanding the complex yet simplistic nature of wellness. Consider also, the overall benefits of wellness as an interconnected method of optimal functioning.

Hettler's Six Dimensions of Wellness Model

Hettler (1976) determined wellness to be "an active process through which people become aware of, and make choices toward, a more successful existence" (National Wellness Institute, 2014; para. 1). Hettler introduced the Six Dimensions of Wellness model that considered the self a holistic entity comprised of six interdependent dimensions. These dimensions include: (a) *emotional*, that is, how positive one feels about self and life; (b) *occupational*, that is, personal satisfaction from work life; (c) *physical*, that is, the desire for physical activity; (d) *spiritual*, that is, the search for life's meaning; *social*, that is, recognition of importance and contributions to society; and (e) *intellectual*, that is, exploration of one's creativity, problem solving, and learning. Using these six dimensions, Hettler encouraged individuals to practice attending to balance of both time and energy.

The Indivisible Self Wellness Model (5-F WEL)

Myers and Sweeney (2005) developed an evidence-based model of wellness known as the Indivisible Self (5-F WEL, 2005). 5-F WEL was developed based on Adler's ideology of a holistic, indivisible self, and focused on five factors of wellness that encompass the whole person (social, essential, physical, spiritual, and coping). *Social factors* include love and friendship. The notion here is that contentment can be found from engaging in activities and relationships that promote positive friendships and provide love and appreciation. According to Myers and Sweeney, maintaining strong friendships and embracing loving relationships bolsters one's chances of success. *Essential factors* are also noted as being necessary for holistic wellness. Myers and Sweeney (2004) explained that this factor is comprised of self-care, gender identity, cultural identity, and spirituality. Self-care focuses on practical strategies for maintaining emotional and physical well-being. It is intentional and purposeful and may extend on a systemic spectrum from stress management to primary care physician support. Both concepts of gender and cultural identity highlight the idea that to be well, individuals should understand and appreciate who they are. Spirituality includes an individual's religious or spiritual beliefs, practices, and connection to something outside him or herself.

Physical factors of wellness include the elements of exercise and nutrition (Sweeney and Myers, 2004). Exercise may positively impact physical and mental health, and is supported through research as an important component of an overall wellness plan. Nutrition, too, may either support or deter from overall wellness. Particularly with students who are moving from living at home to living on a college campus, the management of physical wellness may be a new experience as dining halls and late-night pizzas may replace regular meals. Leisure time, stress management techniques and skills, self-worth, and realistic belief systems comprise the next aspect of wellness: *coping factors* (Sweeney and Myers, 2004). These coping factors relate directly to how an individual manages stress in both the short and long term. Self-worth, which includes how an individual perceives his or her skills, abilities, and strengths, may impact the way an individual views and maintains perspective regarding adversity. For example, an individual with low self-worth may view adversity as something directly related to his or her deficits or weaknesses, while an individual with high self-worth may view the same adverse experiences as unfortunate events that provide opportunities for growth. Similarly, belief systems may positively or negatively impact the perception of challenges, and may support or hinder an individual in coping with stressors. Leisure time and stress management skills also impact an individual's ability to cope with stress. Engaging in a proactive and balanced plan that allows for activities that promote proactive coping with stressors may support overall wellness and resilience amid stress.

The fifth element of wellness identified by Myers and Sweeney (2004) includes *creative factors* such as thinking, emotions, sense of control, work, and sense of humor. These creative factors allow individuals opportunities to think in unique and engaging ways, and may provide outlets for creativity that support wellness. Support systems for emotional wellness may include personal counseling services on campus or in the community.

Wellness versus College Student Challenges

Wellness Concerns

Today's college campus may include significant resources to support students. These wellness resources may include health centers, counseling centers, fitness and recreational opportunities, academic support services, social activities and supports, religious services and organizations, residence life resources, and campus clubs and sports to name a few, and are typically present on all college campuses in some form. Indeed, faculty and staff on college campuses are aware of the impact that wellness can have on transition to college and overall academic success. Student affairs staff tend to be particularly cognizant of concerns related to student wellness. However, despite the availability of resources, college students continue to encounter social and academic concerns such as stress, difficulty with time management, anxiety, transitional concerns, academic difficulties, financial concerns, identity development concerns, lack of academic motivation, and health and wellness concerns. In fact, these are among the top ten student concerns that college housing staff have had to address in their roles supporting students (Reynolds, 2013). Each of these issues alone may negatively impact overall acclimation to the college campus, and many of these issues may occur alongside one another as students' transition to college. These concerns may not only impact student wellness, they may also impact students' academic performance as well. The question that we pose then is if colleges are employing programs to support students, why are students experiencing such significant challenges?

Although we might assume students enroll in college with the hope of being academically successful, nonacademic factors may impact the academic success of students despite their best intentions to make academic progress. A thorough review of the literature identified that nonacademic factors may impact academic performance and attrition in college students. These factors, which include overall emotional health, desire to dropout versus remain in college, and self-report of stress levels all related to student GPA, with lower GPAs associated with greater stress, decision to dropout of college, and poorer overall emotional health (Prichard and Wilson, 2003). Conversely, positive skills related to stress and time management, involvement in campus and college activities, and emotional satisfaction with coursework were demonstrated, alongside academic self-efficacy, to be related to positive academic achievement in the first year of college (Krumrei-Mancuso, Newton, Kim, & Wilcox, 2013). In other words, although supports are in place to address some student concerns, there may be emotional, nonacademic barriers that impede the success of college students. Move with us as we explore further the emotional functioning of college student, including some of these nonacademic factors that may impact overall wellness and adjustment to college.

Mattering as Wellness

Students, who leave home for college may, for the first time in their lives, find themselves in a city or town where they don't know anyone. They may feel alone as they wrestle with firsts, including: first roommate, first less-than-ideal grade, first time being sick away from home, and first trip to a home that has continued to function while he or she has been away at school. All of these experiences may impact the degree to which college students perceive themselves as mattering, and, in some cases, may increase stress and impact adjustment to the college environment. Rayle and Chung (2008) identified that students' beliefs about their mattering in college impacted their experience of academic stress. College peer social support, family support, and perceived mattering to the college were identified by both male and female college students as protective against academic stress. Students who believed they mattered to their family, friends, and school reported experiencing lower levels of academic stress in Rayle and Chung's study. College students' social networks not only help them believe that they matter as they acclimate to a new environment but might also impact the degree to which students cope with academic stress.

Wellness and Risk

Lewis and Myers (2010) reported that coping and physical wellness factors were found to be related to student engagement in drinking and driving behaviors, with increased risk of drinking and driving existing for students who did not prioritize their physical wellness and for those who coped poorly with stressors. Now we see that not only are students feeling the emotional discomfort of college life, but they are also moving toward risky behaviors in order to cope with their negative emotions. To understand the emotional and behavioral wellness patterns of college students, we explored further research focused on at risk behaviors of college students. For instance, Lewis and Myers (2010) found that individuals with lower coping and self-care skills consumed greater quantities of alcohol. Burnett, Sabato, Wagner, and Smith (2014) reported that college students with high substance use and binge-drinking were at risk for engaging in risky sexual behavior. Even more alarming, of the college students included in the study, Burnett and colleagues stated that at least 41% of these students reportedly engaged in "receptive oral sex with men without a condom and without ejaculation" and approximately 84% were engaging in a sexual relationship without knowing the HIV status of their partner. In another study, a discrepancy was found between college students understanding of HIV modes of transmission, their engagement in sexual acts, and their reported perceptions of risks in contracting the disease (Smith, Menn, Dorsett, and Wilson, 2012). Smith and colleagues rightfully attributed this disconnect to students' increased knowledge of advances in HIV treatments, an unfortunate sense of invincibility, and a false sense of security about contracting HIV. This is very disturbing data that makes one wonder about not only the emotional and physical health of college students but also of their overall well-being.

CHALLENGES FACED BY AFRICAN AMERICAN STUDENTS IN HIGHER EDUCATION

As previously mentioned, in this chapter, our focus is on wellness of African American college students. So far we have already discussed substantial difficulties that college students in general experience. Now, let us move on to examine the life of the African American college student. You already have a mental picture of the life of the average college student and so we can safely assume that the life of the African American student may tend to include the aforementioned challenges too. So we know how the college experiences of African American students may be similar to their white counterparts but how might they be different? Previous chapters have highlighted challenges that African American students face either while in college or in preparation for college. It may be best to refresh your memory before we move forward. Take a look back at some of these chapters. In Chapter 1, we learned of the pervasive inequalities that often impede the college advising that African American students may need in order to make informed decisions about college. This chapter reflected on poor school counselor to student ratios as well as counselor inexperience that affects the quality and quantity of service school counselors can afford students. These deficiencies in advising have been shown to significantly impact the decisions that African American students make regarding college and their futures.

In Chapter 10, we looked at a subset of the African American population: first-generation students. We learned that this particular group of students' is most often from low socioeconomic families with little to no support available from family in terms of planning for college. These disadvantages have left first-generation African American college students floundering to survive in academia and distressingly, some drop out. So we can see that preparation for college is a highly significant factor for African American students' educational success in college. In Chapter 7, you were introduced to African American youth with specific learning disabilities. The authors pointed to statistics that suggested that a considerable number of African American students are identified as having disabilities including Attention Deficit Hyperactivity Disorder (ADHD) and learning challenges. The authors also affirmed the need to support systems at the college level to boost the academic performance and increase the diminishing self-worth and self-confidence of these students. Again, in that chapter we are told that without proper assistance, this group of African American students will end up dropping out of college. The next section goes deeper into the college life of the African American student and touches on delicate issues such as health issues, discrimination and racial identity and the impact these variables play on students' well-being.

Physical and Mental Health Risks of African American College Students: The Influence of Perceived Discrimination

In a recent study conducted by Spurgeon and Myers (2010) it was found that African American students at Historically Black Colleges and Universities (HBCUs) scored significantly higher on the coping self factor of wellness (stress management, leisure, and sense of self-worth) than African American students at traditional predominantly white institutions (PWI's). Spurgeon and Myers speculated that this finding may be due to the socially supportive environment at the HBCU as opposed to PWI's. On the other hand, all African American college students (HBCU's and PWI's) in the study scored significantly lower on physical wellness than those of the normed group which implies serious health concerns for African American college students.

Williams and Mohammed (2008) explored the impact of perceived discrimination on health status. The researchers reported that across the majority of the 15 most prevalent causes of death in the United States, African Americans have higher death rates than their Caucasian counterparts. Specifically, mortality rates for African Americans were greater for diabetes, heart disease, hypertension, cancer, stroke, liver cirrhosis, kidney disease, and homicide. The authors identified that perceived discrimination has been found to impact health status across a variety of health conditions. Through meta-analysis, Williams and Mohammed identified relationships between perceived discrimination and stress, anxiety, depression, emotional regulation, psychological distress, intimate partner violence, cardiovascular reactivity, sexual problems, delays in seeking medical care, filling prescriptions, and seeking treatment for physical and mental health concerns. The meta-analysis identifies several studies in which psychological distress was positively associated with self-report of discrimination for African American college students, which is particularly relevant within the context of the present chapter.

Perceived discrimination may not only impact the physical and mental health of African American college students, it may also affect these students' receipt of medical or mental health treatment (Williams & Mohammed, 2008). To promote wellness within this context, the proactive presentation of wellness practices to African American college students may promote engagement with campus-based resources that they may not be inclined to explore on their own. Additionally, based upon the previously described benefits of wellness practices for college students, these practices may also support African American students in reducing physical and psychological risk factors that are detrimental to their health and well-being.

Bridges (2010) explored the impact of racial identity development and psychological coping strategies of African American males at a PWI with the hopes of determining participants' perceptions of how welcoming the institution was based on their racial status (African American males). Most disconcertingly, participants reported often feeling as athletic commodities to the university thus "playing into the stereotype that African American males as athletically gifted but intellectually lazy" (p. 22). Student participants in this study further reflected on incidents of racism, discrimination, stereotypes, and hostility from White individuals in the college community. Despite exposure to these stressful obstacles, these African American college students shared that maintaining a strong sense of racial identity was apropos to their psychological functioning. Similarly, Tovar-Murray, Jenifer, Andrusyk, D'Angelo, and King (2012) determined that African American students with strong racial and ethnic identities reported increased likelihood of attaining their career goals. Tovar-Murray and colleagues further illuminated that racial identity may well serve as a buffer to racially related stressors for African American college students, particularly those who sought support from their ethnic community. The studies listed in this section emphasize the effects of racism and discrimination on the overall wellness of African American college students and underscore the necessity for systemic interventions to support these students as they navigate higher education.

EFFECTIVE STRATEGIES FOR ENHANCING WELLNESS AND MOTIVATION

In reflecting on the range of positive contributions that holistic wellness has on varied situations, it may well be a viable framework for supporting individuals struggling with life situations. In this context, life situations encapsulate events that may be stressful and anxiety-provoking as well as creating impediments to one's overall functioning. Ethnic minorities, particularly African Americans, have historically been marginalized due to institutional forces. Much of what you have read in this book has focused on the negative effects of these forces such as educational, social, and even financial impositions. In this chapter, however, we take a strength-based approach to supporting African Americans in terms of operationalizing wellness as a paradigm for maintaining holistic balance in spite of systemic challenges. Here are two key methods of promoting wellness practices with African American students (or any student population). These two methods may be proposed by a school counselor, college counselor, and college administrators working with African American students.

Learn a Wellness Model

Granello (2013) suggested that counselors working with clients on wellness approaches should introduce the clients to a wellness model. It would be most beneficial to African American students, especially those who have had a negative experience in higher education, to know a model of wellness in order to fully understand the importance of these practices to their academic and social well-being. Considering the significant struggles that students have reported, understanding a wellness model may allow African American students to develop a useful lens for navigating higher education and being successful. Granello further implied that by knowing about a wellness model, a client may develop the ability to understand the relationships between "different but interrelated aspects of his lifestyle" (p. 73). Take for example, the undergraduate African American student, Jason, who describes feelings of isolation, invisibility, and condescension (Haskins, et. al., 2013). If Jason can pinpoint what areas of his functioning are most disadvantaged by these experiences, he may also be able to understand that the connections between his emotional wellness and the occupational and social outcomes. Indeed, understanding a wellness model may equip this student with the ability to shift perspectives in order to recognize marginalization for what it is and subsequently move forward successfully. An initial analysis of wellness may be understood by completing the Five-Factor Wel Inventory (5-F WEL; Myers & Sweeney, 2004). The 5-F WEL presents a comprehensive wellness assessment focused on the alignment of mind, body, and spirit. School counselors and college counselors working with African American students on college readiness are in an ideal position to foster this proactive approach.

Develop a Wellness Plan

Another technique to bolster African American student engagement in wellness practices is to encourage the development of a wellness plan (Granello, 2013). A wellness or self-care plan may create a sense of accountability for these individuals and also allow them a visual method of monitoring progress. A wellness plan is an intentional plan of action to take care of various aspects of health and well-being and should include incremental progress toward building resilience and reducing vulnerability. Again, school counselors and college career counselors may be instrumental in assisting African American students in developing such a plan to address their needs. Conversely, other professionals charged with the supervision of college students such as residence life assistants (RA's), and Deans of colleges, may also be influential in consulting with their African American students about developing self-care plan strategies, hosting seminars on self-care topics, as well as facilitating open group discussions on self-care and college life. As such, a collaborative effort may be made by all stakeholders in promoting wellness and success among African American college students.

Potential Components of a Holistic Wellness Plan

The following section focuses on specific strategies which may be included on a wellness plan and includes evidence-based practices that have been shown to enhance overall wellness. These include mindfulness-based activities, creative arts, wellness courses, spirituality practices, and physical wellness.

Mindfulness-based Activities

Mindfulness-based practices, administered in one 90-minute session, were found to reduce students' reported rates of depression and to increase self-reported acceptance (Danitz & Orsill, 2014). Mindfulness and other acceptance-based practices such as meditation that involve focusing on the present and suspending judgment of thoughts and feelings can be practiced alone or in group settings, and may be practiced in a variety of ways, including within the context of movement-based mindfulness activities.

As previously mentioned in this chapter, exercise and other physical activity can improve fitness, boost mood, and promote overall well-being. In addition to these overall wellness benefits, Caldwell, Harrison, Adams, Quin, and Greeson (2010) demonstrated the impact that movement-based mindfulness courses may have on college students. The researchers found that movement-based activities, such as Pilates or Taiji quan, were demonstrated to increase student mindfulness and to positively impact student sleep patterns. Additional movement-based activities that college students may undertake, such as yoga, tai chi, walking or jogging, may also be explored for their possible physical and mental wellness benefits.

Creative Arts

Activities such as art, dancing, and music may also promote wellness as part of a holistic wellness plan. For example, researchers found that group-based wellness drumming, where group participants played the drums for 45 minutes, reported improved mood directly following the drumming experience (Mungas & Silverman, 2014). Other forms of recreational music, whether playing with a band or practicing solo, may also support overall wellness and help to improve mood.

Wellness Courses

College-based wellness courses, often offered to students as part of a freshman experience, have been demonstrated to positively impact student adjustment and wellness (Conley, Travers, & Bryant, 2013; Lockwood & Wohl, 2012). These courses may provide education on wellness topics, may integrate wellness practices such as relaxation skills, and may include journaling or other reflective practices to support wellness practices throughout the week. Students who desire structure, routine, and facilitated exposure to multiple wellness modalities may find such courses particularly helpful.

Spiritual Practices

Students who engage in spiritual practices aligned with their own belief system reported better physical health, increased physical activity, greater life satisfaction, and reduced likelihood of engaging in high-risk behaviors including excessive alcohol use and tobacco use (Nelms, Hutchins, Hutchins, & Pursley, 2007). Campus-based spiritual and religious organizations may also provide students with opportunities to become connected to the campus and to a network of peers. For students from the African American culture, a cultural group known in the literature for upholding strong spiritual practices, this may well be a most advantageous engagement in in support of ongoing wellness in college.

Physical Wellness

Understanding the connection between physical and mental wellness is critical. Physical wellness encourages more positive behavioral engagement which leads to healthier lifestyles. In their book, *Physical Fitness and Wellness*, Greenberg, Dintiman, and Oakes noted the use of an Awareness inventory which allows individuals to assess their own levels of physical wellness in order to make necessary changes. Greenberg and colleagues continued by emphasizing physical wellness in terms of fitness, nutritional habits, body image, drug use, stress management, and even disease prevention. To reduce adverse effects that these factors may possibly have on African American students, higher education administration needs to place an emphasis on the physical health of their students. This may be accomplished by developing mentoring programs wherein students are connected with individuals in the college community from whom they can seek support. Another strategy to consider is incorporating into the college's website to links to wellness promotion. One such example is Brown University, whose website provides individuals with "answers to questions you always wanted to ask" and includes various topics such as alcohol, tobacco, and other drugs, nutrition and eating concerns, LGBTQ health, and several other relevant topics and resources for support. An additional supportive strategy would be to provide students with a wellness hotline so that students can call in with questions and concerns, particularly those of a sensitive nature that they would not otherwise choose to discuss openly.

Racial Identity Development

Considering the benefits of increased racial development on the psychological well-being and college and career success of African Americans, Spurgeon and Myers (2010) suggested annual start-of-the-year or end-of-the-year programs for upperclassmen geared toward identifying and developing racial identity. Spurgeon and Myers also recommended the support of African American male faculty as positive role models for students. Avenues for developing self-awareness are also noteworthy strategies for promoting self-identity among African American students. Bridges purported that self-awareness includes "an understanding of whom one is as an African American along with an understanding of the history of African Americans, both at the university and in the larger American society." Allowing African American students the opportunity to engage in meaningful, problem-solving, strength-based coping strategies may very well result in greater psychological health, improved wellness, and ultimately, more fruitful career aspirations and destinies.

SUMMARY

African American students encounter significant challenges in higher education. Despite these systemic and political barriers, African American students continue to strive for success. Booker T. Washington (n.d.) once said, "Success is to be measured not so much by the position that one has reached in life as by the obstacles which he has overcome while trying to succeed." School counselors, college counselors, higher education administration and professors play a pivotal role in supporting these students as they meander through their oftentimes stressful educational journeys by encouraging wellness and self-care. Holistic wellness practices can make a difference in the lives of African American students, thus promoting a more fulfilling physical, mental, and social existence.

REFERENCES

Bridges, E. (2010). Racial identity development and psychological coping strategies of African American males at a predominantly White university. *Annals of the American Psychotherapy Association, 13*, 14–26.

Brown University. Health promotion. Retrieved from http://www.brown.edu/Student_Services/Health_Services/Health_Education/nutrition_&_eating_concerns/body_image.php

Burnett, A. J., Sabato, T. M., Wagner, L., & Smith, A. (2014) The influence of attributional style on substance use and risky sexual behavior among college student. *College Student Journal, 48*, 325–336.

Caldwell, K., Harrison, M., Adams, M., Quin, R. H., & Greeson, J. (2010). Developing mindfulness in college students through movement based courses: Effects on self-regulatory self-efficacy, mood, stress, and sleep quality. *Journal of American College Health, 58*, 433–442.

Conley, C. S., Travers, L. V., & Bryant, F. B. (2013). Promoting psychosocial adjustment and stress management in first-year college students: Benefits of engagement in a psychosocial wellness seminar. Journal of American College Health, *61*, 75–86. doi:10.1080/07448481.2012.754757

Danitz, S. B. & Orsillo, S. M. (2014). The mindful way through the semester: An investigation of the effectiveness of an acceptance-based behavioral therapy program on psychological wellness in first-year students. Behavior Modification, 38, 549–566. doi: 10.1177/0145445513520218

Granello, P. F. (2013). *Wellness counseling.* Upper Saddle River, NJ: Pearson Pub.

Haskins, N., Whitfield-Williams, M., Shillingford, M. A., Singh, A., Moxley, R., and Ofauni, C. (2013). The experiences of Black master's counseling students: A phenomenological inquiry. *Counselor Education & Supervision, 52*, 162–178. doi:10.1002/j.1556–6978.2013.00035.x

Krumrei-Mancuso, E. J., Newton, F. B., Kim, E., & Wilcox, D. (2013). Psychosocial factors predicting first-year college student success. *Journal of College Student Development, 54*, 247–266.

Lawson, G., & Myers, J. E. (2011), Wellness, professional quality of life, and career-sustaining behaviors: What keeps us well? *Journal of Counseling & Development, 89*, 163–171.

Lewis T. F. & Myers, J. E. (2010). Wellness factors as predictors of alcohol use among undergraduates: Implications for prevention and intervention. *Journal of College Counseling, 13*, 111–125.

Lewis, T. F. & Myers, J. E. (2012). Wellness factors decrease odds of drinking and driving among college students. *Journal of Addictions and Offender Counseling, 33*, 93–106.

Lockwood, P., & Wohl, R. (2012). The impact of a 15-week lifetime wellness course on behavior change and self-efficacy in college students. *College Student Journal, 46*, 628–641.

Mungas, R. & Silverman, M. J. (2014). Immediate effects of group-based wellness drumming on affective states in university students. *The Arts in Psychotherapy, 41*, 287–292.

Myers, J. E., & Sweeney, T. J. (2004). The Indivisible Self: An evidence-based model of wellness. *Journal of Individual Psychology, 60*, 234–244. doi: 10.1080/09515071003718384

Myers, J. E., Sweeney, T. J., & Witmer, J. M. (2000). The Wheel of Wellness counseling for wellness: A holistic model for treatment planning. *Journal of Counseling & Development, 78*, 251–266.

National Wellness Institute. (2014). *The six dimensions of wellness.* Stevens Point, WI: National Wellness Institute. Retrieved from http://www.nationalwellness.org/?page=Six_Dimensions

Nelms, L. W., Hutchins, E., Hutchins, D., & Pursley, R. J. (2007). Spirituality and the health of college students. *Journal of Religion and Health, 46,* 249–265. doi:10.1080/07448481.2013.824454

Prichard, M. E. & Wilson, G. S. (2003). Using emotional and social factors to predict student success. *Journal of College Student Development, 44,* 18–28.

Rayle, A. D. & Chung, K. (2008). Revisiting first-year college students' mattering: Social support, academic stress, and the mattering experience. *Journal of College Student Retention: Research, Theory, and Practice, 9,* 21–37.

Reynolds, A. L. (2013). College student concerns: Perceptions of student affairs practitioners. *Journal of College Student Development, 54,* 98–104.

Roach, L. F. & Young, M. E. (2007). Do counselor education programs promote wellness in their students? *Counselor Education & Supervision, 47,* 29–045.

Smith, M. L., Menn, M., Dorsett, L., & Wilson, K. (2012). College students' perceptions of HIV risk, importance of protective behaviors, and intentions to change behaviors after attending an HIV/AIDS awareness event. *Texas Public Health Journal, 64,* 23–29.

Spurgeon, S. L. (2009). Wellness and college type in African American male college students: An examination of differences. *Journal of College Counseling, 12,* 33–43.

Spurgeon, S. L. & Myers, J. E. (2010). African American males: Relationships among racial identity, college type, and wellness. *Journal of Black Studies, 40,* 527–543. doi:10.1177/0021934708315153

Tovar-Murray, D., Jenifer, E. S., Andrusyk, J., D' Angelo, R., & Ryan, T. K. (2012). Racism-related stress and ethnic identity as determinants of African American college students' career aspirations. *Career Development Quarterly, 60,* 254–262.

Washington, B. T. (n.d.). Powerful quotes to uplift Black men. Retrieved from https://www.google.com/?gws_rd=ssl#q=African+American+quotes+on+overcoming+obstacles

Williams, D. R. & Mohammed, S. A. (2008). Discrimination and racial disparities in health: Evidence and needed research. *Journal of Behavioral Medicine, 32,* 20–47. doi:10.1007/s10865–008-9185–0

Index

abstract liberalism, 231
academic achievement, 23, 92–93, 101, 116–17, 122, 125, 168, 178–83, 190, 238–44, 261–69, 317–18, 323–27, 344
academic advisement, 4–10, 116
academic rigor, 7–14, 30, 94–102, 109–25.
    See also rigor
ACT, 6–9, 70, 189, 301
Advanced Placement (AP), 7–8, 95–98, 117–25, 136, 296
advocacy, 47, 125, 133, 139–46, 198, 246, 284, 296–300, 357–61
Affirmative Action, 28–29, 109, 228
Agricultural education, 18
American School Counselor Association, 1, 5–6, 9, 76, 114–16, 296
Americans with Disabilities Act (ADA), 32, 133, 142
Amistad Murals, 51–52.
    See also Hale, Woodruff
Armstrong, Samuel Chapman, 21, 44–47
Association of Public and Land Grant Universities, 21
athletics, 228, 282–86, 293, 298, 312–14, 318–22, 327, 329, 332–35

at-risk, 177, 263, 266–69, 281, 345
attribution style, 58–59
attrition, 1, 237–39, 313, 317–18, 334–35, 344

Bachelor's degree, 2, 48, 55, 110–11, 173, 187
Bandura, Albert, 68, 122.
    See also Social Learning Theory
Bronfenbrenner, Urie, 72, 262–63, 268, 272
Brown, Henry Billings, Justice, 24
Brown, Linda, 27
Brown, Oliver, 27
Brown II, 28
Brown v. Board of Education, 25–28, 109, 228
budget, 27, 50, 78–79, 115, 123, 161–64
Bush, George W., 33

campus climate, 188–90, 194, 310–12, 317
Canada, Sy Woodson, 25
career and technical education, 3, 120, 168–73, 175–76, 179–83
career assessment, 9, 145
career counseling, 7, 75–76, 114–15, 357
career development, 4, 6, 55, 85, 112–14, 167, 178–80, 183, 284, 298, 323

355

career exploration, 4–5, 111, 125, 177, 281
career maturity, 4–6
career readiness, 3, 29, 53, 111–15, 141, 175, 268, 279, 297, 317, 323, 332, 334–35, 357
Carvell, Douglass, 29
Centers of Research Excellence in Science and Technology (CREST), 218
Civil Rights Act, The., 30–31, 109, 228
Civil War, the, 19, 21, 39–42, 52, 169–70, 207, 209
Collective Impact Model, 259, 271, 273
college access, x, 6, 9, 11, 29–30, 188
college ambassadors club, 11
college aspiration, 13, 189
college counseling, 4–9, 14, 31
college immersion, 12
college preparation, 1–4, 9–10, 13, 17, 111, 116, 136, 194, 332
college readiness, 3–8, 29, 34, 42, 51–52, 60, 77, 94, 113–17, 244, 279, 302, 333, 335, 349
Comite des Citoyen, 23–24
Common Core State Standards (CCSS), 132
Compromise of 1877, The., 19
cooperative extension, 22–23; programs, 22
core academic skills, 3
course choice, 109, 116, 243
course rigor, 117
Covington, Louisiana, 24
creative arts, 350
Creole, 23–24
Critical Race Theory (CRT), 310–13, 320, 329, 331–32
culture, 3, 5, 8, 10–12, 24, 33, 48, 56–72, 80, 92, 98, 101, 139, 148, 168–69, 181–82, 190–93, 199, 208–12, 215, 219–20, 230–32, 238–40, 262–67, 272, 282–84, 288, 291, 299, 314, 321, 326, 331–32, 351

debt, 153–56, 162–64
deficit thinking, 90
discipline, 96, 115, 117, 228, 287–89, 296–97, 299–300; restorative discipline, 289, 296, 299–300
Draw a Scientist Test (DAST), 60–63
dual enrollment, 7, 117–20, 125
Dubois, W. E. B., 21, 43–44

early admissions, 122
economic class, ii, x
Elementary and Secondary Education Act, 31, 132, 268, 279
Elliott, Kenneth, 29
employability skills, 3, 167, 173–77, 179–83
Evans-Allen Act of 1977, 22
exploitation, 44, 230, 286, 328–29

financial aid, 4, 71, 123–24, 141, 160–64, 173, 189, 200, 228, 244, 301
financial literacy, 32, 153–57, 161, 164
financial management, 155–56
first generation college students, 4, 31, 138, 187–201, 220
Fisk University, 47–49
Flores, Bill, 22
Fourteenth amendment, 23–24, 28; Equal protection clause, 28
Freedman's Bureau, 211

Gaines, Lloyd Lionel, 25
Gaines v. Canada, 25
GEAR UP, 31, 268, 271
gender, 2, 19, 40, 56, 60–62, 71, 112, 114, 145, 169, 180, 198, 215–16, 236–37, 245, 272, 282, 284, 287, 294, 297, 300, 302, 312–21, 327, 329, 333, 335, 342–43, 360
gifted and talented, 87, 89–93, 293–94, 296
gifted child model, 93
goal setting, 122, 147, 169

Gottfredson, Linda, 112–13, 180, 264, 300.
　See also Theory of Circumscription and Compromise
grade point average (GPA), 6, 92, 102, 135–36, 138, 157, 189, 244, 312–13, 344
graduation coaches, 10
grants, 5, 30–32, 123, 157, 160–61, 210, 221, 268, 301

Hale, Woodruff, 51–52.
　See also Amistad Murals
Hampton-Tuskegee Model, 44–48
Harlan, John Marshall, Justice, 25
Hatch, William Henry, 21
Hatch Act of 1887, The., 20–21
high achievers, 87
Higher Education Act, The., 30–31, 208, 268
Historically Black College or University (HBCU), 12, 17, 20–23, 39, 124, 158, 207–21, 347
Historically White Institutions (HWI), 209–15, 218–21
Holland, John, 56, 64.
　See also Theory of Vocational Choice
Homesteaders Act, 18–19
Hopwood, Cheryle, 29
Hopwood v. Texas, 28–29
Howard University, 212
hypermasculinity, 287–88, 302

identity development, 135, 155, 238–40, 282–83, 294, 298, 302, 319, 322, 327, 344, 347, 352
identity reaffirmation, 327
imposter phenomenon, 248, 251
imposter syndrome, 230, 234
incarceration, 8, 280–81
Individualized Education Program (IEP), 33, 133, 135–36, 139–40, 143, 146
Individuals with Disabilities Education Act (IDEA), 32–33, 135–36, 139–40, 143, 146

Industry based certification, 121
institutional caring, 209–10
Intersectionality, 236, 320, 333
intrusive advising, 198–200
Ivy League, 18, 85

Jim Crow, 25–26, 52;
　Era, 25;
　Laws, 25
Johnson, Lyndon B., 30

Kozol, Jonathan, 1

leadership skills, 194, 244
Lever, Asbury Francis, 22
Lincoln, Abraham, 18
Loans, 5, 29–31, 123, 154–57, 159–62, 173, 301;
　Direct Consolidation Loan, 159–60;
　Direct Unsubsidized Loan, 159–60;
　Federal Perkins Loan, 159;
　Student loans, 29, 31, 123, 154–57;
　William D. Ford Federal Direct Loan (Direct Loan) Program, 159
logotherapy, 196–97, 199
Louisiana Separate Car Act, 23–24
low socioeconomic status, 138

Marshall, Thurgood, 26–27
mentor, 4, 9–11, 22, 31, 62, 72, 78, 96, 102, 122, 140, 144–46, 148, 193–94, 198, 214–15, 217, 219, 227–28, 241, 244–47, 266–67, 282–84, 287, 296–99, 302, 314, 351;
　mentoring, 96, 122, 148, 215, 227–28, 241, 244–47, 266–67, 287, 298–99, 314, 351;
　microaggressions, 8, 232, 237;
　microassaults, 232;
　microinsults, 232;
　microinvalidation, 232–33
mindfulness, 350
Mobley, Dennis, 169
Morehouse College, 208
Morrill, Justin Smith, 17

Morrill Land Grant Colleges Act, 18
Morrill-McComas Land Grant Act, 19, 21
motivation, 8–9, 12, 28, 43, 94–96, 99, 101–2, 119, 174, 177, 181–82, 192–94, 197, 242, 245–46, 312, 317, 325, 344, 348

National Association for the Advancement of Colored People (NAACP), 25–27
National Association of State Directors of Career Technical Education Consortium (NASDCTEC), 172
National Collegiate Athletic Association (NCAA) standards, 309, 312–15, 320, 324, 333
National Defense Education Act (1958), The., 29–30
No Child Left Behind (NCLB), 33–34, 134

Obama, Barack, 116
Obama, Michelle, 1, 6, 115
onlyness, 311, 327
othermothering, 209, 214–16, 219

Painter, Theophilis, 26
Paul Quinn College, 208
peer advisor, 243
peer tutor, 243
Pell grants, 31, 157, 163
perseverance, persevere, persistence, 8–9, 72, 75, 138, 147, 175, 187–88, 190, 195, 197, 217, 227, 238, 242–43, 245, 317, 333, 335
Plessy, Homer Adolph, 23
Plessy v. Ferguson, 23
policy, 21, 28, 79, 119, 132, 134, 171, 178, 183, 259–62, 268, 271–73, 289, 310, 319, 331–33
post-secondary degrees, 74, 76, 78
post-secondary education, 10, 30, 76, 111, 131–48, 154, 167, 170, 172, 279, 294, 297, 301

post-secondary training, 1, 4, 53
poverty, 8, 25, 30–31, 72, 80, 94, 110–12, 115–16, 120, 122, 125, 137, 196–97, 259–63, 268, 271–72, 280, 284, 286, 297, 312
Predominantly White Institutions, 12, 237, 241, 247, 310–11, 316–18, 322–24, 326, 328, 347
progress monitoring, 121–22
Proposition 16, 310
Proposition 48, 310
punishment, 288–89

racial identity, 25, 123, 211, 227, 237–41, 247, 282–83, 309, 346–48, 252
racism, 8–9, 43, 47–48, 86, 100–101, 109, 156, 196–97, 230–33, 236–37, 240, 243, 247, 283–84, 310–11, 320, 322, 331, 335, 348; colorblind racism, 231; individual interpersonal racism, 231; institutional racism, 231, 237, 283; systemic racism, 231
Raising Achievement in Mathematics & Science (RAMS), 218
Reach Higher Initiative, 1, 115
Reconstruction Era, 41
recruitment, 78, 227–28, 233, 294, 296, 314–15, 334
Relational Cultural Theory (RCT), 195–96, 199
relationality, 58–59
resilience, 8, 182, 201, 243, 267, 343, 349, 358
retention, 79, 90, 92, 109, 112, 120, 187–90, 193, 195, 197, 199, 201, 210, 214, 218, 227, 238, 241–42, 245, 268, 309
rigor, 5–9, 13–14, 30, 56, 77–80, 94–98, 102, 109, 115–25, 135, 141, 170, 177, 188, 233, 291, 294
rite of passage programs (ROP), 11–12
Rogers, David, 29

SAT, 7, 9, 70, 189, 301
scholarships, 4–5, 7, 25–26, 71, 123–24, 157–58, 161, 221, 231, 286, 301, 322, 330
school choice, 33, 122
school to prison pipeline, 279–80
School to Work Opportunities Act, 170–71
Science, Technology, Engineering, and Math (STEM), 32, 55–56, 60, 62–68, 70, 72–81, 97, 117–18, 141, 157, 216–19, 266, 294–95
Section 504 of the Rehabilitation Act of 1973, 32–33, 133
self-advocacy, 146
self-concept, 56, 58, 63–64, 68–69, 74–76, 100, 112–13, 198, 239, 266
self-determination, 133, 145–46, 148
self-esteem, 96, 214, 246, 266, 268, 319, 328
self-regulation, 101–2
self-regulatory mechanisms, 7
sexuality, 236
Smith, Hoke, 22
Smith-Lever Act of 1914, 22–23
Social Capital Theory, 3;
    aspirational capital, 192;
    capital, 3–4, 6–7, 9–11, 13, 140, 148, 156, 167–68, 191–94, 200–201, 244, 266, 286–87, 298;
    cultural capital, 140, 148, 167–68, 191–92, 244, 266;
    economic capital, 192;
    formal social capital, 4, 6, 9;
    informal social capital, 4, 9;
    navigational capital, 192, 194;
    resistance capital, 192, 194;
    social capital, 3–4, 6–7, 9, 11, 13, 140, 167, 191, 286–87, 298
Social Cognitive Career Theory, 68, 74
Social Learning Theory, 68, 122.
    See also Albert Bandura
Socratic dialogue, 198–99
specific learning disability, 132

spirituality, 56, 58, 182, 208, 212–13, 215, 342–43, 350
spiritual practices, 351
standards blending, 181
stereotype, 8, 60, 93, 99, 102, 118, 134, 144, 230, 233, 279–80, 283–86, 288, 294, 302, 312, 314–16, 324–25, 327, 329, 333–34, 348
stereotype threat, 93, 99, 118, 230, 233, 279, 284–86, 294, 302, 316, 329, 334
stress management, 7, 121–22, 343, 347, 351
student employment, 177–78
Summer Undergraduate Research Experience (SURE), 218
Sweatt, Heman Marion, 26

talent development, 85–86, 89, 94, 96, 98–99, 101;
    talent development paradigm, 94
Taylor v. Wake Forest University, 313
Teacher Education Assistance for College and Higher Education (TEACH) grant, 157
technical careers, 120
technical skills, 174, 281
test bias, 90
Theory of Circumscription and Compromise, 112–13, 180.
    See also Gottfredson, Linda
Theory of Vocational Choice, 56, 64.
    See also Holland, John
time management, 7, 97, 121–22, 178, 193, 333, 344
Title IX, 318–19, 332–33
tokenism, 230, 235–36, 316
top ten percent plan, 29
transition programs, 31, 244
TRIO, 31, 200, 244–45
Tuskegee Institute, 21, 47, 169

University of Missouri Law School, 25
University of Texas Law School, 26
U. S. Congress, 22, 170, 318

U. S. constitution, 23
U. S. Court of Appeals, 29
U. S. Department of Agriculture, 21–22
U. S. Department of Education, 5, 29–30, 32–33, 77, 87, 132, 157–59, 170, 200, 269, 272, 279, 289
U. S. Senate, 18

Village pedagogy, 211–13, 216
Virginia Union University, 208
vocational education, 120, 168–70, 174–75

Washington, Booker Taliferro, 21, 23, 43–45, 48–49, 352. *See also* Booker T. Washington
White planter class, 42
Winston-Salem State University, 212, 218
workforce trends, 168, 171
Work-study programs, 157–58, 160

Xavier University, 208

zero tolerance policies, 288–89, 302
zone of acceptable alternatives, 113

About the Contributors

Brandee Appling is a doctoral candidate at The University of Georgia in the Counseling and Student Personnel Services, P-16 program. She is currently a practicing professional school counselor in Atlanta, GA. Brandee has been a professional school counselor at all three education levels for 10 years.

Christopher T. Belser, MEd, NCC is a doctoral student in the Counselor Education & Supervision program at the University of Central Florida. He served as a professional school counselor in middle schools for three years in Baton Rouge, Louisiana, where he worked heavily with African American males. Belser has taught and written about career development and has presented on a variety of topics at local, state, and national conferences.

Tristen Bergholtz is a professional school counselor from Mount Dora, Florida. She earned a MEd in School Counseling from Louisiana State University. She has provided counseling services to students in grades Pre-K through 12. After earning a bachelor's degree in Interdisciplinary Studies from the University of Central Florida, Tristen served as a Teach For America corps member in Pointe Coupee Parish, Louisiana where she taught high school special education. She has a strong interest in career and college readiness and increasing parental involvement.

Eric M. Brown completed his BS Psychology from Texas A&M, M.Div. at Abilene Christian University, and MEd; Ed.S. in Counseling at University of Florida and currently working on his PhD in Counseling at Old Dominion University. He spent 11 years as a pastor and four years working as a counselor and adjunct instructor of Student Development at Santa Fe College in Gainesville Florida.

Ashley Churbock graduated from The Ohio State University in 2008 with a Bachelor of Arts degree in Psychology. In 2011, Ashley continued on to graduate from Louisiana State University with a Master's degree in Community Counseling. She worked for Communities In Schools and served as a site coordinator at Capitol Middle School in Baton Rouge, Louisiana for 3 years and was awarded the 2013 Diplomas Now, Communities In Schools Site Coordinator of the Year. Ashley returned to Louisiana State University during the 2013–2014 school year to complete her Education Specialist degree in Counseling. She is currently working as the school counselor at a P-12 school, Greater Baton Rouge Hope Academy, which specializes in meeting the needs of special education students.

Jennifer Riedl Cross, PhD is the director of Research at the Center for Gifted Education. With a doctorate in educational psychology, specializing in cognitive and social processes, Dr. Cross is the coeditor, with Tracy L. Cross, of the *Handbook for Counselors Serving Students with Gifts and Talents*. She served as guest editor, with James Borland, of a special issue of *Roeper Review* on the topic of gifted education and social inequality. Her research in the field emphasizes the social aspects of gifted education, from individual coping with the stigma of giftedness to attitudes toward giftedness and gifted education.

Tracy L. Cross, PhD, holds an endowed chair, Jody and Layton Smith Professor of Psychology and Gifted Education, and is the executive director of the Center for Gifted Education at The College of William and Mary. He has published more than 150 articles, book chapters, and columns; made more than 200 presentations at conferences; and published eight books. He received the Distinguished Service Award from The Association for the Gifted (TAG) and the National Association for Gifted Children (NAGC), the Early Leader, Early Scholar and Distinguished Scholar Awards from NAGC, and in 2009 was given the Lifetime Achievement Award from the MENSA Education and Research Foundation. He has edited four journals in the field and is the current editor of the *Journal for the Education of the Gifted*. He served as president of TAG and is currently the president of NAGC.

Jennifer Curry, PhD, Associate Dean for Programs and Services and Associate Professor, teaches in the counselor education program at Louisiana State University where she is the coordinator of the School Counseling program. Her professional experience includes serving as an investigator of Crimes Against Children for the Louisville Police Department and as a professional school counselor in elementary, middle, and high school settings. Her research interests include career and college readiness and school counselor development. She has published over 50 peer-reviewed articles and two books, "*Career Counseling in P-12 Schools*" published by Springer and "*Integrating Play Therapy in Comprehensive School Counseling Programs*" published by Information Age. She has presented her work nationally and internationally on a wide range of school counseling topics at over 50 professional conferences. Additionally, she has served as guest editor of the American School Counselor Association's (ASCA) *Professional School Counseling* journal and as an editorial board member for six years. Dr. Curry has also served as a delegate of ASCA's national assembly, president of the Louisiana School Counselor Association, and president of the national Association for Spiritual, Ethical and Religious Values in Counseling. She is the recipient of the Roger Aubrey Northstar award for the person most likely to change the field of counseling, the American Counseling Association's Ross Trust Award for School Counseling, the Biggs-Pine publication award, ASERVIC's meritorious service award, LSU's College of Education Early Career Award, Louisiana Counseling Association's Advocacy Award, and Louisiana School Counselor's Association's Publication Award.

Jessica Exkano, PhD, currently teaches Technical Writing and College Success Skills at ITI Technical College in Baton Rouge, LA. Her professional experience includes providing college and career-readiness services to low-income, in-school and out-of-school youth through various grant-funded programs at the Louisiana State Youth Opportunities Unlimited project. Her research interests include providing college and career services to low-income youth, obtaining funding for youth programs, and creating partnerships. Jessica received the University Council for Educational Administration's Barbara L. Jackson Scholar award (2012–2014).

Andrea Dawn Frazier has a PhD in educational psychology, and she currently teaches educational psychology and educational research courses in the Department of Counseling, Foundations, and Leadership at Columbus State University. Her research interests encompass the educative experience of students of color and girls, with recent work exploring possible selves and academic self-concept in high-ability African American students and spatial reasoning in elementary-aged children. She is coeditor of "Special Populations in Gifted Education: Understanding Our Most Able Students from Diverse Backgrounds" with Dr. Jaime Castellano.

Michael T. Garrett (Eastern Band of the Cherokee Nation) is a therapist and consultant in the greater Atlanta area. He received his doctorate in Counseling and Counselor Education from UNC-Greensboro. His major research interests include exploring the relationship between cultural values, acculturation, and wellness with implications for developmental, culturally-based therapeutic interventions; strength-based work to improve wellness and resilience of children, adolescents, and adults in families, schools, and communities; better understanding bicultural competence; prevention of school dropout and enhancing school persistence among at risk youth; counseling indigenous and other diverse populations; and spiritual issues in counseling.

Pamela N. Harris is a doctoral student in the Counselor Education and Supervision program at the College of William & Mary. She received both her bachelors and masters degrees at Old Dominion University, where she studied creative writing and counseling. During her seven years as professional school counselor, Pamela created school-wide bullying prevention and character education programs, as well as career development curricula for at risk students. Her clinical and research interests include school-family collaboration, diversity issues, and working with at risk adolescents and their families. Pamela enjoys music, reading, and writing young adult fiction.

Dana C. Hart is the director of the Flores MBA Program at Louisiana State University. He earned a PhD in Educational Leadership and Research in the School of Education at Louisiana State University and maintains a research agenda in historical foundations of higher education in the United States.

Natoya Haskins is an assistant professor at the University of Georgia. Her previous work experience includes school counseling, the United States Army, family counseling, and youth ministry. Her current research interests include African American student and faculty experiences, social justice instrumentation, and the use of critical theories as well as culturally mindful theories to enhance pedagogy.

Nicole R. Hill, PhD, LPC is the chair of the Department of Counseling and Human Services at Syracuse University. Dr. Hill's scholarly interests include working with children and adolescents, multicultural counseling competencies, professional development of faculty and graduate students, and mentoring. She currently serves as Doctoral Program Coordinator and CACREP Liaison. She is committed to leadership and professional engagement that strengthens counseling, counselor education, and supervision as a discipline. Her participation on executive boards of CSI, ACES, and CSJ has contributed to a broader understanding of how to advance the profession through service and advocacy. Before joining the faculty at Syracuse University, she served as interim dean of the Graduate School and Chair of the Department of Counseling at Idaho State University. Her clinical experience is focused on counseling children and adolescents.

About the Contributors

D'Jalon J. Jackson is a second-year doctoral student in the Higher Education program at Louisiana State University (LSU), where she also earned a Bachelor of Science in Kinesiology and a Master of Arts in Counselor Education. She is also pursuing a Certificate of Education Specialist in School Counseling at LSU. Jackson is currently a school counselor at a middle school in Baton Rouge and has previously served as a career and mental health counselor. Her primary research interest includes African American doctoral student attrition rates and resilience factors.

Shandricka E. Jackson is an undergraduate student attending Louisiana State University, where she is working toward a Bachelor of Science in Child and Family Studies and a minor in Professional Leadership. Her anticipated date of graduation is December 2015. Shandricka is a Ronald McNair Undergraduate Research Scholar and a cadet in the Army Reserve Officer Training Corps. In the future, she hopes to be accepted into the Masters of Social Work program at LSU. Shandricka has spent many hours volunteering in nursing homes and homeless shelters and has an affinity for working with war veterans. She is interested in researching social justice and equality for all students.

J. Richelle Joe is a doctoral candidate in Counselor Education and Supervision at the College of William & Mary. She is a National Certified Counselor and holds undergraduate and graduate degrees in psychology, education, and counseling from the University of Virginia and Old Dominion University. Richelle has extensive teaching and counseling experience, including service as a secondary social studies teacher, middle-school counselor, and family counselor. Her professional and research interests include family counseling and school-family collaboration, particularly with families facing multiple life stressors. Additionally, Richelle has a special interest in the impact of HIV/AIDS on individuals and families, and how counselors can be prepared to meet the needs of this population.

Brian Kooyman is a Counselor Education PhD student at the College of William and Mary. Since completing his education as a practitioner in 2011, Brian has worked within the American southeast and abroad in the Russian Federation. Brian's work with minority and international populations continues to influence his perspectives on counseling and his research.

Michele Lopez, MS, NCC is a doctoral student in Counseling and Counselor Education in the Department of Counseling and Human Services at Syracuse University. Her scholarly interests include working with people with disabilities, multicultural counseling competencies, and disability rhetoric in the counseling discourse. Michele currently serves as an instructor in developmental classes for college students, assists faculty in the instruction of master's level classes in her academic department, and serves as a clinical supervisor for counselors who are entering the profession. She currently practices as a professional counselor in a community setting serving clients with disabilities. This practice grounds her view of the counseling work, and strongly informs her view of counselor education as a discipline. As an emerging Feminist Disability Studies scholar, Michele seeks to re-center and legitimize disability in the mental health discourse, honoring the voices of those who have been historically silenced. Michele is also involved in leadership initiatives in the counseling area, serving as the vice-president 2014–2015 of her Sigma Upsilon Chapter of counseling honor society Chi Sigma Iota.

Berlisha R. Morton is a visiting professor of Educational Studies as Colgate University. She utilizes engaged pedagogies in the courses in which she teaches such as Women and Education and Race and Education. She earned a PhD in Educational Leadership and Research at Louisiana State University and maintains a research agenda in womanist histories and womanist pedagogies.

M. Ann Shillingford, PhD., is an assistant professor of Counselor Education at the College of William & Mary in Williamsburg, VA. She has several years of experience as a professional school counselor prior to completing her doctorate at the University of Central Florida. Dr. Shillingford has written several articles and book chapters on multicultural issues particularly those that affect children and youth of color.

Lauren Treacy graduated from Gonzaga University in 2011 with a Bachelor of Arts degree in Psychology, a minor in Sociology, and a concentration in Women and Gender Studies. After graduating, Lauren moved to Louisiana in the fall of 2011 to serve for two years with the education-based non-profit City Year. Through City Year she was able to work with high-need public middle schools in the Baton Rouge area by tutoring, mentoring, and programming for the needs of the ethnically diverse student population. Lauren began attending Louisiana State University in the fall of 2013 to obtain her MEd in School Counseling. She is currently in her second year at LSU and serves as the Chi Sigma Iota honor society LSU chapter president and is a member of the 2014–2015 Louisiana Counseling Association Leadership Academy.

Linwood G. Vereen, PhD, LPC is an associate professor at Syracuse University and Coordinator of the Clinical Mental Health Program.

Dr. Vereen is a longstanding member of the American Counseling Association and has held various leadership positions including serving as the Chair of the Western Region of the American Counseling Association. Beginning in July of 2015, Dr. Vereen will assume the role of President—elect of one of ACA's founding divisions, the Association for Humanistic Counseling. In addition to scholarship dedicated to student athletes, he currently engages in professional and scholarly work focused on humanism as a central tenet of professional counseling, existentialism, humor in counseling, clinical supervisor development, group dynamics, and mindfulness within the small group experience.

Amy E. Williams, MEd, NCC, CSAC, is a doctoral student in the Counselor Education and Supervision program at the College of William and Mary. Her clinical and research interests include substance use and addiction, the impact of addiction on families, and mindfulness and meditation. Before entering the counseling profession, Amy taught elementary school for seven years. Amy's clinical experiences include working with addictions and substance abuse in adolescents, college students, and adults. She has experience working with individuals, groups, and families impacted by substance use disorders. Amy received her BSEd degree in Elementary Education from Lock Haven University of Pennsylvania, her MS degree in Curriculum and Instruction from the University of Scranton, and her MEd in Community and Addictions Counseling from the College of William and Mary.

Cyrus R. Williams III is an assistant professor in the Counseling Department at Regent University. He holds a PhD in Counselor Education from the University of Florida and is a Licensed Professional Counselor. Dr. Williams' primary research interests include: multiculturalism, advocacy counseling, addictive behaviors and career development. Specifically, he focuses on applying non-cognitive variables, such as hope, resilience and strength-based interventions to at risk populations.